Globalization and Trade Integration in Developing Countries

Ahu Coşkun Özer
Marmara University, Turkey

A volume in the Advances in Logistics, Operations, and Management Science (ALOMS) Book Series

Published in the United States of America by
IGI Global
Business Science Reference (an imprint of IGI Global)
701 E. Chocolate Avenue
Hershey PA, USA 17033
Tel: 717-533-8845
Fax: 717-533-8661
E-mail: cust@igi-global.com
Web site: http://www.igi-global.com

Library of Congress Cataloging-in-Publication Data

Names: Ozer, Ahu Coskun, 1981- editor.
Title: Globalization and trade integration in developing countries / Ahu Coskun Ozer, editor.
Other titles: Globalisation and trade integration in developing countries
Description: Hershey : Business Science Reference, [2017]
Identifiers: LCCN 2017027624| ISBN 9781522540328 (hardcover) | ISBN 9781522540335 (ebook)
Subjects: LCSH: Developing countries--Commerce. | Developing countries--Commercial policy. | Bank loans--Developing countries. | Globalization--Developing countries.
Classification: LCC HF1413 .G5836 2017 | DDC 382.09172/4--dc23 LC record available at https://lccn.loc.gov/2017027624

This book is published in the IGI Global book series Advances in Logistics, Operations, and Management Science (ALOMS) (ISSN: 2327-350X; eISSN: 2327-3518)

British Cataloguing in Publication Data
A Cataloguing in Publication record for this book is available from the British Library.

For electronic access to this publication, please contact: eresources@igi-global.com.

Advances in Logistics, Operations, and Management Science (ALOMS) Book Series

ISSN:2327-350X
EISSN:2327-3518

Editor-in-Chief: John Wang, Montclair State University, USA

MISSION

Operations research and management science continue to influence business processes, administration, and management information systems, particularly in covering the application methods for decision-making processes. New case studies and applications on management science, operations management, social sciences, and other behavioral sciences have been incorporated into business and organizations real-world objectives.

The **Advances in Logistics, Operations, and Management Science** (ALOMS) Book Series provides a collection of reference publications on the current trends, applications, theories, and practices in the management science field. Providing relevant and current research, this series and its individual publications would be useful for academics, researchers, scholars, and practitioners interested in improving decision making models and business functions.

COVERAGE

- Computing and information technologies
- Political science
- Information management
- Operations management
- Finance
- Marketing engineering
- Networks
- Services management
- Organizational behavior
- Decision analysis and decision support

IGI Global is currently accepting manuscripts for publication within this series. To submit a proposal for a volume in this series, please contact our Acquisition Editors at Acquisitions@igi-global.com or visit: http://www.igi-global.com/publish/.

The Advances in Logistics, Operations, and Management Science (ALOMS) Book Series (ISSN 2327-350X) is published by IGI Global, 701 E. Chocolate Avenue, Hershey, PA 17033-1240, USA, www.igi-global.com. This series is composed of titles available for purchase individually; each title is edited to be contextually exclusive from any other title within the series. For pricing and ordering information please visit http://www.igi-global.com/book-series/advances-logistics-operations-management-science/37170. Postmaster: Send all address changes to above address.

Titles in this Series

For a list of additional titles in this series, please visit:
https://www.igi-global.com/book-series/advances-logistics-operations-management-science/37170

Supply Chain Management Strategies and Risk Assessment in Retail Environments
Akhilesh Kumar (Indian Institute of Technology Kharagpur, India) and Swapnil Saurav (JDA Softwar, India)
Business Science Reference • ©2018 • 351pp • H/C (ISBN: 9781522530565) • US $225.00

Management Control Systems in Complex Settings Emerging Research and Opportunities
Filippo Zanin (University of Udine, Italy) Eugenio Comuzzi (University of Udine, Italy) and Antonio Costantini (University of Udine, Italy)
Business Science Reference • ©2018 • 190pp • H/C (ISBN: 9781522539872) • US $145.00

Handbook of Research on Applied Optimization Methodologies in Manufacturing Systems
Ömer Faruk Yılmaz (Istanbul Technical University, Turkey & Yalova University, Turkey) and Süleyman Tüfekçí (University of Florida, USA)
Business Science Reference • ©2018 • 449pp • H/C (ISBN: 9781522529446) • US $275.00

Grassroots Sustainability Innovations in Sports Management Emerging Research and ...
Marco Tortora (University of Florence, Italy)
Business Science Reference • ©2018 • 130pp • H/C (ISBN: 9781522535003) • US $145.00

Motivationally Intelligent Leadership Emerging Research and Opportunities
Michael A. Brown Sr. (Florida International University, USA)
Business Science Reference • ©2018 • 139pp • H/C (ISBN: 9781522537465) • US $155.00

Novel Six Sigma Approaches to Risk Assessment and Management
Vojo Bubevski (Independent Researcher, UK)
Business Science Reference • ©2018 • 251pp • H/C (ISBN: 9781522527039) • US $200.00

Enterprise Resiliency in the Continuum of Change Emerging Research and Opportunities
Raj Kumar Bhattarai (Tribhuvan University, Nepal)
Business Science Reference • ©2018 • 186pp • H/C (ISBN: 9781522526278) • US $150.00

For an entire list of titles in this series, please visit:
https://www.igi-global.com/book-series/advances-logistics-operations-management-science/37170

IGI Global
DISSEMINATOR OF KNOWLEDGE

701 East Chocolate Avenue, Hershey, PA 17033, USA
Tel: 717-533-8845 x100 • Fax: 717-533-8661
E-Mail: cust@igi-global.com • www.igi-global.com

Editorial Advisory Board

Table of Contents

Section 2
Trade Policies in Developing Countries

Section 3
Financial Analysis in Developing Countries

Detailed Table of Contents

China is one of the fastest growing economies in the world. To ensure a continual increase in trade, China's contemporary policies are aimed at the creation of new market opportunities for China's companies abroad. The chapter addresses the major challenges of collaboration between China and the countries of Central and Northeast Asia, reviews the milestones of China's trade policies in Eurasia, analyses China's recent trade and development initiative (One Belt One Road project) and its convergence with other integration initiatives in the region, and reviews trade flows between China and the countries of Central Asia (Kazakhstan, Kyrgyzstan, Russia, Tajikistan, Turkmenistan, and Uzbekistan) and Northeast Asia (Democratic People's Republic of Korea, Japan, Mongolia, and the Republic of Korea) during 2015. The chapter is concluded with an analysis of how China can pursue shaping an inter-regional market by looking across national boundaries and with the discussion of structural changes needed for China to ensure its competitiveness in the markets of the studied country.

The EEU was created to strengthen the national economies and capabilities of the member states in global economy by creating the so-called "four freedoms": the free movement of goods, services, capital, and persons. At this stage, the EEU is involved in the creation of free trade zones with countries outside the borders of the Eurasian post-Soviet space that was a reaction of the Eurasian Economic Union on new trends in international trade and the crisis of the WTO. The aim of this chapter is to analyze the internal and external contours of the Eurasian integration in economic and trade cooperation. The first part is devoted to analyzing of the historical background of the EEU creation. The second part evaluates the economic cooperation among the EEU countries. In the third part, the author focuses on the crisis of the WTO and new tendencies in international trade cooperation. And the final part examines the prospects of creation of free-trades zones between the EEU states and other countries.

experiences of Turkey in the 1970-2016 period, the good practices that Turkey has implemented in this respect, topics that Turkey has made mistakes, and the issues that Turkey has suffered are examined with the help of tables and graphs. The most remarkable point in the chapter is the necessity of diversifying countries and markets in the foreign trade because foreign trade has close interaction with political and economic developments and it is always possible that existing markets are being lost or difficulties arise in existing supply sources.

This chapter explores the various dimensions of trade competitiveness in developing countries. After discussing various definitions of competitiveness, the importance of trade competitiveness is discussed in the context of developing countries with reference to the existing literature. Subsequently, major constraints that affect trade competitiveness, particularly macroeconomic conditions, institutional and business environments, and infrastructure, are discussed. Finally, recent empirical findings on trade competitiveness are summarized.

In Turkey, the volume of foreign trade, which was very small in the first years of the republic, raised due to the increasing population and the reviving economy. Imports and exports for Turkey, the proportion of equipment, investment goods, and raw materials that would have been used for industrialization has increased. Another type of trade that is desired to be implemented in Turkey in recent years is free trade. The implementations for free trade also bring the question together with themselves. Does globalization always affect developing countries in a positive correlation with their economies? The data taken from KOF Index of Globalization from ETH Zurich are going to be used to see the relationship with the data coming from imports and exports. Then for all developing countries a classification study is done and the relation of developing countries and Turkey is examined. The purpose of the chapter is to examine the number of imports and exports due to globalization indexes to understand the real impact and the direction of globalization from the perspective of Turkey.

Preface

Globalization has enabled that the borders among the countries have been removed and commercial relations are improved. Also, globalization has enabled to establish trade integrations among the countries by regionally. Trade integrations have been formed in both developed countries and developing countries.

These trade integrations, which are formed among developing countries to reduce the negative effects of globalization on the economy, increase the trade volume among the developing countries. However, there is a debate on that whether the increase in trade volume in integrations is favor of all member countries in the unions or not. In this book, commercial relations in developing countries have been evaluated and economic relations in trade integrations have been analyzed.

In the first section of the book, trade practices and policies in The South East Europe (SEE) countries, China, The Eurasian Economic Union (EEU), Association of Southeast Asian Nations, (ASEAN) are analyzed. Also, in Section 2, chapters based on the evaluations to increase trade in developing countries are included. Finally, in Section 3, financial analyzes on the economies of the developing countries are included.

In Chapter 1, "The Effects of Trade Liberalisation in the SEE Countries: CEFTA 2006 Agreement," Dr. D. Kragulj, M. Parežanin and Dr. S. Jednak state that the importance of trade liberalization within CEFTA 2006 differs from one member country to another. It is the most important market for Bosnia and Herzegovina and Montenegro. It is the most important export market for Serbia and Macedonia. It is the market of moderate importance for Albania, while CEFTA 2006 is a marginal market for Moldova. Trade volume surely should be greater and the member countries should use the chance offered by the trade liberalization. The structure of goods and services in trading is not satisfactory. Member countries trade with the same groups of products. Maybe a specialization for certain products would improve the export performances of the member countries.

In Chapter 2, “Contemporary Foreign Trade Policy of China in the Region of Central and Northeast Asia,” Dr. Vasilii Erokhin explain that in recent decades, China’s foreign trade policy has undergone a transformation to become more pluralized, more transparent, and more market-oriented. Foreign trade has been gradually transforming in line with the country’s broader economic transition towards higher value-added manufacturing and services. Further expansion of China on the global market is caused by the necessity to explore new markets for Chinese goods, to find new investment options for the huge capital accumulated in the country during the decades of economic growth, and to secure sustainable energy and resources supply sources. Countries in Central and Northeast Asia are both very attractive markets and the places of vast hydrocarbon reserves and mineral deposits, that is why China’s policy in the region is aimed at the development of trade and economic relations with them by means of strengthening of existing regional bilateral and multilateral mechanisms and creating a common economic space in Eurasia. As China’s trade and economic expansion in Central and Northeast Asia increases, its influence in the region grows alongside it. Taking into account China’s economic potential, such an expansion promises to become a mutually beneficial arrangement both for China and its neighbors, for whom increasing China’s trade and investments are a catalyst for growth.

In the Chapter 3, “The Eurasian Economic Union in the Context of Transformation of the International Trade System,” Dr. Maria Lagutina analysed the free trade agreements and free trade zones in The Eurasian Economic Union and conclude that a number of Russian experts believe that free-trade agreements between the EEU and other countries would depreciate the value of the EEU itself. The EEU should show to the world that it is an efficient organization capable of attracting trade partners – this is very important in a situation when the WTO is in crisis and leading Western nations are drawing up new rules for the international economy. Even today, one can safely say that the EEU is ready for developing bilateral and multilateral cooperation with many countries and integrationist alliances. Presently the most important direction is the ties with Asian nations, but the reason for this is the West’s lack of willingness to engage in a productive dialog with the EEU.

In Chapter 4, “An Analysis of Trade of the Eurasian Economic Union,” Dr. Ahu Coşkun Özer analyzed the effectiveness of the Eurasian Economic Union and whether this union is effective in developing trade between the member countries. It is stated that Kazakhstan’s economy is dependent on EEU imports and that the economies of Kyrgyzstan and Belarus are completely dependent on EEU for exports and imports. The economic independence of the countries determines the strength of the trade unions. Also, political problems are a handicap for the future of the EEU. Solving the political problems among the countries in the union will also lay the ground for strengthening the economic partnership. EEU members abandoned their national tariffs after their membership in the EEU, and they began to apply single tariffs in foreign trade. The tariff applied within the EEU has been determined on the basis of pre-existing trade tariffs in Russia. These tariffs adversely affected countries with low tariffs on imports, such as Kyrgyzstan, and led to an increase in the prices of imported goods. Russia has enormous power in terms of its share of the trade within the EEU. This shows Russia has economic dominance in the union. This is also the subject of debate about whether the union's members, except Russia, benefit from the customs union. Kazakhstan and Belarus were anxious about the role of the Russia in the union and believed that the customs union was designed by Russian ultra-nationalists.

In Chapter 5, "Who Benefits From Regional Economic Integration? The Case of ASEAN," Dr. Ina Kayser explain that the Association of Southeast Asian Nations was founded despite severe political, economic, cultural and social disparities. Looking at the GDP per capita development, Singapore has nowadays a value 55 times larger than Myanmar. Regional gaps are still prevalent. However, the example of Malaysia's economic transformation shows that ASEAN paved to way for smallest states to economic success. Nonetheless, there is little chance that ASEAN will develop supranational institutions and structures in the very near future. In comparison to other examples of regional economic cooperation, such as the European Union or the Gulf Cooperation Council, this stands out. ASEAN follows its own rules and pace and did achieve a great deal of economic development in the region. Moreover, it triggered political stability and growth as evident from the analysis of GDP development. Thus for the economy, the peoples in the region and as well as for the political systems, ASEAN is very beneficial. The regional institutions of East Asia and the Asia Pacific were built on the back of ASEAN, an organization set up as an alternative regional idea. The core problem is that ASEAN since its formation raised higher expectations that were not met. ASEAN is a high potential region but still falls short of its actual capabilities.

According to the Chapter 6, "Importance of Market Diversification in Foreign Trade: Lessons From Turkey for the Developing Countries," Dr. Sevgi Sezer, market and product diversification in import and export for developing countries are beneficial. Sezer states that the developing countries can learn from Turkey's experience that developing countries can achieve a high and sustainable foreign trade volume. In this context, they should not only settle in certain markets in foreign trade, they should search alternative markets and sign the necessary economic and political agreements. They should also encourage foreign direct investment in the country in order to increase the production and export potential of their countries by providing the necessary support to the domestic firms. It would be beneficial to make foreign direct investments in other countries to ensure the security of supply of energy and food to their countries. While political relations with other countries are maintained, emotional behaviors should be left aside, and national interests should be taken into consideration. All these developments indicate that there is a great benefit for the developing countries to go market and product diversification in their imports and exports so that they can achieve stable foreign trade and economic growth. In this regard, when it is necessary for developing countries it is essential to leave aside profitability, geographical proximity, cultural or nationality closeness factors and they need to act rationally.

In Chapter 7, "Trade Competitiveness in Developing Countries," Dr. Nazlı Karamollaoğlu explores the various dimensions of trade competitiveness in developing countries, explain that maintaining trade competitiveness is fundamental for developing countries given the positive impact of exporting on economic growth and productivity. However, developing nations face many constraints, which means they have a challenging task in maintaining trade competitiveness. Macroeconomic instability, particularly volatile exchange rates and high inflation, put constraints on the competitiveness level. In addition, providing the main elements needed to form a favorable business climate, characterized by strong institutions, financial development, security, infrastructure, is hard for developing countries to achieve. Therefore, in order to establish a solid competitive framework, developing countries' governments must work on these areas in collaboration with the private sector. Challenges may exist but proper implementation of the necessary policies and structural reforms have the potential to contribute to the competitiveness level of developing economies.

In Chapter 8, "The Status of Foreign Trades Under Globalization in Developing and Developed Countries With Turkey," N. Güleç, C. Öztürk, and D. Efendioğlu analyzed the relation between the globalization and positive effects of the developing countries. It is stated that the effects of social globalization on the import and export items of developed countries are more far-reaching than the effects of economic globalization. The implementations for free trade also bring the question together with themselves. Does globalization always effect developing countries in a positive correlation with their economies? The effects of social globalization on the import and export items of developed countries are more far-reaching than the effects of economic globalization. For developing countries, economic globalization is more influential in terms of trade.

According to Chapter 9, "The Relationship Between Non-Performing Loans, Industry, and Economic Growth of the African Economies and Policy Recommendations for Global Growth," by Dr. H. Dinçer, Dr. S. Yüksel, and Z. Adalı, there is a causality relationship between industry volume and economic growth. Dinçer, Yüksel, and Adalı explain that decrease in the industry volume is the main reason of economic recession. The main reason behind this situation is that when there is a problem in the industry, companies will face financial problems and this issue results in decreasing economic growth. Due to this aspect, it was recommended that African countries should focus on industry development in order to provide economic growth. It can also be understood that when the industry is developed in Africa, this will contribute to global trade has an increasing effect on global growth. Also, the decrease in the industry volume is the key reason of high non-performing loans ratio. This issue explains that when industry volume in African countries is decreased, the companies will have lower trade volume. Because of this situation, the profitability of these countries will decline. As a result of this aspect, these parties have problems regarding the repayment of the loans taken by the banks. Thus, it was understood that these countries should also improve their industries to reduce non-performing loans ratio. While considering this result, it can be said that global trade should be developed to have the effective banking system and increase life standards of the people. Owing to this situation, it can be possible to reach global growth.

In Chapter 10, "Analyzing the Impact of Oil Price Fluctuations on Vietnam Stock Market," Dr. H. Viet Khai, L. Minh Sang, P. T. A. Nguyet analyzed the impact of crude oil prices on Vietnam stock market in the period from March 2006 to June 2015. It is stated that the results showed that crude oil prices and Vietnam stock market indices had a long-term relationship. However, when analyzing the long-term and short-term impact, the study results may differ from the results of previous studies. Accordingly, in the short term, crude oil prices and Vietnam stock market indices positively related. In the long term, the results reported the negative relationship between crude oil prices and Vietnam stock market indices. In addition, this study also showed the differences in the impact of crude oil price between the normal period and economic crisis period. The impact of crude oil prices on the stock market in economic crisis period is faster than in the other periods.

All the academic studies in *Globalization and Trade Integration in Developing Countries* assess the impact of globalization on the trade and economies of developing countries. This book is a resource that contains important academic and research results for the business and academic world.

Ahu Coşkun Özer
Marmara University, Turkey

Acknowledgment

This book completed by support of many individuals to whom I would like to express my gratitude.

I thank all the chapter contributors representing six countries and respected universities, research institutes and organizations. I wish to express my sincere thanks to the Editorial Advisory Board and international team of reviewers for sharing their precious time and professional experience and thoughts.

I sincerely thank to IGI Global team and also Maria Rohde for their assistance throughout the book project. I also give my thanks to my spouse Teoman Özer who has always supported me throughout the book development project.

Ahu Coşkun Özer
Marmara University, Turkey

Section 1

Trade Integration in Developing Countries

Chapter 1
Effects of Trade Liberalisation in the SEE Countries:
CEFTA 2006 Agreement

Dragana Kragulj
University of Belgrade, Serbia

Miloš Parežanin
University of Belgrade, Serbia

Sandra Jednak
University of Belgrade, Serbia

ABSTRACT

A key factor for countries in transition is improving their export competitiveness in order to improve the economic performance of the country. The aim of this chapter is an insight into the influence of trade liberalisation within CEFTA 2006 to the member countries. Correlation analysis was used, and bilateral flows between member countries were analysed. The results show a significant influence of trade liberalisation to GDP growth, unemployment rate, public debt, and budget deficit. The results of correlation analysis are not the same for all the member countries. Greater participation in an exchange with other member countries surely would improve poor economic performances of the countries from South-East Europe. Possibilities are present for improving CEFTA 2006 through the further elimination of trade barriers and increase of total trade. The process of the accession to the EU and access to the single market is also determined by the success of CEFTA 2006.

DOI: 10.4018/978-1-5225-4032-8.ch001

INTRODUCTION

Globalisation of world economy and internationalisation of economy life have been on the scene already for a significant period. The rate of interdependence of certain countries of the world in conditions of a complex, international, competitive and global market has been constantly increasing. Wide international market is more and more the condition for placing goods and technical innovations, which stimulates mutual connecting of regions and the world in the economical, but also in the political sense (Kragulj, 2016). Globalization, but also the process of transition, implementation of reforms and various crises have contributed to conclusion of various integrations (Hillman, 2015). The aim of these processes is enlargement of foreign trade flows and reduction of expenses between regions, countries and markets by reduction or elimination of trade bans and barriers, as well as through harmonisation of economic policies (Investopedia, 2017).

Trade integration and liberalisation is the initial step towards the higher levels of integration. Trade liberalisation is elimination and reduction of tariff and non-tariff restrictions that enables free flow of goods and services, i.e. import and export between countries (Lee, 2005). Foreign trade exchange and economic growth, as well as development of the common market are increasing with the establishment of the agreement on trade liberalisation. Different studies show positive effects between the trade liberalisation and the accomplishment of economic growth and increase of export (Haririson, 1996; Kneller et al., 2008; Wacziarg & Welch, 2008, Baldwin & Gu, 2004), while other studies contest the connection (Rodriguez & Rodrik, 2000; Yanikkaya, 2003; Jenkins, 1996). The World Bank and the IMF are proponents of the trade liberalisation due to its positive effects. These organisations perceive the beginning of transition in the SEE countries as implementation of the liberalisation of prices and trade. In order to increase the level of economic and political integration and regional trade, the SEE countries are obliged to be the members of the CEFTA (The Central European Free Trade Agreement) until they become the members of the European Union. CEFTA 2006 is today a unique free trade zone between the SEE countries.

The aim of the paper is to present the effects of trade liberalisation in the SEE countries. The paper will research the volume and structure of export and import between the SEE countries before the accession to CEFTA, as well as the influence of the economic crisis to trade flows between the observed countries. Statistically significant correlation between trade flows and the rate of GDP growth, unemployment rate, public debt and budget deficits will be analysed. Correlation analysis will be used. The results show that export and import between the analysed countries are increased with the accession to CEFTA 2006. The structure of export of the SEE countries is such that raw materials, semifinished products, agricultural products and foodstuff are exported. Such a structure of export is mostly present towards the European Union, while the structure between these countries records some products of higher levels of processing, like industrial products, machines and equipment. With inflow of foreign capital, the structure of export in these countries is being changed and diversified. Serbia has the greatest possibilities since it has the signed agreement on free trade with Russia. However, it is not used sufficiently.

The structure of the paper is as follows. After the introduction, a survey of the literature regarding the effects of the trade liberalisation will be presented. Then a short survey will be presented of the development of the CEFTA and the role of CEFTA 2006 in the process of trade liberalisation of the SEE countries. The fourth part of the paper contains economic performances of the SEE countries as the introduction for the problems with which this chapter is dealing, and then follow the basic problems of the chapter. The sixth part will show the results of the analysis of trade flows of the SEE countries, before their accession to the CEFTA, as well as the period after the economic crisis, while in the next two chapters some of the basic problems and future directions of research will be summarised. The results will be summarised in the conclusion.

BACKGROUND

Effects of Trade Liberalisation

In the macroeconomic area, the concept of economic integration is explained and analyzed in different ways and from different aspects. Some theorists make a distinction between concepts of integration and economic cooperation, in quantitative and qualitative meaning (Balassa, 1961; Šaban & Ušakov, 1971). Integration is defined as achieving the most desirable structure of the international economy where artificial obstacles are removed and deliberately introducing the desired elements of coordination and unification (Tinbergen, 1959). Economic integration can also be defined as the undoing of discrimination among member states and the creation of harmonized and common policies with the aim of raising social wellbeing (Pinder, 1968). Also, integration is defined as a process and as a state of affairs (Balassa, 1961). As a process, integration involves a means to eliminate discrimination between economic units from different national states. As a state of affairs, the integration can be represented as the absence of various forms of discrimination between national economies. Integration can be seen from the lowest to the highest forms of a process that includes: 1) release of trade barriers - trade integration; 2) liberalization of factor movement - factor integration; 3) harmonization of national economic policies - policy integration; and 4) full unification of these policies - total integration (Balassa, 1976). This classification given by Balassa is different from his earlier definition given in the book The Theory of Economic Integration, which includes: 1) Free Trade Area (customs and quantitative restrictions between member states are abolished, but each country retains its own customs duties towards third countries); 2) Customs Union (in addition to the elimination of discrimination in the field of movement of goods in the Union, there is an equalization of customs in trade with third countries); 3) Common market (high degree of economic integration where trade barriers are abolished, as well as restrictions on the movement of factors); 4) Economic Union (in addition to the abolished trade barriers and restrictions on movement of factors, implies a certain degree of harmonization of national policies) and 5) Full Economic Union (implies unity of monetary, fiscal, social and anti-cyclical policy and requires the establishment of a supranational power, whose decisions are binding on member countries) (Balassa, 1961).

Thus, according to the theoretical classification of economic integrations, trade integration takes the lowest level. This initial form of integration represents the process of gradual elimination of trade barriers. However, the contemporary theory does not stay only on short-term effects arising from elimination of customs duties. It studies also long-term effects of trade integration on the volume of production and the size of national income of member countries of the integration. Therefore, there are different effects of the trade liberalisation. Even Viner has introduced two terms: trade creation effect and trade diversion effect. Trade creation effect represents the profit in income accrued due to the increase of trade between the member countries of the integration, as the result of its formation. Trade diversion effect is the loss in income that is accrued due to the decrease of trade with foreign countries in favour of trade with the member countries of the integration (Viner, 1950). Such the comprehension of Viner takes a significant place in the theory of economic policy, since it has been understood that every reduction of customs duties need not to result with trade that is more successful. Kindleberger indicates that elimination of trade barriers between two trade partners will not improve the world efficiency if the effect of trade diversion is stronger than the effect of trade development (Kindleberger, 1974). Such attitudes even today have an important place in trade relations, which is confirmed by numerous studies (Dai et al., 2015; Yang & Martinez-Zarzoso, 2014; Magee, 2016). Haberler had an opposed comprehension in some extent, considering that customs union is always welcomed, even when the third countries are not the issue. It is particularly useful for small countries because it includes the free trade and the international division of labour on the principles of the theory of comparative expenses (Haberler, 1959). Newer studies also recline on his attitudes (Saavedra-Rivano & Estrada, 2016; Tabuchi, 2017). In economic sense, it is extremely important to observe dynamic aspect of the trade integrations theory that investigates interrelations between the size of market of integration and the changes accrued regarding the structure of production, number of employments, investments and, generally, labour productivity. Better use of resources, price reduction of products, improving quality of products, diversification of company's risks, greater returns, competitiveness, inflow of foreign investments, productivity, employment and income are obtained by the trade liberalisation (OECD Report, 2011, Fan at al., 2015). The most important effects of the trade liberalisation are increase of export, wages, employment and obtaining of economic growth. Reallocation of resources among sectors and dislocation of workers from import-oriented sectors to export-oriented sectors are also the effects of the trade liberalisation. Various researches have been performed regarding the investigation of connections between trade liberalisation, employment and wages. Studies give different results. For example, according to Revenga (1995), reduction of tariffs is connected with decrease of employment and increase of average wages, while Baldwinu (2004) in his research comes to the result that trade liberalisation in developing countries may lead to decrease of wages. Egger and Kreickemeier (2007) say that trade liberalisation acts on the selection of the best export-oriented companies, enables the increase of company's profit, but also acts on the wage inequality and the unemployment rate. Opening of the economy attracts foreign direct investments (FDI), while competition, competitiveness and export are increased. Trade liberalisation influences the increase of export through free trade agreement (Cestetpe et al., 2015). Besides, the research shows that trade liberalisation influences the increase of productivity in manufacturing sectors (Turnbull et al., 2016). Developing countries that were focused to agriculture direct their production to industry and specialise for production of the products with lower production costs in comparison with foreign market. The country has a comparative and a competitive advantage, therefore productivity, income and export are increasing and economic growth is accomplished. Comparative advantages and development of infrastructure in the emerging economies are the primary factors influencing the increase of export (Disdier et al., 2013). Certain researches (Liyanaarachchi et al, 2016; Kis-Katos & Sparrow, 2015) showed that trade liberalisation influences the accomplishment of economic growth and greater income, on one hand, and the reduction of poverty, on the other hand. Manni et al. (2012) show that trade liberalisation influences the increase of GDP growth, export and import, as well as that it has positive effects on economic development due to greater openness of economy, but it does not influence the inflation. Manwa & Wijeweera (2016) showed that in the countries of the Southern African Custom Union trade liberalisation has a positive effect on economic growth. Baldwinu (2004) considers that cooperation between countries is necessary, i.e. foreign trade exchange, in order to increase the economic growth. Foreign trade exchange increases the demand for home products and in that way contributes to the increase of economic growth. Hakim & Hamdi (2016) in their research claim that trade liberalisation attracts foreign direct investments, increases the employment and the development of economy. Le & Tran-Nam (in Press) were researching the connection between trade liberalisation, financial modernization and economic development on selected Asia-Pacific countries. They proved that there was a connection between the referred variables, i.e. that trade liberalisation influences the financial modernization and the economic development. In implementation of economic reforms, trade liberalisation has positive effects on economic performances, especially on economic growth. However, its effects are decreasing in periods of national and global crises (Falvey et al., 2012). Naranpanawa & Arora (2014) showed that "trade liberalization has impact on the rich and fast-growing middle-income states and a marginal or negative impact on the poor states". According to the OECD Report (2011), reduction of trade barriers for 50% in G20 economies leads to greater employment, greater real wages and increase of export. CEE countries have opted for European integrative processes. These countries have started their transition towards the market economy with trade liberalisation that is giving positive economic effects. However, the European Union sets specific requirements in front of these countries. These requirements relate to resolving the consequences of conflicts and civil wars at the end of the 20th century as well as establishing regional cooperation between these countries (Kragulj, 2016).

CEFTA 2006 AND TRADE LIBERALISATION OF SEE COUNTRIES

The countries of the Central and Eastern Europe have finished the process of transition. However, the countries of the South-East Europe are still in the process. The process of transition is a multidimensional process that implies many goals that should be achieved. Transition is a process that sums up complex social, economic and political reforms in a country. Radical changes of economic and total social system imply fast leaving of the rigid, centralised, detailed system of planning and accepting, on a democratic basis, a more contemporary and flexible global method of economy. It appeared that the most important issues of strategy and transitional policy are refracted through the program of macroeconomic stability and system transformation (Kragulj, 2005). Likewise, the SEE countries see their economic and political future in the European Union, therefore many reforms conducted imply harmonization with the standards of the united Europe in all spheres of economic and social life. The reforms conducted in that sense should provide positive tendencies of the key, primarily economic indicators, like the gross domestic product growth, the increase of industrial production, the increase of employment and the decrease of unemployment rate, the stability of prices, the reduction of budget deficit and public debt, more favourable flow of foreign trade exchange, the increase of life standard of citizens, etc. Regional cooperation is important for accomplishment of a sustainable development (Baldwin, 2004). Trade liberalisation and privatisation are the key components for the SEE countries and their integration into the EU. Reforms in trade and foreign trade exchange are focused to the elimination of trade restraints (export tariffs, quota systems and administrative restraints of import and export), progress towards the membership in the WTO (World Trade Organization) and the improvement of approach to foreign trade exchange (convertibility of current account and capital account balance). Therefore, the road towards the creation and accession to other contemporary market economies leads, among other things, through strengthening of regional integration and membership in the CEFTA Agreement – the unique multilateral agreement on free trade in the South-East Europe, so-called the Agreement CEFTA 2006 (Kragulj, 2006). The agreement on free trade implies liberalisation of trade on reciprocal basis, which means that all the countries eliminate customs duties for import from the territory of other countries.

The name itself CEFTA – The Central European Free Trade Agreement – describes the Agreement between the countries of the Central Europe. CEFTA was founded by Poland, Hungary and Czechoslovakia on 21 December 1992 in Krakow and implementation of the signed agreement started on 1 March 1993. CEFTA members became also Slovenia (on 1 January 1996), Romania (on 1 July 1997), Bulgaria (on 1 January 1999), Croatia (on 1 March 2003) and Macedonia (in 2006). With the enlargement of the European Union in 2004, 2007, 2011 and 2013, Poland, Hungary, Czech Republic, Slovakia, Slovenia, Romania, Bulgaria and Croatia left this form of trade integration. Today CEFTA represents the agreement defining the unique area of the South-East Europe free trade. CEFTA represents a trade agreement between Albania, Bosnia and Herzegovina, Macedonia, Moldova, Serbia, UNMIK on behalf of Kosovo and Metohija and Montenegro. Namely, as the European Union wanted to stimulate certain countries – candidates for the membership in the EU for the regional cooperation within CEFTA (the Central European Free Trade Area) and BAFTA (the Baltic Free Trade Area), it insists now also on as close as possible mutual economic cooperation between the countries of the Western Balkan, through the process of accession and through the process of stabilisation and association to the EU, with the final goal of future membership in the EU. Actually, the CEFTA Agreement is completely complementary with the Stabilisation and Association Agreement. Signing the Memorandum of Understanding on Trade Liberalisation and Facilitation on 27 June 2001 in Brussels within the Stability Pact for South Eastern Europe by SCG, Romania, Bulgaria, Croatia, Bosnia and Herzegovina, Macedonia, Albania and later Moldavia preceded the establishment of the South-East Europe free trade area. The signatory countries agreed that they would conclude by 31 December 2002 bilateral free trade agreements based on principles and in accordance with the rules of the World Trade Organization, where almost complete trade between these countries would be without any quantitative restrictions and customs duties. Of course, a transitional period was predicted for certain number of sensitive products, where customs duties would be reduced gradually and nulled within the six years period. However, regardless the increase of economic cooperation and trade between the countries in the region, the goals of the Memorandum of regional cooperation were not accomplished in great extent. Although 32 bilateral agreements on free area were concluded by the end of 2005, many agreements were not operational. That was the reason why the decision was made, with the goal of faster improvement of economic cooperation in the region of the Western Balkans and preparations for the accession to the EU, to create a unique multilateral agreement on free trade in the SEE – CEFTA 2006, which would replace practically all the bilateral agreements. The unique agreement under the name CEFTA 2006 was initialled on 9 November and signed on 19 December 2006 in Bucharest. Advantages of CEFTA 2006 concerning the bilateral agreements were huge. When in practice only one agreement functions instead of 32 bilateral agreements, it inevitably leads to the strengthening of trade and, being of special importance, attracts foreign investors to make decisions to invest in the region more easily (Kragulj, 2016). Regarding the old agreement, CEFTA 2006 represents a more modern agreement: it enables trade liberalisation up to 90%, introduces new trade fields like public procurements, services, investments and intellectual property, introduces the rules harmonised with the rules in force in the European Union and strengthens the CEFTA institutions that monitor implementation of the Agreement.

Regarding the issue of trade liberalisation, industrial and agricultural products are comprised in the Agreement, while given benefits differ depending on the products. The greatest liberalisation has been accomplished with industrial products, where 50% to 90% of tariff positions are comprised with duty free regime. Regarding the sensitive products, liberalisation is performed gradually within a transitional period of six years. Several types of liberalisation were predicted for agricultural products regarding the significant importance of this sector for all the countries of the region: a) total elimination of customs duties with the Agreement coming into force or determination of a transitional period; b) reducing customs duties with the Agreement coming into force or determination of a transitional period, and c) introducing customs quotas. The unique multilateral agreement predicted also elimination of all quantitative restraints for import and export, elimination of all export duties and export taxes, ban for using export subventions, elimination of existing trade barriers and harmonisation of existing regulations and standards, simplification of customs procedures, ban for fiscal discrimination, conformation of sanitary and phytosanitary measures with the rules of the World Trade Organisation, etc. Basic characteristics of the unique Agreement are: establishing the free trade zone in the South-East Europe before 31 December 2010; further liberalisation and elimination of all quantitative restraints (except for armaments and military equipment); reduction and gradual elimination of non-customs barriers; principle of non-discrimination (which means that all products are treated in the same way); rule of origin (which means that CEFTA product is treated as domestic product when exported to foreign markets); introduction of diagonal cumulation (which means that products produced in one country member of the Agreement are considered to be domestic products, regardless if they are partly or completely produced in that country); introduction of new fields like public procurements, services, investments, intellectual property, procedures for solving mutual disputes and institutionalisation; current regime of public procurements remains in force until the end of 2010 (which means that domestic companies have a preferential treatment until then); taking over contractual concessions from previous bilateral agreements; introduction of new arbitral mechanisms (Chamber of Commerce and Industry of Serbia, 2017; Kragulj, 2016).

Main trade partners are similar for all the countries of the SEE. These are neighbouring countries and Germany, Italy, Austria and the US for all of the countries. Therefore, countries of the EU are the key foreign trade partner of this region. Countries of the SEE should have increased the share of exchange with the EU to 60% of the total exchange. In time, the coefficient of trade openness has been increased in all of the countries of the SEE. Regional trade takes a significant place in the total exchange. However, the regional exchange in the SEE oscillated in time. Also, a great number of non-tariff and technical barriers obstruct in great extent the trade exchange of these countries, like huge and complicated administration and procedures, incompatibility of domestic standards with international standards, insufficient number of internationally recognised bodies for accreditation and certification, as well as authorised laboratories and institutions, disavowal of quality certificates, corruption (Čokić, 2000). Existence of great number of non-customs tariffs influences the appearance of instability of business in these countries, which has a negative reflection to their economic growth. Economic crisis had consequences for the trade exchange in the region. Export and import were reduced due to reduced domestic demand (Broz et al., 2015). Export of the SEE countries is low. All of the observed countries still have greater import than export. Nikolic (2013) points out that the reason for a poor export of this region is the absence of connection between science, educational policy and industrial policy. Export structure of these countries has not changed much. Non-competitive products and products of lower level of processing, i.e. raw materials and agricultural products have the greatest participation in the export, while products of higher phases of processing have an insignificant participation in the export. FDI are considered the factor that can contribute to the increase of economic growth and export. With inflow of FDI, export structure may change, starting with export of cars or medium- and high-tech products instead of agricultural products. According to Nikolic (2013), the share of medium- and high-tech products in the structure of total export has been increased in certain Balkan countries until 2012, mostly the countries that have become members of the EU or the candidate countries. Economic reforms and trade liberalisation influence the economic growth and accomplishment of better economic performances and possibilities for integration in the EU.

ECONOMIC PERFORMANCES OF SEE COUNTRIES

The countries of the South-East Europe are still in the process of transition and conducting reforms. Any proposal for program of reforms, regardless the situation of the economy, was reduced to the accomplishment of the three basic goals – stabilization, privatization and liberalisation. So-called Washington Consensus was the basis for implementation of all the mentioned programs. The basic goals for conducting reforms, i.e. process of transition, based on that program were set on proposal of international institutions. These are (Stančić & Jednak, 2003): 1) liberalisation (the process that provides free formation of prices and reduction of trade barriers); 2) macroeconomic stabilization (the process when inflation is controlled, with implementation of economic policies that control budget, growth of money supply and credits, as well as establishing a better balance of payment); 3) reconstruction and privatization (the process of creating financial and banking sector, reconstruction and reform of companies and changing ownership of companies into the private property); 4) implementation of social program (programs and care for the poor and reducing poverty) and 5) legal and institutional reforms (the need for redefinition of state in the economy, establishing the rule of law, acts and enactments, as well as construction of necessary institutions for implementation).

Macroeconomic stability was the key for all the countries. Conducting a suitable, mostly consistent fiscal and monetary policy influenced reduction of inflation, fiscal deficit, but also provided macroeconomic stability. Creation and development of private sector was one of the basic prerequisites for development of the market economy. A continuous growth of foreign direct investments was provided in this region. Besides, countries from the EU have become the main trade partner for the SEE countries and the trade has increased significantly. Labour productivity and rate of economic growth were increased, conditioning accomplishment of good economic results. Economies reduced inflation and deficit of fiscal balance and trade balance in time. The goals defined by these countries were increasing the competitiveness and economic policy that should provide accession to the EU, increasing of employment, investments in education and knowledge, increasing economic conditions for more efficient business and others.

The nineties were dramatic years for the South-East Europe. The crises in the period 1998 to 2000 directly or indirectly influenced the implementation of economic reforms. At the beginning of transition, economies of the region had a low level of economic growth and productivity, among other things due to outdated equipment and technology, deficiency of capital, inadequate education and expertise of personnel, as well as great surplus of staff in all companies. For the referred reasons, the total-factor productivity (TFP) had the greatest influence on accomplishment of economic growth in these countries. The greatest rates of economic growth (average growth rate 6.6%) were accomplished in the period 2004-2008 (EBRD, 2014). The best results at the beginning of conducting the economic reforms were in the field of trade liberalisation and foreign trade exchange, while the worst results were in restructuring of companies, privatization of great companies, price liberalisation and reforms of banking sector. In certain countries, the problems of great companies and public sector are still the issue that is to be solved. By the end of the nineties, the greatest achievements were in the field of liberalisation of domestic prices. This liberalisation has increased the rate of inflation. However, most of the countries managed to control it and reduce it with suitable stabilization policies. Low inflation rate in the SEE countries today is the result of the retarded economic growth and reduced demand, stable or reduced prices of energy-generating products and foodstuffs. According to some studies (Kneller et al., 2008; Wacziarg & Welch, 2008), trade liberalisation has a positive influence on economic growth. On the contrary, price liberalisation, reforms regarding companies, policy of competitiveness and development of financial sector had a negative influence on economic growth (Lawson & Wang, 2004). Since the 2000, this region has started to record significant economic, legislative, social and political results. The countries of the region have significantly advanced in implementation of reforms mostly due to the help provided by the EU. The reforms were directed to energy sector, development of public private partnership, restructuring of utilities and infrastructure, as well as development of corporate sector. Certain countries, because of the control and interference of the state, have not accomplished an adequate level of reforms (EBRD, 2014, 2015; Petkovic et al., 2015). Besides, consequences of the economic crisis and the crisis in the eurozone are that these countries in the second half of 2011 retarded the economic activities. Implementation of reforms and improvement of institutions stagnate. Likewise, inflow of FDI and other forms of investments was reduced, which represented a factor of growth and development of this region. With absence of foreign investments, the SEE countries transfered to their own sources of financing. Although in 2013 a mild growth of export was accomplished due to the reduced domestic consumption and investments, the rates of economic growth were decreasing. The drop of consumption and investments was due to fiscal contraction, drop of FDI, uncertainty of investors to invest because of the existing crises. Economic growth below 3% was accomplished in 2014, to drop by 0.5% in 2015 and the average rate of economic growth was 2%. A modest growth was accomplished in 2016, which is expected also in 2017. The SEE countries have accomplished the economic growth due to low prices of goods, increased personal consumption, investments and tourism earnings. According to the EBRD (EBRD, 2015), the GDP *per capita* at the beginning of transition in the observed countries was 15-45% of the GDP EU-15, in the period 2013-2014 it was 35-60% of the GDP EU-15, while it is expected to be 60% of the GDP EU-15 by 2035. The consequence of the reduced economic activity is the decrease of growth rate, production and increase of unemployment, which is still today a great problem of these countries.

MAIN FOCUS OF THE CHAPTER

On basis of the problems and economic performances of the countries of the South-East Europe presented in the previous chapter, the research is directed to the importance of CEFTA 2006 as the possibility for improving the position of international competitiveness. The goal of this chapter is to show if the trade liberalisation within CEFTA 2006 influences the increase of the trade flows volume and the improvement of macroeconomic indicators of the member countries. Effects of the trade liberalisation may be observed through answers to the following research questions:

Q1: Has the volume of trade between member countries increased in comparison to the period before accession to CEFTA 2006? How to estimate bilateral trade flows between member countries?

Q2: Which country has the greatest export and import?

Q3: What goods and services are subject to trade under the free trade zone? Is there a possibility for some form of specialisation of individual countries for export of certain products and services?

Q4: How did global economic crisis affect the trade exchange between the member countries?

Q5: What proportion of foreign trade takes place under CEFTA 2006 in relation to the overall trade exchange?

Q6: Is there a statistically significant correlation between trade flows and the rate of GDP growth, unemployment rate, public debt and budget deficits?

Q7: Are there technical and non-tariff barriers to trade?

Data of the United Nations Statistics Division (2017) were used for the analysis of trade flows. For the correlation analysis, the following data were used: export, import, GDP growth, unemployment rate (World Bank Group, 2017), public debt

(IMF, 2017), budget deficits (Trading Economics, 2017). Croatia was omitted from the analysis because it left CEFTA 2006 with the accession to the EU. The same is valid for UNMIK Kosovo, for which the data are not available in international statistical databases.

RESULTS

In order to observe the effects of trade exchange after establishment of the free trade zone, it is necessary to compare the accomplished trade volume with the period before the signing of the Agreement. The first research issue provides an insight into trade flows between member states before and after the accession of CEFTA 2006. They can also be estimated bilateral trade flows between member states. Likewise, it is necessary also to observe bilateral trade flows between member countries within the two periods. Volume of exchange and bilateral trade flows in the period 2001-2006 and in the period after establishment of CEFTA 2006 from 2007 to 2016 have been observed in this chapter. Analysis has been performed through the prism of the member countries. It should be noted that Serbia and Montenegro were one state until 2006 with the name State Union Serbia and Montenegro (SCG).

In the period 2001-2006, Albania had the export between 1.3 and 3.5 billion dollars, while the import in this period was between 304 and 700 million dollars. After 2007, both export and import significantly increased, with increasing tendency. The import after 2007 in every observed year was over 4.2 billion, while the export was between 1 and 2.5 billion dollars. Until 2007, the foreign trade exchange with SCG was at a low level, while it was increased after the accession to the free trade zone, especially when the issue was the trade exchange with Serbia. Although the total volume of the foreign trade exchange was increased, Albania has a negative balance of trade with almost all of the member countries of this regional integration. The negative balance of trade became even more expressed after the accession to CEFTA 2006. Therefore, bilateral trade relations are not in favour of Albania. The only positive balance of trade is with Montenegro and in some of the years with Moldova, but the volume of exchange with both countries is relatively modest. The main trade partners among the member countries are Serbia, Bosnia and Herzegovina and Macedonia in both observed periods with greater volume of foreign trade exchange. Bosnia and Herzegovina also records the increase of the trade volume after the accession to the integration. The export increased also at the global level after 2007 and was between 4 and 5 billion dollars, while the import was over 12 billion dollars. However, the total import decreased to about 10 billion dollars in the recent years, primarily as the result of favourable trade relations with other members of CEFTA 2006. Bosnia and Herzegovina has a negative balance of trade in both observed periods with Serbia, Macedonia and Moldova, while it has a positive balance with other member countries. The only difference is that it had a negative balance of trade with SCG while it existed and it has a positive balance with Montenegro after 2006.

Increase of total volume of trade is also typical for Macedonia. The export at the global level has increased almost to the level of Bosnia and Herzegovina. The import increased also, but in a significantly smaller volume. In the period 2001-2006, Macedonia was the only country with a positive balance of trade with all the member countries. This trend continued also after the establishment of CEFTA 2006, having a negative balance of trade only with Serbia since 2013.

Bilateral relations of Moldova with other member countries are relatively modest, i.e. it has the lowest volume of trade within CEFTA 2006. A varying level of total import and export in both observed periods is typical for Moldova, so that it is impossible to discuss a trend. The same situation is also with the trade exchange with the member countries in both observed periods.

Serbia and Montenegro were one state in the first observed period. The member countries were the significant foreign trade partners in the total foreign trade exchange in the first period, with the exception of Albania and Moldova. Trade surplus was not present only in the trade with Macedonia. In the period 2007-2016, Serbia has become a dominant exporter to the member countries of CEFTA 2006, especially after 2013. Unlike Serbia, Montenegro has a negative balance of trade with all the member countries.

The second research question is analyzed through coverage of imports with exports. Coverage of imports with exports is shown in the Figure 1. Conclusion may be that most of the member countries accomplish a positive balance of trade in the total trade exchange within CEFTA 2006. The exception is Moldova, which has insufficient covering of import with export. Albania and Montenegro are the leaders regarding this criterion. However, a varying trend of this indicator is characteristic for the referred countries. Other member countries have stable values of indicators with a modest tendency of increase year after year (Chamber of Commerce and Industry of Serbia, 2017).

The next paragraph provides the answer to the third research question. The main subjects of trade within CEFTA 2006 are agricultural products, iron and steel, products of timber and wood industry and foodstuffs. There is no specialization of countries regarding export and import, mostly all of the countries import and export the same products. The exception is bilateral relations of Bosnia and Herzegovina and Moldova, where Bosnia and Herzegovina exports to Moldova only products of the pharmaceutical industry. Trade of services is almost negligible. The exceptions are Albania and Montenegro, where services are prevailing over products in some

Figure 1. Coverage of imports with exports in CEFTA 2006
Chamber of Commerce and Industry of Serbia, 2017.

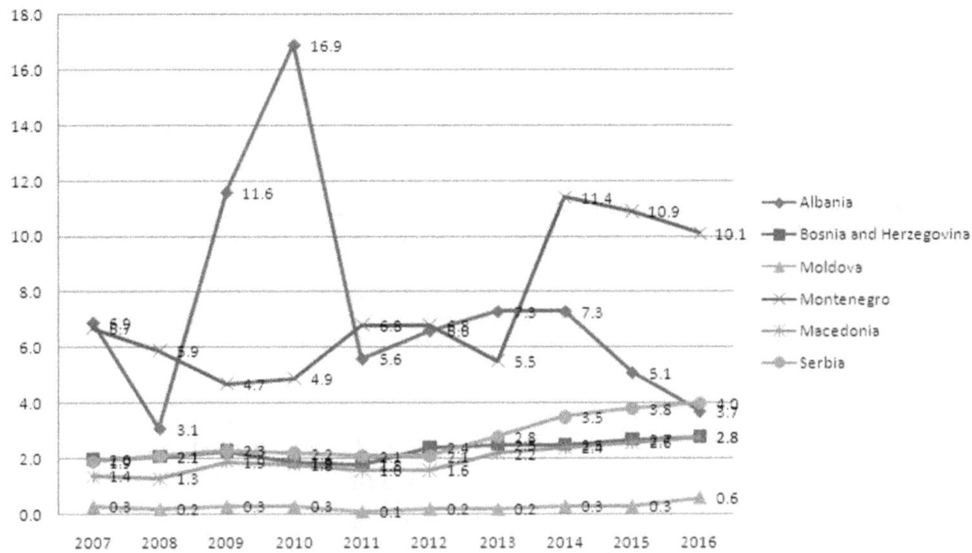

of the observed years. The greatest exporter of services is Serbia (United Nations Statistics Division, 2017).

The fourth research question explains how global economic crisis affected trade exchange between the member countries. Figure 2 shows the total export and import within CEFTA 2006. Effects of the crisis may be noticed on basis of the available data. The beginning of the world economic crisis is characterised by a sudden decrease of trade flows in 2009. However, what is unusual for the global economic flows is that the increase of both export and import among the member countries started after the beginning of the crisis. This may be explained by the fact that the member countries have reoriented the trade exchange from other markets to the market of CEFTA 2006. Thereby, the world economic crisis had positive effects on the increase of the trade exchange between the member countries. Until 2013, the total import was prevailing over the export. After that, both the total export and the total import decrease, the export prevailing over the import. Such a sudden decrease of trade flows is the result of the accession of Croatia in the EU and its leaving the free trade zone.

Fifth research question analyzed proportion of foreign trade takes place under CEFTA 2006 in relation to the overall trade exchange. Table 1 shows the participation of export and import in the common market in relation to the total export and import on the global level. One may say for Bosnia and Herzegovina, Montenegro and Macedonia that CEFTA 2006 is the main trade area regarding both the import

Figure 2. The dynamics of trade flows in CEFTA 2006
United Nations Statistics Division, 2017.

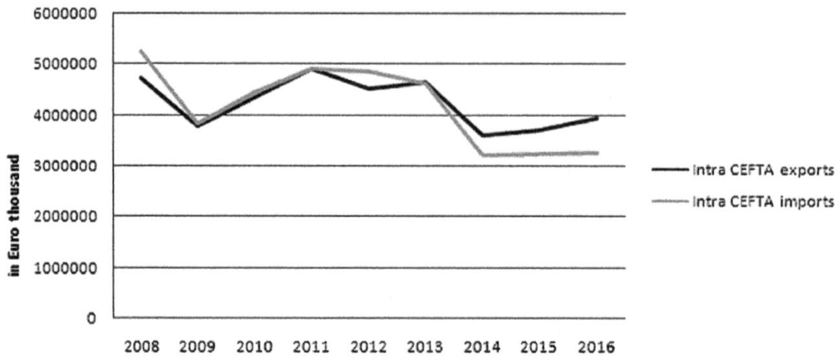

and the export. Volume of import to Macedonia is little lower than to the first two mentioned countries. For Serbia, this market is one of the main export areas, while for Albania it has a moderate importance regarding the trade. CEFTA 2006 has the least importance for Moldova, with almost negligible accomplishments regarding the trade exchange.

The sixth research question analyzed a statistically significant correlation between trade flows and the rate of GDP growth, unemployment rate, public debt and budget deficits.

Correlation analysis given in the Table 2 shows if there is a statistically significant connection between the trade flows (import and export) and macroeconomic variables (unemployment rates, GDP growth rates, public debt and budget deficit). The period was analysed from 2007, when the free trade zone was established, until 2015 – the year for which complete data are available. Influence of the trade flows to macroeconomic indicators of the member countries differs, so that it is impossible to discuss a regularity that is typical for all the observed countries. It is possible to notice on the examples of Albania and Macedonia that there is a statistically significant influence of trade flows to the unemployment rate and the level of public debt. It is unexpected that there is a statistically significant negative correlation between the export and the GDP growth rate of Albania. Explanation primarily may be found in export stagnation of Albania that has a negligible rate of increase. A high level of a negative correlation with the unemployment rate is present at Macedonia, while the correlation is positive at Albania. Albania is characterised by a modest increase of the unemployment rate, while in Macedonia it has a tendency of decreasing. However, Macedonia has a considerably higher unemployment rate. There is a statistically important influence of export to the level of public debt only at Bosnia and Herzegovina, while there is a negative correlation between the import and the

Table 1. Participation of export and import of member countries in total trade exchange within CEFTA 2006 (in % of global export and import of member countries)

	2007	2008	2009	2010	2011	2012	2013	2014	2015	2016
Albania										
Exports	8.66	13.62	6.49	10.37	12.50	12.03	10.87	11.60	14.21	13.57
Imports	6.86	8.33	5.94	9.07	8.64	9.19	7.91	7.90	7.55	6.58
Bosnia and Herzegovina										
Exports	35.81	37.04	35.89	33.62	32.90	29.30	28.27	14.19	13.22	13.14
Imports	29.08	28.90	26.80	27.00	24.98	25.15	23.92	11.44	12.26	12.63
Macedonia, FYR										
Exports	29.55	29.55	37.17	30.39	27.82	24.44	19.91	13.94	12.58	12.55
Imports	11.74	11.29	11.90	11.49	11.38	11.37	11.69	10.32	9.88	9.83
Montenegro										
Exports	28.94	35.43	46.19	39.51	35.41	55.97	60.70	39.14	37.01	39.79
Imports	33.59	34.91	39.22	40.47	43.18	44.39	44.12	37.34	37.79	30.46
Moldova										
Exports	0.65	0.92	0.60	0.45	0.31	0.28	0.18	0.22	0.27	0.52
Imports	0.19	0.25	0.31	0.30	0.37	0.35	0.42	0.60	0.50	0.65
Serbia										
Exports	32.25	33.14	31.56	28.72	27.26	25.15	21.75	19.02	18.59	17.84
Imports	8.16	7.95	8.14	8.68	8.55	7.89	7.15	4.50	4.12	3.99

Source: United Nations Statistics Division, 2017.

budget deficit at Moldova. Such the accomplishment of Moldova is the result of the successful decrease of public debt that was on a high level at the beginning of the observed period (World Bank Group, 2017). Statistically significant influence to the level of public debt may be noticed only on the example of Serbia. There is a negative correlation at Montenegro regarding the import and public debt and budget deficit and a significant positive correlation regarding the export and GDP growth, which is in accordance with expectations.

The seventh research issue provides answers to the possibility of having non-tariff trade barriers. Significant improvement in elimination of trade barriers was accomplished with establishment of CEFTA 2006 and taking over of the obligations from the Agreement. Elimination of customs duties in trade with agricultural and industrial products has a special importance. However, the problem of technical and non-customs barriers remains. A quota system is being introduced in order to protect domestic economy, which has a negative influence on economic performances of

Table 2. Correlation between import and export and GDP growth rate, unemployment rate, public debt and budget deficit

Country	Correlations		Unemployment	GDP Growth	Public Debt	Budget Deficit
Albania	Imports	Pearson Correlation	.755*	-0.516	.764*	0.076
		Sig. (2-tailed)	0.019	0.155	0.017	0.846
		N	9	9	9	9
	Exports	Pearson Correlation	.747*	-.831**	.875**	-0.203
		Sig. (2-tailed)	0.021	0.005	0.002	0.6
		N	9	9	9	9
Bosnia and Herzegovina	Imports	Pearson Correlation	-0.203	0.549	-0.099	-0.125
		Sig. (2-tailed)	0.601	0.126	0.801	0.75
		N	9	9	9	9
	Exports	Pearson Correlation	0.427	-0.088	.774*	-0.169
		Sig. (2-tailed)	0.252	0.822	0.014	0.664
		N	9	9	9	9
Macedonia	Imports	Pearson Correlation	-.893**	0.051	.931**	0.657
		Sig. (2-tailed)	0.001	0.896	0	0.055
		N	9	9	9	9
	Exports	Pearson Correlation	-.889**	0.066	.936**	0.638
		Sig. (2-tailed)	0.001	0.866	0	0.065
		N	9	9	9	9
Montenegro	Imports	Pearson Correlation	-0.587	0.618	-.677*	-.685*
		Sig. (2-tailed)	0.097	0.076	0.045	0.042
		N	9	9	9	9
	Exports	Pearson Correlation	-0.409	.708*	0.122	-0.315
		Sig. (2-tailed)	0.274	0.033	0.755	0.409
		N	9	9	9	9
Moldova	Imports	Pearson Correlation	-0.585	0.463	0.084	-.679*
		Sig. (2-tailed)	0.098	0.209	0.83	0.044
		N	9	9	9	9
	Exports	Pearson Correlation	-0.366	0.211	0.447	-0.305
		Sig. (2-tailed)	0.333	0.586	0.228	0.425
		N	9	9	9	9

continued on following page

Table 2. Continued

Country	Correlations		Unemployment	GDP Growth	Public Debt	Budget Deficit
Serbia	Imports	Pearson Correlation	-0.124	0.195	.696*	0.089
		Sig. (2-tailed)	0.75	0.615	0.037	0.819
		N	9	9	9	9
	Exports	Pearson Correlation	0.23	-0.252	.961**	0.49
		Sig. (2-tailed)	0.552	0.514	0	0.18
		N	9	9	9	9

**. Correlation is significant at the 0.01 level (2-tailed).

*. Correlation is significant at the 0.05 level (2-tailed).

the country (Klimzcak, 2016). Complex customs procedures for export and import of goods represent a greater problem, significantly reducing the possibility for the increase of the total volume of trade (Sowinski & Parker, 2017). Various empirical studies show that regardless the significant improvement in elimination of trade barriers, they still exist and may be reflected especially to the future of the trade within CEFTA 2006 (Toševska-Trpčevska & Tevdovski, 2016).

SOLUTIONS AND RECOMMENDATIONS

Potentials for import and export within the Free Trade Zone are not enough exploited. The increase of trade flows is prevailingly based on enlargement of the already existing trade cooperation before the establishment of CEFTA 2006. However, the world economic crisis showed that CEFTA 2006 is more than a good alternative when other export areas are restricted for import of goods and services. Further development of the Trade Free Zone depends on elimination of barriers, primarily in the domain of complex procedures for export and import of goods. This surely is important, not only from the standpoint of trade development, but also because it is one of the requirements for the accession to the European Union and the World Trade Organization.

Another problem is the institutional support of the member countries to further development of CEFTA 2006. A great deal has to be done for the promotion of export possibilities to this region. International statistical bases do not recognize CEFTA 2006 as a special trade area as it is the case with some other trade integrations. There is a link in the official web pages of national statistical institutions for the trade in CEFTA 2006, which is not in function. A new web portal was launched in the meanwhile, providing information about the trade of the member countries through periodical publications. A database is also present at the site, but only the data for the trade accomplished in 2012 can be seen. It is necessary that national institutions make additional effort in order to create a statistical base for trade flows of the CEFTA 2006 countries, so that it could be recognized in international scopes as the other trade integrations.

FUTURE RESEARCH DIRECTIONS

The analysis displayed in this chapter provides possibilities for the continuation of the research in several directions. Firstly, this chapter deals mainly with the trade exchange within CEFTA 2006. Through the participation of the member countries of the Free Trade Zone in the total trade exchange, it is easy to conclude that other trade regions are dominant for certain countries. A continuation of the research might be based on comparison of trade flows within CEFTA 2006 and trade flows in other international markets. Secondly, it is possible to make a comparative analysis of trade liberalisation effects achieved within the former free trade zone CEFTA and the current CEFTA 2006. Thirdly, it would be interesting to make a separate research for Croatia, which left this Free Trade Zone with the accession to the EU and consider if its trading position and competitiveness has been improved by this or it is now in a worse position.

CONCLUSION

The importance of trade liberalisation within CEFTA 2006 differs from one member country to another. It is the most important market for Bosnia and Herzegovina and Montenegro. It is the most important export market for Serbia and Macedonia. It is the market of moderate importance for Albania, while CEFTA 2006 is marginal market for Moldova. Trade volume surely should be greater and the member countries should use the chance offered by the trade liberalisation. Increase of the foreign trade exchange within CEFTA 2006 followed the world economic crisis and decrease of trade volume, which shows that the market can absorb the goods and the services that are primarily intended for the market of the European Union. Leaving the Free Trade Zone of Croatia has decreased the total trade volume. However, a chance was provided in this way for other members to take over this part of the trade exchange. The structure of goods and services in trading is not satisfactory. Member countries trade with the same groups of products. Maybe a specialization for certain products would improve the export performances of the member countries. Trade flows influence the economic performances of all the member countries. However, the correlation analysis of influences of the trade flows to macroeconomic indicators of the members has not resulted with a unique conclusion. There is a statistically significant correlation of trade flows to economic performances in all of the observed countries, but the influence is different for each country. Work should continue in the next period on further elimination of trade barriers. Foremost, the role of state institutions of the member countries is the key here regarding the simplification and unification of complex technical procedures and regarding the promotion of CEFTA 2006 as an attractive trade region. The main advantage is in the increase of the competitiveness and a form of preparation for the European and other international markets, since there is not much difference between the member countries regarding their economic strength.

REFERENCES

Balassa, B. (1961). *The Theory of Economic Integration. Richard D. Irwin, Inc.*

Balassa, B. (1976). Types of economic integration. In *Economic Integration: Worldwide, Regional, Sectoral* (pp. 17–40). Palgrave Macmillan. doi:10.1007/978-1-349-02571-8_2

Baldwin, J. R., & Gu, W. (2004). Trade liberalization: Export-market participation, productivity growth, and innovation. *Oxford Review of Economic Policy*, *20*(3), 372–392. doi:10.1093/oxrep/grh022

Baldwin, R. E. (2004). Challenges to Globalization. An Overview. In Challenges to Globalization: Analyzing the Economics (pp. 1-14). University of Chicago Press.

Broz, T., Buturac, G., & Tkalec, M. (2015). To what extent does Croatia really cooperate with SEE countries in he fields of foreign trade, direct investment and tourism? *Ekonomska Istrazivanja*, *28*(1), 879–906. doi:10.1080/1331677X.2015.1092703

Cestepe, H., Zildirim, E., & Bahtiyar, B. (2015). The impact of Trade Liberalization on teh Export of MENA Countries to OECD Trade Partners. *Procedia Economics and Finance*, *23*, 1440–1445. doi:10.1016/S2212-5671(15)00427-X

Chamber of Commerce and Industry of Serbia. (2017). *Implementation of CEFTA 2006*. Retrieved May 10, 2017, from http://www.pks.rs/SADRZAJ/Files/CEFTA_ENGLESKI%20DEO.pdf

Čokić, M. (2014). *Aktivnosti Bosne i Hercegovine u cilju realizaciji Centralnoevropskog ugovora o slobodnoj trgovini - CEFTA 2006*. Zbornik radova: II Međunarodna konferencija Bosna i Hercegovina i Euroatlantske integracije Trenutni izazovi i perspektive. Retrieved April 29, 2017, from https://ssrc.ibu.edu.ba/assets/ssrc/userfiles/files/ZBORNIK-TOM-II.pdf

Dai, M., Yotov, Y. V., & Zylkin, T. (2014). On the trade-diversion effects of free trade agreements. *Economics Letters, 122*(2), 321–325. doi:10.1016/j.econlet.2013.12.024

Disdier, A. C., Fontagne, L., & Mimouni, M. (2013). *Tariff Liberalization and Trade Integration of Emerging Countries.* CEPII Working paper No. 2013-36. Retrieved May 8, 2017, from http://www.cepii.fr/PDF_PUB/wp/2013/wp2013-36.pdf

EBRD. (2014). *Transition Report 2014 - Innovation in transition.* Retrieved April 29, 2017, from http://www.ebrd.com/news/publications/transition-report/transition-report-2014.html

EBRD. (2015). *Transition Report 2015-16 - Rebalancing finance*. Retrieved April 29, 2017, from http://www.ebrd.com/news/publications/transition-report/ebrd-transition-report-201516.html

Egger, H., & Kreickemeier, U. (2009). Firm heterogeneity and the labor market effects of trade liberalization. *International Economic Review, 50*(1), 187–216. doi:10.1111/j.1468-2354.2008.00527.x

Falvey, R., Foster, N., & Greenaway, D. (2012). Trade Liberalization, Econmic Crises, and Growth. *World Development, 40*(11), 2177–2193. doi:10.1016/j.worlddev.2012.03.020

Fan, H., Li, Y. A., & Yeaple, S. R. (2015). Trade liberalization, quality, and export prices. *The Review of Economics and Statistics, 97*(5), 1033–1051. doi:10.1162/REST_a_00524

Haberler, G. (1959). The Theory of International Trade. Academic Press.

Hakim, A., & Hamdi, H. (2016). Trade liberalizaction, FDI inflows, environmental quality and ekonomic growth: A comparative analzsis bwteen Tunisaia and Morocco. *Renewable & Sustainable Energy Reviews, 58*, 1445–1456. doi:10.1016/j.rser.2015.12.280

Harrison, A. (1996). Openness and growth: A time-series, cross-country analysis for developing countries. *Journal of Development Economics, 48*(2), 419–447. doi:10.1016/0304-3878(95)00042-9

Hillman, A. L. (2015). 12. Rents and international trade policy. *Companion to the Political Economy of Rent Seeking*, 187.

IMF. (2017). *World Economic Outlook*. Retrieved May 10, 2017, from http://www.imf.org/en/Data

Investopedia. (2017). *Financial dictinary*. Retrieved May 5, 2017, from http://www.investopedia.com/terms/e/economic-integration.asp

Jenkins, R. (1996). Trade liberalization and export performance in Bolivia. *Development and Change*, *27*(4), 693–716. doi:10.1111/j.1467-7660.1996.tb00608.x

Kindleberger, C. (1974). *Međunarodna ekonomija*. Beograd, Srbija: Vuk Karadžić.

Kit-Katos, K., & Sparrow, R. (2015). Poverty, labour market and trade liberalization in Indonezia. *Journal of Development Economics*, *117*, 94–106. doi:10.1016/j.jdeveco.2015.07.005

Klimczak, L. (2016). Trade Liberalisation and Export Performance of the Western Balkans 1. *Montenegrin Journal of Economics*, *12*(2), 45–60. doi:10.14254/1800-5845.2016/12-1/3

Kneller, R., Morgan, C. W., & Kanchanahatakij, S. (2008). Trade liberalisation and economic growth. *World Economy*, *31*(6), 701–719. doi:10.1111/j.1467-9701.2008.01101.x

Kragulj, D. (2005). *Evropski integracioni i tranzicioni procesi*. Beograd, Srbija: Kragulj.

Kragulj, D. (2016). *Ekonomija – Osnovi mikroekonomske i makroekonomske analize*. Beograd, Srbija: Kragulj.

Lawson, C., & Wang, H. (2004). *Economic Transition in Central and Eastern Europe and the Former Soviet Union: Which Policies Worked?* University of Bath.

Le, T. H., & Tran-Nam, B. (in press). Trade Liberalization, Financial Modernizaation and Economic Development: An Emprical Studz of Selected Asia-Pacific Countries. *Research in Economics*.

Lee, E. (2005). *Trade liberalization and employment*. UN.

Liyanaarachchi, T. S., Naranpanawa, A., & Bandara, J. S. (2016). Impact of trade liberalisation on labour market and poverty in Sri Lanka. An integrated macro-micro modelling approach. *Economic Modelling*, *59*, 102–115. doi:10.1016/j.econmod.2016.07.008

Magee, C. S. (2016). Trade creation, trade diversion, and the general equilibrium effects of regional trade agreements: A study of the European Community–Turkey customs union. *Review of World Economics*, *152*(2), 383–399. doi:10.1007/s10290-015-0239-4

Manni, U. H., Naser, M., & Afzal, M. N. I. (2012). Effect of trade liberalization on economidc growth of developing countries: A case of Bangladesh economy. *Journal of Business. Economics &Finance*, *1*(2), 37–44.

Manwa, F., & Wijeweera, A. (2016). Trade liberalisation and economic growth link:The case of Southern African Custom Union countries. *Economic Analysis and Policy*, *51*, 13–2. doi:10.1016/j.eap.2016.05.001

Naranpanawa, A., & Arora, R. (2014). Does trade liberalization promote regional disparities? Evidence from a multiregional CGE model of India. *World Development*, *64*, 339–349. doi:10.1016/j.worlddev.2014.06.001

Nikolić, G. (2013). Tendency of exports technology structure and exports concentration in the Balkan economies 2000-2012. *Industrija*, *41*(3), 7–24. doi:10.5937/industrija41-4186

OECD. (2011). *The Impact of Trade Liberalisation on Jobs and Growth: Technical Note, OECD Trade Policy Papers, No. 107*. Paris: OECD Publishing; doi:10.1787/5kgj4jfj1nq2-

Petkovic, M., Djedovic-Negre, D., & Lukic, J. (2015). Public-Private Partnerships: Interorganizational Design as Key Success Factor. *Mangement. Journal for Theory and Practice Management*, *77*, 1–11.

Pinder, J. (1968). Positive integration and negative integration: Some problems of economic union in the EEC. *The World Today*, *24*(3), 88–110.

Revenga, A. (1995). *Employment and Wages effect of Trade Liberalization.* Policy Reserach Working Paper 1524. The World Bank. Latin America and the Caribbean. Retrieved May 8, 2017, from https://213.154.74.164/invenio/record/10976/files/wps1524.pdf

Rodriguez, F., & Rodrik, D. (2000). Trade policy and economic growth: A skeptic's guide to the cross-national evidence. *NBER Macroeconomics Annual*, *15*, 261–325. doi:10.1086/654419

Saavedra-Rivano, N., & Estrada, M. A. R. (2016). An alternative free trade agreement scheme to developing countries: The micro-free trade territory (MFTT). *Quality & Quantity*, *50*(5), 2293–2311. doi:10.1007/s11135-015-0263-4

Šaban, I. S., & Ušakov, N. A. (1971). *Imperialističeskaja suščnost'zapadnoevropejskoj integracii: meždunarodnopravovye aspekty*. Moskva: Nauka.

Sowinski, C., & Parker, L. (2017). WCO Immediate Release Guidelines State of Application in CEFTA. *Global Trade and Customs Journal*, *12*(5), 196–202.

Stančić, D., & Jednak, S. (2003). Privredna transformacija i privatizacija u Poljskoj. *Management*, *29*, 23–28.

Tabuchi, T. (2017). Comparative advantage in the light of the old value theories. In *A new construction of ricardian theory of international values* (pp. 265–280). Springer Singapore. doi:10.1007/978-981-10-0191-8_9

Tinbergen, J. (1959). *On the Theory of Economic Integration*. Amsterdam.

Toševska-Trpčevska, K., & Tevdovski, D. (2016). Trade Facilitation Indicators and Their Potential Impact on Trade between the Countries of South-Eastern Europe. *Scientific Annals of Economics and Business*, *63*(3), 347–362. doi:10.1515/saeb-2016-0127

Trading Economics. (2017). Retrieved May 12, 2017, from http://www.tradingeconomics.com/

Turnbull, C., Sun, S., & Anwar, S. (2016). Trade liberalisation, inward FDI and productivity within Australia's manufacturing sector. *Economic Analysis and Policy*, *51*, 12–21.

United Nations Statistics Division. (2017). *UN Comtrade Database*. Retrieved May 12, 2017, from https://comtrade.un.org/

Viner, J. (1950). *The Customs Union Issue*. London, UK: Stevens and Son Ltd.

Wacziarg, R., & Welch, K. H. (2008). Trade liberalization and growth: New evidence. *The World Bank Economic Review*, *22*(2), 187–231. doi:10.1093/wber/lhn007

World Bank Group. (2017). *World Bank Open Data*. Retrieved May 12, 2017, from http://data.worldbank.org/

Yang, S., & Martinez-Zarzoso, I. (2014). A panel data analysis of trade creation and trade diversion effects: The case of ASEAN–China Free Trade Area. *China Economic Review*, *29*, 138–151. doi:10.1016/j.chieco.2014.04.002

Yanikkaya, H. (2003). Trade openness and economic growth: A cross-country empirical investigation. *Journal of Development Economics*, *72*(1), 57–89. doi:10.1016/S0304-3878(03)00068-3

KEY TERMS AND DEFINITIONS

CEFTA 2006: Regional agreement defining a unique free trade zone of South-East Europe (i.e., it represents the trade agreement between Albania, Bosnia and Herzegovina, Macedonia, Moldova, Serbia, UNMIK on behalf of Kosovo and Metohija and Montenegro, replacing in practice 32 bilateral agreements in force before).

Economic Integration: Connecting several national economies into a unique economic area, primarily on a regional basis.

Free Trade Agreement: Key condition for creation of free trade areas and customs unions, implying trade liberalisation on reciprocal basis, which means that all countries eliminate customs duties for import from territories of other countries.

Globalization: Evermore integration of goods, services, labour, money, and capital markets in the world, under influence of multinational and transnational companies.

Pearson's Correlation Coefficient: It is widely used measure of the linear correlation between two variables.

Trade Barriers: Process of discrimination in trade that is conducted by various instruments like customs and non-customs barriers, quantitative quotas, administrative restraints, imposing technical and ecological standards, etc. with aim to create unequal conditions in international trade for economic subjects from different countries.

Trade Integration: The lowest form of economic integration where all trade barriers have been eliminated.

Trade Liberalization: Process of eliminating all barriers and trade restrictions with the aim of free business operations.

Transition: Process that sums up complex social, economic, and political reforms in one country.

Transition Countries: Countries that are moving from direct planning to market economy and perform transformation of one-party political system to pluralistic society.

Chapter 2
Contemporary Foreign Trade Policy of China in the Region of Central and Northeast Asia

Vasilii Erokhin
Harbin Engineering University, China

ABSTRACT

China is one of the fastest growing economies in the world. To ensure a continual increase in trade, China's contemporary policies are aimed at the creation of new market opportunities for China's companies abroad. The chapter addresses the major challenges of collaboration between China and the countries of Central and Northeast Asia, reviews the milestones of China's trade policies in Eurasia, analyses China's recent trade and development initiative (One Belt One Road project) and its convergence with other integration initiatives in the region, and reviews trade flows between China and the countries of Central Asia (Kazakhstan, Kyrgyzstan, Russia, Tajikistan, Turkmenistan, and Uzbekistan) and Northeast Asia (Democratic People's Republic of Korea, Japan, Mongolia, and the Republic of Korea) during 2015. The chapter is concluded with an analysis of how China can pursue shaping an inter-regional market by looking across national boundaries and with the discussion of structural changes needed for China to ensure its competitiveness in the markets of the studied country.

DOI: 10.4018/978-1-5225-4032-8.ch002

INTRODUCTION

The unprecedented economic rise of China during 2000-2015, the investment-led growth model of the country, and significant demand for resources created by China provided the drivers for the economic growth and increase of trade flows worldwide (Shah, 2016; Wong, Chi, Tsui, & Tiejun, 2017). Trade and China's investments in infrastructure and manufacturing linked the regions and developed a solid basis for cooperation (Zhang, 2016; Bondaz, Cohen, Godement, Kratz, & Pantucci, 2015). In 2013, China announced a global initiative: One Belt One Road (OBOR) project, a continuation and exportation of the development successes that China has experienced during the 2000s. OBOR focuses on the improvement of connectivity and collaboration among the countries of the world, particularly, in the macro-region of Eurasia. In this region, the collapse of the Soviet Union in the early 1990s along with the gradual opening up of China during the 1980-1990s led to the opening up of previously closed borders from European countries in the West to Asian states in the East (Linn & Tiomkin, 2006). OBOR also aims at the involvement of eastern neighbors of China, i.e. Japan, Republic of Korea, and Mongolia into the global trade and development networks led by China. Such trade policy initiated by China ushered in a new phase of Eurasian development by permitting the integration of the economies of Central and Northeast Asia with each other and with the rest of the world.

Countries of Central and Northeast Asia differ from each other on many parameters, including the economic potential regarding available resources, technologies, and labor force, the level of economic development, and the share in the world trade. Countries of Central Asia (Kazakhstan, Kyrgyzstan, Tajikistan, Turkmenistan, and Uzbekistan) experienced the Soviet-type model of development and underwent considerable economic and political transitions in the early 1990s, from centrally-planned communist regimes to democratic market economies (Khandelwal & Roitman, 2013). Russia, another post-Soviet country, progressed into the well-functioning market economy and remained the key market player in the region of Central Asia, but the process of market reforms for Russia is still incomplete (Erokhin, 2016a). In the Northeast Asia, Japan and the Republic of Korea (South Korea) are considered as one of the most developed economies in the world, high involved in international trade. Mongolia, a landlocked country in the very center of Eurasia, is a lower middle-income economy which specializes in mining and agriculture. Democratic People's Republic of Korea (North Korea) is a socialist state, one of the most closed and centralized economies in the world.

Despite the essential differences between the countries of Central and Northeast Asia, China is one of the largest trading partners for the most of them. For China, further development of trade relations with such different partners requires the establishment of common economic basis, sustainable to economic and geopolitical fluctuations. Contemporary trade policy of China in the region is targeted on development of economic collaboration between Asia and Europe by physical, financial, and economic integration of the entire Eurasian continent with China at its core (Duchatel et al., 2016). Pursuing its economic interests, China aims at solving the most pressing sustainable development challenges in the region of Central and Northeast Asia and promoting a new model of international collaboration using strengthening of existing regional bilateral and multilateral mechanisms and creating a common economic space in Eurasia.

Such trade policy may create a new form of multilateralism which will ensure China's growing leadership in the world, i.e. a focus on long-term investments and infrastructure development. However, in the region of Central and Northeast Asia, such an expansion of China carries not only opportunities but also serious risks. For the countries in the region, especially developing and transition economies, there are many challenges: how to overcome turbulence when opening national markets to international competition, keep existing competitive advantages, prevent "overheating" and "bubbles" in the conditions of growing foreign trade while also maximize effect of trade and economic integration between China and other countries in the region. When increasing its influence in the area using growing trade, China has to remember that not every Eurasian country welcomes such expansion. Most of the countries in Central Asia are afraid to become dependent on trade and economic collaboration with China (Duchatel et al., 2016). Even such developed economies as Japan and the Republic of Korea wary of China's growing dominance in the region and consider China as their most fierce competitor on the global market. On the one hand, countries of Central and Northeast Asia want to enhance their trade turnover and prosperity through establishing closer links with China as the biggest economic power in the region. On the other hand, they want to secure their economic independence. That is why it is so important both for China and its neighbours to create a standard to which integration forces from both sides can be held (Duchatel et al., 2016) and to harmonize actions taken by China and the countries of Central and Northeast Asia with their efforts on the achievement of sustainable development of trade and economic growth.

BACKGROUND

There have been attempts to study China's foreign trade policy or the impact of China's policy on the countries of Central and Northeast Asia. Dohmen (1976), Lu (1997), Mariani (2013), Hamrin and Zhao (1995), Wu (2006), and Liberthal (2004) provided in-depth analysis of foreign trade policy of China in general. Cass,

Williams, and Barker (2003), Lardy (2002), Panitchpakdi and Clifford (2002), and Anderson, Martin, and Van der Mensbrugghe (2010) studied the implications of China's membership in the World Trade Organization (WTO) on both China's internal policies and foreign trade. Recent studies of China's contemporary trade policy by Bondaz et al. (2015), Zhang (2016), Shah (2016), and Wong et al. (2017) all concluded that China could play a meaningful role in furthering the sustainable development in the region of Central and Northeast Asia.

Integration in the macro-region of Eurasia and expansion of China were discussed by Vinokurov and Libman (2012) who concluded that regional integration projects in the post-Soviet area face substantial difficulties in terms of coping with Eurasian economic ties. Khanna and Palepu (2010) studied specifics of development in emerging markets, including China, while other researchers investigated national specifics of integration processes, i.e. Wu (2006) addressed experiences of transition processes amid globalization on the case of China. Many experts recognize specific risks associated with China's trade policy in the region of Central and Northeast Asia. J. Zhang (2016) acknowledges that China's trade and development initiatives, such as OBOR, are the active drivers of the regional and global economy, but warns that the effective implementation of trade policy over the medium-to-long term depends on the responsiveness of both China and the countries in Central and Northeast Asia to the global challenges of sustainable development. As of Wong et al. (2017), despite the China's desire to explore new market opportunities, expansion of China in the region will inevitably face antagonism of the key regional economic powers, i.e. Russia in Central Asia and Japan and the Republic of Korea in Northeast Asia. Fedorenko (2015) investigated mechanisms of intergovernmental cooperation in the region of Central Asia and elaborated on the effects of Eurasian integration on Kazakhstan, Kyrgyzstan, Tajikistan, Uzbekistan, and Turkmenistan. He concluded that regional economic cooperation and trade constituted an essential factor of sustainable growth in Central Asia, but acknowledged the struggle between Russia and China for political and economic dominance in the region. Mariani (2013) emphasized that China's presence in the region of Central Asia was received with varying degrees of acceptance, tolerance, or mistrust among civil society. However, he believed that China's expansion in the region fueled economic growth of Central Asian states.

Despite differing interests in the region, China considers the region of Central and Northeast Asia as a link between itself and the markets of Europe, Asia, and North America. If contemporary China's trade initiatives can be successfully emerged and can involve all countries of the region, it will help shaping a new kind of partnership and increase the role of China as a global actor.

MAIN FOCUS OF THE CHAPTER

China's Foreign Trade

After its foundation in 1949, China gradually carried out economic and trade exchanges with foreign countries (Embassy of the People's Republic of China in the United States of America [China's Embassy in the USA], 2011). China's strategy of "Opening up" was introduced in 1978, and foreign trade has played a central role in China's economic reform process ever since (Solanko, 2016). Following that policy, China has opened wider to the world market, attracted foreign direct investments, and achieved rapid development in foreign trade. In 1978, China accounted for only 1% of the world's total trade (0.76% of the world's total export and 0.82% of the world's total import), while in 2015, China's share in world's total export surpassed the share of the USA (Figure 1).

As a result of the "Opening up" strategy, the structure of China's trade in goods has fundamentally changed. China's export commodity structure shifted from the primary products dominated to manufactured goods dominated in the 1980s, and from

Figure 1. Comparison of China's and the USA's shares in the world's total export and import in 1950-2015, percentage
Source: Author's development based on the United Nations Conference on Trade and Development [UNCTAD] (2017).

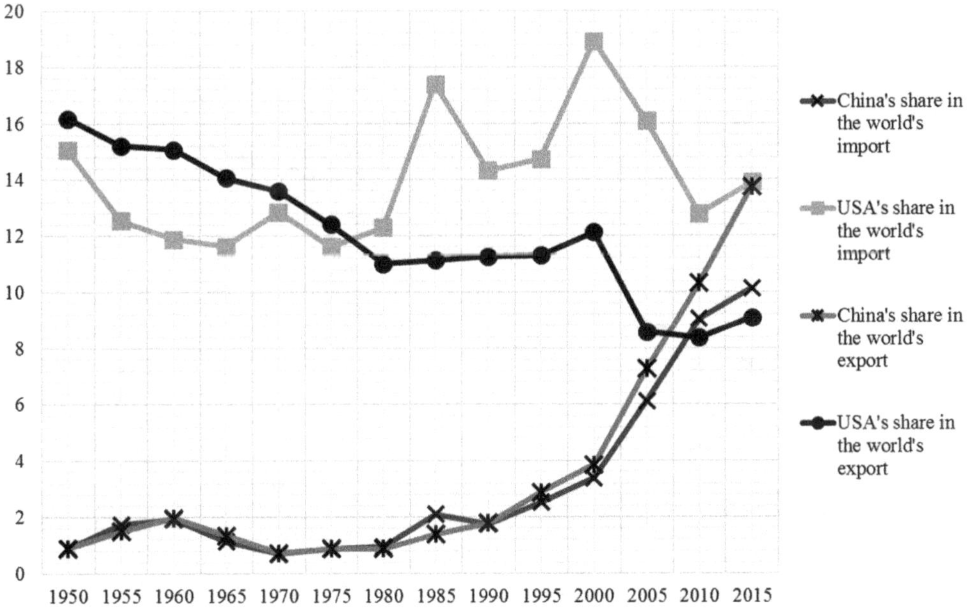

mainly light industrial and textile products to primarily mechanical and electronic products in the 1990s (China's Embassy in the USA, 2011).

In 2001, the country received a new stimulus for the expansion of its foreign trade with the accession to the WTO, an integral part of the policy of opening up and liberalizing the economy. During five years after accession, China's share in the world's total export increased from 4.29% in 2001 up to 7.26% in 2005, in the world's total import from 3.80% up to 6.12%, respectively. China committed to allowing foreign trade operations to all companies, eliminate dual pricing practices for export goods, adhere to agreements on intellectual property rights, allow foreign participation in the major service sectors, and substantially decrease average import tariff levels (Solanko, 2016).

China's export-oriented trade policy of the late 1990s and early 2000s resulted in rapid increase of foreign trade turnover (FTT) in 2005-2015. Within a decade, China's export increased almost threefold from $762.0 billion up to $2.3 trillion (Figure 2).

Major China's trading partners are the USA, the EU, Japan, and ASEAN countries. Altogether, these economies accounted for 48.7% of China's total foreign trade in 2015 (T. Zhang, 2016). In comparison, the aggregated share of all countries of Central Asia, including Russia, was only 2.3% and 2.9% in China's export and import, respectively. Countries of Northeast Asia accounted for 10.6% of China's

Figure 2. China's export, import and foreign trade balance in 2005-2015, $ bln
Source: Author's development based on the United Nations Conference on Trade and Development [UNCTAD] (2017).

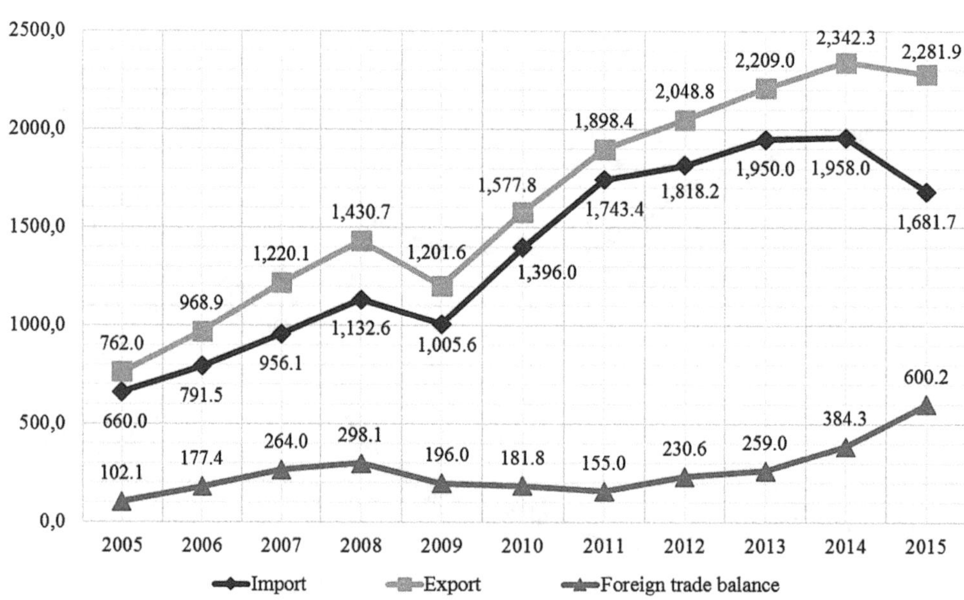

export and 19.3% of China's import (Figure 3). During 2005-2015, the share of the Northeast Asian countries in China's FTT decreased from 20.99% down to 14.28% in favor of the USA and the EU.

To decrease production costs and increase productivity, China continues modernization of the industrial sector. During 2005-2015, the major import item is machinery and transport equipment (over 40% in 2015) (Figure 4). China is one of the world leading importers of natural resources, raw materials, and primary products; the country imports crude materials, mineral fuels, and chemicals.

Machinery and transport equipment and miscellaneous manufactured articles, including traditional labor-intensive products, are China's primary export commodities (Figure 5).

As of T. Zhang (2016), there is a structural upgrading trend in China's foreign trade, emphasizing the increasing exports of several high-tech products, such as medical equipment and instruments, storage batteries and solar batteries, materials technology, and aerospace products. China has benefited from the liberalization of foreign trade and an increase in domestic competition that both have enabled growth in exports of high-quality manufactured goods (Pula & Santabarbara, 2012). As

Figure 3. Shares of the countries of Central and Northeast Asia in China's FTT in 2005-2015, percentage
Source: Author's development based on UNCTAD (2017).
*Note: * Japan, Mongolia, North Korea, and South Korea*
*** Kazakhstan, Kyrgyzstan, Russia, Tajikistan, Turkmenistan, and Uzbekistan*

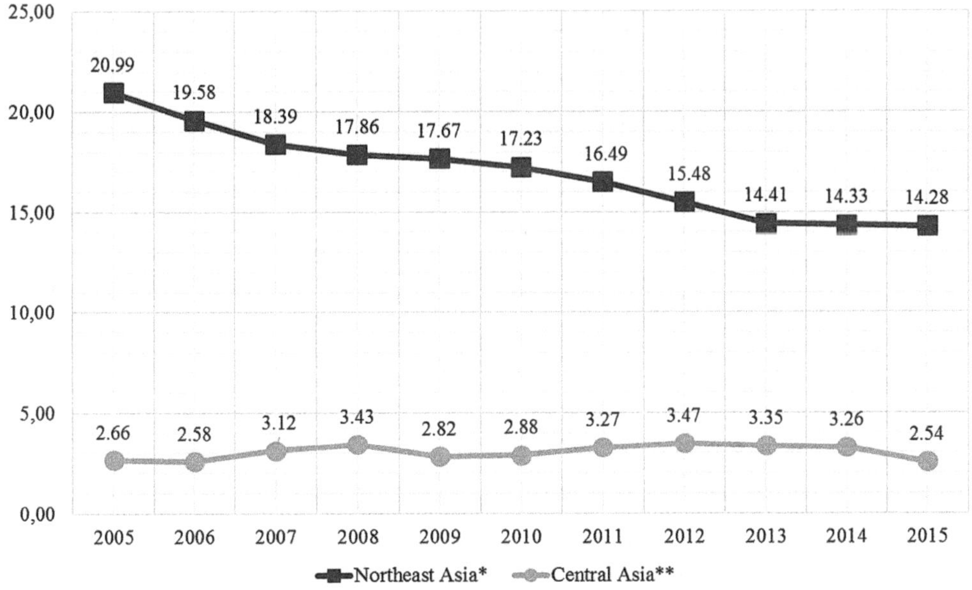

Figure 4. China's major import commodities in 2005-2015, shares in the overall national import, percentage
Source: Author's development based on UNCTAD (2017).

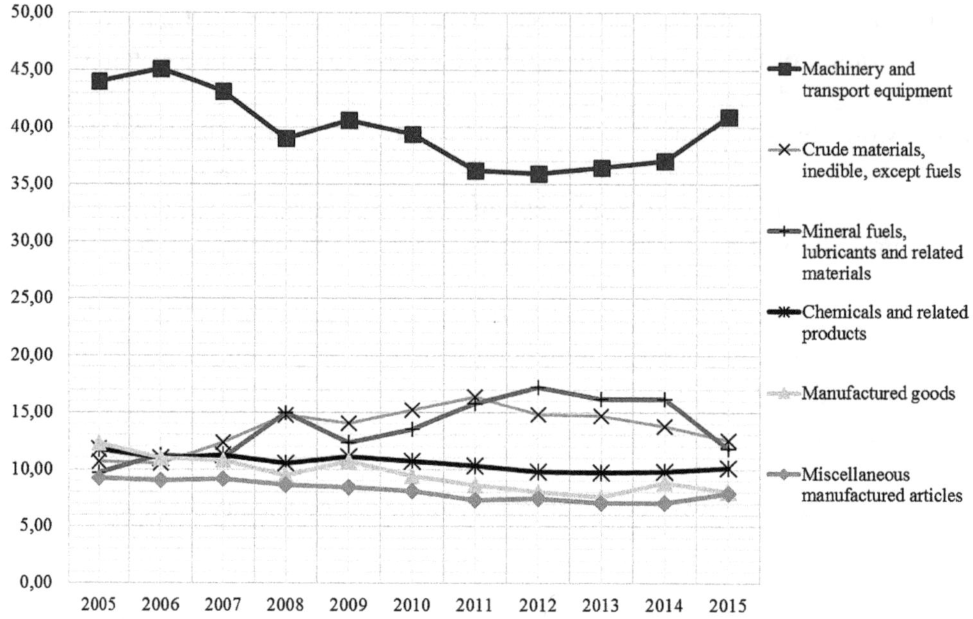

Figure 5. China's major export commodities in 2005-2015, shares in the overall national export, percentage
Source: Author's development based on UNCTAD (2017).

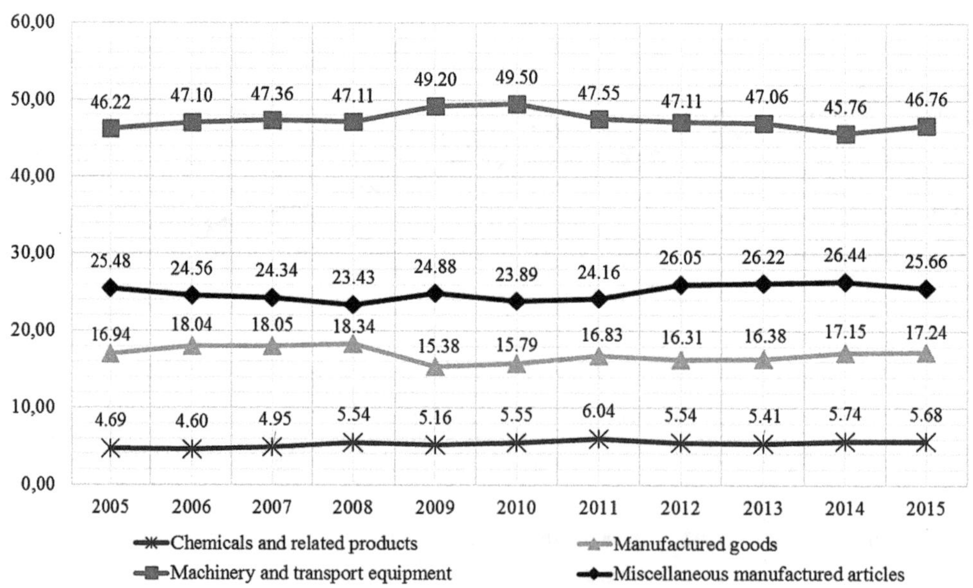

of Solanko (2016), in 1990, only 10% of China's exports was in high-technology goods. By 2000, the share had doubled to around 20%, and in 2014 the share was already closer to 30%. Manufacturing industries in China are now confronted with pressure to relocate: either returning to developed countries for greater efficiency or moving to emerging economies for lower costs (T. Zhang, 2016). China's foreign trade policy aims at restructuring and optimizing of foreign trade by promoting of processing trade, industrial upgrading, and structural optimization, as well as the relocation of manufacturing to China's central and western regions. Some experts (Lemoine & Ünal, 2017; Yuan, 2017) believe that global production chains through processing activities are no longer the primary driver of China's trade performance. As of Lemoine and Ünal (2017), China's development policy should be based on local inputs and domestic demand. Yuan (2017) developed a domestic-market-dominated trade strategy for China. However, having in mind the success of the "opening up" trade policy of the 1980-1990s, Chinese government sees an expansion on the global market as one of the most promising tools to increase exports and support the growth of China's economy.

Contemporary Trade Policies of China: One Belt One Road Initiative

One Belt One Road initiative is a development strategy proposed by the Chinese government in 2013. OBOR focuses on the improvement of connectivity and collaboration among the countries of Eurasia through the increase of China's role in global affairs. Having interregional character, it potentially involves over 50 countries of Asia, Europe, and the Middle East which taken together cover 55% of world Gross National Product (GNP), 70% of global population, and 75% of known energy reserves (Bondaz et al., 2015). China aims at promotion of such cross-continental partnership in five areas: policy communication, road connectivity, unimpeded trade, money circulation, and cultural understanding.

OBOR seeks to rebuild the Silk Road through the development and upgrading of regional infrastructure projects (Shah, 2016). It consists of two routes: the overland Silk Road Economic Belt which goes from China to Europe through the countries of Central Asia and the Middle East to Russia and then to the Eastern, Central, and Western Europe. The second route, the Maritime Silk Road, connects China with Europe through the countries of Southeast Asia, Africa, and the Persian Gulf (Figure 6).

Six international economic cooperation corridors are planned to be established. Silk Road Economic Belt will include the New Eurasia Land Bridge, China-Mongolia-Russia Economic Corridor, China-Central Asia-West Asia Economic Corridor, and China-Pakistan Economic Corridor. Two corridors, China-Indochina

Figure 6. Two OBOR routes: Overland Silk Road Economic Belt and Maritime Silk Road
Source: Silk Road Trade and Travel Encyclopedia, n.d.

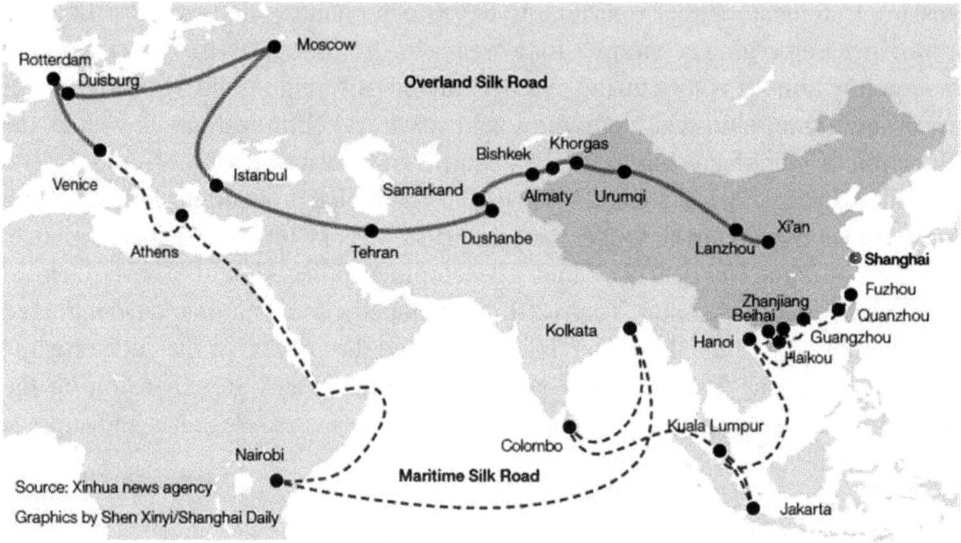

Peninsula Economic Corridor and Bangladesh-China-India-Myanmar Economic Corridor, will compose the Maritime Silk Road. In this chapter, we consider two corridors of the Silk Road Economic Belt, namely New Eurasia Land Bridge and China-Mongolia-Russia Economic Corridor, which unite the countries of Central and North Asia. Technically, OBOR is supposed to connect China with Asian, African, and European states by rail networks, maritime ports, energy pipelines, and other infrastructure projects and provide Chinese goods easier access to the markets of over 50 participating countries.

OBOR and China's Trade Policy in Central Asia

As of Zhang (2016), many of China's production sectors have been facing overcapacity since 2006. Through OBOR China, first, would like to explore new markets of the countries in Eurasia and ensure growing demand for its products, second, give impetus to the accelerated development of China's less developed regions along the borders with Russia, Mongolia, Kazakhstan, Kyrgyzstan, and Tajikistan, and third, explore new investment options for the huge capital accumulated in the country during the previous few decades of economic growth.

Countries of Central Asia have progressed since the collapse of the Soviet Union in 1991 and became attractive markets for Chinese goods. Aggregated import of

Kazakhstan, Kyrgyzstan, Russia, Tajikistan, Turkmenistan, and Uzbekistan increased up to $560 billion in 2015 from only $90 billion in 1995 with Russia's share in total import over 53%. Russia is not a Central Asian state despite the fact that some of its territories geographically lay in Central Asia. Russia has close economic ties with five post-Soviet states of the region. Also, Russia has vital economic and trade interests in the area and considers Central Asia as a region of its geopolitical influence (Bugajski, 2008). However, in 2015, with the global drop in oil prices and Western sanctions in the aftermath of the Ukraine crisis, Russia faced a severe decline of its national currency and purchasing power which taken together decreased its FTT. Annual rates of GDP of the Central Asian countries have also been very fluctuant as the result of the high dependence of those countries on the global demand for natural resources and primary products. Countries of Central Asia are not very much diversified; they are not able to spread risks of lower global demand in particular industries on the entire domestic economy. Aggregated GDP of six countries decreased from $2.2 trillion in 2014 down to $1.6 trillion in 2015, while China continued to grow and reached the peak of $11.2 trillion (UNCTAD, 2017).

Russia's share of the combined GDP of the six countries is about 86%. Second is Kazakhstan with 10%, which totally makes almost 96%. In the pursuit of increasing its economic and geopolitical power in the region, Russia has recently initiated the Eurasian Economic Union (EAEU) between Kazakhstan, Kyrgyzstan, Armenia, and Belarus. Russia's intention is to make the union an alternative to a rather inertial alliance of the Commonwealth of Independent States (CIS) and to turn it into the non-regional bloc. Vietnam joined the free trade zone with the EAEU in 2015. Thailand also expressed its interest in joining the union in the nearest future (Erokhin, 2015).

The union is also open for those Central Asian states, which have not joined it by now (Tajikistan and Uzbekistan), but it seems that Russia will face a fight for the influence on those countries with China's OBOR. Countries of Central Asia expect engagement with China through OBOR to give them access to financial resources, as well as employment opportunities (Kaczmarski, 2015). They even prefer to sign separate bilateral agreements with China rather than using the EAEU as a platform for collective negotiations. OBOR is more attractive for most of the countries in the region since it gives them hope for new markets and new trade opportunities. Countries of Central Asia trade less among themselves than with outside partners, and in 2014-2016 the slowdown of Russia's economy and Western sanctions against Russia have caused trade flows between the Central Asian economies to decline even further (Duchatel et al., 2016). OBOR is expected to facilitate trade between China and the countries of Central Asia and let goods to move from the East to the West without barriers (even bypassing Russia). China is the largest importer of raw goods from Central Asia, and trade with China is growing faster than that with Russia (Kaczmarski, 2015).

Table 1. China's trade with the countries of Central Asia in 2005-2015, $ billion

Countries	2005	2006	2007	2008	2009	2010	2011	2012	2013	2014	2015
Export from China											
Kazakhstan	3.90	4.75	7.45	9.82	7.75	9.32	9.57	11.00	12.55	12.71	8.43
Kyrgyzstan	0.87	2.11	3.67	9.21	5.23	4.13	4.88	5.07	5.08	5.24	4.28
Russia	13.21	15.83	28.53	33.08	17.51	29.61	38.90	44.06	49.59	53.68	34.81
Tajikistan	0.14	0.31	0.51	1.48	1.22	1.38	2.00	1.75	1.87	2.47	1.80
Turkmenistan	0.09	0.16	0.30	0.80	0.92	0.53	0.78	1.70	1.14	0.95	0.82
Uzbekistan	0.23	0.41	0.76	1.28	1.56	1.18	1.36	1.78	2.61	2.68	2.24
Import to China											
Kazakhstan	2.91	3.61	6.43	7.73	6.26	11.11	15.35	14.68	16.05	9.74	5.84
Kyrgyzstan	0.11	0.11	0.11	0.12	0.05	0.07	0.10	0.09	0.06	0.06	0.06
Russia	15.89	17.55	19.69	23.83	21.28	25.91	40.36	44.14	39.67	41.62	33.22
Tajikistan	0.01	0.02	0.01	0.02	0.18	0.06	0.07	0.11	0.09	0.05	0.05
Turkmenistan	0.02	0.02	0.05	0.03	0.04	1.04	4.69	8.67	8.89	9.52	7.83
Uzbekistan	0.45	0.57	0.36	0.33	0.35	1.30	0.81	1.09	1.94	1.60	1.27

Source: UNCTAD, 2017.

Russia is still the major trading partner of China among the countries of Central Asia (Table 1). However, being under the Western sanctions, Russia has been the worst performer among the Central Asian economies regarding trade with China since 2014. In 2015, Russia's import from China decreased by 35.2% compared to 2014, while export to China decreased by 20.2%, respectively.

During the 2000s, lack of comprehensive structural reforms in Russia was masked by a growth fueled by sizeable oil revenues (Erokhin, 2014). Major Russia's export commodities in its trade with China are petroleum and petroleum products (over 60% of Russia's export to China in 2015), cork, wood, coal, coke, and non-ferrous metals (Table 2). China also imports fish, crustaceans, and mollusks from Russia's Far East.

While importing natural resources, raw materials, and primary products from Russia, China delivers to Russia high value-added commodities and high-tech goods, such as telecommunication and sound recording apparatus, electrical machinery and appliances, road vehicles, and manufactures of metal (Table 3). China is also a large supplier of textile yarn and related products, articles of apparel and clothing accessories, and footwear.

Table 2. Structure of China's import from Russia in 2005-2015, percentage

Commodity Groups	2005	2006	2007	2008	2009	2010	2011	2012	2013	2014	2015
Food and live animals	7.17	7.29	7.26	5.50	6.02	5.29	4.14	3.38	3.76	3.53	4.33
Beverages and tobacco	0.00	0.00	0.00	0.00	0.00	0.00	0.00	0.00	0.05	0.05	0.06
Crude materials, inedible, except fuels	20.52	19.83	25.39	24.17	20.39	20.49	21.23	15.54	15.28	13.33	15.86
Mineral fuels, lubricants, and related materials	41.22	53.90	47.49	50.15	44.13	49.59	56.79	66.88	67.76	71.48	60.87
Animal and vegetable oils, fats and waxes	0.00	0.00	0.00	0.00	0.00	0.00	0.00	0.00	0.03	0.02	0.24
Chemicals and related products	13.78	10.66	11.02	10.66	8.46	10.88	7.76	7.00	5.75	4.52	5.27
Manufactured goods	15.10	6.95	7.41	7.81	18.98	12.16	9.32	6.37	6.58	5.74	11.11
Machinery and transport equipment	1.95	1.14	1.12	1.51	1.83	1.27	0.55	0.50	0.48	0.86	1.66
Miscellaneous manufactured articles	0.19	0.17	0.20	0.25	0.23	0.27	0.20	0.27	0.30	0.31	0.42
Commodities and transactions	0.06	0.06	0.05	0.04	0.00	0.00	0.02	0.02	0.03	0.14	0.15

Source: Author's development based on UNCTAD (2017).

Table 3. Structure of China's export to Russia in 2005-2015, percentage

Commodity Groups	2005	2006	2007	2008	2009	2010	2011	2012	2013	2014	2015
Food and live animals	4.77	5.00	3.89	3.75	6.06	4.66	4.50	3.99	3.85	3.91	4.68
Beverages and tobacco	0.08	0.06	0.04	0.06	0.11	0.07	0.08	0.07	0.06	0.04	0.03
Crude materials, inedible, except fuels	0.76	0.51	0.35	0.45	0.46	0.47	0.64	0.48	0.34	0.37	0.46
Mineral fuels, lubricants, and related materials	0.98	0.89	0.70	0.82	0.51	0.74	0.90	0.66	0.58	0.34	0.52
Chemicals and related products	3.64	4.68	4.32	4.92	5.83	5.24	5.32	5.10	5.06	5.29	6.09
Manufactured goods	13.79	17.09	15.72	19.73	18.63	18.61	19.28	19.27	18.79	18.42	17.13
Machinery and transport equipment	19.09	27.59	29.19	35.02	31.09	35.37	38.12	39.77	35.32	33.84	33.65
Miscellaneous manufactured articles	57.05	44.30	45.86	35.20	37.37	34.83	31.08	30.54	35.99	37.75	37.44

Source: Author's development based on UNCTAD (2017).

Second biggest trading partner of China in the region of Central Asia is Kazakhstan. The country performed rather well during 2005-2015 and increased its FTT with China. The country has a strategic position between Asia and Europe, diversified natural resources and actively attracts foreign investments. Its exports, however, essentially depend on oil prices (Erokhin, 2016b). Kazakhstan exports to China petroleum and petroleum products, inorganic chemicals, and non-ferrous metals (Table 4)

Similar to Russia, while Kazakhstan's export to China is made up of mineral fuels and chemicals, the country imports manufactured and technological goods from China (Table 5), particularly electrical machinery and apparatus and manufactures of metal. Kazakhstan's domestic market is also dependent on China's textile yarn, articles of apparel, and clothing accessories.

As for the remaining four countries of Central Asia, their shares in China's FTT are tiny, while the structure of trade flows is similar to Russia and Kazakhstan: China absorbs various kinds of resources and supplies processed goods. Thus, Kyrgyzstan and Tajikistan export non-ferrous metals, metalliferous ores, metal scrap, leather, leather manufactures, textile fibers, and raw hides and skins, while receive electrical machinery and appliances, road vehicles, textile yarn, manufactured clothes, and footwear. Uzbekistan sells to China inorganic chemicals. In 2012, the country

Table 4. Structure of China's import from Kazakhstan in 2005-2015, percentage

Commodity Groups	2005	2006	2007	2008	2009	2010	2011	2012	2013	2014	2015
Food and live animals	0.00	0.00	0.00	0.00	0.00	0.09	0.00	0.34	0.19	1.03	0.86
Crude materials, inedible, except fuels	21.99	16.62	11.20	14.49	17.73	15.30	10.94	10.01	9.60	14.58	8.73
Mineral fuels, lubricants, and related materials	20.27	37.12	50.23	56.02	44.89	52.30	62.93	63.62	62.87	46.92	34.93
Animal and vegetable oils, fats and waxes	0.00	0.00	0.00	0.00	0.00	0.00	0.00	0.00	0.00	0.10	0.17
Chemicals and related products	3.09	4.71	1.87	1.68	7.35	9.36	9.45	8.72	11.65	17.25	25.68
Manufactured goods	54.64	41.55	36.70	27.68	29.71	22.95	16.61	17.30	15.64	20.12	29.62

Source: Author's development based on UNCTAD (2017)

Table 5. Structure of China's export to Kazakhstan in 2005-2015, percentage

Commodity Groups	2005	2006	2007	2008	2009	2010	2011	2012	2013	2014	2015
Food and live animals	1.28	1.04	1.08	1.22	1.56	1.40	1.77	1.73	1.84	1.81	2.74
Crude materials, inedible, except fuels	0.00	0.00	0.14	0.10	0.13	0.11	0.10	0.09	0.08	0.08	0.12
Mineral fuels, lubricants, and related materials	1.79	0.83	0.54	0.82	0.26	0.65	0.94	0.73	1.20	1.57	1.31
Chemicals and related products	3.08	3.33	3.24	3.27	3.51	3.33	3.75	3.82	3.76	3.46	4.52
Manufactured goods	21.03	20.42	21.08	30.31	30.78	21.29	19.79	20.55	20.32	17.72	22.14
Machinery and transport equipment	15.13	18.33	25.41	16.53	17.27	22.15	28.33	31.45	29.12	27.01	30.48
Miscellaneous manufactured articles	57.44	54.79	49.19	48.06	47.14	51.29	44.90	41.73	44.00	48.50	39.05

Source: Author's development based on UNCTAD (2017).

launched gas supplies to China. In exchange, Uzbekistan receives telecommunication and sound recording apparatus, electrical machinery and appliances, iron, and steel. All countries of Central Asia, including Russia and Kazakhstan, have a negative trade balance with China, except Turkmenistan, one of the world richest countries in gas. Turkmenistan's export to China is made up of natural and manufactured gas (98% of overall national export to China in 2015).

As China shifts its economy away from being investment-led to consumption-driven (Shah, 2016), the country explores the markets for its goods and use its excessive savings for the development of regional infrastructure. With the expansion to the west in the form of OBOR initiative, China's overcapacity in industrial sectors can also be used for the development of transport, storage, and distribution infrastructure in the countries of Central Asia. Against the backdrop of economic crisis in Russia and growing dependence on trade with China, countries of Central Asia have no choice but to turn east and consider China's OBOR as an attractive proposal for a trans-continental strategic partnership.

China's Trade With the Countries of Northeast Asia

The development of trade relations between China and the countries in Northeast Asia is influenced by the sharp differences in the size and level of development of the economies in the region (Schott & Goodrich, 2001). China is one of the leading economies in the world; Japan has been an industrial power since the late 1970s; South Korea is a rapidly developing country, while North Korea is a small and underdeveloped country. China is industry driven, relatively advanced economies of Japan and South Korea are services driven (De, 2006), whereas Mongolia and North Korea specialize in the extraction of natural resources and agricultural production.

Due to the high level of economic development of Japan and South Korea, these two countries lead in a trade with China in the region. Japan's share is 5.9% of China's total export and 8.5% of China's total import in 2015, while South Korea received 4.5% and supplied 10.4%, respectively (Table 6).

Japan and South Korea have equal FTTs in a trade with China – $279 bln and $276 bln in 2015, respectively. China supplies to Japan electrical machinery and appliances, telecommunication and sound recording apparatus, office machines and automatic data processing machines, road vehicles, manufactures of metal, articles of apparel, clothing accessories, and footwear (Table 7). Machinery, transport equipment, and manufactures goods taken together made up 84.6% of China's export to Japan in 2015.

Table 6. China's trade with the countries of Northeast Asia in 2005-2015, $ bln

Countries	2005	2006	2007	2008	2009	2010	2011	2012	2013	2014	2015
Export from China											
Mongolia	0.32	0.43	0.68	0.91	1.06	1.45	2.73	2.65	2.45	2.22	1.57
North Korea	1.08	1.23	1.39	2.03	1.89	2.28	3.16	3.53	3.63	3.52	2.95
South Korea	35.11	44.52	56.43	73.93	53.68	68.77	82.92	87.67	91.16	100.33	101.47
Japan	83.99	91.62	102.06	116.13	97.91	121.04	148.27	151.63	150.13	149.41	135.90
Import to China											
Mongolia	0.54	1.15	1.35	1.53	1.34	2.55	3.70	3.94	3.51	5.10	3.78
North Korea	0.50	0.47	0.58	0.76	0.79	1.19	2.48	2.50	2.93	2.87	2.51
South Korea	76.82	89.72	103.75	112.14	102.55	138.34	162.72	168.73	183.07	190.11	174.56
Japan	100.41	115.67	133.95	150.60	130.94	176.74	194.57	177.83	162.25	162.84	143.09

Source: UNCTAD, 2017.

Table 7. Structure of China's export to Japan in 2005-2015, percentage

Commodity Groups	2005	2006	2007	2008	2009	2010	2011	2012	2013	2014	2015
Food and live animals	8.55	8.12	7.42	5.88	7.03	6.82	6.66	7.10	6.73	6.67	6.77
Beverages and tobacco	0.07	0.08	0.08	0.05	0.07	0.05	0.04	0.05	0.05	0.04	0.04
Crude materials, inedible, except fuels	1.69	1.56	1.34	1.48	1.35	1.44	1.38	1.33	1.25	1.29	1.24
Mineral fuels, lubricants, and related materials	3.71	3.00	2.86	4.10	1.65	1.68	2.08	1.63	1.22	0.97	1.13
Animal and vegetable oils, fats and waxes	0.04	0.04	0.03	0.05	0.03	0.02	0.02	0.03	0.04	0.02	0.03
Chemicals and related products	4.57	5.20	5.97	6.52	5.09	6.28	7.43	5.86	5.61	5.97	6.20
Manufactured goods	13.32	13.78	13.23	13.40	11.98	12.16	13.78	12.37	11.90	12.43	12.24
Machinery and transport equipment	37.14	38.25	39.18	38.98	39.43	42.09	39.04	41.33	43.33	44.57	44.48
Miscellaneous manufactured articles	30.40	29.45	29.17	28.85	32.52	28.79	28.85	30.30	29.90	28.05	27.87
Commodities and transactions	0.51	0.57	0.67	0.71	0.85	0.70	0.68	0.01	0.00	0.00	0.00

Source: Author's development based on UNCTAD (2017).

As distinct from China's trade with Central Asia where China supplies manufactured goods in exchange of natural resources and primary products, the structure of China-Japan FTT is shifted in favor of manufactured and high value-added goods. China is one of the largest importers of Japan's electrical machinery and appliances, telecommunication and sound recording apparatus, professional and scientific instruments, and road vehicles and specialized machinery (Table 8).

The structure of trade between China and South Korea is more or less similar to trade with Japan. Major China's export commodities are telecommunication and sound recording apparatus, electrical machinery and appliances, professional and scientific instruments, iron and steel, articles of apparel and clothing accessories, and footwear (Table 9).

In exchange, China imports high-tech goods (electrical machinery and appliances, professional and scientific instruments, telecommunication and sound recording apparatus), organic chemicals, and petroleum products (Table 10).

Table 8. Structure of China's import from Japan in 2005-2015, percentage

Commodity Groups	2005	2006	2007	2008	2009	2010	2011	2012	2013	2014	2015
Food and live animals	0.29	0.29	0.24	0.21	0.27	0.27	0.13	0.16	0.19	0.22	0.30
Beverages and tobacco	0.01	0.01	0.01	0.01	0.01	0.01	0.01	0.02	0.01	0.01	0.06
Crude materials, inedible, except fuels	2.82	2.64	2.73	2.80	3.10	2.66	2.77	3.22	3.38	2.92	2.67
Mineral fuels, lubricants, and related materials	1.28	1.36	1.57	3.19	1.62	1.32	1.24	1.19	1.15	1.05	0.82
Animal and vegetable oils, fats and waxes	0.01	0.01	0.01	0.01	0.01	0.01	0.01	0.01	0.01	0.01	0.01
Chemicals and related products	12.91	12.81	13.72	13.04	14.11	13.15	13.30	14.14	16.18	15.19	14.91
Manufactured goods	15.58	15.41	15.11	15.42	15.06	14.29	14.11	13.93	13.86	13.93	13.74
Machinery and transport equipment	55.93	56.86	56.11	54.25	54.83	57.55	57.65	55.49	52.80	53.97	54.76
Miscellaneous manufactured articles	10.95	10.44	10.38	10.98	10.84	10.47	10.64	11.76	12.31	12.39	12.50
Commodities and transactions	0.23	0.18	0.13	0.11	0.14	0.27	0.15	0.09	0.10	0.31	0.25

Source: Author's development based on UNCTAD (2017).

A remarkable growth in China's trade with South Korea and Japan has resulted in robust growth of the economies in Northeast Asia. However, the region is still characterized by its low level of regional integration (De, 2006) due to the distinctions of economic potentials of Northeast Asian countries. Mongolia and North Korea are far less developed and industrialized compared to Japan and South Korea, and China's trade with those countries is different to trade with Japan and South Korea. China imports metalliferous ores, metal scrap, coal, coke, petroleum and petroleum products (particularly, from Mongolia), and articles of apparel and clothing accessories (particularly, from North Korea), while it exports iron, steel, specialised machinery, and electric current to Mongolia and telecommunication and sound recording apparatus, petroleum and petroleum products, and road vehicles to North Korea.

In addition to the economic reasons, the development of trade and economic integration among the countries of Northeast Asia has been delayed owing to political factors. During the 1980-1990s, most prominent were the political and ideological barriers that separated China from its neighbors (Schott & Goodrich, 2001), while today there are continuing military tensions between North Korea and countries of the region, particularly South Korea.

Table 9. Structure of China's export to South Korea in 2005-2015, percentage

Commodity Groups	2005	2006	2007	2008	2009	2010	2011	2012	2013	2014	2015
Food and live animals	7.18	5.51	5.55	3.45	4.26	4.32	4.26	3.88	3.96	3.96	3.62
Beverages and tobacco	0.09	0.04	0.05	0.04	0.06	0.04	0.04	0.05	0.05	0.07	0.07
Crude materials, inedible, except fuels	2.45	2.07	1.91	1.72	1.58	1.72	1.70	1.65	1.50	1.46	1.12
Mineral fuels, lubricants, and related materials	6.61	5.19	4.72	4.95	4.12	2.86	2.88	2.47	2.17	2.11	1.65
Animal and vegetable oils, fats and waxes	0.06	0.04	0.04	0.03	0.04	0.04	0.04	0.02	0.03	0.03	0.02
Chemicals and related products	6.47	6.83	7.02	6.48	7.19	8.04	8.90	7.73	7.87	7.90	7.53
Manufactured goods	27.52	30.63	31.08	33.09	21.36	23.15	24.68	21.82	19.70	20.96	18.76
Machinery and transport equipment	35.81	35.30	36.49	39.23	48.81	46.45	43.21	48.06	50.34	48.02	49.75
Miscellaneous manufactured articles	13.79	14.43	13.17	10.81	12.51	13.30	14.28	14.22	14.30	15.51	17.40
Commodities and transactions	0.03	0.02	0.02	0.01	0.02	0.01	0.04	0.07	0.02	0.01	0.05

Source: Author's development based on UNCTAD (2017).

Contemporary China's trade and development policies in the region of Northeast Asia are aimed at the promotion of economic collaboration between countries and thus improving political relations among the former adversaries and current competitors. For example, Mongolia is one of the key states for the expansion of OBOR initiative to the west. China-Mongolia-Russia Economic Corridor is considered as one the directions for expansion of trade relations between China and Russia with the involvement of Mongolia, while South Korea and Japan may contribute to the development of Maritime Silk Road initiative.

SOLUTIONS AND RECOMMENDATIONS

Most of the countries of Central and Northeast Asia have abundant natural and labor resources and high agricultural potential. Russian is still widespread in the region since Soviet times, and most of the people in Kazakhstan, Kyrgyzstan, Tajikistan, Turkmenistan, Uzbekistan, and even some people in Mongolia speak Russian. The countries have traditional close economic, trade and social ties between themselves. The major threats to the development of trade among the countries of the region are

Table 10. Structure of China's import from South Korea in 2005-2015, percentage

Commodity Groups	2005	2006	2007	2008	2009	2010	2011	2012	2013	2014	2015
Food and live animals	0.27	0.21	0.25	0.26	25.35	0.25	0.31	0.29	0.31	0.31	0.38
Beverages and tobacco	0.01	0.01	0.02	0.02	0.03	0.02	0.02	0.04	0.04	0.05	0.07
Crude materials, inedible, except fuels	1.09	1.04	1.19	1.24	1.28	1.16	1.32	1.14	0.89	0.80	0.76
Mineral fuels, lubricants, and related materials	4.57	6.48	6.29	8.87	5.35	5.67	7.82	6.84	5.60	5.02	3.77
Animal and vegetable oils, fats and waxes	0.00	0.01	0.01	0.00	0.00	0.00	0.01	0.01	0.00	0.01	0.00
Chemicals and related products	17.04	16.63	17.18	17.53	17.30	15.91	16.80	16.54	16.90	15.69	14.70
Manufactured goods	14.77	12.96	11.39	10.92	11.11	9.52	8.98	8.21	8.61	12.72	7.39
Machinery and transport equipment	45.77	47.37	47.22	45.09	46.86	48.90	47.16	49.90	53.68	52.52	59.50
Miscellaneous manufactured articles	16.39	15.16	16.29	15.93	17.45	18.26	16.94	15.85	13.89	12.82	13.28
Commodities and transactions	0.09	0.14	0.16	0.14	0.37	0.29	0.61	1.17	0.08	0.05	0.15

Source: Author's development based on UNCTAD (2017).

low diversification of output and export, dependence on fossil-fuel exports, weak infrastructures, low effective demand on domestic markets, and corruption. These weaknesses are common for all countries of Central Asia and some countries in Northeast Asia, particularly, Mongolia and North Korea.

China is interested in continuing its economic expansion abroad and exploring new markets for its goods. In order to ensure sustainable growth and mutual beneficial character of trade both for China and its trading partners, China's trade policies have to be aimed at:

- Expansion of investment and trade cooperation, optimization of trade structure and cultivation of new growth points for economy and employment.
- Facilitation of mutual investment, the launch of major investment cooperation projects and jointly building of industrial parks and cross-border economic cooperation zones.
- Improvement of interconnection in logistics and transportation, and collaboration on infrastructure construction projects.
- Development of trade-facilitating mechanisms in ripe areas, formulation of standard policies in the fields of common interests.

- Enhancement of financial cooperation through the Silk Road Fund and the Asian Infrastructure Investment Bank.

To increase benefits from international trade, both China and its neighbors have to transform economic growth drivers, seize current opportunities, reduce dependence on factors of production (investment and labor), increase reliance on innovation and quality, modernize and diversify. The major challenge for the sustainable development of trade between China and the countries of Central and Northeast Asia would be the development and implementation of trade policies that take into account evolving technologies, new financing mechanisms, multi-stakeholder contributions/ partnerships, and cross-border cooperation.

FUTURE RESEARCH DIRECTIONS

There are certain threats to the perspectives of OBOR and other China's trade and development initiatives in the region of Central and Northeast Asia, most of which are related to sustainability in its different dimensions. The first is a sustainability of institutions. Being a very ambitious project, OBOR involves many countries and requires significant coordination among various markets, customs regulations, financial systems, etc. Given such a complicated project, the second dimension of sustainability is economic capacity of China itself. With slowing economy and shrinking reserves, would China be able to avoid exporting its domestic economic troubles to the neighbors? The third dimension is environmental sustainability. China suffers from air, water, and land pollution. The question is what environmental standards will be applied to those infrastructure and construction projects which China wants to develop across the Central and Northeast Asia. In all those spheres, further researches are required to deliver sustainability to the development of trade relations between China and the countries of the macro-region of Eurasia.

CONCLUSION

In recent decades, China's foreign trade policy has undergone a transformation to become more pluralized, more transparent, and more market-oriented. Foreign trade has been gradually transforming in line with the country's broader economic transition towards higher value-added manufacturing and services.

Further expansion of China on the global market is caused by the necessity to explore new markets for Chinese goods, to find new investment options for the huge capital accumulated in the country during the decades of economic growth, and to secure sustainable energy and resources supply sources. Countries in Central and Northeast Asia are both very attractive markets and the places of vast hydrocarbon reserves and mineral deposits, that is why China's policy in the region is aimed at the development of trade and economic relations with them by means of strengthening of existing regional bilateral and multilateral mechanisms and creating a common economic space in Eurasia. China should ensure that such trade initiatives as OBOR establish a clearly defined mechanism for collaboration between all involved countries taking into account the differences in various fields of national regulations. Implementation of particular trade policies has to be ensured on a long-term basis by all participating countries and has to be integrated into all infrastructure, transport, and construction projects. Financial and economic sustainability is also important, especially in the view of China's slowdown in 2016. Interregional financial institutions have to be established and supported by the countries of Central and Northeast Asia to ensure financial stability in the region.

As China's trade and economic expansion in Central and Northeast Asia increases, its influence in the region grows alongside it. Taking into account China's economic potential, such an expansion promises to become a mutually beneficial arrangement both for China and its neighbors, for whom increasing China's trade and investments are a catalyst for growth.

ACKNOWLEDGMENT

This chapter is a part of the project HEUCFJ170901 funded by Harbin Engineering University, China

REFERENCES

Anderson, K., Martin, W. J., & Van der Mensbrugghe, D. (2010). China, the WTO, and the Doha Agenda. *China & World Economy*, 1–18.

Bondaz, A., Cohen, D., Godement, F., Kratz, A., & Pantucci, R. (2015). *One Belt, One Road: China's Great Leap Outward*. London: European Council on Foreign Relations.

Bugajski, J. (2008). *Expanding Eurasia: Russia's European Ambitions*. Washington, DC: CSIS.

Cass, D. Z., Williams, B., & Barker, G. R. (2003). *China and the World Trading System: Entering the Millennium*. New York, NY: Cambridge University Press. doi:10.1017/CBO9780511494482

De, P. (2006). *Trade in Northeast Asia: Why Do Trade Costs Matter?* Munich: Leibniz Institute for Economic Research.

Dohmen, H. (1976). China's Foreign Trade Policy. *Inter Economics*, *11*(7), 197–201. doi:10.1007/BF02929005

Duchatel, M., Godement, F., Liik, K., Shapiro, J., Slavkova, L., Stanzel, A., & Tcherneva, V. (2016). *Eurasian Integration: Caught between Russia and China*. Retrieved April 17, 2017, from http://www.ecfr.eu/article/essay_eurasian

Embassy of the People's Republic of China in the United States of America. (2011). *China's Foreign Trade*. Retrieved April 17, 2017, from http://www.china-embassy.org/eng/zt/bps/t943740.htm

Erokhin, V. (2014). Foreign Trade in Russia: Existing Distortions and Potentials of Regional Competitiveness in View of Liberalization. *International Journal of Sustainable Economies Management*, *3*(3), 1–18. doi:10.4018/ijsem.2014070101

Erokhin, V. (2015). Contemporary Reshaping of Eurasian Integration: Russia's Policies and their Implication for the EU and EurAsEC. *Procedia Economics and Finance*, *22*, 402–411. doi:10.1016/S2212-5671(15)00313-5

V. Erokhin (Ed.). (2016a). *Global Perspectives on Trade Integration and Economies in Transition*. Hershey, PA: IGI Global. doi:10.4018/978-1-5225-0451-1

Erokhin, V. (2016b). Rising Economic Powers among Economies in Transition: Is There Enough Space on the Global Market? In V. Erokhin (Ed.), *Global Perspectives on Trade Integration and Economies in Transition* (pp. 1–25). Hershey, PA: IGI Global. doi:10.4018/978-1-5225-0451-1.ch001

Fedorenko, V. (2015). *Eurasian Integration: Effects on Central Asia*. Washington, DC: Rethink Institute.

Hamrin, C. L., & Zhao, S. (1995). *Decision-making in Deng's China: Perspectives from Insiders*. Armonk, NY: M.E. Sharpe.

Kaczmarski, M. (2015). *China and Russia: Two Approaches to Integration*. Retrieved April 17, 2017, from http://thediplomat.com/2015/03/china-and-russia-two-approaches-to-integration/

Khandelwal, P., & Roitman, A. (2013). *The Economics of Political Transitions: Implications for the Arab Spring*. Washington, DC: International Monetary Fund.

Khanna, T., & Palepu, K. G. (2010). *Winning in Emerging Markets: A Road Map for Strategy and Execution*. Boston, MA: Harvard Business Press.

Lardy, N. R. (2002). *Integrating China into the World Economy*. Washington, DC: Brookings Institution Press.

Lemoine, F., & Ünal, D. (2017). China's Foreign Trade: A "New Normal". *China & World Economy*, *25*(2), 1–21. doi:10.1111/cwe.12191

Liberthal, K. (2004). *Governing China: From Revolution Through Reform*. New York, NY: W. W. Norton.

Linn, J. F., & Tiomkin, D. (2006). The New Impetus towards Economic Integration between Europe and Asia. *Asia Europe Journal*, *4*(1), 31–41. doi:10.1007/s10308-006-0046-6

Lu, N. (1997). *The Dynamics of Foreign-Policy Decisionmaking in China*. Boulder, CO: Westview Press.

Mariani, B. (2013). *China's Role and Interests in Central Asia*. London: Saferworld.

Panitchpakdi, S., & Clifford, M. L. (2002). *China and the WTO: Changing China, Changing World Trade*. Singapore: J. Wiley & Sons.

Pula, G., & Santabarbara, D. (2012). *Is China Climbing Up the Quality Ladder?* Helsinki: Bank of Finland, Institute for Economies in Transition.

Schott, J. J., & Goodrich, B. (2001). Economic Integration in Northeast Asia. *Proceedings of the KIEP/KEI/CKS Conference on The Challenges of Reconciliation and Reform in Korea*.

Shah, A. (2016). Building a Sustainable "Belt and Road." *Horizons, 7*. Retrieved April 17, 2017, from http://www.cirsd.org/en/horizons/horizons-spring-2016--issue-no-7/building-a-sustainable-%E2%80%98belt-and-road-

Silk Road Trade and Travel Encyclopedia. (n.d.). *Maps*. Retrieved April 18, 2017, from http://www.ipekyollari.com/OBOR/2XinhuaOBOR.jpg

Solanko, L. (2016). *Opening up or Closing the Door for Foreign Trade – Russia and China Compared*. Helsinki: Bank of Finland, Institute for Economies in Transition.

United Nations Conference on Trade and Development. (2017). Statistics Database [Data file]. Retrieved April 17, 2017, from http://unctad.org/en/Pages/Statistics.aspx

Vinokurov, E., & Libman, A. (2012). *Eurasia and Eurasian Integration: Beyond the Post-Soviet Borders*. Retrieved April 17, 2017, from http://www.eabr.org/general/upload/CII%20-%20izdania/Yerbook-2012/a_n5_2012_10.pdf

Wong, E., Chi, L. K., Tsui, S., & Tiejun, W. (2017). One Belt, One Road: China's Strategy for a New Global Financial Order. *Monthly Review. An Independent Socialist Magazine, 68*(8). Retrieved April 17, 2017, from: https://monthlyreview.org/2017/01/01/one-belt-one-road/#en1

Wu, Y. (2006). *Economic Growth, Transition and Globalization in China*. Cheltenham, UK: Edward Elgar Publishing Limited.

Yuan, P.-H. (2017). Trade Strategy Adjustment of China after the Financial Crisis. *Chinese Economy, 50*(2), 112–118. doi:10.1080/10971475.2016.1227171

Zhang, J. (2016). *What's Driving China's One Belt, One Road Initiative?* Retrieved April 17, 2017, from http://www.eastasiaforum.org/2016/09/02/whats-driving-chinas-one-belt-one-road-initiative/

Zhang, T. (2016). *China's Foreign Trade in 2016: Identifying Trends and Opportunities*. Retrieved April 18, 2017, from http://www.china-briefing.com/news/2016/12/22/chinas-foreign-trade-2016-identifying-trends-opportunities.html

ADDITIONAL READING

Akyüz, Y. (2005). *Trade, Growth and Industrialization: Issues, Experiences and Policy Challenges*. Penang, Malaysia: Third World Network.

Bairoch, P., & Kozul-Wright, R. (1996). *Globalization Myths: Some Historical Reflections on Integration, Industrialization and Growth in the World Economy*. Geneva: UNCTAD.

Boehringer, C., & Rutherford, T. (1999). *Decomposing General Equilibrium Effects of Policy Intervention in Multi-Regional Trade Models: Method and Sample Application*. Retrieved April 21, 2014, from http://EconPapers.repec.org/RePEc:zbw:zewdip:5249.

Bussière, M., Delle Chiaie, S., & Peltonen, T. A. (2014). Exchange Rate Pass-Through in the Global Economy: The Role of Emerging Market Economies. *IMF Economic Review, 62*(1), 146–178. doi:10.1057/imfer.2014.5

Chang, H.-J., & Nolan, P. (1995). Europe versus Asia: Contrasting Paths to the Reform of Centrally Planned Systems of Political Economy. In H.-J. Chang & P. Nolan (Eds.), *The Transformation of the Communist Economies* (pp. 3–45). London: Macmillan. doi:10.1007/978-1-349-23916-0_1

Dawson, T. C. (2003). *Globalization, the Transition Economies, and the IMF*. Vienna: Joint Vienna Institute.

Devereux, M. (1999). Growth and the Dynamics of Trade Liberalization. *Journal of Economic Dynamics & Control*, *23*(5-6), 773–795. doi:10.1016/S0165-1889(98)00043-8

Erokhin, V. (2014). Trade Relations within and between the Countries of the Former Soviet Union. In V. Erokhin (Ed.), *International Trade from a Russian Perspective*. London: Henry Stewart Talks Ltd. Retrieved April 18, 2017, from http://hstalks.com/?t=MM1883816

Erokhin, V. (2016). Similarities and Differences of Rural Development in the Regions of Northeastern China and Far East of Russia. In *Proceedings of International Research Conference "Agro-energy for Sustainable Agriculture and Rural Development"*. Nitra, Slovakia: Slovak University of Agriculture.

Estevadeordal, A., Freund, C., & Ornelas, E. (2008). Does Regionalism Affect Trade Liberalization Toward Nonmembers? *The Quarterly Journal of Economics*, *124*(4), 1531–1575. doi:10.1162/qjec.2008.123.4.1531

Gill, I. S., Izvorski, I., Van Eeghen, W., & De Rosa, D. (2014). *Diversified Development: Making the Most of Natural Resources in Eurasia*. Washington, DC: World Bank. doi:10.1596/978-1-4648-0119-8

Kierzkowski, H. (2000). Challenges of Globalization: The Foreign Trade Restructuring of Transition Economies. *Russian & East European Finance and Trade*, *36*(2), 8–41.

Kose, M. A., & Prasad, E. (2010). *Emerging Markets: Resilience and Growth amid Global Turmoil*. Washington, DC: Brookings Institution Press.

Kukushkina, J., & Ostrovskaya, E. (2013). Current Issues and Prospects of Eurasian and European Economic Integration. *International Organizations Research Journal*, *8*(4), 214–228.

McMillan, J., & Naughton, B. (1992). How to Reform a Planned Economy: Lessons from China. *Oxford Review of Economic Policy*, *8*(1), 130–143. doi:10.1093/oxrep/8.1.130

Molchanov, M. (2016). Russia's Leadership of Regional Integration in Eurasia. In S. Kingah & C. Quiliconi (Eds.), *Global and Regional Leadership of BRICS Countries* (pp. 113–133). Cham: Springer International Publishing. doi:10.1007/978-3-319-22972-0_7

Obydenkova, A. (2011). Comparative Regionalism: Eurasian Cooperation and European Integration. The Case for Neofunctionalism? *Journal of Eurasian Studies*, *2*(2), 87–102. doi:10.1016/j.euras.2011.03.001

Raynolds, L., Murray, D., & Wilkinson, J. (2007). *Fair Trade: The Challenges of Transforming Globalization*. London: Routledge.

Santacreu, A. M. (2015). *The Economic Fundamentals of Emerging Market Volatility*. St. Louis, MO: Federal Reserve Bank of St. Louis.

Shah, A. (2010). *Deregulation or Protectionism?* Retrieved April 18, 2017, from http://www.globalissues.org/article/43/deregulation-or-protectionism

Syroezhkin, K. (2007). China in Central Asia: From Trade to Strategic Partnership. *Central Asia and the Caucasus*, *45*(3), 40–51.

Tukmadiyeva, M. (2013). Xinjiang in China's Foreign Policy toward Central Asia. *The Quarterly Journal*, 87-110.

R. Vos, & M. Koparanova (Eds.). (2011). *Globalization and Economic Diversification: Policy Challenges for Economies in Transition*. London: Bloomsbury Academic. doi:10.5040/9781849665742

Zelenko, O. (2012). *Trade Policy Options of CIS Countries: Twenty Years After*. Rotterdam: Erasmus University.

KEY TERMS AND DEFINITIONS

Developing Economies: The countries, progressing toward becoming advanced, but still lacking market efficiency and sustainable market mechanisms, having greater domestic and external risks due to political instability, infrastructure problems, and currency volatility.

Eurasian Economic Union: The union of Armenia, Belarus, Kazakhstan, Kyrgyzstan, and Russia established in 2014 for effective promotion of free movement of goods, services, capital, and labor between participating countries.

Foreign Trade: The system of international commodity-money relations composed of foreign trade activities of all countries worldwide.

One Belt One Road Initiative: A development strategy proposed by the Chinese government in 2013 and focused on the improvement of connectivity and collaboration among the countries of Eurasia through the increase of China's role in global affairs.

Trade Liberalisation: A process of reduction or elimination of constraints in the sphere of international trade, including reduction or removal of customs tariffs, import quotas, abolishment of multiple exchange rates, and simplification of administrative requirements to import and export operations.

Trade Protectionism: A set of measures to limit imports or promote exports by putting up barriers to trade that countries use to limit unfair competition from foreign industries.

Chapter 3
The Eurasian Economic Union in the Context of Transformation of the International Trade System

Maria Lagutina
Saint Petersburg State University, Russia

ABSTRACT

The EEU was created to strengthen the national economies and capabilities of the member states in global economy by creating the so-called "four freedoms": the free movement of goods, services, capital, and persons. At this stage, the EEU is involved in the creation of free trade zones with countries outside the borders of the Eurasian post-Soviet space that was a reaction of the Eurasian Economic Union on new trends in international trade and the crisis of the WTO. The aim of this chapter is to analyze the internal and external contours of the Eurasian integration in economic and trade cooperation. The first part is devoted to analyzing of the historical background of the EEU creation. The second part evaluates the economic cooperation among the EEU countries. In the third part, the author focuses on the crisis of the WTO and new tendencies in international trade cooperation. And the final part examines the prospects of creation of free-trades zones between the EEU states and other countries.

DOI: 10.4018/978-1-5225-4032-8.ch003

INTRODUCTION

The Eurasian Economic Union (EEU) was created to strengthen the national economies and capabilities of the member states in global economy by creating the so-called 'four freedoms': the free movement of goods, services, capital and persons. It was founded during a period of the global economic instability and geopolitical changes in Eurasia that have affected the situation inside the EEU (Kuzmina, 2017).

The emergence of the EEU in January 2015 marked a new phase of joining the Eurasian countries into the global economic space. At the moment, membership consists of five states: Armenia, Belarus, Kazakhstan, Kyrgyzstan and Russia, four of which are members of the World Trade Organization (WTO). However, the accession of the EEU occurred at different times and on different terms: for example, Armenia, Kyrgyzstan and Russia joined in the EEU as a WTO member, while Kazakhstan entered this structure as a member of the EEU and on more liberal external partner conditions than in the EEU. All this creates political and economic difficulties for the harmonization of internal rules of trade of the EEU and WTO. At this stage of the EEU is actively involved in the creation of free trade zones with countries outside the borders of the Eurasian post-Soviet space that was a reaction of the EEU on new trends in international trade and the crisis of the WTO.

The creation of free trade zones of the EEU is largely determined by current geopolitical situation in the world. Thus, the European direction in connection with the political crisis 2014-2015 in relations with Russia and the subsequent sanctions war, making unpromising the creation of a free trade zone with the EU. In this regard, for the development of the EEU is very important the creation of free trade zones with countries in the Asia-Pacific region that will allow the EEU countries to form their own stable trade space.

The aim of this chapter is to analyze the 'internal' and 'external' contours of the Eurasian integration in economic and trade cooperation of the EEU. This can be achieved by means of analyzing the existing economic cooperation among the EEU countries and prospects of the creation of free-trade zones of the EEU with other countries.

Our analysis is based mainly on analytical materials of Eurasian Economic Commission, the Chamber of Commerce and Industry of the Russian Federation and Russian International Affairs Council etc. We have used a case study approach for data collection, mainly through the study of official documents and by reviewing annual reports.

This chapter consists of four parts. The first part is devoted to analyzing of the historical background of the EEU creation. The second part evaluates the economic cooperation among the EEU countries as on bilateral, as on multilateral levels. In the third part, the author focuses on the crisis WTO and new tendencies in international trade cooperation. And the final part examines the prospects of creation of free-trades zones between the EEU states and other countries, which are located outside of the EEU space.

BACKGROUND

What Is Eurasian Economic Union?

A determinant factor in the EEU establishment was awareness of the post-Soviet states' need for blending in with the global economic space as equal partners on condition of mutually advantageous cooperation, rather than raw-material appendage and peripheral states. In this regard, the Western sanctions policy merely affirms aspirations among the EEU nations to enhance their economic status within the global scope.

As the Russian expert M. Lapenko notes, "Partially, the Eurasian integration idea was put into practice in *the Eurasian Economic Community (EurAsEC)* in 2000" (Lapenko, 2014, 134-135 pp.), where Belorussia, Kazakhstan, Russia and Tajikistan acceded to. From all integrational structures of the post-Soviet space the EurAsEC proved to be the most effective integrational entity. Over the years of its functioning a kind of ideological core got crystallized out, leaders whereof were ready to assume new accountability and give in part of their freedoms to a supranational body for the sake of speeding up economic development of their countries. This core was constituted by Belorussia, Kazakhstan and Russia. Precisely these states established *the Customs Union (CU)* in 2010, and after that passed over to the next integrational stage – *the Common Economic space (CES)* (2012).

On May 29, 2014 the integrational processes within the framework of the EurAsEC came onto a qualitatively new tier – in Astana the leaders of the three states concluded a Treaty on establishment of *the Eurasian Economic Union (EEU)*, which came into effect on January 1, 2015 (Dogovor o Evraziyskom ekonomicheskom soyuze, 2014). In October 2014 the EurAsEC activity was ceased, which was replaced by the EEU. The CU and CES featured pillars of the EEU.

Beginning of the Treaty on the Eurasian Economic Union on January 1, 2015 featured a landmark in evolution of the Eurasian integration (Dogovor o Evraziyskom ekonomicheskom soyuze, 2014), which represents a completely new page of regulatory and economic integration in the Eurasian space. Conclusion of the Treaty heralded on set of concerted economic and industrial policy that the leaders of Belorussia, Kazakhstan and Russia have been aspiring to. The institutional section of the Treaty stipulated the functioning principles of the union, as well as its growth areas.

Today the EEU is an international organization of regional economic integration, which has the international personality and established by the Treaty on the Eurasian Economic Union (Official site of Eurasian Economic Commission). According to the text of the Treaty, the coordinating bodies in the union system are: the Supreme Eurasian Economic Council (the Supreme Council), the Eurasian intergovernmental Council (the Intergovernmental Council), the Eurasian Economic Commission (the Commission), the Court of the Eurasian Union (the Court of the Union). The hallmark of the new Treaty is an access of the business communities to elaborating drafts of regulations by the Eurasian Economic Commission (EEC). In its turn, the Eurasian Commission is assigned with the role of a permanently standing body. According to the official web-site, the Eurasian Economic Commission is a "permanently functioning supranational regulatory authority of the Customs Union and Common Economic Space" (Official site of Eurasian Economic Commission). Activity by the EEC runs along the two levels – the interstate one and direct collaboration with business. Furthermore, in the future other supranational bodies are set to be established as well (for instance, the EEU Parliament and Foreign Ministers Council of the EEU, etc.).

As we mentioned before, at the moment membership consists of five states: Armenia, Belarus, Kazakhstan, Kyrgyzstan and Russia. Meanwhile, yet in 2012, about 35 countries, including India, Syria, Iran, New Zealand, etc., said they were interested in creating a free-trade zone with the EEU nations. Vietnam recently signed a free-trade agreement with the EEU. In addition, negotiations are underway about expanding trade ties between the EEU and MERCOSUR, ASEAN and other integrationist blocs. So, the prospects of the expansion of the EEU's economic ties appear to have both regional and global dimensions.

MAIN FOCUS OF THE CHAPTER

'Internal Contour' of the Eurasian Integration: Economic Cooperation Among the EEU Countries

Today the EEU covers an area of more than 20 million square kilometers with a population of more than 179 million people (Official site of Eurasian Economic Union). The EEU's economic potential accounts for about 2.7% of the world's GDP, about 3% of the world's export and about 2.5% of the world's import, but mostly its potential is the potential of Russia – the alliance's biggest national economy (Kuvshinova, 2016).

The EEU's chief objective is providing its participating nations with so called "four freedoms": free movement of goods, capital, services and labor. Presently the EEU has already accomplished the first stage of economic integration – free movement of goods, services and labor (Dogovor o Evraziyskom ekonomicheskom soyuze, 2014). First of all, the abolishment of several customs restrictions and duties simplified trade in goods and services among the EEU countries. The single market of services applies to many areas – for instance, construction, commerce, agriculture, etc. – and is gradually expanding. Integration within the EEU means a gradual unification of sector-specific policies (in electric power sector, industry, agriculture, etc.), as well as integration of markets (for instance, markets of medical products and devices, drugs, oil and oil products, etc.), and there are plans to set in place, by 2025, a supranational trade regulator at the EEU, as well as a supranational financial megaregulator (Kuvshinova, 2016).

The EEU was created for the purpose of comprehensive modernization, cooperation, and strengthening the national economies' competitiveness, as well as creating conditions for sustained development and, consequently, improving living standards in the member states (Official site of Eurasian Economic Commission). So, we can point up the following advantages of the integration for the EEU member states:

- Free movement of goods, services, capital and labor within the EEU;
- Abolishment of customs and transportation control within the EEU;
- Abolishment of customs duties in intra-EEU (trade within the EEU) and unification of customs procedures;
- Unification of regulations regarding customs tariffs and other barriers in trade with third countries protects the EEU producers' interests;
- Unification of technical requirements, sanitary and phytosanitary measures;
- Legal guarantees to investors, protection of investment;
- System of protection of export-oriented businesses;
- The EEU's principles agree with the WTO's norms.

In 2016 the volume of intra-EEU trade was 42.5 million USD, which is 6% less than the corresponding indicator for 2015. In 2016, of all the EEU member countries only Armenia and Russia saw their imports grow, by 8.7% and 1%, respectively. In contradistinction to this, imports from the EEU members to Kyrgyzstan declined by 23.2%, to Belarus, by 10.7%, and to Kazakhstan, by 13.8% (Vzaimnaya torgovlya tovarami, 2016). In our opinion, this trend has resulted not from a weakened integration drive within the EEU but, rather, from opportunistic changes in the economies of the EEU members and the world: the crisis of 2014-2015 and the drop in prices of oil and other exports from the EEU countries negatively affected the volumes of trade among the nations.

In the structure of intra-EEU trade the following items have the largest shares of the market:

- Mineral products (33.4% of intra-EEU trade), with 81.7% of the total supplied by Russia.
- Machines, tools and transportation vehicles (16.4%), with 60% of the total supplied by Russia and 37.1%, by Belarus.
- Alimentary products and agricultural commodities (15.5%), with 54.8% of the total supplied by Belarus and 34% by Russia;
- Metals and metalware (10.6%), with 67.2% of the total supplied by Russia (Shein, 2015).

Trade transactions between Russia and Belarus, and between Russia and Kazakhstan, account for the largest share of intra-EEU trade. The shares of sales within the above mentioned pairs of countries in the overall intra-EEU trade volume are 57% and 33%, respectively (Barieri, izyatia I ogranicheniya EAES, 2016). So, the EEU's other countries account for about 20% of the overall trade volume.

Russia and Belarus

Russia's leading economic partner, Belarus is Russia's number one trade partner within the EEU. According to a Belarusian expert Alexander Shpakovsky, the Republic of Belarus arguably has a key role in Eurasian integration processes since it is "a real industrial oasis of the EEU: our country produces 17% of all of the world's combine harvesters, 6% of tractors, 6.4% of flax fiber, and 2.8% of potato; BelAZ accounts for up to 30% of the world's dump trucks. <...> As for cutting-edge technologies, Belarus exports more IT services than any other CIS country. Belarus has a High Technologies Park, builds an industrial park together with China and a nuclear power plant together with Rosatom" (Shpakovsky, 2014). So, Belarus is very interested in finding new markets for its products.

During the last five years the development of integration processes, including those within the EEU, has strengthened significantly the economic cooperation between the countries. The volume of trade transactions between Russia and Belarus in 2000-2015 grew nearly threefold, from 9.3 to 27.5 million USD (Rossiysko-belorusskoe torgovo-ekonomicheskoe sotrudnichestvo, 2015). According to an information on the Belarusian Foreign Ministry's web site, imports from Russia prevail, accounting for over 60% of the foreign trade turnover

The structure of Russian exports to Belarus is dominated by gas and oil products (oil, natural gas, oil products, electric power); machines, tools and transportation vehicles; chemical products, plastics, caoutchouc; metals and metalware; alimentary products.

Russian imports include alimentary products; agricultural commodities; mineral products; chemical products, plastics, caoutchouc; textiles, textile products and footwear; metals and metalware (Torgovo-ekonomicheskoe sotrudnichestvo Rossii I Belorussii, 2017).

Russia is the main investor to the Belarusian economy. So, as of January 1, 2015, Belarus had more than 2,000 firms with Russian investment, including about 1,300 joint ventures (Rossiysko-belorusskoe torgovo-ekonomicheskoe sotrudnichestvo, 2015). One of Russia's largest investors in Belarus is OAO Gazprom; other Russian players on Belarusian market include Lukoil, Rosneft, etc. Russian banks with a significant presence in Belarus include Sberbank of Russia, Vnesheconombank, VTB, Alfa-Bank. As the integration processes intensify, a whole series of new integration projects is in the making, the biggest among them being the creation of the Russian-Belarusian holding Rosbelavto using KAMAZ's and MAZ's assets, as well as establishing industry-specific cooperation with such Belarusian companies as OAO Minsk Wheel Tractor Plan (Minsky zavod traktornykh tyagachei), OAO Peleng, OAO Integral and OAO Grodno Azot (Rossiysko-belorusskoe torgovo-ekonomicheskoe sotrudnichestvo, 2015).

Still, a close look at the Russian-Belarusian economic interactions also reveals several problems and stumbling blocks: first of all, they include an obvious asymmetry in Russian-Belarusian trade – Russia exports to Belarus raw materials while Belarus exports to Russia mostly finished products.

Russia and Kazakhstan

Russia is Kazakhstan's biggest trade partner: the share of the bilateral trade in Kazakhstan's overall foreign trade volume is about 20% (the average annual volume of mutual sales amounts to about 21 billion USD) (Characteristics of Kazakh-Russian relations). In recent years, given the difficult economic and geopolitical context, the trade volume between two countries somewhat declined, although Kazakhstan still has more than 5,600 businesses with Russian investment (for instance, Lukoil, Gazprom, Rusal, Polymetal, EuroChem, etc.). Kazakhstan is attractive for Russian business for the following reasons: tax advantages, the convenience of doing business, the speed of introducing new technical requirements, etc. The structure of Russian imports in Kazakhstan is dominated by engineering: machines, tools, transportation vehicles, chemical products, metals, mineral products, alimentary products, timber, pulp and paper products, etc.

And for Russia, Kazakhstan is one of the main foreign trade partners (2nd largest among the CIS countries, 9th among the world's countries). As for the presence of

Kazakh businesses on the Russian market, today Russia has more than 3,000 businesses with Kazakh investment (for instance, Milk Project, drug manufacturer NOBEL-AFF Kazakhstan, producer of construction materials Alina, etc.) (Prezident TTP RF Sergey Katirin: Kazakhstan – nadejniy partner, 2016). Today Kazakh companies are becoming notable players in Russia, although so far Russian businesses have had a more prominent presence in Kazakhstan than Kazakh businesses in Russia. Kazakhstan's exports to Russia mostly include mineral products, metals and metalware, chemical products, machines, food stuffs, etc. The Kazakh players, meanwhile, are interested in promoting joint ventures in Kazakhstan more actively, and Kazakh businesses are interested in geographically expanding their presence on the Russian market (not only in areas near the border but in other Russian regions as well).

Kazakhstan's industrialization program (so called "Kazakhstan's Industrialization Map") has produced 20 completed big joint investment projects, 4 currently in the making, and 3 planned projects (Official visit of Vladimir Putin to Kazakhstan, 2015). Cooperation between Russian and Kazakh businesses has produced, inter alia, the following projects: Rosselmash opened offices in Kazakhstan and services its combine harvesters; AvtoVAZ participates in the construction of a new plant in Kazakhstan; Transmashholding together with Kazakhstan Railways and the French company Alstom built in Astana a locomotive construction plant; a project to set up a joint venture assembling multi-purpose helicopters Ka-226T is underway; oil from Kazakhstan is exported via a pipe of the Caspian Pipeline Consortium state-owned by Russia and Kazakhstan; a joint venture of Gazprom and Kazakhstan's gas monopoly KazMunaiGaz, KazRosGas supplies gas from the Karachaganak Field to Gazprom Dobycha Orenburg for processing; joint Kazakh-Russian-Kyrgyz venture ZAO Zarechnoe, which mines uranium in Kazakhstan, etc.

So, the economic relations between Russia and Kazakhstan now have a mixed record: along with obvious achievements and stories of success, some problems remain unresolved. In 2010-2016 sales volumes between Kazakhstan and Russia were changing dynamically – reaching its peak in 2012-2013, they then declined sharply by 44% (export) and 45% (import). Mainly, the enterprise that received maximum advantage from the Eurasian Economic Space is AvtoVAZ: its imports to Kazakhstan grew tenfold (in 2010-2014) (EAES I Tamojenniy soyuz: komu vigodno? 2016). Still, Russia and Kazakhstan are countries with a huge potential in terms of resources, which holds promise for their future development not only in a bilateral format but also in the context of integration processes in the EEU.

As for intra-EEU trade not involving Russia, the volume of these transactions is low, and presently this is one of the main problems of the development of integration within the EEU.

Belarus and Kazakhstan

The volume of Belarusian imports to Kazakhstan was steadily growing since 2012 up to the difficult year 2015, whereas the exports have declined since 2010 nearly six fold (EAES I Tamojenniy soyuz: komu vigodno? 2016). Over recent years Belarus has penetrated the Kazakh market in several areas: machines, tools, plastics and plastic articles, alimentary products, agricultural products, chemical products, etc. A decline in the volume of Kazakh exports to Belarus affected the structure of exports: whereas in 2010 oil, ferrous metals and aluminum were the main export commodities, in 2015 oil deliveries to Belarus were practically at a zero level, and this was reflected in the structure of exports – ferrous metals and aluminum were the staples. So, in 2010-2016 Belarus in general improved its balance of trade with Kazakhstan. The existence of the EEU and Customs Union did not significantly affect Kazakhstan's imports. Main beneficiaries of Belarus's accession to the EEU are the country's producers of food stuffs – the volume of its deliveries to Kazakhstan grew appreciably.

When Armenia and Kyrgyzstan joined the Treaty on the EEU in 2015, this development did not have a noticeable impact on the structure and volume of intra-EEU trade because these two countries' markets are small. The pairs Kyrgyzstan-Armenia and, in ascending order, Armenia-Kazakhstan account for the smallest shares of intra-EEU trade: 0.001% and 0.01%, respectively (Barieri, izyatia I ogranicheniya EAES, 2016). It is still too early to evaluate the efficiency and achievements of Armenia and Kyrgyzstan because they have been members only for a very short time.

The EEU unites national economies of varying size, with different economic legislation and different levels of economic openness. Therefore, the development of this integration project is held back by internal limitations. According to the Russian expert Elena Kuzmina (2016), these limitations include the following factors: first, with many of their sectors identical, the EEU's largest national economies are mutually competitive on the EEU and global markets, which creates structural limitations for the development of mutual trade; second, the Eurasian institutions develop quickly and quite well; however, there is but a mere handful of cooperative industrial projects; most of the already existing projects are bilateral, few were started within the EEU; third, integration mostly occurs in the traditional sectors of economy that are exhausting their potential: electric power, chemical industry and petrochemicals, iron and steel; fourth, one of the EEU's main objectives, set out in the Treaty, was cooperative modernization and diversification of industry, but the work in this direction is still proceeding quite slowly.

On the whole, it is obvious that the creation and functioning of an integration project so big as the EEU should be evaluated after it has been afoot for a longer period of time, and problems and the signs of a crisis we are witnessing at this stage are natural. Yet, the existing crisis opens up for the EEU countries certain prospects and opportunities for diversification of industry and cooperation with third countries.

'External Contour' of the Eurasian Integration: The Crisis WTO and New Tendencies in International Trade Cooperation

While the 'internal contour' of the Eurasian integration is stagnating due to some objective reasons, the EEU should actively promote the so-called 'external contour' of integration (Tkachuk, 2016): the creation of a network of free trade zones (FTA) and Preferential Trade and Economic Cooperation Agreements in Eurasia.

The EEU is taking shape as global trade undergoes a serious transformation. As is well known, during the last decades the World Trade Organization (WTO) has been the main regulator of global trade. Under Article XXIV of the General Agreement on Tariffs and Trade (GATT), facilitation is the universal principle of international trade. Advantages accorded to one of the participants ought to be automatically applied to all others, although Article XXIV provides for three exceptions: customs unions, free trade zones, and the least developed nations, which enjoy a system of preferences. So, these three exceptions cannot be construed as violations of the WTO's rules (The text of General Agreement on Tariffs and Trade (GATT), 1947). Elaborating these provisions, the WTO member states since 2001 have been discussing measures to liberalize global trade between countries with different levels of development (the Doha Round). The setbacks along the road to a compromise caused the interested parties to look for new forms of trade agreements, bringing about a proliferation of free-trade zones. As for the prospects of development of these free-trade zones, one fears that with the reach of the free-trade zones being so global international business simply would not need the WTO: new rules are being drawn up and they can become an instrument for squeezing economies that are not parties to the integration initiatives out of the common system of international trade and industry, because only parties to the agreements will enjoy preferences and advantages.

In view of this, the creation of matching free-trade zones with the Pacific Rim economies is very important for the development of the EEU – this will help Russia to form its stable trade space. Besides, given the current conditions, it is important to draw up and enshrine into law rules for trade and investment in the EEU, to develop links between the EEU and the EU, as well as the EEU and the integration initiatives spearheaded by China and other BRICS countries, and lay down rules for these countries and blocs (O Trans-Tikhookeanskom partnerstve, 2015).

It can be argued that creating free-trade zones is now the most important element of economic policies in many countries, and there are objective reasons for this:

- A free-trade zone shapes up cooperation arrangements tailored specifically for this zone's participants, and this is practically impossible to achieve within the WTO;
- The apparent futility of the negotiations about further simplifying the trade and striking a balance between the interests of developed and developing nations (the Doha Round) leads to the formation of regional trade preferences;
- Signing up for a free-trade zone, a country gains a wider access for its companies to markets of goods and services of partner countries and, so, increases its exports;
- Free-trade zones generate additional inducements to produce goods and services and, so, countries that do not create their own networks of agreements may put their businesses' at a competitive disadvantage on global markets and find themselves squeezed out of global industrial chains (Voskresenskiy, 2014).

Pursuant to the Treaty on the EEU, decisions about signing international agreements on behalf of the EEU, including free-trade agreements, are the purview of the Supreme Eurasian Economic Council, consisting of the heads of the EEU member states. Besides, the approval process for such agreements involves certain formal steps inside the member states, as stipulated in these countries' national laws. When such agreement comes under the purview of both the member states and the EEU as such, the agreement should be signed by each of the EEU member states, as well as by the EEU (Voprosy I otvety po Soglasheniyu o svobodnoy torgovle mezhdu Evraziyskim ekonomicheskim soyuzom I Sotsialisticheskoy Respublikoy Vietnam).

Of special interest is the fact that it was European countries –members of the European Free Trade Association (EFTA): Switzerland, Norway, Liechtenstein and Iceland – who first showed an interest in the possibility of signing free-trade agreements with the Customs Union member states. In 2011, the Customs Union was among the EFTA's top 10 trade partners (The European Free Trade Association). However, the sanctions against Russia "froze" the negotiations about the free-trade zone both with the EFTA and New Zealand.

Despite the present-day crisis in the Russian-European relations there still objectively exists a foundation of mutual interest, on the part of the EU and the EEU, in integration and interaction: "it is predicated on territorial proximity to each other, substantial trade flows, considerable potential of the investment ties, issues of economic security, the EEU's interest in the transfer of European technologies, unresolved questions of cross-border infrastructure development, and existence of neighboring countries with common borders" (Vinokurov, 2014). These factors have not been eliminated as the EU - Russia cooperation ground to a halt; in fact, they account for the situation when losses caused by the anti-Russian sanctions turn out to be a burden not for Russia alone but - likely equally - for the EU countries as well.

According to analysts from the Eurasian Development Bank (EDB), deep economic integration with the EU is extremely important and very promising:

- The European Union is the largest trade partner for Russia and Kazakhstan; Russia, for its part, is the EU's third largest trade partner.
- The EU could make a substantial contribution to the modernization of the EEU states.
- In the present situation of a political crisis in relations with Western countries, the EEU initiates several free-trade agreements with partners outside the post-Soviet space (for example, with the EFTA and Vietnam), and in this context the EU should be regarded as a major long-term partner.
- The Ukrainian problem could be resolved through extensive economic cooperation between the EU and the EEU, which makes this cooperation even more important (Vinokurov, 2014).

However, in the judgment of E.Vinokurov, the EEU is interested not just in signing an agreement on free trade but in designing a far-reaching comprehensive treaty with the EU states: "the prototypes of potential integration between the EU and the EEU are quite diverse – from the Deep and Comprehensive Free Trade Area (DCFTA) to the Comprehensive Economic and Trade Agreement (CETA). The Transatlantic Trade and Investment Partnership (TTIP) (even without the United States) is modeled after the latter" (Vinokurov, 2014, p.12).

Unfortunately, now there are not any formal links between the supranational bodies of the EEU and the EU and the reason of this is the reluctance of the EU to enter into such official negotiations (Torgovaya politika EAES, 2016), because of the difficult geopolitical situation in Eurasia.

Therefore, today Asia is the key region where the EEU countries seek to establish free-trade zones. President V. Putin brought up this point in his speech at the Asia-Pacific Economic Cooperation forum, emphasizing the fact that "the coordination of integration efforts in Eurasia and the Asia-Pacific region will be useful for everyone, and in the future it will be possible to speak about a fruitful dialog between members of the burgeoning Eurasian Economic Union and the APEC, with the participation of other regional alliances" (Press-konferentsiya po itogam foruma ATES, 2012). Elaborating on this topic, one can also review the results of a meeting of the Eurasian Intergovernmental Council in Kazakhstan (2015), when the EEU and *Vietnam* signed a free-trade agreement. According to experts from the EEU, a free-trade zone with Vietnam "gives the EEU businesses access to markets of the entire Asia-Pacific region, both in terms of direct sales and indirectly, as suppliers in a supply chain. Today the staple of global trade is goods produced by fairly long chains, and inclusion into such chains is very important for the development of businesses" (Voskresenskiy, 2014). The free-trade agreement with Vietnam includes as trade of goods, as trade of services and investment. Undeniably, it is yet early to assess even preliminary results of a free-trade zone with Vietnam. However, Vietnam was one of the 11 countries that signed, in October 2015, the Trans-Pacific Partnership Agreement, and due to this, the Vietnam-EEU free-trade agreement creates certain connections between the EEU's and TPP's markets. One can only note that the creation of a free-trade zone between Vietnam and the EEU member states can significantly augment the EEU's internal market. Even now Vietnam has a population of about 100 million, and these people are interested in hi-tech goods produced at the EEU member states.

The year 2015 has seen a reinvigoration of trade between Russia and *Egypt*, which may lead to the creation of a free-trade zone between Egypt and the EEU. Egypt already has 400 businesses with Russian investment, and several promising projects are in the works. An investment fund with the participation of Russia, Egypt and UAE, now in the making, can do much good (Latukhina, 2015).

The Supreme Eurasian Economic Council at a session decided to begin negotiations between the EEU and *Israel* about a free-trade zone (EAES I Izrail nachinayut peregovory o sozdanii zony svobodnoy torgovli, 2015).

The work of joint task groups set up to explore the practicability of free-trade agreements with *India* and *Iran* is nearing completion. Free-trade zones with Iran and India would more than double the volume of these countries' trade with the EEU. Nearly all EEU countries (except Kyrgyzstan) are participants of the international North South Transport Corridor, setting the scene for a free trade between the EEU and Iran. India's economic ties with the EEU countries develop along similar lines. As is well known, the Indian economy is relatively competitive in comparison with the Western economies. This circumstance is certain to increase the significance of the India-EEU free trade zone for all participating countries (Zona svobodnoy torgovli EAES – Indiya – Iran, 2015).

It is important to stress that one of the goals of the creation of a global free-trade zone in the Asia-Pacific region (Trans-Pacific Partnership) is reducing *China's* competitiveness with relation to USA and Japan. So, it appears that representatives of the EEU and China have begun talks about a free-trade zone just in time. The parties are looking into the regulatory issues and designing the framework for joint infrastructural projects, which is expected to be reflected in the linking up of "the EEU projects and the Silk Road initiative" (EAES I Kitay nachinayut peregovory o sozdanii zony svobodnoy torgovli, 2015).

In September 2013 China's president Xi Jinping announced that the country was launching a project called One Belt, One Road (OBOR) (Videnie i deystvie, napravlennie na prodvizhenie sovmestnogo stroitelstva…, 2015). What China proposes is not just a classic integration project – it is a mega-project comprising diverse initiatives (from economic to cultural), which will supposedly result in the creation of "Big Eurasia", stretching from the Pacific to the Baltic and Mediterranean Seas.

The crisis in relations with the West objectively forced Russia to intensify its relations with China. As a result, Russia and China officially agreed to harmonize the Eurasian Economic Union and the Silk Road Economic Belt: on May 8, 2015 Russian president Vladimir Putin and Chinese president Xi Jinping signed a Joint Statement of Russian Federation and People's Republic of China on Cooperation in Harmonization of Eurasian Economic Union and Silk Road Economic Belt, thus setting in stone the Russian-Chinese plans to expand the economic cooperation in Eurasia.

Mongolia is discussing a free-trade agreement with the EEU. As the Mongolian president Tsakhiagiin Elbegdorj puts it, "why should you buy meat in Australia or New Zealand, when Mongolia can supply quality products and Mongolian cashmere is every bit as good as the products of Italian and other international producers" (Mongoliya mozhet zakluchit dogovor o zone svobodnoy torgovli s EAES, 2015). The EEU plans negotiations with Syria regarding possible commercial and economic cooperation, although the question of creating a free-trade zone with Syria has not been discussed yet. Nor have there been any moves to create a free-trade zone with *Turkey* (EAES ne vedet peregovory s Siriey o sozdanii zony svobodnoy torgovli, 2015).

In April 2017 *South Korea* and the EEU have begun negotiations on conclusion of free-trade agreement. According to the Korea International Trade Association the trade turnover between two actors amounted to more than 14,19 billion US dollars in 2016 (Korea I Evraziyskiy ekonomicheskiy soyuz nachali peregovori po soglasheniyu o svobodnoy torgovle, 2017). Korea exported to the EEU cars and spare parts, synthetic resins, plastic products and metal plate. Meanwhile, energy resources such as crude oil, oil, coal and natural gas were imported into Korea from countries of the EEU. Korean and Russian experts see rich potential in development of cooperation between South Korea and the EEU.

Thus, it is not only countries geographically close to the EEU that show an interest in cultivating preferential contacts with it. According to Valentina Matvienko, after a visit of a group of Russian members of parliament to *Latin America* it became clear that "Ecuador and some other Latin American countries are interested in creating a free-trade zone with the EEU since they understand the potential. Ecuador will be chairing the Community of Latin American and Caribbean States (CELAC), and we expect this organization to help us in cultivating ties with the region's integrationist organizations" (Matvienko, 2015). The cooperation with Latin American's countries and integration groups is one of priorities on external agenda of the EEU. Negotiations with regional representatives were beginning since the autumn 2014. There are two format of negation's process: the Memorandum of cooperation between the EEU and the Latin America's countries (for example, Chile, Brazil and Mexico) and the Memorandum of cooperation between the EEU and the Latin America's regional organizations (for example, MERCOSUR, Andean Community of Nations). The Latin America's vector of cooperation seems as one of the most profitable for the EEU.

SOLUTIONS AND RECOMMENDATIONS

Nowadays the main goal of the EEU development is its full integration into the global trade system and in this context the members of the EEU build a system of partnerships, primarily at the level of concluding FTA agreements, with the countries with which they have a good level of political dialogue. Meanwhile, the EEU countries have different approaches to formats of its international ties; besides that they have different degree of readiness to take the obligations on trade of services and investments. For example, in the case of FTA with Vietnam now only Russia took these obligations.

Today the EEU has a major challenge to formulate its approaches to building relationships with the two main actors in the Greater Eurasia – China and the European Union. The 'conjugation' between the EEU and the EU is an elusive idea, because the crisis between Russia and the Western countries. The EU prefers to develop and support the bilateral relationships with the members of the EEU. As a result the project of 'conjugation' between the EEU and the Chinese project 'One belt, one Road' is more profitable on this stage.

The EEU should not repeat the mistakes of the EU geopolitical enlargement with the countries of the Eastern Europe. Thus, from my point of view, the EEU should keep the current number of members and try to develop its trade transactions (not only between Russia and Belarus, and between Russia and Kazakhstan, but also fully including Kyrgyzstan and Armenia). Meanwhile, the opportunities for a growth in foreign trade with the third countries (not from the post-Soviet area) and different integration associations are one of the general expectations for all members of the EEU for the near perspective (for example, in Latin America and Africa). There are the expectation of expanding the list of countries and blocs outside of the post-Soviet area, with which the EEU will sign as the preferential agreements, as non-preferential agreements on trade.

Thus, the EEU has a big potential for development its international trade connections, but in the same time it is obvious that the potential in this direction is still not implemented completely. Unfortunately, for example, a free trade zone with Vietnam does not contain any serious possibilities to increase mutual trade turnover.

Thus, it is important that the ongoing negotiations on creating free trade zones would bring some benefits not only in political and image sphere, but in economic as well.

FUTURE RESEARCH DIRECTIONS

Taking into account the latter trends in the development of the international cooperation of the EEU with the third countries and international blocs, it is interesting to evaluate the prospects of cooperation between the Latin America and the EEU in the context of the conjugation of the EEU and the Chinese project "One belt, one road". It is known that China has a great interest in the Latin America and actively invests in the extractive industries of the states in this region. Moreover, recent years China became a strong competitor in economic sphere of the region to the main partner of most countries in the Latin America - the USA. Today China is a key partner for Chile, Peru, Colombia, Mexico, Brazil and Argentina. In this context, the project of conjugation of the EEU and "One belt, one road" may expand in the Latin American region in the future.

CONCLUSION

However, a number of Russian experts believe that free-trade agreements between the EEU and other countries would depreciate the value of the EEU itself. For instance, Vasily Koltashov believes that "the EEU's foundation is the Russian market. Free trade zones would bring advantages to many countries, opening up for them our market. Nevertheless, what would Russia sell to them? Grain, fertilizers, oil, metals are the staple of our commerce. As we can see, the range of goods is modest. The produce of the defense industry does not count for it can be sold without any zones. There are no high hopes presently. Free-trade zones as such will not contribute to the development of our economy" (Ekspert: zony svobodnoy torgovli mogut obestsenit EAES, 2015). I believe that the EEU should show to the world that it is an efficient organization capable of attracting trade partners – this is very important in a situation when the WTO is in crisis and leading Western nations are drawing up new rules for international economy. Even today, one can safely say that the EEU is ready for developing bilateral and multilateral cooperation with many countries and integrationist alliances. Presently the most important direction is the ties with Asian nations, but the reason for this is the West's lack of willingness to engage in a productive dialog with the EEU.

REFERENCES

Barieri, izyatia I ogranicheniya EAES. (2016). [Barriers, Exceptions and Limitations of the EEU]. Eurasian Economic Commission. Analitical paper. Retrieved 14 May, 2017, from https://barriers.eaeunion.org/api/info/document/38/file

Characteristics of Kazakh-Russian relations. (n.d.). Embassy of the Republic of Kazakhstan in the Russian Federation. Retrieved 12 April, 2017, from http://www.kazembassy.ru/ru/dvustoronneesotrudnichestvo/harakteristikaotnoshenii

Dogovor o Evraziyskom ekonomicheskom soyuze. (2014). [The Treaty on the Eurasian Economic Union]. Signed in Astana on May 29. Retrieved 12 April, 2017, from http://www.eaeunion.org/files/history/2014/2014_2.pdf

EAES I Izrail nachinayut peregovory o sozdanii zony svobodnoy torgovli. (2015, October 16). [The EEU and Israel begin the negotiations on creating a free trade zone]. *Kommersant.ru*. Retrieved from https://www.kommersant.ru/doc/2834675

EAES I Kitay nachinayut peregovory o sozdanii zony svobodnoy torgovli. (2015, May 12). [The EEU and China begin the negotiations on creating a free trade zone]. *GazetaNova.RU*. Retrieved from http://gazetanova.ru/politics/9163-eaes-i-kitay-nachinayut-peregovory-o-sozdanii-zony-svobodnoy-torgovli.html

EAES I Tamojenniy soyuz: komu vigodno? (2016). [The EEU and Customs Union: who benefits?]. Retrieved 21 April, 2017, from http://kazdata.kz/04/2016-03-eaes-ts-kazakhstan-torgovye-otnosheniya.html

EAES ne vedet peregovory s Siriey o sozdanii zony svobodnoy torgovli. (2015, October 12). [The EEU does not negotiate with Syria on the establishment of a free trade zone]. Expert center on WTO issues. Retrieved from http://www.wto.ru/2015/10/12/еаэс-не-ведет-переговоры-с-сирией-о-соз/

Ekspert: zony svobodnoy torgovli mogut obestsenit EAES. (2015, June 2). [An expert: free trade areas can reduce the EEU]. Sovet Federatsii. Retrieved from http://svpressa.ru/economy/news/123895/

Korea I. Evraziyskiy ekonomicheskiy soyuz nachali peregovori po soglasheniyu o svobodnoy torgovle. (2017, April 11). [Korea and the Eurasian Economic Union began negotiations on free trade agreement]. Retrieved from http://russian.korea.net/NewsFocus/Business/view?articleId=145305

Kuvshinova, O. (2016, December 14). *Snijenie baryerov v torgovle stran EAES mojet uvelichit ih tovarooborot na chetvert* [The reduction of trade barriers in the EEU countries could increase their turnover by a quarter]. Retrieved from https://www.vedomosti.ru/economics/articles/2016/12/14/669499-snizhenie-barerov

Kuzmina, E. M. (2016). Eurasian Economic Union in the New Economy. *Management consulting, 10*. Retrieved 12 May, 2017, from https://cyberleninka.ru/article/n/evraziyskiy-ekonomicheskiy-soyuz-v-novyh-ekonomicheskih-usloviyah

Kuzmina, E. M. (2017, June 15). *Ekonomicheskoe razvitie stran EAES I perspektivi ekonomicheskoy integrazii do 2025 goda* [Economic development of the EEU countries and prospects of economic integration by 2025]. Working paper. Retrieved from http://russiancouncil.ru/papers/EAEU2025-Policybrief-ru.pdf

Lagutina, M. (2017). Improving relations with Russia and Ukraine. In A. Amighini (Ed.), *China's Belt and Road: a Game Changer?* (pp. 53–75). Milan: ISPI.

Lagutina, M., & Vasilyeva, N. (2016). *The Russian Project of Eurasian Integration. Geopolitical Prospects*. Lexington Books, Rowman and Littlefield.

Lapenko, M. (2014). Ukrainskiy krizis I ego vliyanie na realizatsiu proekta sozdaniya Evraziyskogo ekonomicheskogo soyuza [Ukrainian crisis and its influence on the development of the Eurasian economic union]. *Connections, 14*(1). Retrieved from http://connections-qj.org/ru/article/ukrainskiy-krizis-i-ego-vliyanie-na-realizaciyu-proekta-sozdaniya-evraziyskogo

Latukhina, K. (2015, August 26). Putin: EAES I Egipet mogut sozdat zonu svobodnoy torgovli [Putin: the EEU and Egypt can create a free trade zone]. *Rossiyskaya gazeta*.

Matvienko, V. (2015, January 13). *Ryad stran Latinskoy Ameriki proyavlyaut interes k sozdaniyu zony svobodnoy torgovli s EAES* [The number of countries in Latin America show its interest to creating a free trade zone with the EEU]. Sovet Federatsii. Retrieved from http://council.gov.ru/press-center/news/50386/

Mongoliya mozhet zakluchit dogovor o zone svobodnoy torgovli s EAES. (2015, May 8). [Mongolia may sign an agreement on free trade zone with the EEU]. BNEWS.KZ. Retrieved from http://bnews.kz/ru/news/post/266141/

O Trans-Tikhookeanskom partnerstve. (2015, October 5). [About the Trans-Pacific partnership]. Russian research center of APEC. Retrieved from http://apec-center.ru/о-транстихоокеанском-партнерстве/

Official visit of Vladimir Putin to Kazakhstan. (2015, October 15). Embassy of the Republic of Kazakhstan in the Russian Federation. Retrieved from http://www.kazembassy.ru/ru/mpolitika/7376-2015-10-15-07-19-47

Press-konferentsiya po itogam foruma ATES. (2012, September 9). [Press conference on the results of the APEC forum]. President of Russia. Retrieved from http://kremlin.ru/events/president/transcripts/16432

Prezident, T. T. P. RF Sergey Katirin: Kazakhstan – nadejniy partner. (2016, October 14). [President of CCI of Russia Sergei Katyrin: Kazakhstan is a reliable partner]. The Chamber of Commerce and Industry of the Russian Federation. Retrieved from https://tpprf.ru/ru/news/prezident-tpp-rf-sergey-katyrin-kazakhstan-nadezhnyy-partner--i156458/

Rossiysko-belorusskoe torgovo-ekonomicheskoe sotrudnichestvo. (2015). [Russian-Belorussian trade and economic cooperation]. Retrieved 18 June, 2017, from http://belarus.mid.ru/spravocnye-materialy/-/asset_publisher/9CH6VzS6hIWV/content/rossijsko-belorusskoe-torgovo-ekonomiceskoe-sotrudnicestvo

Shein, N. B. (2015). *Nekotorie itogi vzaimnoy torgovli stran-chlenov EAES v 2015 godu* [Some results of mutual trade of member countries of the EEU in 2015]. Retrieved 18 June, 2017, from https://riss.ru/analitycs/34092/

Shpakovsky, A. (2014). *Evraziyskaya integraziya yavlyaetsya dlya Belorusi bezalternativnim vektorom* [Eurasian integration is the only vector for Belarus]. Retrieved 18 June, 2017, from http://www.postkomsg.com/expert_opinion/202548/

The European Free Trade Association. (2016). Retrieved 15 June, 2017, from http://www.efta.int/about-efta/european-free-trade-association

The text of General Agreement on Tariffs and Trade (GATT). (1947, October 30). Retrieved from https://www.wto.org/english/docs_e/legal_e/gatt47_e.pdf

Tkachuk, S. (2016, May 13). *EAES I vse-vse-vse. Vneshniy kontur stanovleniya evraziyskoy integrazii* [The EEU and all. The external contour of the formation of the Eurasian integration]. Retrieved from https://aftershock.news/?q=node/400139

Torgovaya politika EAES. (2016, June 28). [Trade policy of the EEU]. Retrieved from http://eurasiancenter.ru/expert/20160628/1004383194.html

Torgovo-ekonomicheskoe sotrudnichestvo Rossii I Belorussii. (2017, March 30). [Trade and Economic Cooperation of Russia and Belarus]. Retrieved from http://www.tks.ru/news/nearby/2017/03/30/0003

Videnie i deystvie, napravlennie na prodvizhenie sovmestnogo stroitelstva "Ekonomicheskogo poyasa Shelkovogo puti" i "Morskogo Shelkovogo puti 21 veka". (2015, March 23). [Vision and action aimed at promoting the joint construction of "Economic belt of the Silk road" and "Maritime silk road of the 21st century"]. The official site of the Embassy of the Republic of China in the Russian Federation. Retrieved from http://ru.china-embassy.org/rus/zgxw/t1257296.htm

Vinokurov, E. (2014, October 14). *Evropeyskiy I Evraziyskiy soyuzy: povod dlya integratsii* [The European and Eurasian unions: the reason for integration]. TASS Informational agency of Russia. Retrieved from http://tass.ru/opinions/1597482

Vinokurov, E. (2014). *Kolichestvenniy analiz ekonomicheskoy integratsii Evropeyskogo soyuza I Evraziyskogo ekonomicheskogo soyuza: metodologicheskie podkhody. Doklad #23* [Quantitative analysis of economic integration of the European Union and the Eurasian Economic Union: methodological approaches. Paper #23]. ZII EABR.

Voprosy I otvety po Soglasheniyu o svobodnoy torgovle mezhdu Evraziyskim ekonomicheskim soyuzom I Sotsialisticheskoy Respublikoy Vietnam. (n.d.). [Questions and answers about the Agreement on the free trade between the Eurasian Economic Union and the Socialist Republic of Vietnam]. Retrieved 14 June, 2017, from http://www.eurasiancommission.org/ru/act/trade/dotp/sogl_torg/Documents/Вопросы%20и%20ответы%20по%20Соглашению%20о%20свободной%20торговле%20между%20странами%20ЕАЭС%20и%20Вьетнамом.pdf

Voskresenskiy, M. (2014, July 17). *Integratsiya, shag vtoroy: zony svobodnoy torgovli v EAES* [Integration, the second step: a free trade zone in EEU]. Evraziyskiy kommunikatsionniy centr. Retrieved from http://eurasiancenter.ru/economyexperts/20140717/1003589939.html

Vozvrashchenie Makkindera – Vengriya prisoedinyaetsya k "Shelkovomu puti." (2015, September 16). [The return of Mackinder – Hungary joins the "Silk road"]. War and Peace. Retrieved from http://www.warandpeace.ru/ru/commentaries/view/105060/

Vzaimnaya torgovlya tovarami. Statistika Evraziyskogo ekonomicheskogo soyuza. (2016). [Mutual trade of goods. Statistics of the Eurasian Economic Union]. Statistical Bulletin. Eurasian Economic Commission. Moscow. Retrieved 18 June, 2017, from http://www.eurasiancommission.org/ru/act/integr_i_makroec/dep_stat/tradestat/publications/Documents/Int_III_2016.pdf

Zona svobodnoy torgovli EAES – Indiya – Iran. (2015, October 5). [A free trade zone of the EEU — India — Iran]. NOVORUSMIR.RU. Retrieved from http://novorusmir.ru/archives/4260

KEY TERMS AND DEFINITIONS

Common Market: A group formed by countries within a geographical area to promote duty free trade and free movement of labor and capital among its members.

Economic Integration: Process in which two or more states in a broadly defined geographic area reduce a range of trade barriers to advance or protect a set of economic goals.

Eurasian Development Bank (EDB): An international financial organization established to promote economic growth in its member states, extend trade and economic ties among them, and to support integration in Eurasia.

Eurasian Economic Commission (EEC): The permanent regulatory body of the Eurasian Economic Union (EAEU), which aimed to ensure the functioning and development of the EAEU and developed proposals for the further development of integration.

Eurasian Economic Union (EEU): An international organization for regional economic integration that has international legal personality and is established by the Treaty on the Eurasian Economic Union.

One Belt, One Road (OBOR): The Chinese infrastructure mega-project which aimed at connectivity with Europe via Central Asia to increase trade between the Asia Pacific Region (APR) and Europe. It consists of two components: the land transportation infrastructure (known as Silk Road Economic Belt [SREB] or the One Belt) mostly via high speed trains and the sea transportation infrastructure (known as the Maritime Silk Road) via trans-ocean ships.

World Trade Organization (WTO): The only global international organization dealing with the rules of trade between nations based on the WTO agreements; the goal is to help producers of goods and services, exporters, and importers conduct their business.

Chapter 4
An Analysis of Trade of the Eurasian Economic Union

Ahu Coşkun Özer
Marmara University, Turkey

ABSTRACT

After the creation of the Eurasian Economic Union in 2015, the Customs Union and the Common Economic Space between Russia, Belarus, and Kazakhstan represented two of the most important regional integration projects launched in the post-Soviet era. However, even though institutions, customs unions, and a common economic space have been established, it has become a matter of debate whether this union is effective in developing trade between the member countries. Russia has enormous power in terms of its share of the trade within the EEU. This shows Russia has economic dominance in the union. This is also the subject of debate about whether the union's members, except Russia, benefit from the customs union. In this chapter, the answers to these questions have been investigated by evaluating the commercial activities and macroeconomic variables of the member countries of the Eurasian Economic Union.

INTRODUCTION

After the Second World War, trade liberalization and the elimination of barriers to world trade began. In the context of these developments, the General Agreement on Tariffs and Trade was signed in 1947. Initiatives have been created to shape trade unions among the countries of the European Union and the Eurasian Economic Union (EEU). These supranational bodies were formed by countries in the Eurasian region after the collapse of the Soviet Union.

DOI: 10.4018/978-1-5225-4032-8.ch004

The customs union within the EEU has been established but it has been a matter of debate whether this union will function as the European Union and other similar trade associations do. According to research carried out, the EEU does not operate as effectively as other trade associations because the member countries' populations, land areas, and trade rates in the union are not homogenously distributed. The trade rates of the countries in the EEU vary between member states, but these ratios range from 45% to 55%. It is also a topic of debate whether the operation of the union has strong structures and standards.

In this study, the establishment history of the EEU, trade potentials of the EEU, and trade rates between the member countries of the EEU have been evaluated. A general assessment has been made on the effectiveness and potential in world trade of the EEU.

BACKGROUND

The scientific literature contains investigations of the aims of the Eurasia Economic Union and its impact on member states. Rivera and Garashchuk (2016) state that the EEU was created more as an economic rather than political union; however, the analysis of trade proves the contrary to be true: integration in the post-Soviet area is thereby considered as nothing but another attempt on the part of Russia to return its leadership in the region and strengthen its position at the international level. According to the Sakaev (2016), the central purpose of the EEU is to try to maintain control over the post-Soviet geopolitical space and to prevent the implementation of alternative integration projects. Also, Dreyer and Popescu (2014) think that the EEU is a rival project to the EU's Eastern Partnership and that the Kremlin seeks to establish a new center of power in an increasingly multipolar world. In scientific literature, it is claimed that the primary purpose of the EEU is economic, but it is necessary to have political affiliation to realize this aim. There have been attempts to establish similar trade associations in the region of the Eurasia but the EEU is the only trade association officially established in the region.

There is research on the effects of the Eurasian Customs Union on the economies of the member countries. According to Carneiro (2013), Russia, a member of the Eurasian Economic Union, acts conservatively. Russia applied high levels custom tariffs for the non-member countries. The tariffs to be applied to non-member countries within the EEU have been determined on the basis of Russian standards. Kazakhstan is a country implementing liberal economic policies, has increased tariffs by around 100 percent for the countries outside of the EEU.All member states have applied high levels of customs tariffs for non-EEU countries and it caused to reduce their imports from countries, except Russia. This means a significant increase in Russia's exports.

According to Carneiro (2013), the Russian market has not provided any significant benefit to Kazakhstan and Belarus, which are members of the Eurasian Economic Union. After the Customs Union, the trade of these two member countries has not increased significantly. Kazakhstan have begin to do benefit and cost analysis on membership of EEU. it is necessary to fulfill commitments given to member states in order to build strength of the Eurasian Economic Union.

As mentioned above, it is very natural for the EEU members to increase exports and imports because the Eurasian Economic Union should shift imports from outside into the union by creating a trade-distorting effect. However, interests of the trade union should be priority within the trade and economic unions, the interests of the countries are in second rank after the interests of the trade union. If only one or a few countries are profitable in the trade union, the other countries are only serving for that country's interests, then that caused to detriment in the trade union. While Russia offers serious benefits from this unity, the interests of other countries are not at the same level with Russia. This causes to make cost-benefit analysis for the countries in the union.

There are countries that are considering leaving the EEU so there is a need for studies on how the EEU has influenced the economies of the member states since the day it was established. Studies on this subject are limited in the literature.

FOCUS OF THE CHAPTER

Issues, Controversies, Problems

It has become a matter of debate whether the EEU is effective in fostering trade between the member countries. In this study, the answers to these questions have been sought by evaluating the commercial activities and macroeconomic variables of the member countries of the EEU. Statistical data has been examined and commercial relations within the Eurasian Economic Union have been evaluated and analyzed the benefits of the EEU to its members.

History of Eurasian Economic Union

The first real practical step in the formation of the Eurasian Union has been the creation of the customs union within Belarus, Kazakhstan, and Russia in 2010. The customs union, as a form of exclusively economic integration, aims to facilitate the economic cooperation of the member states. An agreement on the common economic space, which is to come into force in 2012, has been also signed. The subscription of the declaration on the establishment of the Eurasian Union by leaders of Russia, Kazakhstan, and Belarus on November 18, 2011 should be unquestionably considered the main achievement of the implementation of the Eurasian community in an economic sense. This event, and an active discussion between the leaders of the three countries, clearly demonstrates their intent to develop the potential for integration on a Eurasian basis. Vladimir Putin, being the Prime Minister, said in an interview with the newspaper Izvestia, "Now from the Customs Union, we are taking a step to the Common Economic Space. We are creating a huge market with over 165 million consumers, with the unified legislation, free movement of capitals, services and labor power (Raikhan, 2013)." When it is evaluated from this point of view, the EEU constitutes a large market. It is seen that EEU has both political and economic dimensions. Formalization of the EEU has taken 4 years from the formation of the concept of the union. Although implementations of the trade union have begun 2010, the agreement was signed in 2014.The member countries of the EEU have joined the union in different years.

The EEU is a political and economic union established on May 29, 2014 by a treaty signed by the leaders of Belarus, Kazakhstan, and Russia (Tasch & Barbara, 2014). The treaty, which included Armenia to EEU, was signed on October 9, 2014. (Druzhinin & Aleksei, 2014). The union was officially established on January 1, 2015. Kyrgyzstan's full membership to the Eurasian Union become effective as of May 1, 2015, when the protocols were approved. Member countries are Belarus, Armenia, Kazakhstan, Kyrgyzstan, and Russia. Trade relations in the EEU are based on the market potential, which depends on the population and resources of the member countries.

The EEU has approximately 175 million people and a gross domestic product of over $4 trillion. The EEU requires the free movement of goods, capital, services, and people and provides for common transport, agriculture, and energy policies, with provisions for a single currency and greater integration in the future. The EEU institutions include the Eurasian Commission, which is the executive body, the Court of the EEU, and the Eurasian Development Bank (Gharabegian, 2015).

There are countries considering joining the EEU in the future, but there is uncertainty about how the participation of the countries will affect the EEU. For example, possible candidates are the People's Republic of China, EU, India, Iran, Zimbabwe, Tunis, and Turkey.

The economy of the EEU has been predicted to grow by 25% by 2030 (Iglauer, 2014). It is estimated that China's membership of the EEU will stimulate this economic growth but China's membership will affect the power balances in the EEU. According to the trade rates, China is the largest trading country in the EEU. Yang and Wang (2014) states that China sees the Silk Road Economic Belt as contributing to the economic growth of the EEU by bridging the regional economies of the EEU and the Asia-Pacific, thereby offering an economic stimulus to both regions. Prior to the launch of the EEU in January 2015, the establishment of a customs union in 2010 between Russia, Kazakhstan, and Belarus stimulated trade between these countries and China. In 2012, China accounted for 114.6 billion USD in trade with Russia, Kazakhstan and Belarus, and China became the largest trading partner with the customs union (Yang & Wang, 2014). For the future perspectives, the membership of China in the EEU will affect the power balances in the union, also participation of China in the EEU can increase the power of union in the world.

China and the Eurasian Economic Union are expected to work towards establishing a free trade zone in order to improve relations between the China and the members of the Eurasian Economic Union. At the same time, China and EEU will create cross-border zones for economic cooperation and industrial parks to facilitate economic integration, thereby China and EEU will facilitate the economic integration (Zhong, 2015).

Also, India has started to study possible free trade with the Eurasian Union in starting in the beginning of 2017. It is expected that free-trade agreement will also serve to develop trade between India and other countries of the EEU. India's trade value with the EEU countries is about $10 billion.

Trade in EEU

According to official European Economic Community (EEC) statistics, \after the creation of the customs union within Belarus, Kazakhstan, and Russia in 2010, the initial creation of the customs union coincided with a boost in intra-regional trade, which was up by 32.1% in 2011 to some $62 billion and by a further 7.5% in 2012. Since then, however, the trend has been strongly downwards, falling by 5.5% in 2013, 11% in 2014, and 25.8% in 2015. By 2015, trade among EEU members was down to $45 billion. In the period from January to April 2016, trade was down 18.4 per cent year-on-year (Crisis Group Report, 2016).

According to the National Bank of Kazakhstan statistics, Kazakhstan experienced a 28.8 percent decline in foreign trade with Russia, a 48.4% decline with China, and 41.5% decline with Europe. These differences relate primarily to the structure of trade (China and Europe are both importers of Kazakh oil and gas) rather than any impact of the EEU (as mentioned in the 2016 Crisis Group Report). Trade between the member countries has increased in the first year of the customs union, but trade rates have declined in subsequent years.

When the EEU member countries' trade tendencies are evaluated, it is observed that the import and export rates between the member countries vary significantly. When the 2014 data is evaluated, Russia's 7% of total exports and imports are in the

EEU counties. 9% of Kazakhstan total exports, and 36% of the total imports are in the EEU. It also accounts for 20% total exports of Armenia. Russia also accounts for 46 percent of Kyrgyzstan's imports and 33% of exports and 44% of the exports of Belarus and 55% of imports in the EEU. In the foreign trade, while the Eurasian Economic Union has great importance for Kyrgyzstan and Belarus, other member countries of the EEU are much more involved with countries outside the EEU. This data shows that the trade rates among the member countries are relatively high. These rates demonstrate the dependence of the countries within the EEU on each other.

However, these rates are still high compared to the EU, which is one of the other commercial unions. For example, France is the main trading partner of Germany,

Table 1. Foreign trade of the countries of the EEU, million of US dollars

	2014 (Million US Dollars) of Which				2015 (Million US Dollars) of Which			
	Total	CIS	Thereof EAEU	Other Countries	Total	CIS	Thereof EAEU	Other Countries
Armenia								
Exports	1547,3	357,1	324,7	1190,2	1485,3	286,3	256,3	1199
Imports	4424,4	1363,1	1154,6	3061,3	3239,2	1096,9	968,6	2142,3
Balance	−2877,1	−1006	−829,9	−1871,1	−1753,9	−810,6	−712,3	−943,3
Belarus								
Exports	36080,5	21107,5	16178,4	14973	26660,4	14076,2	11006,7	12584,2
Imports	40502,4	24187,1	22293,5	16315,3	30291,5	18342,8	17204,2	11948,7
Balance	−4421,9	−3079,6	−6115,1	−1342,3	−3631,1	−4266,6	−6197,5	635,5
Kazakhstan								
Exports	79459,8	11052,5	7155	68407,3	45955,8	7908,3	5120,4	38047,5
Imports	41295,5	17547	14940,5	23748,5	30567,7	13062	11203,6	17505,7
Balance	38164,3	−6494,5	−7785,5	44658,8	15388,1	−5153,7	−6083,2	20541,8
Kyrgyzstan								
Exports	1883,7	893,4	637,6	990,3	1646,4	741,2	509,8	905,2
Imports	5734,7	2896,1	2646,5	2838,6	3937,7	2048,9	1879,1	1888,8
Balance	−3851	−2002,7	−2008,9	−1848,3	−2291,3	−1307,7	−1369,3	−983,6
Russia								
Exports	501472,1	64801,6	37720,3	436670,5	346048,4	45352,2	28823,2	300696,2
Imports	292000	35883,8	23179,6	256116,2	184810,4	21284,7	14181	163525,7
Balance	209472,1	28917,8	14540,7	180554,3	161238	24067,5	14642,2	137170,5
EAEU, total								
Exports	620443,4	98212,1	62016	522231,3	421796,3	68364,2	45716,4	353432,1
Imports	383957	81877,1	64214,7	302079,9	252846,5	55835,3	45436,5	197011,2
Balance	236486,4	16335	−2198,7	220151,4	168949,8	12528,9	279,9	156420,9

Zbarskaya & Gabdrakhimova, 2016.

and Germany exports 9% of total exports to France. Germany is the main trading partner of France, with 17% of its exports going to Germany (Eurostat, 2014).

When the commercial trends in recent years are evaluated, developments in the economies of Russia and Kazakhstan and oil prices affect trade in the EEU. It is difficult to assess the EEU's direct impact on trade because its introduction coincided with an economic slowdown in Russia and Kazakhstan and sharp currency devaluations. According to the National Bank of Kazakhstan, the decline in oil and commodity prices skewed figures sharply downwards (e.g., mineral resources were two-thirds of EEU exports and one-third of trade within the EEU in 2015). Thus, foreign trade for EEU members declined with all major partners, both within and outside the EEU (Crisis Group Report, 2016, p.10). Tariff regimes applied separately by the countries within the EEU have been removed, and a single tariff has been implemented. However, this tariff is already in practice in Russia.

According to the GAIN report (2016) and Tarr (2016), the EEU replaced its members' individual tariff regimes with a single external tariff. In most cases, this was based on pre-existing Russian trade tariffs, which were relatively high and therefore raised levies on imports for the more open economies of Kyrgyzstan, Kazakhstan, and Armenia. However, there have been transition arrangements for tariffs on many goods. Armenia (until 2022) and Kyrgyzstan (until 2020) have arrangements in place to retain former tariffs for a transitional period on some imports that are only used inside the country (Crisis Group Report, 2016, p. 11)

Nevertheless, for countries such as Kyrgyzstan, which had low tariffs on its consumer-goods trade with China, the result has been higher prices on Chinese imports and difficulties for wholesale and re-export trade. Russian goods, on the other hand, have become cheaper, largely due to the weaker ruble (Crisis Group interviews, 2016). At this point, efficiency is discussed in other countries in the EEU, except Russia. Inequalities exist about the distribution of import customs taxes.

First, there is a constant debate on sharing the benefits of the customs union among member states. According to the mechanism of the distribution of import customs duties between the member countries, Belarus gets 4.70% while Kazakhstan's and Russia's shares are 7.33% and 87.97% respectively (Golam, 2013) It is seen that the benefits from the EEU for the other member countries is low while considering the commercial dominance of Russia within the EEU.

Many observers have doubts and suspicions about Russia's true political and ideological goals and objectives in creating the customs union. Oppositions in Kazakhstan and Belarus are concerned about Russian's role and place in the union and believe that the creation of the customs union is a design by Russian ultra-nationalists and Neo-Eurasianists to restore Russian hegemony and are underpinned by imperial goals of restoring of the USSR (Golam, 2013).

When the EEU is compared to other trade associations, differences between it and other associations like the EU can be seen. Considering that Germany is the most populous member state in the EU, it is still a fact that the proportion of the population in the EU is not so high compared to Russia in the Eurasian Economic Union.

The most populous country in the EU is the western Germany and this ratio is 32 per cent of the total union, it is thought that this ratio is balanced with the population of Italy and France. (Blokmans, Kostanyan & Vorobiov, 2012).

However, Russia's dominance in the market in the customs union and its share in the market are quite high compared to other countries in the union. This ratio appears to be imbalanced when compared to the distributions in other economic unions.

It is seen that Russia is dominant in the customs union and the common economic area with 84 percent market share, and also when it is evaluated by the volume of the economies of member countries in customs union, there are differences between the member countries. For example, Russia's gross domestic product accounted for over 88% of the customs union's GDP in 2009, while West Germany's share barely exceeded 40% before the creation of the EEC (Blokmans, Kostanyan & Vorobiov, 2012).

If a functional economic union want to be created, the problem of transportation between countries should be solved and infrastructure inadequacy problem should be resolved. Because the logistics is important for the trade, transportation distances between the member countries constitutes one of the most important problems in the EEU.

When the distances between economic centers are evaluated, it is considered that transportation costs are in the EEU considerably higher than the customs union in the EU. It is believed that there is a significant asymmetry in distance of the economic centers between Russia and Belarus and the economic centers of Russia

Table 2. Comparison of the distances between major economic centers in the EEC and the EAEU

Trade Flows Distance,	km
EEC	
Paris–Frankfurt	573
Frankfurt–Amsterdam	438
EEU	
Moscow–Minsk	717
Moscow–Astana	2,700

Blockman, Kostanyan & Vorobiov, 2012.

and Kazakhstan, and it affect intra-union trade flows. (Blockman, Kostanyan, & Vorobiov, 2012).

Foreign Trade of Armenia

The total foreign trade volume of Armenia is approximately $4.724B, and about a third of this figure is from export. Also, according to the 2015 data, 17% of Armenia's exports go to member countries of the EEU. Approximately 30% of the total imports to Armenia come from other members of the EEU.

According to the statistics, in 2014, Armenia exported in total $1.62B and imported in total $4.28B, it caused trade deficit of $2.65B. The gross domestic product of Armenia was $11.6B in 2014 and its gross domestic product per capita was $8.07k. When statistics are evaluated in terms of exported products, copper ore is the top exported product of Armenia at $303 m, hard liquor at $160 m, gold at $160 m, ferroalloys $132 m and rolled tobacco at $115 m. Top imported product of Armenia is petroleum gas at $423 m, it is followed by refined petroleum at $294 m, cars at $195 m, gold at $143m, and diamonds at $143 m. The top export destinations of Armenia are Russia ($307 m), China ($181 m), Canada ($173 m), Germany ($160 m) and the United States ($92.5 m). The top import origins are Russia ($989 m), China ($403 m), Georgia ($254 m), Turkey ($227 m) and Iran ($194 m) (Atlas Media MIT, n.d.).

Foreign Trade of Kazakhstan

The total foreign trade volume of Kazakhstan in 2015 was approximately $76.522B dollars, which constituted exports of 45.955m dollars. When the foreign trade of Kazakhstan is considered from different countries, 17% of total exports and 43%

Table 3. Exports and imports of Armenia with the countries of the EEU (million US dollars)

Exports		Imports		Balance		% as of 2014		Country
2014	2015	2014	2015	2014	2015	Exports	Imports	
9	6,8	31	25,7	−22	−18,9	75,4	82,7	Belarus
7	4,2	0,6	0,4	6,4	3,8	59,9	68,1	Kazakhstan
0,4	0,4	0,1	0,1	0,3	0,3	98,5	127,9	Kyrgyzstan
308,3	244,9	1122,9	942,4	−814,6	−697,5	79,4	83,9	Russia
324,7	256,3	1154,6	968,6	−829,9	−712,3	78,9	83,9	Total

Zbarskaya & Gabdrakhimova, 2016.

of total imports happen between the independent state community (Azerbaijan, Armenia, Belarus, Georgia, Kazakhstan, Kyrgyzstan, Moldova, Russia, Tajikistan, Turkmenistan, Uzbekistan and Ukraine) where members of the EEU also participate. According to the assessment in terms of country groups, OECD countries are in the first place in exports to Kazakhstan, and European Union member countries are in the second place.

When the products exported by Kazakhstan are evaluated, crude petroleum is the first product with exported value $39.7B, it is followed by refined petroleum with $3.6B, petroleum gas with $3.51B, radioactive chemicals ($2.26B) and refined copper ($1.99B). The main income of the country is based on the export of underground natural resources. The industry based on the extraction of raw has been developed in Kazakhstan. The export revenues of the country depends on the high world oil prices.

The Kazakhstan economy is based on imports. Because the majority of production in the country is concentrated in the oil and gas sectors, production in consumption goods and capital goods do not meet the domestic demand. Products produced in domestic markets cannot compete with imported goods.

The main import items of Kazakhstan are automotive, petroleum oils, pharmaceuticals and aircraft. Cars are the first product most imported with $2.32B, refined petroleum is the second imported product ($1.49B), it is followed by packaged medicaments with $1.1B and planes, helicopters, and spacecraft ($842 m) and computers ($682 m) (Atlas Media MIT, n.d.).

Kazakhstan's main trading partners are China, the Netherlands, Russia, France, Italy, and Germany. China is the most exported destination of Kazakhstan (export value is $9.9B, %14), Kazakhstan export petroleum oils and natural gas to China.

Table 4. Foreign trade of Kazakhstan by country groups

2014 Exports	2014 Imports	2014 Balance	2015 Exports	2015 Imports	2015 Balance	
79459,8	41295,5	38164,3	45955,8	30567,7	15388,1	Total
11052,5	17547	–6494,5	7908,3	13062	–5153,7	CIS
7155	14940,5	–7785,5	5120,4	11203,6	–6083,2	EAEU
51732,9	13989,4	37743,5	28557,8	10555,6	18002,2	OECD
44681,1	8634,9	36046,2	24445,5	6879,6	17565,9	EU-28
17333,1	21712,4	–4379,3	10306,7	16005,3	–5698,6	BRICS
4541,7	234,7	4307	2661,2	163,7	2497,5	EFTA
988,2	211,6	776,6	626,5	181,1	445,4	OPEC

Zbarskaya & Gabdrakhimova, 2016.

Table 5. Export and import of Kazakhstan

Kazakhstan	Total	CIS	Thereof EAEU	Other Countries
Exports 2015	45956	7908	5120,4	38048
Imports 2015	30568	13062	11204	17506
Balance 2015	15388	−5154	−6083	20542

Zbarskaya & Gabdrakhimova, 2016.

The second destination is the Netherlands (export values is $6.84B, %10), it is followed by Russia (export value is $6.68B, %9.8). France and Italy are the other countries Kazakhstan exported. Kazakhstan's most imported countries are Russia, China, Germany, United States and France. Russia is the first country Kazakhstan mostly imported, the share of the Russia is %33 and import value from Russia is $13.8B. China is the second most importing country ($7.8B;%18), it is followed by Germany ($2.32B,%5.5), the United States ($1.9B,%4.5) and France ($1.12B,%2.7) (Atlas Media MIT, n.d.).

Foreign Trade of Kyrgyzstan

The 2015 export share of Kyrgyzstan by the main partner countries are China (34%), Kazakhstan (21%), Russia (10%), Uzbekistan (9%), the United Arab Emirates (6%), Turkey (5%), and 15% rest of the countries. Import shares by the main partner countries in 2015 are Russia (32%), China (26%), Kazakhstan (14%), Turkey (4%), and the rest of the countries (24%) *(Zbarskaya & Gabdrakhimova, 2016).*

According to the Economic Complexity Index (ECI), Kyrgyzstan is in 104th range between the most complex economies. In 2014, Kyrgyzstan exported $1.09B and imported $9.3B, resulting in trade deficit of $8.2B. Gross domestic product of Kyrgyzstan was $7.4B in 2014 and its gross domestic product per capita was $3.32k (Atlas Media MIT, n.d).

Table 6. Foreign trade of Kyrgyzstan in 2015, million US dollars

Kyrgyzstan	Total	CIS	Thereof EAEU	Other Countries
Exports 2015	1646,4	741,2	509,8	905,2
Imports 2015	3937,7	2048,9	1879,1	1888,8
Balance 2015	−2291	−1308	−1369	−983,6

Zbarskaya & Gabdrakhimova, 2016.

Table 7. Kyrgyzstan export by country groups

2014 (Million Dollars)			2015 (Million Dollars)			
Exports	**Imports**	**Balance**	**Exports**	**Imports**	**Balance**	
1883,7	5734,7	−3851	1646,4	3937,7	−2291,3	Total
893,4	2896,1	−2002,7	741,2	2048,9	−1307,7	CIS
637,6	2646,5	−2008,9	509,8	1879,1	−1369,3	EAEU
711,5	1470,9	−759,4	687,3	719,4	−32,1	OECD
58,6	583,6	−525	50,1	319,8	−269,7	EU-28
157,7	2996,1	−2838,4	193,7	2315,5	−2121,8	BRICS
575,6	20,4	555,2	562,1	20	542,1	EFTA
168,4	22,4	146	119,7	15,7	104	OPEC

Zbarskaya & Gabdrakhimova, 2016.

Exports of the Kyrgyzstan depend on the import performance of the neighbors. Products Kyrgyzstan exported are precious and semi-precious metals, chemicals, textiles, mineral products, beverages and tobacco, machinery and equipment.

Gold is the top exported product with value $445 m, it is followed by radioactive chemicals ($58.3 m), scrap copper ($52.8 m), dried legumes ($50.3 m) and precious metal ore ($40 m) Major import products of Kyrgyzstan are mineral products, machinery and chemicals. Refined petroleum is the first product imported. The value of the imported refined petroleum is $1.01b. The second product is knit men's suits with value $483 m, it is followed by knit women's suits, lightly mixed woven cotton and cars. (Atlas Media MIT, n.d). Trade partners of Kyrgyzstan are Switzerland, Russia, Kazakhstan, China, and Turkey.

Table 8. Exports and imports of Kyrgyzstan with the countries of the EEU, million US dollars

Exports		Imports		Balance		As% of 2014 (Current Prices)		Country
2014	**2015**	**2014**	**2015**	**2014**	**2015**	**Exports**	**Imports**	
0,1	0,2	0,3	0,3	−0,2	−0,1	163,2	131,6	Armenia
6,5	5,6	89,7	50,6	−83,2	−45	86,3	56,4	Belarus
508,7	347,7	776,7	566	−268	−218,3	68,4	72,9	Kazakhstan
122,3	156,3	1779,8	1262,2	−1657,5	−1105,9	127,8	70,9	Russia
637,6	509,8	2646,5	1879,1	−2008,9	−1369,3	80	71	Total

Zbarskaya & Gabdrakhimova, 2016.

Foreign Trade of Russia

Russia is the 10th largest export economy in the world and the 27th most complex economy, according to the economic complexity index. Russia has foreign trade surplus $154B in 2014 with export value $449B and import value $295B (Atlas Media MIT, n. d.).

Economic power of the Russian based on natural resources and human power. Rich natural resources is the basic building block of the economy. Foreign trade of Russia is based on oil and natural gas export so oil prices are driving force of the economy. High level of oil prices keep the economic growth of Russia. But overvalued exchange rates negatively affects growth in non-natural resources sectors in Russia.

The top exported products of Russia are crude petroleum, coal briquettes, raw aluminum. The export value of the crude petroleum is $155B, refined petroleum is $88.3B, petroleum gas is $35.9B, coal briquettes is $12.7B and raw aluminum is $7.64B. Top imported products of Russia are cars, packaged medicaments, vehicle parts, planes, helicopters, spacecraft and computers (Atlas Media MIT, n. d.).

The top export destinations of Russia are China with export value $39.3B, the second destination is the Netherlands with export value $39B, it is followed by Germany (export value $29.8B), Italy (export value $22.9B) and Japan (export value $21.5B). The top import destinations are China, Germany, the United States, Belarus and Italy(Atlas Media MIT, n. d.).

Approximately 8% of Russia's exports in 2015 have been to the countries within the Eurasian Economic Organization. Also, 7.6% of the imports have gone to member states of the EEU.

Russia's most exported country is the Netherlands. The Netherlands is ranked in the first as the top country of Russia's exports and import by 11.69% in 2015.

Table 9. Exports and imports of Russia with the countries of the EEU, million US dollars

Exports		Imports		Balance		As% of 2014 (Current Prices)		Country
2014	2015	2014	2015	2014	2015	Exports	Imports	
1094	1050,9	314	209,6	780	841,3	96,1	66,8	Armenia
20605	15603,7	15346,3	9004,5	5258,7	6599,2	75,7	58,7	Belarus
14277,3	10866,2	7445,4	4895,2	6831,9	5971	76,1	65,7	Kazakhstan
1744	1302,4	73,9	71,7	1670,1	1230,7	74,7	97,1	Kyrgyzstan
37720,3	28823,2	23179,6	14181	14540,7	14642,2	76,4	61,2	Total

Zbarskaya & Gabdrakhimova, 2016.

Russia provides 8.24% of total exports to China. Sand Italy and Germany follow these countries (about 4% of Russia's exports are made to these countries). Russia imports 15% of its total imports from China. China is followed by Germany at 10% and the USA by 6%. (World Bank World Integrated Trade Solutions, 2015).

Foreign Trade of Belarus

It is stated that Belarus is planning to pull out of the EEU because of the deteriorating bilateral relations with Russia.

Minsk's main hope for the EEU is that it will provide Belarus with a stable supply of oil and so will enable Minsk to save as much revenue as possible from sales. For this reason, the common market for oil has been Belarus's focus during the talks on the creation of the EEU. This common oil market will only come about in 2025, but Russia has proposed a temporary compromise: after long discussions in 2014, Belarus will receive an additional $1.5 billion—a duty that it previously paid to Moscow for the export of oil. The figure represents about 2% of Belarus's GDP (Astapenia, 2015).

As relations between Putin and Belarusian President Alexander Lukashenko worsen, rumors are swirling in Russian media that Minsk is planning a grand divorce in which Belarus would pull out of Russia's EEU and the Collective Security Treaty Organization. Minsk is refusing to pay a $550 million gas debt that Moscow claims it is owed, and Belarus just irked Russia by granting five-day visa-free travel to citizens of 80 countries (Center for Balkan and Black Sea Studies, 2017).

Table 10. Exports and imports of Belarus with the countries of the EEU, million US dollars

Exports		Imports		Balance		As% of 2014 (Current Prices)		Country
2014	2015	2014	2015	2014	2015	Exports	Imports	
29,2	27,8	9,4	7,6	19,8	20,2	95,1	81,6	Armenia
879,4	525,1	87,4	49,4	792	475,7	59,7	56,5	Kazakhstan
88,8	55,4	6,5	4	82,3	51,4	62,3	62,1	Kyrgyzstan
15181	10398,4	22190,2	17143,2	−7009,2	−6744,8	68,5	77,3	Russia
16178,4	11006,7	22293,5	17204,2	−6115,1	−6197,5	68	77,2	Total

Zbarskaya & Gabdrakhimova, 2016.

Table 11. Foreign trade of Belarus (million US dollars) 2015

	Total	CIS (Community of Independent States)	Thereof EAEU	Other Countries
		Belarus		
Exports	26660	14076	11007	12584
Imports	30292	18343	17204	11949
Balance	−3631	−4267	−6198	635,5

Zbarskaya & Gabdrakhimova, 2016.

SOLUTIONS AND RECOMMENDATIONS

After the cold war, the disintegration of the Soviet Union reshaped the power balance in world politics. It is a common view that competing against the USA, which is the dominant power in world politics and economics is only possible by creating new regional associations.

The European Union project is not new, but it has developed in accordance with this objective. In this context, Russia has struggled to build a structure like the EU with regional countries to restore the economic and political power it had in the Soviet era and create a force against the West (i.e., USA and EU).

Considering the economic and political balance in the world, there is a strong case to be made that such balances have recently changed in favor of Asia.

When the China and Indian economies are considered, if China, India, and other countries in this region become members of the EEU, the Eurasian Economic Union may become a counterbalancing force to the United States and the EU.

If this potential is to be transformed into reality, the common interests of every member of the EEU should be considered. Otherwise, the disintegration of the EEU may result. When we evaluate the world power balance, it is a fact that the EEU should operate more effectively in the world.

FUTURE RESEARCH DIRECTIONS

There are countries that are considering leaving the EEU, and others are considering joining the EEU. It is possible to conduct research on specific hypotheses about how the EEU will be influenced by the separation of member countries from the union and participation of the new countries considering to joining the union.

CONCLUSION

The formation of the customs union of the EEU, which took place in 2010, resulted in a large market with a population of 175 million and a GDP is 4 trillion dollars. It is estimated that the EEU's economy will grow by 25% by 2030.

A single foreign exchange within the EEU is an aim of the union, and it is expected that the EEU will expand its membership in the future. A major research topic focuses on how the participation of countries such as China, India, Tunisia, and Turkey, which are considering to joining the union, will affect the future of the union.

When trade trends in the union are evaluated, it is seen that Kazakhstan's economy is dependent on EEU imports and that the economies of Kyrgyzstan and Belarus are completely dependent on EEU for exports and imports. The economic independence of the countries determines the strength of the trade unions. The GDP of the nations in the EEU are not high. Also political problems are a handicap for the future of the EEU. Solving the political problems among the countries in the union will also lay the ground for strengthening the economic partnership. Also, countries within the union do not have a technological structure that can produce high value-added products that can compete in international markets. It is also necessary to regulate the roads of transport between countries so as to facilitate trade between member countries. These factors are decreasing the power of the EEU.

EEU members abandoned their national tariffs after their membership in the EEU, and they began to apply single tariffs in foreign trade. The tariff applied within the EEU has been determined on the basis of pre-existing trade tariffs in Russia. These tariffs adversely affected countries with low tariffs on imports, such as Kyrgyzstan, and led to an increase in the prices of imported goods.

Russia has enormous power in terms of its share of the trade within the EEU. This shows Russia has economic dominance in the union. This is also the subject of debate about whether the union's members, except Russia, benefit from the customs union. Kazakhstan and Belarus were anxious about the role of the Russia in the union and believed that the customs union was designed by Russian ultra-nationalists.

When the EEU is compared with the other trade associations such as the EU, it is seen that the EEU is far from homogenous in terms of many elements, such as trade rates of the countries, and distances between EEU members.

REFERENCES

Armenia Trade Statistics. (n.d.). Retrieved February 17, 2017, from http://atlas.media.mit.edu/en/profile/country/arm/

Astapenia, R. (2015). *Belarus and Eurasia Economic Union: The view from Minsk.* Retrieved March 28, 2017, from http://www.ecfr.eu/article/commentary_belarus_and_the_eurasian_economic_union_the_view_from_minsk

Blockmans, S., Kostanyan, H., & Vorobiov, I. (2012, December). *Towards a Eurasian Economic Union: Integration and cooperation.* CEPS Special Report No. 75.

Center for Balkan and Black Sea Studies. (n.d.). *Belarus reportedly mulls leaving the Eurasian Economic Union as relations with Russia worsen.* Retrieved February 3, 2017, from http://bulgariaanalytica.org/cbbss/?p=10497

Cheng, A., & Lim, H. (n.d.). China and The Eurasian Economic Union: Prospects for The Silk Road Economic Belt. *IPP Review*. Retrieved February 15, 2017, from http://ippreview.com/index.php/Home/Blog/single/id/18.html

Crisis Group. (2016). *The Eurasian Economic Union: Power, Politics and Trade.* Europe and Central Asia Report N°240. Retrieved January 1, 2017, from https://d2071andvip0wj.cloudfront.net/240-the-eurasian-economic-union-power-politics-and-trade.pdf

Dreyer, I., & Popescu, N. (2014). *The Eurasian Customs Union: The economics and the politics*. European Union Institute for Security Studies. Retrieved January 15, 2017, from http://www.iss.europa.eu/uploads/media/Brief_11_Eurasian_Union.pdf

Druzhinin, A. (2014). Armenia Joins Eurasian Economic Union. *Sputnik International*. Retrieved January 12, 2017, from https://sputniknews.com/world/20141010193914853-Armenia-Joins-Eurasian-Economic-Union/

Eurostat, International trade in goods in 2014 EU's top trading partners in 2014. (n.d.). Retrieved January 1, 2017, from http://ec.europa.eu/eurostat/documents/2995521/6760204/6-27032015-AP-EN.pdf

Francisco, C. G. (2013). *What promises does the Eurasian customs union hold for the future? Economic premise. No. 108.* Washington, DC: World Bank.

GAIN Report on Eurasian Economic Union One Year On. (n.d.). Retrieved February 20, 2017, from https://gain.fas.usda.gov/Recent%20GAIN%20Publications/Eurasian%20Economic%20Union%20One%20Year%20On_Moscow_Russian%20Federation_3-11-2016.pdf

Gharabegian, A. (2015). The Eurasian Economic Union and Armenia. *The Armenian Weekly.* Retrieved February 10, 2017, from http://armenianweekly.com/2015/10/20/the-eurasian-economic-union-armenia/

Golam, M. (2013). The concept of 'Eurasia': Kazakhstan's Eurasian policy and its implications. *Journal of Eurasian Studies*, *4*(2), 160–170. doi:10.1016/j.euras.2013.03.006

Iglauer, P. (2014). Eastern interest in Eurasian economic deal. *Asia Times*. Retrieved February 11, 2017, from http://www.atimes.com/atimes/Central_Asia/CEN-01-110614.html

Kazakhstan: Balance of Payments and External Debt for 2015. (n.d.). Retrieved January 1, 2017, from http://bit.ly/29vI5wQ

Kazakhstan Trade Statistics. (n.d.). Retrieved January 12, 2017, from http://atlas.media.mit.edu/en/profile/country/kaz/

Kyrgyzstan Trade Statistics. (n.d.). Retrieved February 17, 2017, from http://atlas.media.mit.edu/en/profile/country/kgz/

Raikhan, S. (2013). Eurasian idea of N.A. Nazarbayev as the basis of modern integration. In *Procedia of Social and Behavioral Sciences, 2nd Cyprus International Conference on Educational Research* (*Vol. 89*, pp. 377-386). Academic Press. doi:10.1016/j.sbspro.2013.08.863

Rivera, P. P., & Garashchuk, A. (2016). The Eurasian Economic Union: Prospective regional integration in the post-Soviet space or just geopolitical project? *Eastern Journal of European Studies*, *7*, 91.

Russia Trade Statistics. (n.d.). Retrieved February 3, 2017, from http://atlas.media.mit.edu/en/profile/country/rus/

Sakaev, V. T. (2016). The political demography of the Eurasian Economic Union. *Journal of Economics and Economic Education Research*, *17*, 169–177.

Tarr, D. G. (2016). The Eurasian Economic Union among Russia, Belarus, Kazakhstan, Armenia and the Kyrgyz Republic: Can it succeed where its predecessor failed? *Eastern European Economics*, *54*(1), 1–22. doi:10.1080/00128775.2015.1105672

Tasch, B. (2014). Russia, Kazakhstan, Belarus sign treaty creating huge economic bloc. *Time Magazine*. Retrieved January 12, 2017, from http://archive.is/4CCJd

The Eurasia Economic Union. (n.d.). Retrieved January 12, 2017, from https://tr.wikipedia.org/wiki/Avrasya_Ekonomik_Birli%C4%9Fi

The Eurasian Economic Commission Statistics. Figures are for Russia, Kazakhstan and Belarus for 2011-2014. (n.d.). Retrieved January 1, 2017, from www.eurasiancommission.org/ru/act/integr_i_makroec/ dep_stat/tradestat/analytics/Pages/default.aspx

World I. T. S. Russian Federation Exports by Country and Region 2015. (n.d.). Retrieved March 25, 2017, from http://wits.worldbank.org/CountryProfile/en/Country/RUS/Year/LTST/TradeFlow/Export/Partner/all/

Yang, S., & Wang, S. (2014). Development and impacts of the Customs Union of Russia, Belarus and Kazakhstan. *China Institute of International Studies*. Retrieved February 15, 2017, from http://www.ciis.org.cn/english/2014-09/23/content_7254454.htm

Zbarskaya, I. A., & Gabdrakhimova, R. K. (2016). *Foreign Trade of Countries of The Commonwealth of Independent States 2015*. Moscow, Russia: Interstate Statistical Committee of the CIS.

Zhong, N. (2015). China vows to enhance trade with Eurasian bloc. *China Daily*. Retrieved February 15, 2017, from http://www.chinadaily.com.cn/world/cn_eu/2015-05/11/content_20676192.htm

KEY TERMS AND DEFINITIONS

Common Economic Space: In addition to the Customs Union, if labor and capital are free-moving, it is called as the common economic space. The common economic space is the next phase of the customs union in the form of economic integration. The contents of the customs union are also available in the common economic space. In summary, customs tariffs and quotas are removed between member countries in the common economic space. Common customs tariffs are applied against non-member countries and labor and capital move freely.

Customs Union: A customs union is a type of economic integration in which customs tariffs and quotas are cleared among member countries and common customs tariffs are applied against non-member countries. The customs union creates distorting and increasing effects for foreign trade among member countries. Member countries become more profitable to trade with each other than other countries with the removal of customs duties. For this reason, member countries prefer trade with countries in the customs union rather than other countries so the diversion effect of this customs union boosts foreign trade in the union. Goods are in free movement between member countries in the customs union. Goods move freely between member countries without custom tariffs and quotas.

Eurasian Development Bank: The Eurasian Development Bank aims to develop trade and economic relations between the countries that are members of the EEU. Thus, it supports the integration in Eurasia and provides financial support to increase the production and trade of all member countries.

European Union: The six European countries (The Netherlands, Luxembourg, the Federal Republic of Germany, France, and Italy), which are called the six, have established three communities under the names the European Coal and Steel Community, the European Atomic Energy Community, and the European Economic Community(EEC). They are trying to maximize economic interests by forming a coalition under the aim of the European Coal and Steel Community in the coal field. The purpose of the European Atomic Energy Society is to conduct research on atomic energy, provided that it is used in useful areas. It is aimed to form an economic area and finally to achieve political unity with EEC. In 1965, these three communities were united and called the EC (European Community). In 1992, the name of the European Community became the European Union. The European Union, which has 28 members, is based on the Treaty of Rome, signed in 1957. Nineteen of these 28 countries have removed their national currency from being the official currency. These 19 countries are using Euro as their official currency. Therefore, these 19 countries are called the euro zone (euro area). The EU, where the new member has joined as many times as the nominee, has been in a distressed situation in recent years. Some EU member states, especially Britain, have begun to make cost benefit analysis on their situation. As a result of the referendum, the exit of the UK from the EU is ongoing.

Tariff: Taxes imported during the entry of the imported goods are called customs tax (tariffs). Tariffs are the means of foreign trade policy. Tariffs are used especially in countries that want to protect domestic producers. When tariffs are raised in the countries, the price of imported goods increases. Thus, domestic commodities can compete with imported commodities. In some cases, the tariffs are reduced and the domestic producers are directed to compete and increase efficiency.

Trade Liberalization: The liberalization of foreign trade is applied by removing or reducing customs tariffs and non-tariff instruments. In this application, the domestic production is not protected by tariffs or other means. Completely free-trade-based trading is done. Firms compete in terms of price, quality, and cost, without government protection.

Trade Union: Many trade unions can be established to promote foreign trade and economic relations among member countries. One of these trade unions, which is called the forms of international integration, is free trade agreements. In free trade agreements, customs taxes are removed between member countries. Thus, foreign trade is increased among the member countries. Some of the most prominent examples of free trade agreements in the world are NAFTA (North American Free Trade Agreement), APEC (Asia Pacific Economic Cooperation Organization), et al. Examples of other international economic unions include the Customs Union, the Common Economic Space, the Economic Union. The European Union is the most prominent example of economic union in the world.

Chapter 5
Who Benefits From Regional Economic Integration?
The Case of ASEAN

Ina Kayser
IST University of Applied Sciences, Germany

ABSTRACT

This chapter analyses ASEAN as an example of regional economic integration throughout the decades. ASEAN was founded as a means of stability in a region with great threats to regional security. Its member states could hardly vary more in terms of economic impact, political systems, and culture. Nonetheless, ASEAN became one of the most vibrant economic regions in the world following its own ASEAN Way. This chapter analyzes the shift from a security-focused functional community toward a successful economic cooperation. Since its formation, ASEAN's development was driven by its rhetorical strength rather than the actual implementation of measures. Nonetheless, as of today, ASEAN managed to partly overcome this rhetoric dilemma, becoming the third largest market worldwide.

INTRODUCTION

Founded in 1967 by Indonesia, Malaysia, the Philippines, Singapore and Thailand to regionally counterbalance growing communist influence in East Asia, ASEAN (Association of South East Asian Nations) is nowadays not only an alliance for regional security, but also a growing economic partnership. Today, ASEAN encompasses ten member states: Brunei Darussalam joined in 1984, Vietnam in 1995, Laos and Myanmar in 1997 and Cambodia in 1999.

DOI: 10.4018/978-1-5225-4032-8.ch005

In the light of ASEAN's 50th anniversary, this chapter focuses on the economic development of member economies and the expansion of the region as a whole. The ASEAN region is among the top performing economies worldwide and an increasingly important location of international trade and investment. If ASEAN was a single country, it would rank third in terms of the largest economy in Asia and seventh in the world (ASEAN Secretariat 2015). Yet the region has been subject to a serious economic crisis in 1997/8 and was affected by the 2008/9 global financial crisis. The region is characterized by considerable diversity regarding country sizes, historic roots, political systems and economic performance. But precisely because of its heterogeneity, the region offers many prospects and opportunities to the business community and general public (ASEAN Secretariat, 2015).

BACKGROUND

The discussion on regional economic integration is well established in economic literature and does not provide a distinct meaning of the concept of integration, reaching from dimensions of social integration to international cooperation and trade integration (Balassa, 1961). Balassa (1961; 2011) provides a framework to cluster the stages of economic integration which is well established in academic literature. He proposes a differentiation in free trade area, customs union, common market, economic union, monetary union, fiscal union, and the hitherto non-existent complete economic integration. A free trade area removed tariffs and quotas internally and has national tariffs retained against other countries. An example is NAFTA. A customs union additionally has common external tariffs such as Mercosur. In a common market, a free movement of production factors, goods and services is possible. An example is the EU before the European Monetary Union came into place. The economic union aims at the harmonization of some national policies and transfers decision making for some national policies to a supranational level, such as the competition policy in the EU. A monetary union has a single common currency as well as a single central bank (as the European Central Bank in the EU). Moreover, a fiscal union aims at harmonizing taxes, which is the case to some degree in the EU as well. Finally, a political union has an entire democratic body at supranational level. This form of regional integration is not existent to this date. Contrastingly, Tinbergen (1954) merely postulates the distinction between positive and negative integration. Thereby, positive integration promotes common policies and economic institutions to actively enable integration whereas negative integration aims at reducing trade barriers and thus passively strengthening integration. Given that increased economic integration most likely will imply both positive and negative integration, Balassa's view delivers a more detailed approach to cluster certain stages of integration and is therefore the basis of this research.

After the growing influence of communism in Vietnam in the late 1950s and the fading power of the Southeast Asia Treaty Organization (SEATO) (Goodman, 1996), some of the relatively young East Asian countries were in fear of their recently obtained independence. The absence of a regional power comparable to the People's Republic of China (PRC) or Japan and the regional location between the Soviet Union and the United States (US) as global superpowers triggered the wish for regional unity and stability. The leading motivation of the founding nations of ASEAN was to form a unitary voice that would be heard and recognized internationally. The urge to achieve collective strength pushed the focus on regional differences in the background.

The issues of individual vulnerability and the potential for regional states to lose their only recently gained sovereignty were emphasized by the spread of internal communist uprisings that made the shift of Vietnam into the system of the Soviet Union even more intimidating for the smaller South East Asian states.

Moreover, Indonesia faced a regime collapse by the second half of the 1960s. Indonesia's President Sukarno was the source of regional animosity in the entire South East Asian region. Most notably, he disapproved the foundation of the Malaysian state in 1963, thereby triggering the so called Konfrontasi clash in the region and the invasion of Indonesian troops into Malaysia (Jones, 2001). Following these events, Indonesia threatened to withdraw from the UN in 1965 if Malaysia took seat in the Security Council (Jones, 2001). This period of Konfrontasi showed the depth of regional hostility. The role of Indonesia in the region was problematic to the formation of ASEAN. Indonesia seemed to be an internal threat to the region, because President Sukarno followed the idea of a greater Indonesia. When President Sukarno resigned, his successor President Suharto shifted Indonesian foreign policy away from regional animosity to a more amicable and cooperative climate.

Efforts to rebuilt confidence in Indonesia as a regional partner began with the formation of ASEAN in 1967. Notably, ASEAN is an agreement to explicitly give a unified frame to a region that is diverse within. This is a major difference to other regional agreements such as the European Union or the Gulf Cooperation Council with common grounds in regards to political and economic systems, culture and history. The main driver to form ASEAN for its five founding states was thus to guarantee internal security and autonomy by collectively defending each other from the growing influence of the Soviet Union, the US, the PRC, and Japan in South East Asia. Against this background, this chapter analyses the question whether such a divers and deeply divided region can profit from regional integration as a whole without the absence of truly binding agreements and governing institutions. To tackle the research question, this chapter will analyse the decades of ASEAN's development in detail and draw on the shift from a security bloc to an economic cooperation.

THE FIRST DECADE: 1967-1976

By the mid-1970s, ASEAN had emerged as the predominant economic and political grouping of states in the region. Thereby its actions follow its unique ASEAN Way, in reaching full consensus-based unanimous decisions rather than majority-based resolutions. Critics cynically argue that the unanimity rule makes ASEAN nothing but a talking shop (Yuzawa, 2012, p.77).

In economic terms, the regional was relatively insignificant with minor GDP shares in the region (see Table 1). For example, Malaysia's economy was largely dependent on agricultural and commodity exports and the way to a modern economy had yet to be paved (Koen, 2017).

In 1971, ASEAN foreign ministers formally endorsed the Zone of Peace, Freedom and Neutrality (ZOPFAN) in Southeast Asia. However, the endorsement did not lead to efforts towards its implementation due to the members' concerns about the consequences for regional security if a superpower vacuum arose. The Third ASEAN Summit in Manila in 1987 did call for the establishment of a Nuclear Weapons Free Zone in Southeast Asia (NWFZ). But again no resolution was passed because of the reservations of some dialogue partners.

In the wake of the fall of Saigon in February 1976, the Bali Summit of ASEAN leaders concluded with two important agreements. The first was the ASEAN Concord, by which each state committed to eliminate threats posed by subversion to their internal stability. The second was the Treaty of Amity and Cooperation in Southeast Asia, which postulated respect for sovereignty, non-interference in domestic affairs, and peaceful settlement of disputes. However, in line with the ASEAN Way, the Treaty contained no provision for sanctions against its breaching.

The Bali Summit marked a breaking point because it clearly signalled that the ASEAN vision of regional order in South East Asia was driven by an inward focusing concept of stability. Another significant outcome was the rejection of the alliance option, which was shaped by the ASEAN states' declared commitment to achieve autonomy from great power competition and intervention. It was also aimed at rendering the external security linkages of the individual ASEAN states less provocative to opponents like Vietnam and the PRC.

At the time of ASEAN's formation, economic cooperation was viewed as a means to build common interests and to reduce threat perceptions. The organisation began to focus increasingly on economic issues in the second half of the 1970s.

Table 1. Regional development 1967-1976

Year	GDP per Capita (Current US$)																				
	Brunei Darussalam*		Indonesia		Cambodia*		Lao PDR*		Myanmar*		Malaysia		Philippines		Singapore		Thailand		Vietnam*		World	
	Absolute	% YOY	Absolute	% YOY	Absolute	% YOY	Absolute	% YOY	Absolute	% YOY	Absolute	% YOY	Absolute	% YOY	Absolute	% YOY	Absolute	% YOY	Absolute	% YOY	Absolute	% YOY
1967	1.112,32		n/a		134,30		n/a		n/a		308,93		187,11		516,29		137,92		n/a		585,37	
1968	1.235,54	11,08%	n/a	n/a	138,76	3,32%	n/a	n/a	n/a	n/a	319,33	3,37%	199,94	6,85%	566,54	9,73%	161,01	16,74%	n/a	n/a	621,39	6,15%
1969	1.233,85	-0,14%	53,52	n/a	143,81	3,64%	n/a	n/a	n/a	n/a	315,36	-1,24%	207,43	3,75%	625,72	10,45%	166,92	3,68%	n/a	n/a	650,22	4,64%
1970	1.360,85	10,29%	65,03	21,51%	156,83	9,05%	n/a	n/a	n/a	n/a	320,97	1,78%	224,62	8,29%	708,27	13,19%	174,79	4,71%	n/a	n/a	687,14	5,68%
1971	1.301,40	-4,37%	74,57	14,68%	141,82	-9,57%	n/a	n/a	n/a	n/a	344,40	7,30%	241,70	7,60%	812,27	14,68%	186,88	6,92%	n/a	n/a	740,22	7,72%
1972	1.380,42	6,07%	79,69	6,85%	102,30	-27,87%	n/a	n/a	n/a	n/a	354,23	2,85%	186,77	-22,73%	925,29	13,91%	192,13	2,81%	n/a	n/a	796,88	7,65%
1973	1.455,42	5,43%	79,15	-0,67%	135,32	32,27%	n/a	n/a	n/a	n/a	379,57	7,15%	201,03	7,64%	1.070,82	15,73%	194,26	1,11%	n/a	n/a	861,78	8,14%
1974	1.909,38	31,19%	90,84	14,77%	68,96	-49,04%	n/a	n/a	n/a	n/a	440,07	15,94%	211,40	5,16%	1.263,66	18,01%	209,36	7,77%	n/a	n/a	976,53	13,32%
1975	2.924,97	53,19%	130,98	44,18%	93,99	36,30%	n/a	n/a	n/a	n/a	652,62	48,30%	258,36	22,21%	1.684,34	33,29%	269,85	28,90%	n/a	n/a	1.165,24	19,32%
1976	6.953,44	137,73%	202,43	54,55%	77,82	-17,21%	n/a	n/a	n/a	n/a	789,63	20,99%	343,24	32,85%	2.339,57	38,90%	332,12	23,07%	n/a	n/a	1.314,12	12,78%

World Bank, 2017.

* Brunei Darussalam joined ASEAN in 1984; Cambodia in 1999; Lao PDR and Myanmar in 1997 and Vietnam in 1995.

Economic cooperation received a at least a rhetorical improvement at the Bali summit of 1976 in the light of a rising attractiveness of the PRC when ASEAN members decided to deepen their cooperation. However, little changed in practice. The ASEAN Industrial Projects (AIP) scheme – whereby one large industrial project was designated for each country and the products of the project enjoyed preferential treatment in member countries that was launched subsequently was notable for its failure.

ASEAN started off on everything but a common economic ground. The GDP per capita in Singapore was 6.3 times larger than the GDP of the Philippines (see Table 1). The world recovered after the recession and stagflation in the early 1970s, inflation was high and demand began to rise again. Generally speaking, the founding nations were not hit as hard by the recession as the non-members, but profited largely from its end. The hope of a more stable environment with Suharto's election in Indonesia and the wake of the Vietnamese war triggered this perception.

THE SECOND DECADE: 1977-1986

Still, the success of trade cooperation was rather unremarkable. GDP growth rates were heterogeneous (see Table 2). This underlines that there was no common ground to start from and no common direction of growth. On account of the varyingly strong economic and political systems in the member states a mutual approach to growth was needed to pursue a joint economic path. Contrastingly, the Preferential Trade Arrangement established in 1977 was partly illogical as members offered tariffs concessions on products that were either not produced or traded in the region. The ASEAN Industrial Complementation (AIC) scheme, which was initially proposed by the automobile industry, was launched in 1981 and sought to realize economies of scale at a region-wide level by the tariff-free exchange of components among the various automotive plants located in the region. The AIC was only marginally more successful than the AIP. The Japanese government was the scheme's main funder while Japanese car manufacturers were its main beneficiaries. The ASEAN Industrial Joint Venture (AIJV) scheme, which was launched in 1983 offering tariff concessions to products produced jointly by firms from two or more member countries, was also rather unsuccessful. To narrow the focus, Ravenhill (1995, p. 853) argues: "National jealousies over competing plans for import substituting industries, poor project preparation, and excessive bureaucratisation have stymied ASEAN's various efforts at industrial cooperation."

Brunei Darussalam joined ASEAN in 1984 by the time it became an independent political entity after gaining independence from Britain. ASEAN is the first international organization Brunei joined, placing high emphasis on its membership

Table 2. Regional development 1977-1986

Year	GDP per Capita (Current US$)																				
	Brunei Darussalam*		Indonesia		Cambodia*		Lao PDR*		Myanmar*		Malaysia		Philippines		Singapore		Thailand		Vietnam*		World	
	Absolute	% YOY	Absolute	% YOY	Absolute	% YOY	Absolute	% YOY	Absolute	% YOY	Absolute	% YOY	Absolute	% YOY	Absolute	% YOY	Absolute	% YOY	Absolute	% YOY	Absolute	% YOY
1977	9.968,14	17,18%	333,59	19,95%	n/a	n/a	n/a	n/a	n/a	n/a	1.019,21	16,21%	450,12	11,79%	2.845,88	3,16%	445,32	13,75%	n/a	n/a	1.701,31	11,08%
1978	10.765,32	8,00%	365,80	9,66%	n/a	n/a	n/a	n/a	n/a	n/a	1.240,05	21,67%	506,09	12,43%	3.193,33	12,21%	528,51	18,68%	n/a	n/a	1.969,23	15,75%
1979	15.010,65	39,44%	356,81	-2,46%	n/a	n/a	n/a	n/a	n/a	n/a	1.570,87	26,68%	596,40	17,84%	3.899,57	22,12%	589,75	11,59%	n/a	n/a	2.251,21	14,32%
1980	25.530,41	70,08%	491,44	37,73%	n/a	n/a	n/a	n/a	n/a	n/a	1.770,17	12,69%	684,65	14,80%	4.926,96	26,35%	682,77	15,77%	n/a	n/a	2.495,66	10,86%
1981	21.925,79	-14,12%	566,43	15,26%	n/a	n/a	n/a	n/a	n/a	n/a	1.763,36	-0,38%	731,73	6,88%	5.595,24	13,56%	720,90	5,58%	n/a	n/a	2.511,68	0,64%
1982	20.795,04	-5,16%	583,53	3,02%	n/a	n/a	n/a	n/a	n/a	n/a	1.843,04	4,52%	741,79	1,38%	6.075,60	8,59%	742,70	3,02%	n/a	n/a	2.441,09	-2,81%
1983	18.227,22	-12,35%	512,85	-12,11%	n/a	n/a	n/a	n/a	n/a	n/a	2.033,02	10,31%	645,46	-12,99%	6.629,94	9,12%	797,93	7,44%	n/a	n/a	2.478,55	1,53%
1984	17.439,58	-4,32%	525,23	2,41%	n/a	n/a	490,91	n/a	n/a	n/a	2.213,70	8,89%	594,03	-7,97%	7.223,40	8,95%	817,87	2,50%	n/a	n/a	2.525,48	1,89%
1985	15.797,48	-9,42%	516,87	-1,59%	n/a	n/a	643,09	n/a	n/a	n/a	1.979,16	-10,59%	565,76	-4,76%	6.995,10	-3,16%	747,49	-8,60%	239,43	n/a	2.611,64	3,41%
1986	10.280,77	-34,92%	474,78	-8,14%	n/a	n/a	469,41	-27,01%	n/a	n/a	1.709,71	-13,61%	535,24	-5,40%	6.793,54	-2,88%	813,10	8,78%	437,13	82,57%	3.037,89	16,32%

World Bank, 2017.

* Brunei Darussalam joined ASEAN in 1984; Cambodia in 1999; Lao PDR and Myanmar in 1997 and Vietnam in 1995.

(Thambipillai, 1998, p. 80) South East Asian economic regionalism has been disorganized by the overwhelming importance of export markets beyond South East Asia and ASEAN members' competing economic profiles.

THE THIRD DECADE: 1987-1996

Economically, The ASEAN region became a vibrant economic area at that time as evident from Table 3. The regions GDP grew steadily and the economies of Indonesia, Malaysia and Thailand took off with major growth rates. Trade and investment increased in the region and ASEAN actively engaged in new markets and growing economic competition (Zaw, 2001).

ASEAN's stated objective is to promote multilateral cooperation in economic, social, cultural, educational and academic fields. Thus, ASEAN shifted away from being a mere security cooperation that it has predominantly been for the past 25 years. The Bangkok Declaration was, however, not a treaty with legal obligations and the informal operating style largely continued. It operates by consensus and is supported by a small level of bureaucracy, though this changed partly in 1992. ASEAN went through its first major overhaul in 1992 when its members decided to strengthen the ASEAN Secretariat and enter into a free trade agreement, the ASEAN Free Trade Area (AFTA) (Singapore Declaration; ASEAN, 1992). From a historical perspective, this is the first articulation of the concept of ASEAN economic integration, revealed in the Framework Agreement on Enhancing ASEAN Economic Cooperation signed in Singapore in 1992 (ASEAN, 1992). The establishment of AFTA was an attempt to increase the exchange of goods between the ASEAN countries. At the fourth meeting of the ASEAN member countries in Singapore in January 1992, members agreed to set up a free trade zone with duties between 0% and 5% within 15 years (effective by January 1993). In more detail, they agreed to reduce tariffs on intra-ASEAN trade in manufactured and processed agricultural foods ranging from zero to five percent within fifteen years; the transition period was later antedated at the fifth AFTA Council Meeting and reduced to ten years (ASEAN, 1994). AFTA has fully entered into force since January 2003.

However, the tariff reduction plans are tempered by the provision that allows members to exclude products on a variety of grounds. Thus, most studies on the effects of AFTA showed rather modest economic gains to flow from the agreement (Clarete et al., 2003, pp. 126).

Economists tend to explain the emergence of trade blocs as an institutionalisation of efforts to realize efficiency gain through greater competition (e.g., Snorrason, 2012). They pay little attention to the role of the state in the creation of trade blocs. Contrastingly, Bowles and MacLean (1996) reject such a line of analysis and argue

Table 3. Regional development 1987-1996

Year	GDP per Capita (Current US$)																				
	Brunei Darussalam*		Indonesia		Cambodia*		Lao PDR*		Myanmar*		Malaysia		Philippines		Singapore		Thailand		Vietnam*		World	
	Absolute	% YOY	Absolute	% YOY	Absolute	% YOY	Absolute	% YOY	Absolute	% YOY	Absolute	% YOY	Absolute	% YOY	Absolute	% YOY	Absolute	% YOY	Absolute	% YOY	Absolute	% YOY
1987	11.672,00	13,53%	442,00	-6,90%	n/a	n/a	279,00	-40,56%	n/a	n/a	1.927,00	12,71%	579,00	8,18%	7.531,00	10,86%	936,00	15,11%	594,00	35,89%	3.396,00	11,79%
1988	11.084,00	-5,04%	482,00	9,05%	n/a	n/a	149,00	-46,59%	n/a	n/a	2.050,00	6,38%	644,00	11,23%	8.902,00	18,20%	1.123,00	19,98%	402,00	-32,32%	3.735,00	9,98%
1989	11.954,00	7,85%	530,00	9,96%	n/a	n/a	173,00	16,11%	n/a	n/a	2.194,00	7,02%	705,00	9,47%	10.380,00	16,60%	1.295,00	15,32%	97,00	-75,87%	3.853,00	3,16%
1990	13.702,00	14,62%	585,00	10,38%	n/a	n/a	204,00	17,92%	n/a	n/a	2.417,00	10,16%	715,00	1,42%	11.864,00	14,30%	1.508,00	16,45%	98,00	1,03%	4.262,00	10,62%
1991	14.002,00	2,19%	632,00	8,03%	n/a	n/a	235,00	15,20%	n/a	n/a	2.627,00	8,69%	715,00	0,00%	14.505,00	22,26%	1.717,00	13,86%	143,00	45,92%	4.442,00	4,22%
1992	15.381,00	9,85%	682,00	7,91%	n/a	n/a	251,00	6,81%	n/a	n/a	3.081,00	17,28%	814,00	13,85%	16.144,00	11,30%	1.930,00	12,41%	144,00	0,70%	4.647,00	4,62%
1993	14.678,00	-4,57%	828,00	21,41%	253,00	n/a	287,00	14,34%	n/a	n/a	3.396,00	10,22%	816,00	0,25%	18.302,00	13,37%	2.213,00	14,66%	189,00	31,25%	4.656,00	0,19%
1994	14.221,00	-3,11%	912,00	10,14%	270,00	6,72%	325,00	13,24%	n/a	n/a	3.686,00	8,54%	939,00	15,07%	21.578,00	17,90%	2.498,00	12,88%	230,00	21,69%	4.927,00	5,82%
1995	16.047,00	12,84%	1.026,00	12,50%	322,00	19,26%	363,00	11,69%	n/a	n/a	4.280,00	16,12%	1.061,00	12,99%	24.937,00	15,57%	2.856,00	14,33%	288,00	25,22%	5.386,00	9,32%
1996	16.914,00	5,40%	1.137,00	10,82%	318,00	-1,24%	377,00	3,86%	n/a	n/a	4.744,00	10,84%	1.160,00	9,33%	26.263,00	5,32%	3.057,00	7,04%	337,00	17,01%	5.425,00	0,72%

World Bank, 2017

* Brunei Darussalam joined ASEAN in 1984; Cambodia in 1999; Lao PDR and Myanmar in 1997 and Vietnam in 1995.

that the formation of AFTA was the result of three interrelated factors. Firstly, it was ASEAN's response to changes in the international political economy, particularly the economic slow-down of the early 1980s, the Plaza Accord in 1985 which realigned major currencies, the collapse of the Soviet bloc, and the formation of trade blocs elsewhere in the world. Secondly, there was a shift in the internal power structures within the ASEAN states towards business interests. Lastly, the concern of ASEAN leaders to maintain ASEAN's identity in a post-Cold War Greater East Asia was a driver toward increasing economic integration (Bowles & MacLean, 1996).

Similarly, Ravenhill (1995) suggests different reasons underlying the establishment of AFTA. Firstly, ASEAN was looking for a new raison d'être following the end of the Cold War and the associated threat through communism that had bound the ASEAN countries since ASEAN's beginning. Secondly, AFTA was a defensive move against the possibility of the collapse of GATT/WTO Uruguay Round negotiations. Thirdly, there were fears that foreign investment on which much of ASEAN economic success was built would in future go toward Mexico to take advantage of NAFTA or to the PRC to participate in the rise of the world's potentially largest market. Finally, by the end of the 1980s, the ASEAN economies had become more balancing and generally more efficient as a result of unilateral trade liberalisation and deregulation.

At the beginning, AFTA developed slowly, Indonesia and the Philippines feared, for example, to lose their control over their domestic markets in a too rapid economic integration. In July 1995, the Foreign Ministers of the ASEAN countries agreed on a reduction of the deadline to eight years, which was formally adopted at the ASEAN summit in Bangkok in December.

At the beginning, economic cooperation was viewed as a means to build common interests and to reduce threat perceptions. The organisation began to focus on economic issues more concretely since the 1990s with the growing spread of the WTO and the formation of APEC. The formation of NAFTA in 1994 and the threat an integrated Mexico posed to Southeast Asia's largest final export destination as a wake-up call as did the rising attractiveness of China from the late 1970s and especially from the early 1990s onwards.

Since the mid-1990s, ASEAN has sought to expand its economic cooperation to include contiguous regions or states first signing an economic cooperation with the Australia-New Zealand Closer Economic Partnership pact and leading the formation of the Asia-Europe Meeting (ASEM) in 1996.

With the shift of security issues in the region and the fading influence of communism since the end of the Vietnam war, ASEAN changed its policy toward a more constructive engagement in the region. Consequently, in 1995, Vietnam became the first Indochinese country to join ASEAN. Joining ASEAN had vital social, political, economic and military implications for Vietnam (Chauhan, 2013). Vietnam's membership of the grouping integrated its security with the whole of

Southeast Asia and created a favourable environment for economic development (Chauhan, 2013). In more detail, Vietnam's global image rose, leading to increased cooperation with multiple players in the region access to trade with super powers like the United States and China (Chauhan, 2013).

THE FOURTH DECADE: 1997-2006

The economic vibrancies of the third decade came to an end during the fourth as evident from Table 4. A major slump in economic growth is observable for all ASEAN member economies. The Asian Financial crisis of 1997 and 1998 led to recession and dramatically decreasing investment in the region. Especially Thailand and Malaysia were affected by the crisis, though the entire region encountered a downward spiral (Table 4). ASEAN as a whole was not able to provide a regional answer to the crisis due to its informal and consensus-based decision making style. Hence, some academic observers predicted its decline (e.g. Rueland 2000). On economic-political grounds, ASEAN is a stabilizer for the region. Hence, ASEAN was not solely interested to survive the crisis. The major economies of East Asia, namely Japan, China and South Korea, supported ASEAN during that time to ensure their economic interests in the region were preserved (Krapohl, 2016).

ASEAN and North East Asian leaders have increasingly focussed on enhancing ASEAN's long ties to North East Asia through an increasingly formal ASEAN+3 arrangement since 1997 (Japan, South Korea, and China). Since its early days, ASEAN has attempted to strengthen its global influence and relations with extra-regional powers through a process of ASEAN-led dialogue partner relations. ASEAN has invited extra-regional dialogue partners like the United States, Japan and the European Union to participate in informal talks after the annual ASEAN Conference of the heads of states. From the mid-1990s, ASEAN and the three North East Asian states (ASEAN+3) have worked to strengthen these dialogue partner relationships through more frequent and more public meetings. These three states now are officially invited as observers to ASEAN Conferences and relevant bureaucratic working groups. Moreover, ASEAN +3 have committed to work together to come up with joint positions in a similar way as APEC does. In 2005, ASEAN also became the central organization in the newly formed East Asia Summit including China, Japan, Korea, India, Australia, and New Zealand.

Despite all criticism during the crisis, ASEAN focused on strengthening economic integration in the region and successfully maintained its unique approach (Stubbs, 2014). Vietnam experiences a period of unsuspected economic incline since its integration into ASEAN in 1995 with major GDP growth rates (Table 4). In 1997, Laos and Myanmar joined ASEAN in the wake of the crisis. Membership in ASEAN

Table 4. Regional development 1997-2006

Year	GDP per Capita (Current US$)																					
	Brunei Darussalam*		Indonesia		Cambodia*		Lao PDR*		Myanmar*		Malaysia		Philippines		Singapore		Thailand		Vietnam*		World	
	Absolute	% YOY	Absolute	% YOY	Absolute	% YOY	Absolute	% YOY	Absolute	% YOY	Absolute	% YOY	Absolute	% YOY	Absolute	% YOY	Absolute	% YOY	Absolute	% YOY	Absolute	% YOY
1997	16.779,00	-0,80%	1.064,00	-6,42%	304,00	-4,40%	345,00	-8,49%	n/a	n/a	4.586,00	-3,33%	1.127,00	-2,84%	26.386,00	0,47%	2.480,00	-18,87%	361,00	7,12%	5.334,00	-1,68%
1998	12.785,00	-23,80%	464,00	-56,39%	268,00	-11,84%	248,00	-28,12%	n/a	n/a	3.228,00	-29,61%	967,00	-14,20%	21.824,00	-17,29%	1.856,00	-25,16%	361,00	0,00%	5.240,00	-1,76%
1999	14.206,00	11,11%	671,00	44,61%	295,00	10,07%	277,00	11,69%	n/a	n/a	3.457,00	7,09%	1.088,00	12,51%	21.796,00	-0,13%	2.044,00	10,13%	374,00	3,60%	5.362,00	2,33%
2000	18.155,00	27,80%	780,00	16,24%	300,00	1,69%	324,00	16,97%	187,00	n/a	4.005,00	15,85%	1.040,00	-4,41%	23.793,00	9,16%	2.016,00	-1,37%	433,00	15,78%	5.460,00	1,83%
2001	16.617,00	-8,47%	748,00	-4,10%	320,00	6,67%	326,00	0,62%	134,00	-28,34%	3.879,00	-3,15%	958,00	-7,88%	21.577,00	-9,31%	1.897,00	-5,90%	449,00	3,70%	5.358,00	-1,87%
2002	17.017,00	2,41%	900,00	20,32%	338,00	5,63%	320,00	-1,84%	139,00	3,73%	4.133,00	6,55%	1.001,00	4,49%	22.017,00	2,04%	2.094,00	10,38%	477,00	6,24%	5.496,00	2,58%
2003	18.759,00	10,24%	1.066,00	18,44%	361,00	6,80%	363,00	13,44%	213,00	53,24%	4.431,00	7,21%	1.011,00	1,00%	23.574,00	7,07%	2.349,00	12,18%	531,00	11,32%	6.096,00	10,92%
2004	22.132,00	17,98%	1.150,00	7,88%	407,00	12,74%	418,00	15,15%	213,00	0,00%	4.925,00	11,15%	1.080,00	6,82%	27.405,00	16,25%	2.643,00	12,52%	607,00	14,31%	6.780,00	11,22%
2005	26.338,00	19,00%	1.263,00	9,83%	472,00	15,97%	476,00	13,88%	240,00	12,68%	5.564,00	12,97%	1.197,00	10,83%	29.870,00	8,99%	2.874,00	8,74%	699,00	15,16%	7.247,00	6,89%
2006	31.158,00	18,30%	1.590,00	25,89%	538,00	13,98%	591,00	24,16%	288,00	20,00%	6.195,00	11,34%	1.395,00	16,54%	33.580,00	12,42%	3.351,00	16,60%	797,00	14,02%	7.754,00	7,00%

World Bank, 2017.

* Brunei Darussalam joined ASEAN in 1984; Cambodia in 1999; Lao PDR and Myanmar in 1997 and Vietnam in 1995.

was anticipated to have long term effects on economic development. Despite the Asian crisis, Vietnam remained the only member economy with positive growth rates, whereas Laos and Myanmar faced severe recession.

Laos had been given until 2008 to meet the AFTA goals which was supposed to foster investment and trade but also required government reforms (Stuart-Fox, 1998). ASEAN was fairly unknown in Laos at the time it became a member and most of the population was reluctant about the membership (Stuart-Fox, 1998). Myanmar had higher expectations of its membership with regard to its international legitimacy and economic development than Laos.

By 1999, Cambodia became the tenth member of ASEAN. For Cambodia, membership was a challenge as it was lagging behind of the other member economies and required a range of economic and administrative reforms.

By 2003 against the predictions, most ASEAN members have satisfied their first round of intra-regional tariff cuts covering over 60% of tariff lines despite the Asian Financial Crisis and the shortened deadlines. Thailand has effectively gained concessions from Malaysia for not fulfilling its commitments to liberalize access to its auto industry, showing a new willingness to use AFTA and its dispute settlement mechanism to encourage preferential liberalization.

THE FIFTH DECADE: 2007 UNTIL TODAY

Though the implementation of AFTA was completed in 2010, many expectations were not met. The aim of a single internal market with fully liberalized trade of goods, services and movement of workers still seems to be afar. Critics argue that the rather weak norms and structures of ASEAN hinder further economic integration (Aggarwal & Chow, 2010). This view is challenged by others who argue that there is no conflict between integration goals and institutional framework, but rather in the wording of ASEAN initiatives (Acharya, 1998). The terminology of blueprints is sometimes ambiguous and different interest groups put different spins on it. This ambiguous terminology leads to rising expectations in the private sector and amongst the governments of non-ASEAN nations that were not met yet. An example is the terminology of a common market versus a single market. Whereas a single market is defined as the absence of any tariffs and other trade barriers, a common market leaves much more space for interpretation. This conflict in terminology rises criticism especially from the private sector, claiming that member states hinder the realization of a single internal market. This leads to a huge conflict between politics and business representatives.

The global financial crisis did not affect all member economies equally (see Table 5). Vietnam, Myanmar, Laos and Indonesia were still able to promote growth in contrast to the capital-intensive economies of the other member states.

As of today, ASEAN only reached the free trade area stage of economic integration, following Balassa's (2011) criteria. Nonetheless on account of the ASEAN Way, ASEAN itself states that "ASEAN moves towards greater cohesion and integration by 2015 and beyond" (ASEAN Secretariat 2015), aiming at implementing a single market and a customs union. Economically, the GDP in the region has nearly doubled since its formation to 2015, with a combined GDP of over US$2.5 trillion, while the average GDP per capita grew by almost 80% to over US$4,000 (ASEAN Secretariat 2015). Likewise, the region has become a fast growing investment destination, accounting for 11% of total global foreign direct investment (FDI) inflows in 2014 as compared with just 5% in 2007 (ASEAN Secretariat 2015). The ASEAN Economic Community (AEC) accounts for one of the three pillars of ASEAN's formation. It combines a number of agreements such as AFTA and initiatives to promote strong economic integration and the reduction of trade barriers between the Member States in order to promote prosperity in the region.

SOLUTIONS AND RECOMMENDATIONS

In the past 50 years, ASEAN advanced from a security alliance toward increased integration in trade and investment. AFTA was developed in 1992 and evolved into the AEC by 2003.

In retrospective, ASEAN has concluded over 300 international agreements regarding regional economic cooperation. However, all of these are worded in the ASEAN Way, mostly without any legally binding parameters. Therefore, economic cooperation still follows largely a recommendation-based structure and the implementation of agreements is not mandatory but on a rather voluntary basis. Younger agreements tend to be more detailed and more specific regarding cooperation and involve timelines for implementation and reassessment. Nonetheless, the ASEAN Way of cooperation is still persistent, and its mentality remains even unchanged when the ASEAN Charta came into effect in 2008. The Charta is meant to be a constitutional instrument to further strengthen the region. It provides an institutional and legal framework for ASEAN and is actually a truly legally binding agreement of the ten member states.

On account of Tables 1-5, GDP growth in Malaysia has averaged 6.4% since ASEAN's formation, more than other member economies. Though it is not the strongest economy in the alliance, it considerably profited from its membership. During the past 50 years, the Malaysian economy has experienced a distinct transformation

Table 5. Regional development 2007-2015

Year	GDP per Capita (Current US$)																				
	Brunei Darussalam*		Indonesia		Cambodia*		Lao PDR*		Myanmar*		Malaysia		Philippines		Singapore		Thailand		Vietnam*		World	
	Absolute	% YOY	Absolute	% YOY	Absolute	% YOY	Absolute	% YOY	Absolute	% YOY	Absolute	% YOY	Absolute	% YOY	Absolute	% YOY	Absolute	% YOY	Absolute	% YOY	Absolute	% YOY
2007	32.708,00	4,97%	1.861,00	17,04%	629,00	16,91%	711,00	20,30%	398,00	38,19%	7.241,00	16,88%	1.679,00	20,36%	39.224,00	16,81%	3.963,00	18,26%	919,00	15,31%	8.628,00	11,27%
2008	37.798,00	15,56%	2.168,00	16,50%	743,00	18,12%	900,00	26,58%	624,00	56,78%	8.487,00	17,21%	1.929,00	14,89%	39.721,00	1,27%	4.385,00	10,65%	1.165,00	26,77%	9.345,00	8,31%
2009	27.726,00	-26,65%	2.263,00	4,38%	735,00	-1,08%	948,00	5,33%	718,00	15,06%	7.312,00	-13,84%	1.837,00	-4,77%	38.578,00	-2,88%	4.231,00	-3,51%	1.232,00	5,75%	8.748,00	-6,39%
2010	34.852,00	25,70%	3.125,00	38,09%	783,00	6,53%	1.139,00	20,15%	958,00	33,43%	9.069,00	24,03%	2.145,00	16,77%	46.570,00	20,72%	5.112,00	20,82%	1.334,00	8,28%	9.482,00	8,39%
2011	46.378,00	33,07%	3.648,00	16,74%	879,00	12,26%	1.298,00	13,96%	1.151,00	20,15%	10.428,00	14,99%	2.372,00	10,58%	53.094,00	14,01%	5.539,00	8,35%	1.543,00	15,67%	10.407,00	9,76%
2012	46.974,00	1,29%	3.701,00	1,45%	946,00	7,62%	1.445,00	11,33%	1.137,00	-1,22%	10.835,00	3,90%	2.605,00	9,82%	54.451,00	2,56%	5.915,00	6,79%	1.755,00	13,74%	10.499,00	0,88%
2013	43.971,00	-6,39%	3.632,00	-1,86%	1.025,00	8,35%	1.701,00	17,72%	1.135,00	-0,18%	10.971,00	1,26%	2.786,00	6,95%	55.618,00	2,14%	6.225,00	5,24%	1.908,00	8,72%	10.664,00	1,57%
2014	41.024,00	-6,70%	3.500,00	-3,63%	1.095,00	6,83%	1.755,00	3,17%	1.227,00	8,11%	11.306,00	3,05%	2.873,00	3,12%	56.007,00	0,70%	5.970,00	-4,10%	2.052,00	7,55%	10.795,00	1,23%
2015	30.555,00	-25,52%	3.346,00	-4,40%	1.159,00	5,84%	1.818,00	3,59%	1.161,00	-5,38%	9.768,00	-13,60%	2.904,00	1,08%	52.889,00	-5,57%	5.815,00	-2,60%	2.111,00	2,88%	10.058,00	-6,83%

World Bank, 2017.

* Brunei Darussalam joined ASEAN in 1984; Cambodia in 1999; Lao PDR and Myanmar in 1997 and Vietnam in 1995.

from dependence on agriculture and commodity exports to a more differentiated economy with strong global ties (Koen, 2017).

FUTURE RESEARCH DIRECTIONS

Future research should focus on the uniqueness of the region and the question whether this unique way can last in the coming years. Digitalization is revolutionizing our economic systems making more agile management and governance vital to economic growth. As evident from this research, ASEAN has an ongoing history of consensus-based decision-making. As the historic perspective shows, these processes can be troublesome and protracted. ASEAN will face severe challenges to encounter the shifts in economic markets. The key question that arises is whether the ASEAN Way can adapt to the age of digitalization.

CONCLUSION

ASEAN was founded despite severe political, economic, cultural and social disparities. At the beginning, economic cooperation was viewed as a means to build common interests and to reduce threat perceptions. The organisation began to focus on economic issues more concretely since the 1990s with the growing spread of the WTO and the formation of APEC. Looking at the GDP per capita development, Singapore has nowadays a value 55 times larger than Myanmar. Regional gaps are still prevalent. However, the example of Malaysia's economic transformation shows that ASEAN paved to way for smallest states to economic success. Nonetheless, there is little chance that ASEAN will develop supranational institutions and structures in the very near future. Most political decision makers still refuse to accept some sort of supranational governing institution and this is also not part of ASEAN's Charta. These supranational institutions seem, however, to be vital to the realization of a single market. The historic analysis presented in this chapter shows that ASEAN was always rich in visions and rhetoric attempts, but actual realization of plans and transformation of the region fell short of expectations. Nonetheless, integration happens, but in small steps as evident from the historic analysis. In comparison to other examples of regional economic cooperation, such as the European Union or the Gulf Cooperation Council, this stands out. ASEAN follows its own rules and pace and did achieve a great deal of economic development in the region. Moreover, it triggered political stability and growth as evident from the analysis of GDP development. Thus for the economy, the peoples in the region and as well as for the political systems, ASEAN is very beneficial. The regional institutions of East Asia and the Asia Pacific were built on the back of ASEAN, an organization set up as an alternative regional idea. The core problem is that ASEAN since its formation raised higher expectations that were not met. ASEAN is a high potential region but still falls short of its actual capabilities.

REFERENCES

Acharya, A. (1998). Culture, security, multilateralism: The 'ASEAN way' and regional order. *Contemporary Security Policy*, *19*(1), 55–84. doi:10.1080/13523269808404179

Aggarwal, V. K., & Chow, J. T. (2010). The perils of consensus: How ASEAN's meta-regime undermines economic and environmental cooperation. *Review of International Political Economy*, *17*(2), 262–290. doi:10.1080/09692290903192962

ASEAN. (1992). *Singapore Declaration*. Retrieved from http://asean.org/?static_post=singapore-declaration-of-1992-singapore-28-january-1992

ASEAN. (1994). *Joint Press Statement. The Fifth AFTA Council Meeting*. Retrieved from http://asean.org/?static_post=asean-economic-community-asean-free-trade-area-afta-council-press-releases-the-5th-afta-council-ministerial-meeting-1994

Balassa, B. (1961). Towards a Theory of Economic Integration. *Kyklos*, *1*(1), 1–5. doi:10.1111/j.1467-6435.1961.tb02365.x

Balassa, B. (2011). *The Theory of Economic Integration (Routledge Revivals)*. London: Routledge.

Bowles, P., & MacLean, B. (1996). Understanding Trade Bloc Formation: The Case of the ASEAN Free Trade Area. *Review of International Political Economy*, *3*(2), 319–348. doi:10.1080/09692299608434358

Brueckner, M. (2017). *The rise of the middle class and economic growth in ASEAN*. Canberra: Centre for Economic Policy Research, Australian National University. doi:10.1596/1813-9450-8068

Chauhan, S. (2013). *Vietnam's role in ASEAN*. Retrieved from http://www.eastasiaforum.org/2013/10/23/vietnams-role-in-asean/

Clarete, R., Edmonds, C., & Seddon Wallack, J. (2003). Asian regionalism and its effects on trade in the 1980s and 1990s. *Journal of Asian Economics*, *14*(1), 91–129. doi:10.1016/S1049-0078(02)00242-7

Goodman, A. (1996). Vietnam and ASEAN: Who Would Have Thought it Possible? *Asian Survey*, *36*(6), 592–600. doi:10.2307/2645793

Jones, M. (2001). *Conflict and Confrontation in South East Asia, 1961-1965: Britain, the United States, Indonesia and the Creation of Malaysia*. Cambridge, UK: Cambridge University Press. doi:10.1017/CBO9780511497346

Koen, V. (2017). *Malaysia's economic success story and challenges.* OECD Economics Department Working Papers, 1369. Paris: OECD Publishing.

Krapohl, S. (2016). *Regional Integration in the Global South: External Influence on Economic Cooperation in ASEAN, MERCOSUR and SADC*. Berlin: Springer.

Pangestu, M., & Ing, L. Y. (2016). ASEAN: Regional integration and reforms. *Asian Economic Papers*, *15*(2), 1–28. doi:10.1162/ASEP_a_00424

Ravenhill, J. (1995). Economic Cooperation in Southeast Asia: Changing Incentives. *Asian Survey*, *35*(9), 850–866. doi:10.2307/2645786

Rueland, J. (2000). ASEAN and the Asian crisis: Theoretical implications and practical consequences for Southeast Asian regionalism. *The Pacific Review*, *13*(3), 421–451. doi:10.1080/09512740050147942

ASEAN Secretariat. (2015). *A Blueprint for Growth. ASEAN Economic Community 2015: Progress and Key Achievements*. Jakarta: ASEAN Secretariat.

Snorrason, S. (2012). *Asymmetric Economic Integration: Size Characteristics of Economies, Trade Costs and Welfare*. Heidelberg, Germany: Physica. doi:10.1007/978-3-7908-2861-0

Stuart-Fox, M. (1998). Laos in 1997: Into ASEAN. *Asian Survey*, *38*(1), 75–79. doi:10.2307/2645470

Stubbs, R. (2014). ASEAN's leadership in East Asian region-building: Strength in weakness. *The Pacific Review*, *27*(4), 523–541. doi:10.1080/09512748.2014.924229

Thambipillai, P. (1998). Brunei Darussalam and ASEAN: Regionalism for a small state. *Asian Journal of Political Science*, *6*(1), 80–94. doi:10.1080/02185379808434116

World Bank. (2017). *GDP per capita*. Available from http://data.worldbank.org/data-catalog/world-development-indicators

Yuzawa, T. (2012). The Fallacy of Socialization? Rethinking the ASEAN Way of Institution-building. In R. Emmers (Ed.), *ASEAN and the Institutionalization of East Asia* (pp. 75–88). London: Routledge.

Zaw, A. (2001). *ASEAN-Burma relations. Challenges to Democratization in Burma - Perspectives on multilateral and bilateral responses*. Washington, DC: National Democratic Institute.

ADDITIONAL READING

Cuyvers, L., De Lombaerde, P., & Verherstraeten, S. (2005). *From AFTA towards an ASEAN economic community... and beyond. Centre for ASEAN studies*. CAS.

Mattli, W. (1999). *The logic of regional integration: Europe and beyond*. Cambridge: Cambridge University Press. doi:10.1017/CBO9780511756238

Oejendal, J. (2001). South East Asia at a Constant Crossroads: An Ambiguous New Region? *Schultz et al., Regionalization in a Globalising World*, 160.

Schirm, S. A. (2002). *Globalization and the New Regionalism: Global Markets. Domestic Politics and Regional Cooperation*. Cambridge: Cambridge University Press.

S. Tay, J. P. Estanislao, & H. Soesastro (Eds.). (2000). *A new ASEAN in a new millennium*. Centre for Strategic and International Studies.

Tinbergen, J. (1954). *International economic integration*. Amsterdam: Elsevier.

KEY TERMS AND DEFINITIONS

ASEAN Free Trade Area: Trade bloc agreement to facilitate trade without tariffs and other trade barriers aiming at dismantling 98% of all tariffs in the region.

ASEAN Way: Unique way of supranational governance by making decisions only by the means of mutual consensus rather than governing institutions.

ASEAN+3: Dialogue forum of the 10 ASEAN member states together with China, Japan, and South Korea.

ASEAN+6: Anticipated regional economic partnership between the ASEAN economies and Australia, China, Japan, South Korea, India, and New Zealand. ASEAN+6 has the potential to become the world's largest free trade area.

East Asian Summit: Annual summit of 16 heads of states of the region as well as the United States of America and Russia.

Regional Integration: Effort reduce regional barriers in economic, political, social, or cultural terms.

South-East Asian Region: Countries within the region delimited by the borders of India, China, New Guinea, and Australia.

Zone of Peace, Freedom, and Neutrality: First important mutual consensus-based declaration of ASEAN to promote peace and stability in the region.

Section 2

Trade Policies in Developing Countries

Chapter 6
Importance of Market Diversification in Foreign Trade:
Lessons From Turkey for the Developing Countries

Sevgi Sezer
Uludag University, Turkey

ABSTRACT

It is of great importance for developing countries to diversify their markets and products in their exports and imports in order to achieve stable foreign trade and economic growth. This chapter presents lessons that developing countries need to learn from the foreign trade experiences of Turkey. In this context, the foreign trade experiences of Turkey in the 1970-2016 period, the good practices that Turkey has implemented in this respect, topics that Turkey has made mistakes, and the issues that Turkey has suffered are examined with the help of tables and graphs. The most remarkable point in the chapter is the necessity of diversifying countries and markets in the foreign trade because foreign trade has close interaction with political and economic developments and it is always possible that existing markets are being lost or difficulties arise in existing supply sources.

DOI: 10.4018/978-1-5225-4032-8.ch006

INTRODUCTION

The Benefits of Free Foreign Trade

The idea that free foreign trade enhances the wealth of all countries begins with Adam Smith's book The Wealth of Nations published in 1776. In his book, Smith states that free foreign trade increases the division of labor and specialization in the countries, which positively affects productivity and production. Thus, all citizens in a country will have the opportunity to consume more goods and services, and the level of welfare of the people will rise. According to Smith's Absolute Advantage Theory, which is expressed in his book, each country should concentrate on the production of the goods that it can produce the cheapest, consume as much as it needs from the products it obtains and, the rest of the product should be sold to other countries and products that are not produced should be bought from these countries. When all countries follow a similar policy, the production, consumption and welfare of each country will increase. In the following years, Smith and his followers, who are called Classical Economists, have emphasized freedom of enterprise and free foreign trade in the countries by saying "let do, let pass"[1] (Kaboub, 2001). In other words, people or entrepreneurs must be able to produce whatever they want, wherever they want, and sell it in the country whichever they want. From this point of view, it can be said that Adam Smith's ideas actually corresponds to the behavior of today's multinational companies, and from this aspect they also become the source of ideas for these companies.

Developments in information and communication technologies and the prevalence of mass media have begun to homogenize the taste and preferences of consumers and make individuals more willing to buy goods and services produced in other countries[2]. This situation brought globalization in the sense of consumption. On the other hand, international companies are struggling to reduce their costs and maximize profits by following a vertical production strategy[3]. This has brought about the phenomenon of globalization in the sense of production (Islam, 2015). Developing countries should also keep in mind that they can not stay out of this globalization and they should make production and consumption strategies and foreign trade organizations accordingly.

Implementing free foreign trade policies and directing domestic producers to foreign markets is one of the most important factors that accelerate the economic growth of countries (UNCTAD, 2004). This is also supported by the "Export-Led Growth Model" developed in the 20th century, and the model states that countries must undertake an effort to increase their exports by abandoning efforts to produce everything they need (Giles and Williams, 2010). At this point, knowing and applying international marketing methods in order to benefit from foreign markets is of great importance for countries. On the other hand, countries that implement protectionist foreign trade policy cause local firms to be inefficient and domestic consumers to consume lower quality goods at higher prices. Domestic companies that want to benefit from this situation do not want to deal with the pressure of foreign competition, they do not try to improve themselves and introduce new product or production techniques. Even bribes are given to politicians, corruption and unfair gains can occur in order to maintain this situation (World Bank, 1996). However, this harms the firm and the country's economy in the long run and makes them more inefficient and small-scale. Companies and countries that want to grow, increase profits and become a world-class brand have to turn to international markets (Porter, 1998).

In the document prepared by the European Commission (2012), the main benefits of free foreign trade for developing countries are as follows:

1. While free foreign trade can help to increase development, and reduce poverty by creating growth through increased commercial opportunities and investments, it can also expand the productive base through private sector development.
2. Free foreign trade can increase competitiveness by reducing the input costs of developing countries, increasing the value added of their products and advancing the global value chain.
3. Free foreign trade facilitates product diversification by allowing developing countries to access new markets and new materials that create new production opportunities.
4. Free foreign trade encourages innovation by attracting foreign direct investments to the country, accelerating research and development activities in the country, facilitating the exchange of information, technology and investment.
5. Free foreign trade increases the market network of companies, increases the supply of goods and services, allows companies to benefit from economies of scale, and reduces unit production costs. This allows domestic consumers to access products at a lower price.
6. With the increase of competition and the development of commercial partnerships, which are provided by free foreign trade, the world's leading products and efficient production techniques become widespread.
7. Free foreign trade contributes to reduce government spending by diversifying the supply of goods and services, strengthening competition for public contracts.
8. Free foreign trade strengthens ties among countries, bringing people together in peaceful and mutually beneficial markets, trade fairs, international trade conventions, and contributes to global peace and stability.
9. Free foreign trade creates new and high-income employment opportunities by increasing the number of economic sectors that create stable jobs and generally generate high incomes (European Commission, 2012).

In order to be able to have the benefits of free foreign trade, it is necessary for countries to stop trading only with certain countries and to definitely go to market diversification, that is, to establish foreign trade links with different countries and country groups. In this way, any problem with one of the trading partners can immediately be tolerated with the others.

BACKGROUND

Diversification of the Market in Foreign Trade

As the foreign trade of the countries increases, the number of the countries where the foreign trade is realized and the number of products that is traded need to increase. Foreign trade made only in certain countries can be seriously affected by an economic or political negativity that the country may be experienced with these countries, which can lead to hard-to-recover losses (Alesina et al., 1996). Similarly, the concentration in certain products in foreign trade can also be a problem in the long run, and countries may be in a difficult situation when the demand structure changes or new competitors enter the market in the related product group[4]. The diversification of exported products or the availability of imported products from different countries provides various advantages in export and import (European Commission, 2012). Market and product diversification in export and import show itself in the form of decrease of concentration. It should be targeted that concentration in foreign trade has a decreasing trend over time. Concentration seems to be low in the developed countries with high foreign trade volume (State Institute of Statistics Prime Ministry Republic of Turkey, 2003).

Free foreign trade creates new business opportunities for local companies by opening new markets, removing unnecessary barriers and facilitating exports, and there is no objection to this (European Commission, 2016). Now the main question here is which country or group of countries will be involved in the foreign trade. Since the primary purpose for companies is to maximize profits, the answer to this question will of course be the countries where the highest profits are earned with the least cost. For this reason, the countries with the lowest transportation costs and the countries with high national income or per capita income will be preferred. The availability of sea or rail transportation also provides a significant advantage to reduce transportation costs. The cost of international transportation by rail is 2.5 times more than the cost of transportation by sea. By road, it is 4 times more expensive than the cost of shipping and by air 12 times more expensive than the cost of shipping (Energy Efficiency Association, 2017). In other words, for a cargo that can be transported by sea with a cost of \$100, it has to be paid \$250 by rail,

$400 by road, and $1200 by air. In this respect, companies prefer maritime and rail transport in the foreign trade as much as possible.

Another important determinant in the foreign trade is customs taxes and quotas. While the customs tax briefly expresses the taxes and fees paid when a particular good passes through a customs border (Rajsekhara, Hulle and Jansen, 1999), quota refers to the limitations on quantity or value of goods to be imported or exported (Levin Institute, 2017). Countries are making economic cooperation agreements with each other in order to get free foreign trade by getting rid of the customs taxes and quotas. The first ones that come to mind from these agreements are as follows: The Customs Union Agreement between the members of the EU and the candidate countries, The North American Free Trade Agreement (NAFTA) between the United States, Canada and Mexico, and The Economic Cooperation Organization Trade Agreement (ECOTA), which was established between Turkey, Iran and Pakistan in 1985 and signed within the scope of the Economic Cooperation Organization which was expanded in 1992 with the participation of Afghanistan, Azerbaijan, Kazakhstan, Kyrgyzstan, Tajikistan, Turkmenistan and Uzbekistan after the collapse of the Union of Soviet Socialist Republics (Turker, 2017). In such economic cooperation agreements, the free movements of goods and services among the countries included in the union is allowed, while a common customs tariff is applied for the countries outside the union. Thus, efforts are being made to increase the level of welfare of the Union by increasing free foreign trade among the member countries of the Union.

Countries do not have to adhere to only one international free trade agreement. Countries can also participate in free foreign trade unions established by different groups of countries in order to obtain trade advantageously with different countries. For example, Turkey signed the Economic Cooperation Organization Trade Agreement with the Middle East and Central Asian Countries in 1992 and signed the Customs Union Agreement in 1995 to trade freely with the member countries of the European Union. Nowadays, Turkey is on the agenda to participate in the Shanghai Cooperation Organization formed by China, Russia, Kyrgyzstan, Tajikistan, Kazakhstan and Uzbekistan. Similarly, the United States, which is included in NAFTA, and the European Union, which has a customs union, are planning to sign the Transatlantic Trade and Investment Partnership (TTIP) agreement (European Union, 2015).

Political developments are effective in foreign trade as well as economic developments. For example, the 1st Gulf War of the United States against Iraq in 1991 and the 2nd Gulf War of 2003 significantly reduced Turkey's exports to Iraq. Similarly, the Arab Spring uprisings, which started in Tunisia in 2010 and affected North Africa and Middle East Countries, have also led to a deterioration of Turkey's good relations with this region and a significant decline in foreign trade (Gocer and Cinar, 2015). After Turkey downed Russian warplane due to violation of its air space in 2015, the embargo imposed on Turkish goods by Russia and the vegetables that

Turkey sends to this country remained unsold and some of them went to waste. However, if there were alternative markets where these products could be sold, this export loss would not be experienced by Turkey.

Considering the import side of the incident, especially a problem to be experienced in the import of compulsory goods for the manufacturing industry such as energy, intermediate goods and raw materials, has the potential to deeply influence many sectors, especially the manufacturing industry. For this reason, it is necessary for countries to diversify their imports. For example, Russia threatened to cut natural gas for Turkey and European countries due to its claim of involvement of European countries in Ukraine's internal affairs in 2014, and the aircraft crisis with Turkey in November 2015. In such cases, alternative import sources are needed.

Countries can make foreign direct investments in different countries so that the tension in the international arena does not threaten the security of energy and food supply. Investments made by China in the Persian Gulf are aimed at ensuring energy security while investments in African countries are also aimed at securing industrial raw materials and food supply (Cinar and Gocer, 2014). The reason why the US has not left the Middle East for years is to have oil resources in the region (Beaver, Beaver and Wilsey, 2017) and the Russian and Iranian policies toward Syria are also due to their willingness to share oil resources in Syria (Durden, 2016). Moreover, in recent years, some countries are trying to ensure their food supply. For example, Saudi Arabia has an effort to produce wheat on its behalf by leasing land from the Konya Plain and Israel makes production on its behalf in the land covered by the South-East Anatolia Project (Yildiz, 2007).

There is a great benefit for developing countries to go market diversification in their imports and exports so that they can achieve stable foreign trade and economic growth (Vijayasri, 2013). In this regard, for countries who want to achieve stable foreign trade and economic growth, it is essential to leave aside profitability, proximity, cultural or national factors and these countries need to act rationally when it is necessary.

Market diversification does not only involve the exchange of final goods and services with different countries. It also includes dividing production processes among different countries according to the most economic output components. At this point, responsibility is not only on government administrators but also on company managers. By following the vertical production strategies, it is necessary for companies to consider that they do not have to carry out the production in one country at all, and that they should be directed to the country where they can produce each part of the product at the most efficient price and the best quality (Miyamoto, 2014). At the same time, it is useful for companies to regulate production scales by planning to sell goods in all the countries of the world, not just targeting consumers in their own countries.

According to new trade theories developed by Paul Krugman in the 1980s, nowadays, foreign trade is no longer carried out by countries, but by multinational companies (Krugman, 1979a; 1979b; 1980). In this context, companies that want to sell goods in different countries make foreign direct investments in those countries and thus constitute a value chain by selling their own products in their own stores in different countries of the world. Another innovation introduced by new trade theories is the concept of intra-industry trade[5]. Within the framework of classical foreign trade theories, foreign trade between the underdeveloped country and the developed country is inter-industry trade, whereas in the case of intra-industry trade, countries with similar development levels sell the same kind of products to each other and purchase from each other[6]. This situation will increase the productivity and product quality of domestic companies by forcing domestic companies to compete with international companies (Krugman, 1991).

Some studies on market diversification in foreign trade as follows: Sattar (2015) expresses that countries that have achieved structural change in exports through increased export diversification have grown faster and more extensively, and Ahmed, Islam and Al-Amin (2013) argue that with market diversification in foreign trade, firms' export targets will grow, production quantities will increase and thus they will benefit from economies of scale. While Erkan (2014) states that for many developing countries, market diversification in foreign trade plays an important role in exporting traditional products, exporting non-traditional (innovative) products and converting traditional markets to non-traditional (competitive) markets, Goldfarb (2006) explains that it would be wrong to put all the eggs in the same basket in foreign trade as in the stock market, and it is absolutely necessary to make market diversification. Bacchetta, Jansen, Piermartini and Amurgo-Pacheco (2007) state that market diversification in exports would absorb external shocks. Cadot, Carrère and Strauss-Kahn (2013) state that the diversification of countries in foreign trade will affect countries' income and economic growth positively.

Developing countries need to learn some lessons from the foreign trade experiences of Turkey, which is among the emerging economies and considered to be among the 20 largest economies in the world. In in the next section, the foreign trade experiences of Turkey in the 1970-2016 periods, the good practices that Turkey has implemented in this respect, topics that Turkey has made mistakes and the issues that Turkey has suffered are examined with the help of tables and graphs.

MAIN FOCUS OF THE CHAPTER

Foreign Trade and Market Diversification in Turkey

Turkey has clearly faced the negative effects of not doing market diversification in foreign trade on the time, and because of this, it is a country that has experienced significant economic losses. Since Turkey did not diversify its markets before 2008 global economic crisis, its exports decreased by 23%, unemployment rose up to 16.1% and economy shrank by 4.8% in this crisis. In 2009 and afterwards, they took lessons from their experiences in this crisis and went on diversification of their foreign trade markets (country and country groups). Developing countries should also take this negative experience that Turkey has been facing into account, and should diversify their markets in foreign trade. This will make them more resistant to internal and external economic shocks.

Until 1980, Turkey had adopted the economic growth model based on import substitution, and after this date, Turkey has adopted the export-driven economic growth model. At the beginning of the 1980s, foreign exchange trading and foreign exchange accounts were not allowed in Turkey, and companies could only supply foreign exchange needs through the Central Bank. In such a structure, Turkey generally had an economic tendency that produces and exports textile products. With the decision numbered 32, adopted in 1983, and the amendment made in 1989, the Turkish Lira was fully convertible[7], making it legitimate for citizens to hold foreign exchange and to trade foreign exchange in the free market. Distribution of Turkey's exports according to country groups in 1970-2016 periods is shown in Table 1.

Table 1. Distribution of Turkey's exports by country groups (%)

	EU28	Other European Countries	Total European	American Countries	African Countries	Near and Middle East Countries	Other Asian Countries	Australia and New Zealand	Total (Billion US Dollar)
1970	60	16	76	9.8	1.4	7.9	4.5	0.12	0.588
1980	57.3	12.1	69.4	4.8	3.7	18.9	2.9	0.09	2.9
1990	57.7	9.1	66.8	8.3	5.8	12.5	6	0.22	13.0
1995	57.7	9.8	67.5	8.3	5.1	11.1	7.7	0.25	21.2
2000	59.2	6.9	66.1	13.6	5.2	9.7	4.9	0.51	26.5
2005	59.1	8.1	67.2	8.5	5.2	14.5	4.3	0.38	70.3
2010	46.5	9.8	56.3	5.3	8.2	20.5	7.5	0.35	113.9
2016	47.9	6.8	54.7	6.56	8	22	6.8	0.52	142.5

Source: Turkish Statistical Institute (2017).

Figures 1-8 are obtained when the data in the table are to be examined in detail with pie charts.

According to Figure 1, while 60% of Turkey's exports were made to EU member countries in 1970, it is seen that the share of exports made to all European countries was as high as 76%. It is seen that 10% of the exports were made to the American countries, 8% to the Near and Middle East countries and 4.5% to the other Asian countries. At that time, the exports to the African countries were at a very low level of 1.4%. The distribution of Turkey's exports among the country groups in 1980 is shown in Figure 2.

According to Figure 2, the share of European countries in Turkey's exports in 1980 decreased to 69.4% from 76% in 1970, the share of the American countries decreased from 9.8% to 4.8%. On the other hand, the share of the Near and Middle East countries in Turkey's exports increased from 7.9% in 1970 to 18.9% in 1980, and the share of African countries increased from 1.4% to 3.7%. In other words, in this period, it can be said that the market diversification has started to take place partially in foreign trade. The distribution of Turkey's exports among the country groups in 1990 is shown in Figure 3.

In the 1980-1990 period, the Turkish economy experienced significant transformations. In 1980, the economic growth model based on import substitution was turned into an export-led growth model, and the Turkish Lira became fully convertible. The economic structure deteriorated with the military coup of 1980. After the Turgut Ozal came to power in 1983, implementation of liberal policies relieved the Turkish economy and opened the economy to foreign markets. In this period, Europe's share in Turkey's exports partially declined to 66.8% from 69.4% and the share of Near and Middle East decreased from 18.9% to 12.5%, while the share of America increased from 4.8% to 8.3%, Africa's share from 3.7% to 5.8%,

Figure 1. Distribution of Turkey's exports among country groups in 1970 (%)

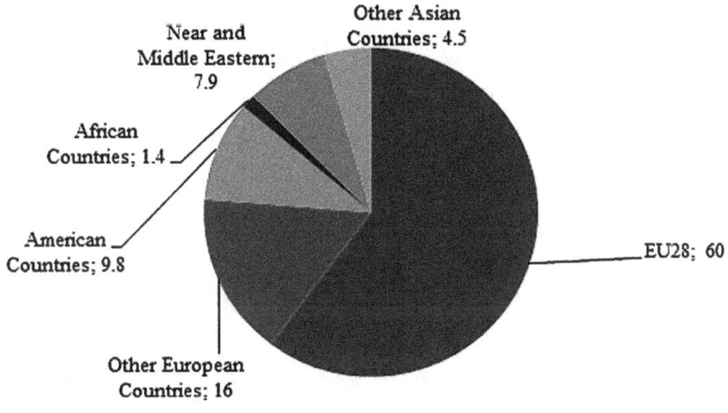

Figure 2. Distribution of Turkey's exports among country groups in 1980 (%)

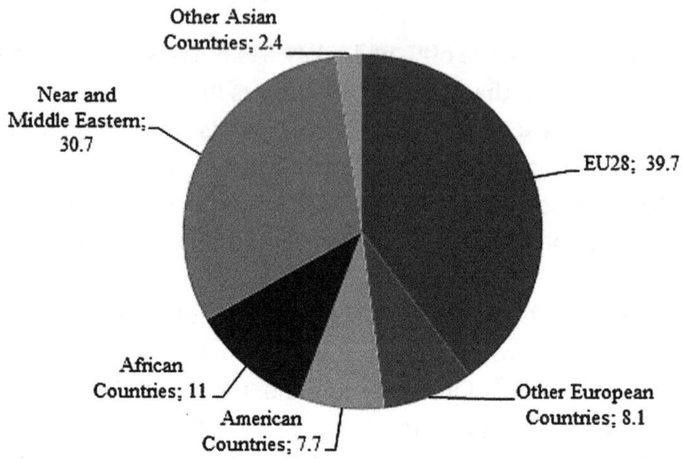

Figure 3. Distribution of Turkey's exports among country groups in 1990 (%)

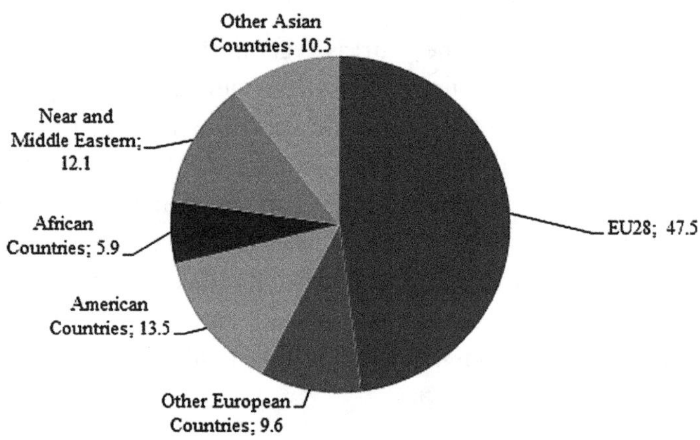

and the share of other Asian countries from 2.9% to 6%. The cause of the decline in the share of the Near and Middle East in Turkey's exports was the war between Iran and Iraq in the 1980-1988 period, in which at least 1 million people from two countries died and a total of$150 billion was lost. In addition to the loss of security of the region due to this war, the purchasing power of the people living in that region had fallen (Ebrahimzadeh, Fattahi and Nejad, 2006). This had led to a decrease in Turkey's exports to that region.

Turkey signed a Customs Union agreement with the European Union countries in March 1995 and this agreement came into force on 1 January 1996. In this regard, it is useful to look at the foreign trade in 1995 in order to see the situation before the Customs Union agreement was introduced. The distribution of Turkey's exports among the country groups in 1995 is shown in Figure 4.

According to Graph 4, the share of the Near and Middle East countries in Turkey's exports continued to decrease in 1995 and the share of other Asian countries increased partially. The reason for the declining share of the Near and Middle East countries was the invasion of Kuwait by Iraq in 1991 (1st Gulf War), and the increase of insecurity in the region and the fall of purchasing power with the US-launched Desert Shield Operation, which aimed to remove Iraqi forces from Kuwait. The reason for the increase in the share of other Asian countries in this period is that India's liberalization initiative in 1991 and its inclusion in the World Trade Organization in 1995 made it easier for Turkey to sell goods to India and to that region (Peng, Wang and Jiang, 2008). The distribution of Turkey's exports among the country groups in 2000 is shown in Figure 5.

As seen in Figure 5, since the first years of implementation of the Customs Union agreement, the share of the EU in the foreign trade of Turkey has increased and the share of the other European Countries not included in this union has decreased. This situation is called "Trade Diversion Effect" in the international economic literature (Soloaga and Winters, 2001). The share of the Near and Middle East continued to decline. Interestingly, exports to the countries in the America increased rapidly in this period. The distribution of Turkey's exports among the country groups in 2005 is shown in Figure 6.

As seen in Figure 6, while the share of European countries in Turkey's exports was still at 67% in 2005, there was a relative decrease in the share of the USA and an increase in the share of the Near and Middle East countries. The reason why the share of the Near and Middle Eastern countries in Turkey's exports increased in this

Figure 4. Distribution of Turkey's exports among country groups in 1995 (%)

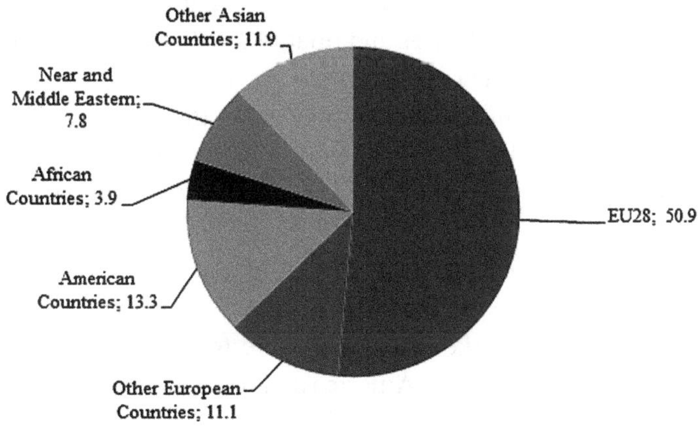

Figure 5. Distribution of Turkey's exports among country groups in 2000 (%)

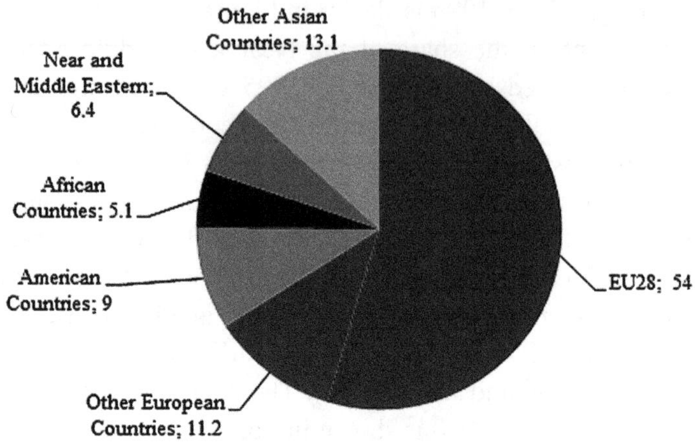

Figure 6. Distribution of Turkey's exports among country groups in 2005 (%)

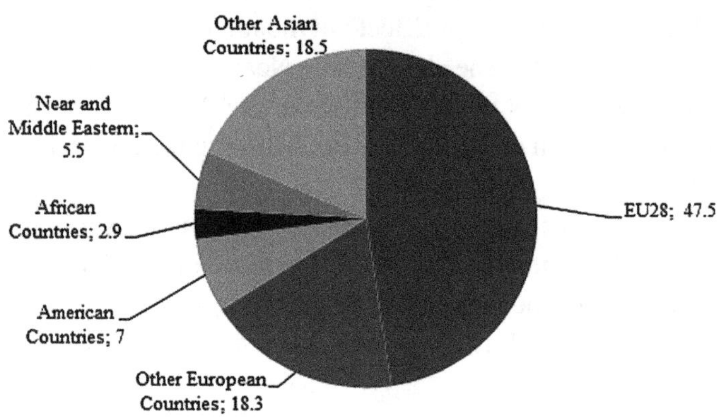

period is the efforts of the Justice and Development Party, which came into power in November 2002, to develop the ties and relations with this geography. While the share of the EU countries in Turkey's exports remained same, it is observed that some of the lost markets in the accession process to the Customs Union regained and thus the share of the other European countries in Turkey's exports increased somewhat. The distribution of Turkey's exports among the country groups in 2010 is shown in Figure 7.

It is important to emphasize on this figure. Because in 2007, just before the global financial crisis in 2008 that started in the US housing market and affected the whole world, 66.4% of Turkey's exports were to Europe, 14.1% to Near and Middle East, 5.6% to Africa, 5.2% to America and 4.9% to other Asian countries. As

Figure 7. Distribution of Turkey's exports among country groups in 2010 (%)

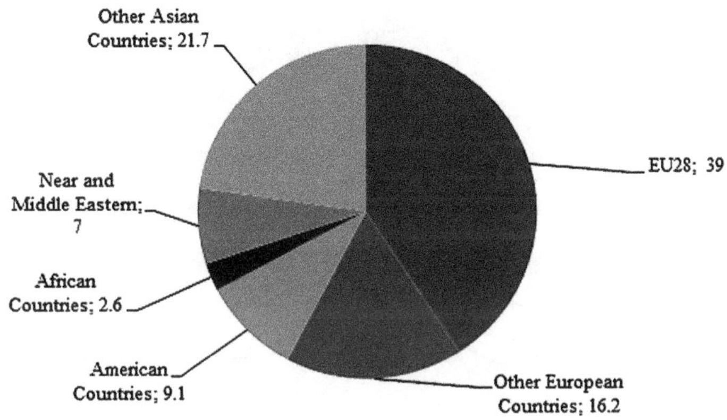

the purchasing power of Europe and America was adversely affected by the global financial crisis of 2008, Turkey could not sell the goods to these countries and the total exports of Turkey decreased by 22.7% in 2009. This situation led companies to lay off workers[8] to cut production because companies had a high level of stock and were unable to find an additional warehouse to store their products, so that Turkish economy shrank by 4.8%. This has led companies and government officials responsible for Turkey's economy to seek new markets. Turkey has been accelerated to make new foreign trade agreements with the countries of Russia, Central Asia and Far East, especially Africa. As can be seen from Figure 7, while the share of EU and American countries in Turkey's exports decreased in 2010, the share of other European countries, Africa, Near and Middle East and other Asian countries increased significantly. These efforts continued increasingly and in 2012, 50.2% of exports were made to Europe, 27.8% to Near and Middle East, 8.8% to Africa, 6.3% to America and 6.9% to other Asian countries. With the effect of these measures, Turkey's exports rose to $ 152.5 billion in 2012 from $ 102 billion in 2009, and the economy grew 9.2% in 2010 and 8.8% in 2011 (The Central Bank of the Republic of Turkey, 2017). *The negative experience of the Turkish economy during the crisis of 2009 has taught the companies and government officials responsible for Turkey's economy that it is absolutely necessary to search for alternative markets rather than merely adhering to specific markets.* With the creation of alternative markets, the impact of shrinkage is minimized by creating new markets in response to shrinking market. The distribution of Turkey's exports among the country groups in 2016 is shown in Figure 8.

By the year 2016, the European countries were still unable to get rid of the 2008 debt crisis and the economic recession after the global economic crisis, resulting in Turkey's exports to this region falling to 54.7%. On the other hand, as a result

Figure 8. Distribution of Turkey's exports among country groups in 2016 (%)

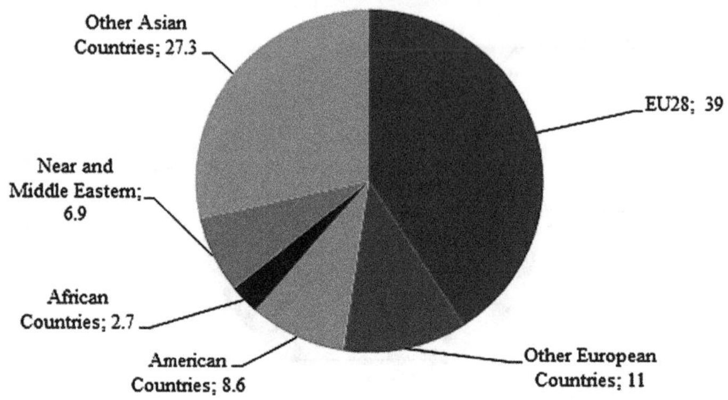

of increasing economic ties with Iran and Qatar, the share of the Near and Middle Eastern countries in Turkey's exports has increased, and the impact of the US, which rapidly emerged from the global crisis, has also increased the share of American countries in Turkey's exports. The reason for the decline in Turkey's exports to other Asian countries in 2016 is the political tensions with Russia after the shooting down of a Russian warplane, which violates the Turkish border in November 2015, and the embargo imposed on Turkish goods by Russia. Table 2 shows the changes in the distribution of Turkey's imports by country groups during 1970-2016 periods.

Figure 9-16 are created to examine the data in Table 2 in detail

As seen in Figure 9, in 1970, 65.6% of Turkey's imports were from European countries, while 23.6% of imports in the same period were covered by American countries. Interestingly, the share of oil-rich Near and Middle Eastern Countries in

Table 2. Distribution of Turkey's imports by country groups (%)

	EU28	Other European Countries	Total European	American Countries	African Countries	Near and Middle East Countries	Other Asian Countries
1970	55	10.6	65.6	23.6	1.33	5.2	3.3
1980	39.7	8.1	47.8	7.7	11	30.7	2.4
1990	47.5	9.6	57.1	13.5	5.9	12.1	10.5
1995	50.9	11.1	62	13.3	3.9	7.8	11.9
2000	54	11.2	65.2	9	5.1	6.4	13.1
2005	47.5	18.3	65.8	7	2.9	5.5	18.5
2010	39	16.2	55.2	9.1	2.6	7	21.7
2016	39	11	50	8.6	2.7	6.9	27.3

Source: Turkish Statistical Institute (2017).

Figure 9. Distribution of Turkey's imports among country groups in 1970 (%)

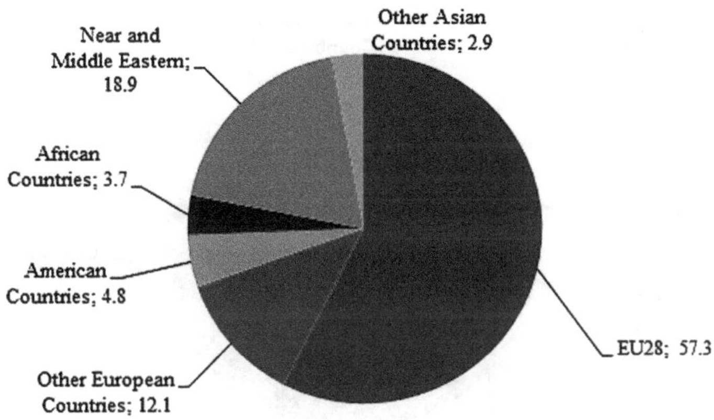

Turkey's imports was quite low at 5.2% in this period. The distribution of Turkey's imports among the country groups in 1980 is shown in Figure 10.

In this figure, a remarkable difference is noticed when compared to the previous figure. In 1980, the share of EU member countries in Turkey's imports declined considerably. It is estimated that this may be the military coup that took place in Turkey on 12 September 1980. A significant decline in the 1980s is also observed in the share of American countries. However, the share of Africa and the countries of the Near and Middle East increased dramatically. It is estimated that the reason for this increase is the open, export-oriented liberal economic policies implemented by Turgut Ozal, who came to power in 1983, and the increased demand for energy and raw materials with the accelerated economic growth in this period. The distribution of Turkey's imports among the country groups in 1990 is shown in Figure 11.

Figure 10. Distribution of Turkey's imports among country groups in 1980 (%)

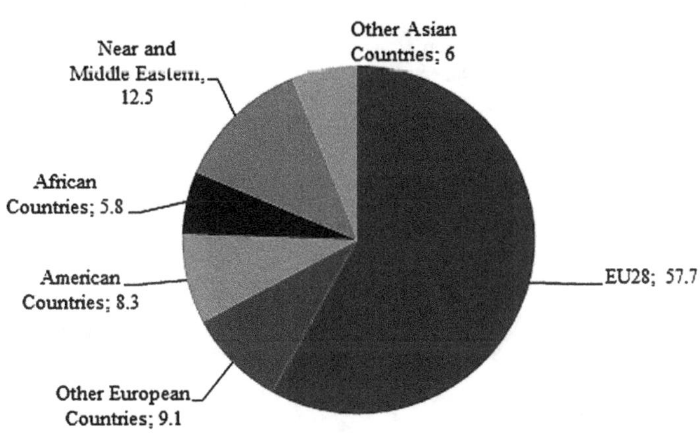

Figure 11. Distribution of Turkey's imports among country groups in 1990 (%)

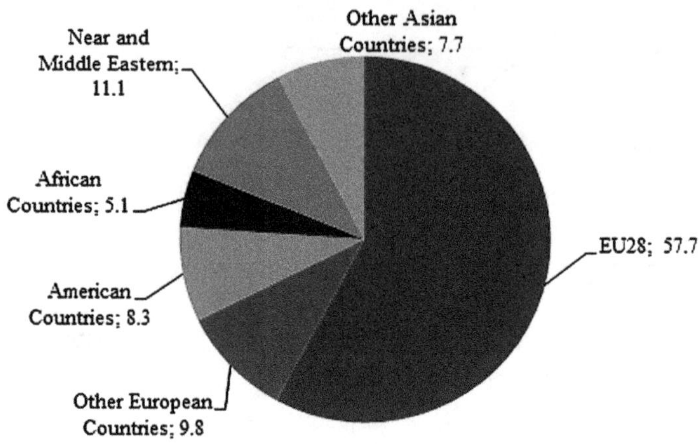

By 1990, the share of European countries in Turkey's imports increased again, while the share of Africa, the Near and Middle East countries decreased. Another noteworthy point is the increase in the share of other Asian countries. This increase is attributed to China's policy of participating to foreign markets, which started in 1978, Russia's efforts to move to the free economy starting in 1989[9], and India's participation in world markets. Distribution of Turkey's imports among the country groups in 1995 is shown in Figure 12.

1995 is critical from four perspectives. Firstly, Turkey experienced an economic crisis on 5 April 1994 and the Turkish Lira was devalued by 76.2%, which deeply affected foreign trade. The second is the 1st Gulf War in the 1990-1991 periods. The third is India's membership to the World Trade Organization in 1995, which made it

Figure 12. Distribution of Turkey's imports among country groups in 1995 (%)

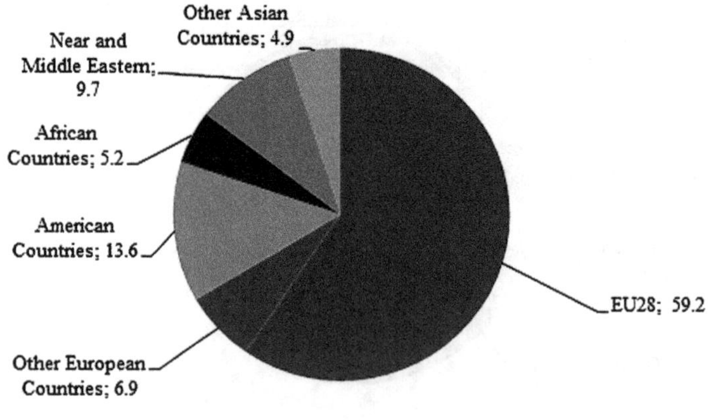

easier for India to sell its products to the world. Lastly, Turkey signed the Customs Union Agreement with the EU in March 1995. When the table is viewed in the light of those information, the reasons for the decrease in imports from African countries and Near and Middle East countries, but the increase from imports from the European Union and other European countries will be better understood. The distribution of Turkey's imports among the country groups in 2000 is shown in Figure 13.

By the year 2000, imports from EU countries increased rapidly due to the Customs Union agreement, which took place on 1 January 1996, while imports from other countries generally declined, which is a good example of the trade diversion effect of the Customs Union. The distribution of Turkey's imports among the country groups in 2005 is shown in Figure 14.

When examining the 2005 import rates, the following events should be considered. After the membership of China to the World Trade Organization in 2001, cheap Chinese commodities began to enter many markets. As a result of the foreign exchange crisis experienced in Turkey in February 2001, the dollar was devalued by about 56% in the free market. After the terrorist attack on September 11, 2001 in the twin towers of the World Trade Center in the United States, the United States intervened for the 2nd time in Iraq (2nd Gulf War). Lastly, Turkey began the negotiations for full EU membership in 2004. The decrease in imports from the countries of Africa and Near and Middle East in 2005 and the increase in the share of other Asian countries will be better understood in this framework. The distribution of Turkey's imports among the country groups in 2010 is shown in Figure 15.

While examining the data in 2010, it is necessary to consider the effects of the 2008 global economic crisis and the search for new markets in the process of emergence from this crisis. It should be noted that imports from the EU have decreased and imports from other Asian countries, including China, India and Russia, have

Figure 13. Distribution of Turkey's imports among country groups in 2000 (%)

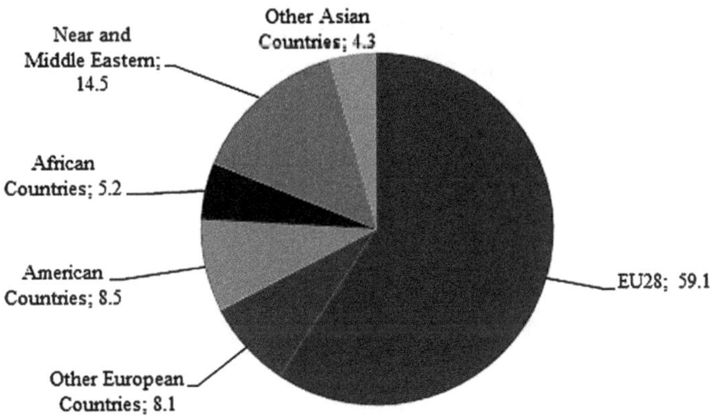

Figure 14. Distribution of Turkey's imports among country groups in 2005 (%)

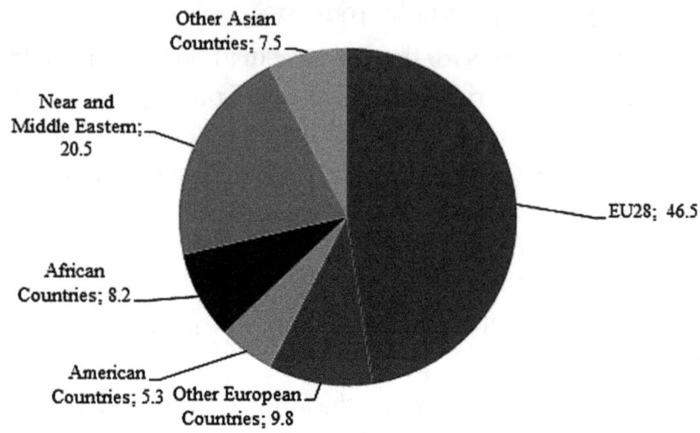

Figure 15. Distribution of Turkey's imports among country groups in 2010 (%)

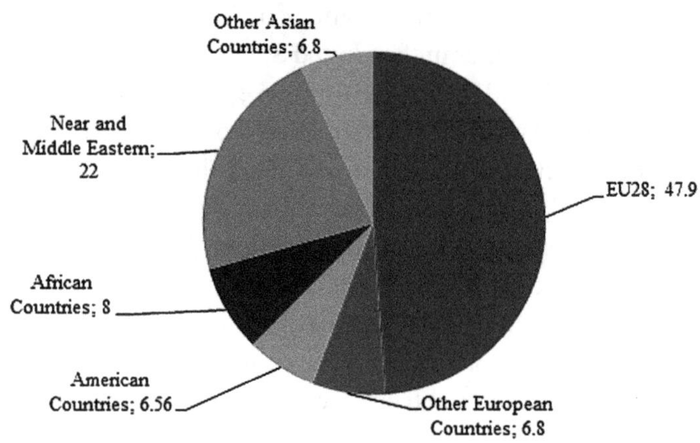

continued to increase. When foreign trade agreements are signed between countries, only the goods to be mutually traded are taken into consideration, not the goods that only one country sells to the other. For this reason, it is seen that Turkey, which is looking new markets for its exports and turning its direction to Asian and African Countries in order to get out of the 2008 global economic crisis, is committed to import more goods than the counterparts in this period, and the imports from the Near and Middle East and other Asian Countries are seen to increase rapidly. The distribution of Turkey's imports by country groups in 2016 is presented in Figure 16.

The same is true for the year 2016, while imports from other Asian countries have increased significantly, imports from other European countries have declined

Figure 16. Distribution of Turkey's imports among country groups in 2016 (%)

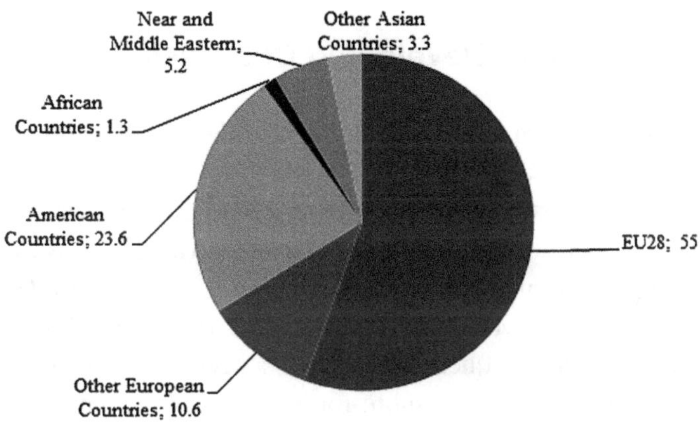

substantially. This may be due to the fact that in May 2013 the US dollar rapidly appreciated against the US dollar after the US Federal Reserve announced that the FED would end its expanding monetary policy in the exit process from the global crisis and move into a restrictive monetary policy, which has made the imports from European countries relatively more expensive. Also, China has become an important import center for Turkey with cheap intermediate goods and final goods.

In the 2000s, 66% and 55.2% shares of European countries in Turkey's exports and imports, respectively, tended to decrease in recent years. This is good for the country. While Turkey continues to research new markets, it should not lose its market share in Europe, which has high purchasing power and technological level. Otherwise, the foreign trade with the Middle East and African countries will mostly return to the inter-industry trade, which makes exporters in Turkey susceptible to laziness or laxity. In the long run, this creates many disadvantages.

When we briefly mention the other important problems that Turkey has experienced in foreign trade, it is seen that imports of Turkey are higher than its exports. The reasons for this are that the production is highly dependent on imported intermediate inputs and that the exported products are generally low values added products such as textiles, unprocessed agricultural products and raw materials (Akbaş ve Şentürk, 2013). Turkey needs to be able to produce and export high value added products by focusing on the R&D (Research-Development) and innovation. For imports, national hydroelectric power stations and nuclear power should be developed instead of imported natural gas in electricity generation, the ways of producing domestic demand for intermediates needed for industry should be investigated, and the ways of producing high-tech machinery and equipment in the country should be investigated.

SOLUTIONS AND RECOMMENDATIONS

Policy Suggestions for Developing Countries

Firstly, the necessary information for revealing the place of developing countries in the world is presented in Table 3.

Of the 206 countries listed by the World Bank in 2016, 46 are developed, 132 are developing and 60 are the least developed countries. In Table 3, 81.8% of the world's population is in the developing countries, producing 39.2% of world GDP, 41.4% of world exports and 41.5% of world imports. This data are rather low compared to the population of the countries in question. There is a need for these countries to work harder, to produce more and to do more foreign trade. In recent years, especially China has achieved this and China, which has become one of the most important actors of world trade since its accession to the World Trade Organization in 2001, has become one of the locomotives of the economic growth of the world[10]. The main issues that developing countries need to do in order to increase their foreign trade can be listed as follows:

1. It is absolutely necessary to adopt free foreign trade and to abandon closed, overprotective economic models.
2. To develop the necessary economic and political cooperation with other countries in order to overcome customs taxes and quotas that prevent free foreign trade. To sign bilateral free trade agreements. To be included in as many free foreign trade zones and economic cooperation as possible. In doing so, however, without killing the domestic industry, the necessary measures must be taken until the infant industry and domestic producers can develop and become competitive in the international market.

Table 3. Global macroeconomic data (2016)

	Population (Million)	Percent of World (%)	GDP (Billion US Dollar)	Percent (%)	Export (Billion US Dollar)	Percent of World (%)	Import (Billion US Dollar)	Percent of World (%)
Developed Economies	1050.2	14.1	43188.9	58.2	11724.8	55.5	11649.3	55.9
Developing Economies	6077.5	81.8	29044.5	39.2	8748.1	41.4	8654.4	41.5
Least Developed Economies	976.8	13.1	933.9	1.3	201.9	1.0	293.1	1.4
World	7432.7	100	74176.9	100	21110.5	100	20837.4	100

Source: UNCTAD (2017a); World Bank (2017).

3. Applying a stable exchange rate regime to enable foreign trade to be carried out in a sustainable manner.
4. Making the country's money convertible through the world's currencies, allowing citizens and businesses to hold foreign exchange, trade in foreign currencies, or enable foreign currency transactions.
5. To facilitate the foreign trade of the companies, to prepare the infrastructure such as the port and the transportation network necessary for this issue.
6. To provide the necessary export incentives to the firm. To pay VAT refunds to the firm on time.
7. Do not just settle for inter-industry foreign trade, but also guide domestic firms to the intra-industry trade, and make the necessary education, incentives and investments in this field.
8. Do not settle for foreign trade with certain country groups, and develop foreign trade with different countries and country groups. While struggling not to lose the current market share, to continue to search for new markets constantly.
9. While continuing the market search for foreign trade, preferring countries with high per capita income.
10. In this regard, proximity, political, cultural and religious sensitivities should be left to one side and act as rational as possible, and long-term foreign trade plans should be developed[11]. To be as calm and logical as possible while maintaining relationships with other states[12].
11. To save domestic production from being dependent on imported intermediate goods.
12. To be able to produce and export technology-intensive and high value-added products by giving importance to R&D and innovation.
13. To provide country diversity in imports and ensure supply security in areas such as food, medicine, defense industry and energy.
14. To give importance to product diversity in foreign trade.

It should not be forgotten that one of the most important causes of internal conflicts, social explosions[13], terrorist attacks, suicide bombings and other criminal cases in countries is poverty[14]. In this regard, it would be useful that policy makers in the underdeveloped and developing countries should promote, facilitate foreign trade, and guide companies in this issue in order to increase the income of citizens and countries.

Countries have to remember that Free Trade Agreements have not only positive but also negative impacts on trade and the economy as well as having social, environmental and cultural implications. For example; the liberalization of imports to be initiated before the domestic baby industries fully developed and can compete with other companies in the world may cause these firms to fail and withdraw from the market. It would be more beneficial for the country in the long run to maintain their production instead of imported cheap and poor quality goods[15].

In addition, one of the most important requirements for achieving the expected return from free foreign trade is to increase the diversification of products for trade. Taking into account the globalization of individuals' demands and preferences, widening the product range will ease holding and growing in foreign markets. It is also important that the prices of the products offered to foreign markets are competitive. It should not be forgotten that nowadays e-trade makes it for people to access the goods in different countries as easy as pressing a few button on the keyboard. Moreover, retail sector operations run by multinational corporations are able to offer products all over the world to consumers. It is beneficial for domestic companies that operate in foreign markets to consider these points.

FUTURE RESEARCH DIRECTIONS

Future work on this topic should be supported also with an econometric analysis. For this, an index can be formed that measures the degree of market diversification of countries in foreign trade. The relationship between this index and net export exports can be analyzed econometrically. If subsequent researchers will take seriously into account this topic, it will be useful for them.

CONCLUSION

Free foreign trade is one of the most important means of increasing the prosperity of all countries by using countries' natural resources, labor force and technology in the most effective way, providing the division of labor and specialization in the production of certain products and increasing production and consumption. This hypothesis is true when we look at the developments in the world, it is clear that the level of income of countries that started free trade in the early years and signed more free foreign trade agreements with other countries in this respect is higher than nations living in a closed economic structure based import substitution. The best example of this is South Korea and North Korea. While South Korea is the 11th largest economy in the world today, North Korea is a country with no economic success, which is on the agenda only with the weapons it produces and the threats of war it has made.

In the scope of foreign trade, especially the country and market diversification are emphasized in this study. Although Turkey has been advocating free foreign trade since its founding in 1923, it has indeed succeeded in doing free foreign trade after the 1980s. Turkey, which traded mostly with neighboring countries or close countries before 1980, signed the customs union agreement with the European Union in 1995 and started to do free foreign trade with this group of countries. In this process, the share of European countries in the foreign trade of Turkey has started to increase rapidly. However, with the global economic crisis in 2008, the economic stagnation in these countries significantly reduced Turkey's exports, unemployment rose to 16.2% in February 2009, and the Turkish economy shrank by 4.8%. The Turkish government and businessmen, who are now looking for a new market, have started to focus on the Middle East, Africa, Central Asia and Russia markets. However, the Arab Spring events in North Africa and the Middle East since December 2010 have also adversely affected these markets. Tension with Russia due to the downing of the Russian warplane by Turkey for the violation of the Turkish airspace in November 2015 caused the loss of the Russian market.

It is not enough to just look at the volume of the export. It is also important to ensure supply security in areas such as imported food, energy, raw materials, semi-finished goods, advanced technology machinery and equipment, medical supplies, and defense industry products. In the Cyprus Operation of 1974, as a result of the arms embargo imposed to Turkey by the USA, the planes and the weapons became unusable. When the threat of cutting off natural gas sent by Russia to Turkey is on the agenda after downing of Russian jet by Turkey in 2015, Turkish politicians helplessly said "In that case, we burn cow dung". However, Turkey imports 97% of the natural gas it needs and uses this natural gas both in the industry and in the heating and kitchen of the residences. Even a considerable portion of the electricity Turkey uses is generated by using natural gas. Therefore, a natural gas interruption has the potential to deeply affect the whole country's economy and people's health.

As it is seen from these examples, commercial relations and international political relations are in close interaction. It is then necessary for the developing countries to learn from Turkey's experience so that they can achieve a high and sustainable foreign trade volume. In this context, they should not only settle in certain markets in foreign trade, they should search alternative markets and sign the necessary economic and political agreements. They should also encourage foreign direct investment in the country in order to increase the production and export potential of their countries by providing the necessary support to the domestic firms. It would be beneficial to make foreign direct investments in other countries to ensure the security of supply of energy and food to their countries. While political relations with other countries are maintained, emotional behaviors should be left aside, and national interests should be taken into consideration.

All these developments indicate that there is a great benefit for the developing countries to go market and product diversification in their imports and exports so that they can achieve stable foreign trade and economic growth. In this regard, when it is necessary for developing countries it is essential to leave aside profitability, geographical proximity, cultural or nationality closeness factors and they need to act rationally.

REFERENCES

Ahmed, R., & Islam, T., & Al-Amin. (2013). The effects of market diversification activities on Bangladesh RMG export. *International Journal of Economics and Financial Issues*, *3*(4), 938–948.

Akbas, Y. E., & Sentürk, M. (2013). Dependency of import and export of Turkey: An empirical application for selected countries. *Ege Academic Review*, *13*(2), 195–208.

Alesina, A., Ozler, S., Roubini, N., & Swagel, P. (1996). Political instability and economic growth. *Journal of Economic Growth*, *1*(2), 189–211. doi:10.1007/BF00138862

Bacchetta, M., Jansen, M., Piermartini, R., & Amurgo-Pacheco, A. (2007). *Export diversification as an absorber of external shocks.* Retrieved May 5, 2017, from http://www.etsg.org/ETSG2007/papers/ jansen.pdf

Beaver, B., Beaver, J., & Wilsey, M. (2017). *The Middle East: United States policy and relations in the latter half of the 20th century.* Retrieved August 6, 2017, from https://web.stanford.edu/class/e297c/war_peace/middleeast/hcentury.html

Cadot, O., Carrère, C., & Strauss-Kahn, V. (2013). Trade diversification, income, and growth: What do we know? *Journal of Economic Surveys*, *27*(4), 790–812. doi:10.1111/j.1467-6419.2011.00719.x

Cinar, S., & Gocer, I. (2014). Towards a new cold war: Global energy policies. Adnan Menderes University. *Journal of Institute of Social Sciences*, *1*(2), 16–29.

Dunya. (2014). *We bought a $ 1.4 billion toy from China.* Retrieved August 6, 2017, from https://www.dunya.com/ihracat/cin039den-14-milyar-dolarlik-oyuncak-aldik-haberi-234563

Durden, T. (2016). *The oil-gas war over Syria (In 4 Maps).* Retrieved August 6, 2017, from http://www.zerohedge.com/news/2016-10-24/oil-gas-war-over-syria-4-maps

Ebrahimzadeh, M.H., Fattahi, A.S. & Nejad, A.B. (2006). Long-term follow-up of Iranian veteran upper extremity amputees from the Iran-Iraq War (1980-1988). *Journal of Trauma-Injury Infection & Critical Care, 61*(4), 886-888.

Energy Efficiency Association. (2017). *Cost in transportation systems*. Retrieved April 16, 2017, from http://www.enver.org.tr/tr/icerik/ulasim/15

Erkan, B. (2014). Product and market diversification in Turkey's foreign trade. *International Journal of Advances in Management and Economics, 3*(1), 1–15.

European Commission. (2012). *10 Benefits of trade for developing countries*. Retrieved May 04, 2017, from http://trade.ec.europa.eu/doclib/docs/2012/january/tradoc_148991.pdf

European Commission. (2016). *Report from the Commission to the Council and the European Parliament on trade and investment barriers and protectionist trends*. Brussels, COM(2016) 406 Final. Retrieved October 11, 2017, from http://trade.ec.europa.eu/doclib/docs/2016/ june/tradoc_154665.pdf

European Union. (2015). *Inside TTIP, The transatlantic trade and investment partnership (TTIP) towards an EU–US trade deal, An overview and chapter-by-chapter guide in plain English*. Retrieved May 03, 2017, from http://trade.ec.europa.eu/doclib/docs/2015/july/tradoc_153635.pdf

Giles, J. A., & Williams, C. L. (2010). Export-led growth: A survey of the empirical literature and some non-causality results. *The Journal of International Trade & Economic Development. An International and Comparative Review, 9*(3), 261–337.

Gocer, I. (2013). *Productivity and macroeconomic effects of foreign direct investment: The case of Turkey, China and India* (Unpublished PhD dissertation). Adnan Menderes University, Social Sciences Institute, Department of Economics.

Gocer, I., & Cinar, S. (2015). The reasons of Arab Spring, its international dimension and impacts on Turkey's foreign trade and tourism incomes. *The Journal of KAU, IIBF, 6*(10), 51–68.

Goldfarb, D. (2006). *Too many eggs in one basket? Evaluating Canada's need to diversify trade*. C.D. Howe Institute, Commentary, No: 236.

Islam, R. (2015). *Globalization of production, work and human development: is a race to the bottom inevitable?* UNDP Human Development Report Office, Think Piece.

Kaboub, F. (2001). The demise and rebirth of laissez-faire capitalism. *Oeconomicus, 4*, 83–86.

Korkmaz, P. (2013). *View from London*. Retrieved May 05, 2017, from https://perihankorkmaz.wordpress.com/2013/06/17/ulkelerin-dostlari-ve-cikarlari/

Krugman, P. (1979a). Increasing returns, monopolistic competition and ınternational trade. *Journal of International Economics*, *9*(4), 469–479. doi:10.1016/0022-1996(79)90017-5

Krugman, P. (1979b). A model of balance-of-payment crises. *Journal of Money, Credit and Banking*, *11*(3), 311–325. doi:10.2307/1991793

Krugman, P. (1980). Scale economies, product differentiation, and the pattern of trade. *The American Economic Review*, *70*(5), 950–959.

Krugman, P. (1981). Intra-industry specialization and the gains from trade. *Journal of Political Economy*, *89*(5), 959–973. doi:10.1086/261015

Krugman, P. (1991). Increasing returns and economic geography. *Journal of Political Economy*, *99*(3), 483–499. doi:10.1086/261763

Levin Institute. (2017). *Trade and globalization*. Retrieved May 03, 2017, from http://www.globalization101.org/uploads/File/Trade/tradeall.pdf

Miyamoto, Y. (2014). *Strategic outsourcing and quality choice: Is a vertical integration model sustainable?* Retrieved October 11, 2017, from http://web.iss.u-tokyo.ac.jp/~matsumur/miyamoto2014.pdf

Peng, M. W., Wang, D. Y. L., & Jiang, Y. (2008). An institution-based view of international business strategy: A focus on emerging economies. *Journal of International Business Studies*, *39*(5), 920–936. doi:10.1057/palgrave.jibs.8400377

Porter, M. E. (1998). *Competitive advantage of nations*. New York: The Free Pres. doi:10.1007/978-1-349-14865-3

Rajsekhar, B., Hulle, F. V., & Jansen, J. C. (1999). Indian wind energy programme: Performance and future directions. *Energy Policy*, *27*(11), 669–678. doi:10.1016/S0301-4215(99)00031-2

Sattar, Z. (2015). *Strategy for export diversification 2015-2020*. Retrieved May 04, 2017, from http://www.plancomm.gov.bd/wp-content/uploads/2015/02/7_Strategy-for-Export-Diversification.pdf

Smith, A. (1776). An Inquiry into the Nature and Causes of the Wealth of Nations (5th ed.). London: Methuen & Co., Ltd. doi:10.1093/oseo/instance.00043218

Soloaga, I., & Winters, L. A. (2001). Regionalism in the nineties: What effect on trade? *The North American Journal of Economics and Finance*, *12*(1), 1–29. doi:10.1016/S1062-9408(01)00042-0

State Institute of Statistics Prime Ministry Republic of Turkey. (2003). *Concentration in foreign trade*. Retrieved May 18, 2017 from www.turkstat.gov.tr/IcerikGetir.do%3Fistab_id%3D90

The Central Bank of the Republic of Turkey. (2017). *Electronic data delivery system*. Retrieved May 19 from http://evds.tcmb.gov.tr/index_en.html

Turker, M. (2017). *Economic cooperation organization trade agreement and last development*. Retrieved May 03, 2017 from http://www.mfa.gov.tr/ekonomik-isbirligi-teskilati-ticaret-anlasmasi-_economic-cooperation-organization-trade-agreement-ecota_-ve-son-gelismeler-.tr.mfa

Turkish Statisticial Institute. (2017). *Statistical tables and dynamic interrogation*. Retrieved May 04, 2017, from http://www.tuik.gov.tr/PreTablo.do?alt_id=1046

UNCTAD. (2004). *Exports of services and economic growth in developing countries. United Nations Conference on Trade and Development*. Retrieved October 11, 2017, from http://unctad.org/en/docs/ditctncdmisc20036_en.pdf

UNCTAD. (2017a). *United Nations Conference on Trade and Development*. Retrieved May 05, 2017, from http://unctadstat.unctad.org/wds/TableViewer/tableView.aspx?ReportId=97

UNCTAD. (2017b). *United Nations Conference on Trade and Development*. Retrieved May 19, 2017, from http://unctadstat.unctad.org/wds/TableViewer/tableView.aspx

UNCTAD. (2017c). *United Nations Conference on Trade and Development*. Retrieved May 19, 2017, from http://unctadstat.unctad.org/wds/TableViewer/downloadPrompt.aspx

Vijayasri, G. V. (2013). The importance of international trade in the world. *International Journal of Marketing. Financial Services & Management Research*, *2*(9), 111–119.

World Bank. (1996). *The political economy of corruption-causes and consequences*. Retrieved October 11, 2017, from http://siteresources.worldbank.org/EXTFINANCIALSECTOR/Resources/282884-1303327122200/074ackerm.pdf

World Bank. (2017). Retrieved May 05, 2017, from http://data.worldbank.org/indicator/NY.GDP.MKTP.CD?view=chart

Yıldız, F. (2007). *Yabancı Uyruklu Gerçek ve Tüzel Kişilere Taşınmaz Mal Satışı. 21. Yüzyıl.* Nisan/Mayıs, 123-136.

KEY TERMS AND DEFINITIONS

Developing Countries: Countries that are not yet highly industrialized.

Emerging Market Economies: An emerging market economy describes a nation's economy that is progressing toward becoming more advanced, usually by means of rapid growth and industrialization.

Free Trade: Free trade is the economic policy of not discriminating against imports from and exports to foreign jurisdictions.

Inter-Industry Trade: The exchange of different products belonging to a different industry. The term is usually applied to international trade where different types of goods or services are both imported and exported.

International Trade: International trade is the exchange of capital, goods, and services across international borders or territories. It is the exchange of goods and services among nations of the world.

Intra-Industry Trade: The exchange of similar products belonging to the same industry. The term is usually applied to international trade where the same types of goods or services are both imported and exported.

Market Diversification: Market diversification is a strategy to enter into new markets or new countries.

Stable Economic Growth: An economic situation that displays only minor fluctuations in output growth and exhibits a consistently low inflation rate.

ENDNOTES

1. The word is originally French and has the form of "laissez-faire, laissez-passer".
2. There is no country where burgers, Coca Cola and jeans have not entered into.
3. Vertical production strategy is that different stages of production take place in different countries. In this type of investment, the foreign firm either transforms the intermediate goods produced in the country into the final goods to be sold in other countries or tries to produce intermediate goods for final production in other countries. The decisive factor for this type of investment is input costs.

4 For example, while Turkey was one of the major textile exporters in the world in the 1990s, India in 1995 and China in 2001 entered the World Trade Organization and began to sell cheap goods to the world quickly, and Turkey began to lose its relative superiority and market share in this sector so the textile factories in the country have started to lose money, even to go bankrupt and people became unemployed. At this point, it is necessary to increase the product variety in the export.

5 For example, in the 1980s, Turkey exported fabrics and bought electronic devices.

6 Perhaps the most important contribution of the Customs Union agreement in 1995 has been to this area. With this agreement, customs barriers with European countries have been removed, and high-technology foreign products have rapidly started to enter the Turkish market. As a consequence of this, Turkish firms have had to improve themselves and they have started to produce more qualified and more technology-intensive products. Turkey was transformed from a textile exporting country in the 1990s to the country that mainly exports automotive products in the 2010s. The fact that Turkey imports both Mercedes brand cars from Europe and sells its own automobiles such as Tofas and Renault to European countries is a good example of intra-industry trade. This is also the dynamic impact of the Customs Union.

7 To make it easy to change with the other country's money, or to allow it.

8 Unemployment in Turkey reached 16.2% in February 2009, the highest level ever.

9 Mikhail Gorbachev's policies of openness (Glasnost) and restructure (Perestroika) to participate in foreign markets have been effective. Gorbachev, trying to establish a more socially oriented market economy by creating a more liberal and democratic environment for the Soviets, aimed to increase productivity and eliminate waste at the same time with his reforms.

10 By the end of 2016, China ranked the first with 21 trillion US$ exports and the second with 15.8 trillion US$ imports (UNCTAD, 2017b). With 11 trillion US $ of GDP, it is also the world's second largest economy (UNCTAD, 2017c).

11 As British Prime Minister David Cameron said, "Britain has no friends, only national interests" (Korkmaz, 2013). Other countries should accept this as an example to them.

12 After Turkey downed the Russian jet in a fury on 24 November 2015, Turkey could not be able to sell goods to this country, and lost many tourists from this country, which forced Turkey to apologize repeatedly and make a lot of political concessions.

13 The main reason for the Arab Spring that started in Tunisia in 2010 and affect all the North African and Middle Eastern countries is the poverty, unemployment and lack of democracy in the region. The reason for the start of events was the process that started in Tunisia. Mohammad Bouazizi, a college graduate and an unemployed young man, lost his life in the hospital after he set himself on fire in front of the municipal building on 18 December 2010, because the municipal police officers broke up his desk and tortured him while he was a peddler (Gocer and Cinar, 2015).

14 There is a proverb in Turkish saying "Hungry dog drills the oven". That is, when a person is hungry and poor, he becomes available to get into a bad path.

15 With China joining the World Trade Organization in 2001 and making it easier to sell goods to the world, 92% of toy manufacturers in Turkey have left production and imported cheap toys from this country. This situation has led to production, employment and foreign exchange loss in the country. Moreover, despite the fact that harmful chemical substances are detected in children's toys imported from China, healthy local products cannot be replaced by them (Dunya, 2014).

Chapter 7
Trade Competitiveness in Developing Countries

Nazlı Karamollaoğlu
MEF University, Turkey

ABSTRACT

This chapter explores the various dimensions of trade competitiveness in developing countries. After discussing various definitions of competitiveness, the importance of trade competitiveness is discussed in the context of developing countries with reference to the existing literature. Subsequently, major constraints that affect trade competitiveness, particularly macroeconomic conditions, institutional and business environments, and infrastructure, are discussed. Finally, recent empirical findings on trade competitiveness are summarized.

INTRODUCTION

Over the last quarter century, trade has been accepted as a central driver of growth and development for developing countries. The share of developing countries in trade flows has increased tremendously, now making up almost 40 percent of world trade. With this huge expansion of trade, international competition has greatly increased. In today's world, to be able to survive in global markets, developing countries need to stay competitive.

In general, competitiveness has been defined as the measure of a country's advantage in selling its products in international markets (Organisation for Economic Cooperation and Development [OECD], 2014). Nevertheless, the definition of competitiveness is not unique. For this reason, in the first section of this chapter, we present different perspectives on how to measure competitiveness. After that,

DOI: 10.4018/978-1-5225-4032-8.ch007

with reference to the existing literature, we focus on the importance of trade competitiveness for developing economies. In this regard, the growth enhancing effect of trade, the impact of different trade policies on economic growth, as well as the link between productivity and exporting is discussed. Subsequently, major challenges for developing countries to maintain their competitiveness level in international markets are outlined. In this framework, the potential impact of macroeconomic instability, in particular focusing on exchange rate and inflation, is assessed. In addition to macroeconomic imbalances, other challenges related to institutional and business environments, as well as infrastructure are also presented. Finally, recent empirical evidence on various dimensions of trade competitiveness using firm-level micro data is discussed. This line of research is interesting, not only for understanding the dynamics of trade competitiveness in the context of developing countries, but also for developing policy recommendations.

BACKGROUND

Trade policy and its potential to enhance growth has been at the center of the economic debate since the Mercantilist view in the 17th century. Since that time, views have changed dramatically. In the early days, trade policies favoring "import substitution" were predominantly believed to achieve growth prospects. However, after the 1970s and 1980s saw the failure of import-substitution strategies, export promotion and outward oriented policies became popular instead.

Trade is a major element of economic growth and poverty reduction. In fact, the idea that trade is an engine for growth dates back to Adam Smith and David Ricardo. Adam Smith considers trade to be a positive-sum game. During the trading process, if countries specialize in the production of goods in which they have absolute advantages, all parties win (as cited in Moon, 2000). The other famous classical economist, David Ricardo, in his famous work "On the Principles of Political Economy and Taxation" also stressed the role of free trade in promoting efficiency and productivity in the economy. Ricardo, by building on Smiths' absolute advantage theory, claimed that all countries gain from free trade by producing what they are best at in comparison to other countries.

During the 17th and 18th centuries, before the free trade argument, mercantilism was the dominant economic philosophy. During this time, a large number of development economists favored the protectionist view with the aim of protecting domestic industries and jobs from foreign competition. Throughout this period, protectionist trade policies in the form of import substitution were dominant. In the context of this import substitution type of industrialization, it was argued that a country should attempt to reduce its reliance on imported goods through the domestic production of industrialized products. Proponents of this view strongly believed in the protection of infant industries; nascent domestic industries that need protection against international competition until becoming mature and competitive. In this regard, foreign imports are replaced by local production.

The 1980's Latin American Debt crisis was a turning point in reshaping the policy debate favoring protectionism. Anecdotal evidence showed that import substitution policies, which were dominant in Latin American countries, were unsustainable. When contrasted with the strong trajectories of their East Asian counterparts, which had aggressively implemented outward oriented strategies, it was evident that the Latin American countries' growth trajectories were weak. Table 1 from Edwards (1993, p.1360) illustrates this sharp contrast between the growth rates of Selected East Asian and Latin American Countries. The solid growth rates experienced in East Asian countries which were conducting outward oriented strategies put protectionism and its impact on promoting growth into the center of discussion regarding trade policy.

The impact that trade policy has on promoting growth has been an important debate in the second half of the twentieth century. The vast body of empirical work that was conducted during the 1970s and 1980s emphasized the role of export promotion policies in promoting growth. Since then, it has been argued that export expansion contributes to economic growth by increasing the rate of capital formation and enhancing the growth of factor productivity (Kavoussi, 1984). These policies are now considered to be the best development strategies for developing countries.

Amongst the earlier and most well-known work, Michaely (1977), using a sample of 41 developing countries, reported a positive relationship between proportional per capita income growth and the proportional increase in the ratio of exports to GNP. His results document that this relationship was very strong for the 23 most developed countries in his sample. However, there was no relationship with the poorest countries in the study, implying that growth is only affected by export performance once countries achieve a minimum level of development. A subsequent study by Balassa (1978), based on a group of 11 developing countries that already had an industrial base, tested the hypothesis that export-oriented policies lead to better growth performance than policies favoring import substitution. The results of his study document a significant and positive relationship between economic growth and export performance. Chow (1987), based on a sample of eight Newly Industrializing Countries (NICs), shows that for the majority of these countries, there is robust bidirectional causality between the growth of exports and the development of manufacturing industries. These findings suggest that an increase in exports not only promotes the growth of national income but also leads to industrial development, thus supporting the export-led growth strategies. Tyler (1981) documents a significant positive association between economic growth and exports as well as various other economic variables, including the growth of manufacturing output and investment, based on a large sample of developing countries. Similarly, Kavoussi (1984) shows that export expansion is associated with better economic performance for both low and middle-income countries. Kavoussi (1984) also stresses that the rise in productivity resulting from export expansion is an important cause of the positive correlation between the growth rates of exports and GNP.

Although export promotion was the dominant view in the literature during this time, there are a small number of studies, which cast doubt on the efficacy of export-promotion policies in fostering economic growth. Singer and Gray (1988) highlight the fall in external demand regarding the export-growth link. They document that when external demand is weak, the positive impact of outward-oriented policies

Table 1. Growth and exports in Latin America and East Asia: 1965-1989 (percentage distribution)

	Annual Rate of Growth of Real GDP		**Annual Rate of Growth of Manufacturing**		**Annual Rate of Growth of Exports**	
	1965-80	**1980-89**	**1965-80**	**1980-89**	**1965-80**	**1980-89**
Selected Latin American Countries						
Argentina	3.5	-0.3	2.7	-0.6	4.7	0.6
Brazil	8.8	3.0	9.8	2.2	9.3	5.6
Chile	1.9	2.7	0.6	2.9	7.9	4.9
Colombia	5.8	3.5	6.4	3.1	1.4	9.8
Mexico	6.5	0.7	7.4	0.7	7.6	3.7
Peru	3.9	0.4	3.8	0.4	1.6	0.4
Venezuela	3.7	1.0	5.8	4.9	-9.5	11.3
Latin America & Caribbean (Average)	6.0	1.6	7.0	1.5	-1.0	3.6
Selected East Asian Countries						
Hong Kong	8.6	7.1	n.a.	n.a.	9.5	6.2
Indonesia	8.0	5.3	12.0	12.7	9.6	2.4
Korea	9.6	9.7	18.7	13.1	27.2	13.8
Malaysia	7.3	4.9	--	8.0	4.4	9.8
Singapore	10.1	6.1	13.2	5.9	4.7	8.1
Thailand	7.2	7.0	11.2	8.1	8.5	12.8
East Asia (Average)	7.2	7.9	10.6	12.6	10.0	10.0

Source: Edwards (1993, p.1360).

disappear, particularly for poorer developing countries. They also argue that outward-oriented policies are not always an effective policy choice. Rodriguez and Rodrick (2000) find little evidence that open-trade policies (in the form of lower tariff and nontariff barriers to trade) are significantly associated with economic growth. Later work by Yanikkaya (2003) investigates the relationship between economic growth and a wide variety of trade-openness measures. These are divided into two categories: measures of trade volumes; and measures of trade restrictions. Unlike the vast body of empirical studies, while the results for various measures of trade volumes are generally consistent with the literature, Rodriguez and Rodrick's (2000) results illustrate that trade barriers are positively and significantly associated with growth. This suggests that trade barriers can actually be beneficial for economic growth.

The availability of firm-level data also presented the link between export participation and productivity. Amongst the earlier work, Aw and Hwang (1995), based on micro-level data on the Taiwanese electronic industry, documented that there are significant differences in productivity levels between exporters and non-exporters. With the increasing availability of longitudinal-plant or firm-level data, literature further documented the existence of considerable divergence in productivity levels among establishments in similar industries (Bernard & Jensen 1995, 1999, 2004a, 2004b; Baldwin & Gu, 2003). This evidence formed the foundation of the New-New trade theory, which was first presented in Melitz (2003). Within the context of the New-New trade model, cross-firm heterogeneity has been accepted as the major driver of international trade. In this framework, there exist barriers to engaging in export activity, and only firms with productivities above a certain level, called threshold productivity, are able to export. The recent literature on heterogeneous firms highlights that exporters are, on average, more productive, capital intensive, larger, and pay higher wages than non-exporters (Bernard, Jensen, & Lawrence, 2007). This line of literature has also documented that at an aggregate level, exporting contributes to productivity growth at industry level as well as at country level.

MAIN FOCUS OF THE CHAPTER

General Overview of Competitiveness

In general, competitiveness has been defined as a measure of a country's advantage in selling its products in international markets (OECD, 2014). However, no single definition of competitiveness has gained general acceptance in the literature. The concept of competitiveness is broad and multifaceted, including both price and non-price factors, and can be analyzed at three different levels: national or macroeconomic level; sector level; or firm or micro-economic level.

Price-related factors that are used while measuring competitiveness are indices relating to the terms of trade, unit labor cost, and the real effect of exchange rates. An increase or appreciation of these factors often creates a cost disadvantage for domestic producers in international markets, which diminishes the countries' or firms' competitive positions. According to Lall (2001), this approach "assumes underlying structural factors, such as productivity, innovation, and skills, are constant or irrelevant and focuses on short-term macroeconomic factors that affect relative prices of national goods and services relative to other countries". In addition to price-related factors, qualitative measures, referred to as non-price factors, have often been considered when measuring countries' competitiveness levels. These include factors, such as technology, the performance of public institutions, the macro-economic environment, education, and the business environment.

A common approach to measuring macro-level competitiveness is to build an index, which constitutes both price and non-price related factors. In this framework, competitiveness is measured as a combination of a set of factors, policies, institutions, strategies, and processes, that determine the level of sustainable productivity (World Economic Forum, Global Competitiveness Report, 2014). A well-known index for competitiveness is the Global Competitiveness Index (GCI) developed by Xavier Sala-i-Martín in collaboration with the World Economic Forum. The GCI includes over one hundred indicators belonging to 12 main groups, spanning from institutions, infrastructure, macroeconomic environment, education, and labor and goods market efficiency, to financial market development and innovation, all of which are closely related to the concepts that affect productivity and long-term prosperity

The realm of this chapter is to investigate the concept of trade competitiveness. Trade competitiveness deals with a country's (or sector's, or firm's) position, performance, and capabilities in the export markets (World Bank, 2014). When we measure "trade competitiveness", the conventional approach is to use indicators, such as the level of openness (total exports and imports in goods and services as a percentage of GDP), or the growth of exports over a given period (International Trade Centre [ITC], n.d.

). This type of quantitative measurement has the advantage of being accessible for many countries at a more disaggregated level (at either industry or product level), which enables us to analyze trade dynamics in more detail for a broader set of countries. However, taking into consideration metrics that are only based on exports and export performance is not sufficient when measuring trade competitiveness. Solid export performance does not always result in higher rates of GDP growth, therefore other measures, both qualitative and quantitative, such as interdependencies between imports and exports, international flows of capital, investment, and human capital also need to be considered when measuring trade competitiveness (World Bank, 2014).

The World Bank has introduced a useful approach to measure trade competitiveness, known as the Trade Competitiveness Diagnostic (TCD). There are two components of the TCD, namely Trade Outcome Analysis and Competitiveness Diagnostics. Trade Outcomes Analysis presents a summary of trade performance and trade competitiveness, while Competitiveness Diagnostics focus on understanding the underlying policies and structural dynamics that shape observed performance. The first component, Trade Outcome Analysis, provides a quantitative and qualitative assessment of historic trade performance. This involves identifying four major channels through which a country's trade competitiveness can be measured. These channels are: (1) the intensive margin which measures the value of exported goods for existing products and markets; (2) the extensive margin which measures the value of exported goods for different products and markets[1]; (3) the quality margin which represents the quality and sophistication of exports; and (4) the sustainability margin which measures the entry and survival of new exporters. The second component of the TCD is Competitiveness Diagnostics. In this component, market access, supply-side factors, and trade-promotion infrastructure are all considered. Market access focuses on the external trade policy environment, including tariffs and quantitative restrictions, which may facilitate or constrain exporters from entering and maintaining competitiveness in export markets. Supply-side factors cover factors that influence private-sector investment and participation in exports, and factor conditions that contribute to the cost and quality of production including land and infrastructure intermediate inputs. Trade promotion infrastructure, on the other hand, represents government interventions (such as export promotion policies and special economic zones) which are implemented in an attempt to address market failures.

Another useful index is the Trade Performance Index (TPI), which measures trade competitiveness. This was developed by the International Trade Centre (ITC). One major difference between the World Bank's approach and the TPI is that the TPI is based purely on quantitative metrics of export performance. Using several quantitative performance indicators, the TPI provides information on a country's general trade profile, current trade performance, and changes in recent export performance.

In addition to macro/country-level competitiveness, competitiveness can be analyzed at a more disaggregated level, such as at the level of firm or product. Porter (1998) argues that as wealth is created at the microeconomic level, then competitiveness can be ascertained from the point of each individual firm. Porter (2007) also stresses the importance of a broader set of factors for a healthy economy, which include sound macroeconomic, political, legal, and social circumstances. However, he states that while these conditions are necessary, they are not sufficient on their own. He, therefore, strongly advocates improvement at a micro level. According to Porter (1998; 2007), company strategies and operating practices as well as the quality of the microeconomic business environment are extremely important. Even if macroeconomic, political, legal, and social reforms are present, these reforms will not be successful if there is no improvement at the microeconomic level.

Challenges to Competitiveness

Developing country exporters face several limitations that negatively impact their potential to engage in export activities. In particular, macroeconomic stability is an important factor for trade competitiveness, as exchange rates and inflation are major channels through which developing countries' trade competitiveness may be affected.

The exchange rate is an important determinant of trade competitiveness because, as a result of the depreciation of a domestic currency, the value of exported goods denominated in a foreign currency decreases, which subsequently results in an increase in foreign demand. This effect is often referred as the competitiveness channel.[1] Although domestic currency depreciation is preferable due to its impact on the foreign value of domestic products in international markets, when analyzing the impact of exchange rates on export competitiveness, other channels play an important role. For example, the production processes of developing countries are highly dependent on intermediate goods which are often imported. This means that if currency depreciation occurs, the production costs of companies that rely on these imported, intermediate inputs increase. This leads to a cost disadvantage, which is referred to as the cost of production channel. This cost of production channel operates inversely to the competitiveness channel. Added to this, most developing countries suffer from high dollarization rates, which leads to the inability of these countries to borrow internationally in their own currency. Eichengreen and Haussman (2010) refer to this situation as "original sin", as when such a currency mismatch occurs, the subsequent currency depreciation results in an increase in the book value of debt which negatively affects firm-level financial variables.[2] This results in the need for the continued financing of sunk costs to increase exports, which then leads to a contractionary effect on exports, referred to as the balance sheet channel. If one considers the real exchange rate to be a measure of competitiveness, one should also take into account the competitiveness channel, cost of production channel, and balance sheet channel. Therefore, the total effect of the exchange rate on competitiveness is ultimately determined by the relative magnitude of the counterbalancing effects of these three channels. Literature examining the link between the volume of exports and real exchange rates show that, in general, exchange rates have an insignificant effect on trade volumes. However, studies using more disaggregated level, sectoral or firm level data, often find exchange rate depreciations have a significant (and positive) impact on trade volumes. Among these studies, Dekle and Ryoo (2007) and Dekle, Jeong, and Ryoo (2009) document a significant relationship between export volumes and exchange rates. Similarly, Forbes (2002) examines the results of large devaluations on firms' performances, and finds that, on average, export sales increase by 4 percent, one year after each devaluation episode.

As mentioned previously, price stability is another important factor involved in export competitiveness, as high and unstable price levels have a direct effect on real exchange rates. Empirical research has shown that this leads to high inflation which has a negative impact on exports. For example, Gylfason (1999), using data covering 160 countries from 1985-94, documents that high inflation has been associated with low exports and sluggish growth. In addition to the effects of the real exchange rate on inflation, Gylfason (1999) also stresses the distortive capacity of inflation on production, as it drives a wedge between the returns on real and financial capital as well as having a negative impact on real interest rates; this then negatively impacts savings and the quality of investment.

Developing countries frequently suffer from an unfavorable business climate. Dethier, Hirn, and Straub (2010) stress that a favorable business or investment climate is important for attracting investment, as well as for creating new opportunities for trade and access to new technologies. Similarly, Balchin (2008), based on data covering eight African countries, suggests that a country's business climate is closely associated with its probability for exporting. Dollar, Hallward-Driemeier, and Mengistae (2006), based on firm-level surveys on several developing countries, document that a sound investment climate has a positive impact on both exports and foreign investment.

Amongst the most notable, Hall and Jones (2001) bring attention to the concept of social infrastructure described as the set of institutions and government policies that determine the economic environment of a country. They believe that a country's long-term economic performance is determined primarily by the social infrastructure. That a country should have strong institutions has been widely stressed as being an important factor in the performance of international trade (Levchenko, 2007; Dollar and Kray, 2003). Levchenko (2007), using data on U.S. imports, examines the link between institutional quality and international trade. The empirical results provide evidence that institutional differences, measured by institutional dependence and institutional quality, are an important determinant of trade flows. Anderson and Marcouiller (2002) stress the role of corruption and imperfect contract enforcement in reducing international trade. Estimating a structural model of import demand, they document that poor institutions have a negative impact on trade similar to that of tariffs. Dutt and Traca (2010) investigated the impact of corruption on trade. Their results document that corruption has a negative impact on bilateral trade for the majority of countries, but when the level of tariffs is high, corruption can have a positive impact on trade. It is presumed this may happen as corrupt officials in high tariff environments may allow exporters to avoid paying tariffs. Linders, Slangen, De Groot, and Beugelsdijk (2005), based on a sample of bilateral trade flows between 92 countries, found that institutional distance negatively effects bilateral trade through increasing transactional costs between partners from dissimilar institutional settings.[3] The study also reports that if the institutional quality of importing and exporting partners increases, then the trade among them also increases.

Financial health has also been reported as an important constraint regarding the trading behavior of firms. Among firm-level empirical studies, Bellone, Musso, Nesta, and Schiavo (2010), using French data, found strong evidence that less credit-constrained firms self-select into export. Likewise, Forlani (2008) found that the probability for export was negatively and significantly affected by financial constraints in a panel of Italian firms. Muûls (2008) found the same with Belgian firms. Berman and Hericourt (2010) in their study using a large cross-country, firm-level database on developing and emerging economies, show that a firm's access to finance positively affects their entry decision into the export market. Manova (2013) also stresses the role of financial development in increasing a country's exports. Minetti and Zhu (2011), utilizing survey data from Italian manufacturing firms that provide a firm-specific measure of credit rationing, found that the probability for export is 39% lower for credit-rationed firms and that credit- rationing reduces foreign sales by more than 38%.

Finally, the quality of infrastructure, through its impact on transportation costs, has also been stressed as an important determinant of trade performance. Limao and Venables (2001) highlight the close relationship between infrastructure and transport costs, especially for non-coastal countries. Their analysis, based on a data covering African trade flows, indicate that a low level of trade is largely associated with poor infrastructure. Wilson, Mann, and Otsuki (2005) investigated the impact of several trade facilitation measures, namely port efficiency, the customs environment, the regulatory environment, and service sector infrastructure on trade flows. They found that both the imports and exports of a given country increase with improvements to these trade facilitation measures. Similarly, Nordas and Piermartini (2004) and Francoise and Manchin (2013), reported that the quality of infrastructure is an important determinant of trade performance.

Empirical Literature on Trade Competitiveness

Elucidating the sources of export growth is important in order to understand which main channels affect a country's level of competitiveness. In a simple framework, a given country's export growth may result from the expansion of trade of existing products (the intensive margin) or entering new export markets or selling new products (the extensive margin). Literature examining the contributions of both of these margins on export growth presents inconclusive results. Among existing studies, regarding the effect of the intensive margin, Amurgo-Pacheco (2008) opines that export growth is mostly explained by growth at the intensive margin. Similarly, Besedes and Prusa (2011) argue that developing countries should improve their performance in the intensive margin if they want to increase their exports. Their study shows the contribution of the extensive margin to export growth, in the form of establishing new partners and markets, only has a short-term impact on exports and a negligible impact on a country's long-term export growth. They therefore conclude that the extensive margin is only of moderate importance. However, a number of researchers argue the reverse. Hummels and Klenow (2005), report that for larger economies, it is the extensive margin, which accounts for 60 percent of exports. In addition, Evenett and Venables (2002) opine that a third of the growth of exports of developing countries between 1970 and 1997 could be attributed to the sales of existing exports to new trading partners. They refer to this expansion as geographic spread, which is dependent on the geographic and linguistic proximity between trading partners. These conflicting findings are often purported to be due to the differences in the measurement of these two margins.

Developing countries' exports tend to be limited to a few products, which can result in volatile export revenues. It has therefore been argued that policies which support export diversification may create a more stable income inflow. Amurgo-Pacheco (2008) shows that the level of export diversification between developed and developing countries differs.[4] The results of their study show that export diversification is on the rise among developing countries and, when comparing two different dimensions of export diversification (product and geographical), it is geographical diversification that actually matters more than product diversification.[7]

Another set of papers investigate the impact of specific economic policies on export performance in developing countries. For example, Martincus and Carballo (2008) investigated the effects of export promotion activities (EPAs) in Peru over the period 2001-2005. The authors stress that informational problems are more severe when firms attempt to expand along the extensive margin rather than attempting to expand along the intensive margin. The empirical results document that export promotion activities have been effective in increasing exports, primarily along the extensive margin. However, the study fails to identify any impacts of such policies on the intensive margins of exports. In a later study, Martincus and Carballo (2010) investigated the impact of trade promotion activities using disaggregated export data on Chilean exporters over the 2002-2006 period. The study highlights the fact that the impact of export promotion activities can differ over the distribution of export performance measured by the growth of exports for the intensive margin and by the growth of the number of countries and number of products for the extensive margin. For the intensive margin, the impact is mostly concentrated at the lower tail of the distribution, while for the extensive margin, the impact is at the lower and upper ends of the distributions. Martincus and Carballo (2010) imply that smaller firms seem to benefit the most from export promotion actions. Seker (2011), using a dataset that comprises a wide set of countries with different income levels, investigated the link between investment climate and export performances. The study reports that regulatory quality, customs efficiency, quality of infrastructure, and access to finance is associated with increasing export performance. The study also reports a comparatively high impact on improvements in the investment climate on the export performance of countries that are relatively more constrained in access to foreign markets. This implies that for closed economies, efforts toward the development of a favorable investment climate should be an important policy objective in order to increase export levels and catch up with countries with liberal trade policies. Based on different country groupings, Hallaert, Cavazos-Cepeda, and Kang (2011) study attempts to measure the impact of binding constraints on trade expansion. Their study shows that in small and vulnerable economies, increasing the number and quality of roads has an important impact on trade and on economic growth. On the other hand, restrictive trade policies (measured by custom tariffs) seem to have a greater impact on the trade performance of landlocked countries, rather than coastal countries. For commodity exporters, the study reports that the tariff regime is a major constraint to trade performance.

In today's world, the dynamics of international trade is changing. With globalization, interconnectedness between economies has been increasing, and Global value chains (GVCs) play an increasing role in international trading activities. In this new set-up, the production process has been fragmented into separate countries. Existing research identifies that developing countries' participation in GVCs has been increasing in recent years. This is important, as much theoretical and empirical literature has documented that a country's participation in GVCs can improve its productivity performance. For example, Baldwin and Yan (2014), based on Canadian firm level-data found strong empirical evidence of a causal link between GVC participation and firm-level productivity. The study reports that Canadian manufacturing firms which joined the GVCs became more productive than those that did not. Similarly, Giovannetti, Marvasi, and Sanfilippo (2015) show that even small and less productive firms, if involved in production chains, can take advantage of the reduced costs of entry and economies of scale, and that this enhances their ability to export. Country-specific structural factors, such as geography, size of the domestic market and level of development, are found to be key determinants of GVC participation. Low import tariffs, engagement in regional trading agreements, logistics performance, intellectual property protection, the quality of infrastructure, as well as the quality of institutions (particularly for developing countries) are major policy tools which are estimated to have strong impacts on GVC integration (Kowalski, Gonzalez, Ragoussis, & Ugarte, 2015).

SOLUTIONS AND RECOMMENDATIONS

As the constraints they face are numerous, maintaining trade competitiveness is a challenging task for developing countries. Obtaining a well-functioning institutional framework, financial development, an absence of corruption and crime, and a strong regulatory framework are key for developing countries in order to establish a favorable business climate for domestic and foreign investors. Moving into the fourth industrial revolution has had the effect of putting innovation and technology to the fore of these competitiveness efforts. Therefore, just as human capital, through its impact on innovative activity, is an important factor for competitiveness for developing countries, technology, too, is important determinant for competitiveness.

Instead of building full supply chains, domestically developing countries have the option of joining GVCs to become competitive. Therefore involvement in global value chains will also bring economic benefits in the form of increasing productivity, advanced skills, and a more sophisticated and diversified export portfolio (Kowalski et al. 2015).

Finally, macroeconomic instability through its impact predominantly on prices may diminish a country's competitive position, thus a stable exchange rate and low inflation are key to help developing countries.

FUTURE RESEARCH DIRECTIONS

The impact of trade on generating growth is an extensively studied research topic in the context of both developing and developed countries. Firm-level micro-data from developing countries which has recently become available means it is now possible to extend the research by analyzing the sources of export growth from different angles. This will make this line of research very fruitful. Despite the availability of micro-data on exports and imports at firm or very disaggregated industry level, the comparability of the existing studies remains a challenge due to the differences in the data (units of analysis, sampling processes), the execution of the empirical model, or differences in the definitions of trade margins. Regarding future research, cross-country studies, with comparable techniques and data, will be useful to reconcile currently conflicting evidence in the literature.

CONCLUSION

In this chapter, with reference to the existing literature, the various aspects of trade competitiveness were investigated in the context of developing countries. It was highlighted that maintaining trade competitiveness is fundamental for developing countries given the positive impact of exporting on economic growth and productivity. However, developing nations face many constraints, which means they have a challenging task in maintaining trade competitiveness. Macroeconomic instability, particularly volatile exchange rates and high inflation, puts constraints on the competitiveness level. In addition, providing the main elements needed to form a favorable business climate, characterized by strong institutions, financial development, security, infrastructure, is hard for developing countries to achieve. Therefore, in order to establish a solid competitive framework, developing countries' governments must work on these areas in collaboration with the private sector. Challenges may exist but proper implementation of the necessary policies and structural reforms have the potential to contribute to the competitiveness level of developing economies.

REFERENCES

Ali, R., Alwang, J. R., & Siegel, P. B. (1991). *Is export diversification the best way to achieve export growth and stability? A look at three African countries* (World Bank Working Paper No. 729). Retrieved from World Bank website: http://documents.worldbank.org/curated/en/635281468774612514/pdf/multi0page.pdf

Amurgo-Pacheco, A. (2008). *Patterns of export diversification in developing countries* (World Bank Policy Research Working Paper No. 4473). Retrieved from World Bank website: https://openknowledge.worldbank.org/bitstream/handle/10986/6447/wps4473.pdf?sequence=1

Anderson, J. E., & Marcouiller, D. (2002). Insecurity and the pattern of trade: An empirical investigation. *The Review of Economics and Statistics*, *84*(2), 342–352. doi:10.1162/003465302317411587

Aw, B. Y., & Hwang, A. R. M. (1995). Productivity and the export market: A firm-level analysis. *Journal of Development Economics*, *47*(2), 313–332. doi:10.1016/0304-3878(94)00062-H

Balassa, B. (1978). Exports and economic growth: Further evidence. *Journal of Development Economics*, *5*(2), 181–189. doi:10.1016/0304-3878(78)90006-8

Balchin, L. (2008). Trade-related business climate and manufacturing export performance in Africa: A firm-level analysis. *Journal of Development Perspectives*, *4*(1), 32–66.

Baldwin, J. R., & Gu, W. (2003). Export-market participation and productivity performance in Canadian manufacturing. *The Canadian Journal of Economics. Revue Canadienne d'Economique*, *36*(3), 634–657. doi:10.1111/1540-5982.t01-2-00006

Baldwin, J. R., & Yan, B. (2014). *Global value chains and the productivity of Canadian manufacturing firms* (Statistics Canada Economic Research Paper No. 090). Retrieved from Statistics Canada website http://www.statcan.gc.ca/pub/11f0027m/11f0027m2014090-eng.pdf

Bellone, F., Musso, P., Nesta, L., & Schiavo, S. (2010). Financial constraints and firm export behaviour. *World Economy*, *33*(3), 347–373. doi:10.1111/j.1467-9701.2010.01259.x

Berman, N., & Héricourt, J. (2010). Financial factors and the margins of trade: Evidence from cross-country firm-level data. *Journal of Development Economics*, *93*(2), 206–217. doi:10.1016/j.jdeveco.2009.11.006

Bernard, A. B., & Jensen, J. B. (1999). Exceptional exporter performance: Cause, effect, or both? *Journal of International Economics*, *47*(1), 1–25. doi:10.1016/S0022-1996(98)00027-0

Bernard, A. B., & Jensen, J. B. (2004a). Exporting and Productivity in the USA. *Oxford Review of Economic Policy*, *20*(3), 343–357. doi:10.1093/oxrep/grh020

Bernard, A. B., & Jensen, J. B. (2004b). Why some firms export. *The Review of Economics and Statistics*, *86*(2), 561–569. doi:10.1162/003465304323031111

Bernard, A. B., Jensen, J. B., & Lawrence, R. Z. (1995). Exporters, jobs, and wages in US manufacturing: 1976-1987. *Brookings papers on economic activity. Microeconomics*, *1995*, 67–119.

Bernard, A. B., Jensen, J. B., Redding, S. J., & Schott, P. K. (2007). Firms in international trade. *The Journal of Economic Perspectives*, *21*(3), 105–130. doi:10.1257/jep.21.3.105

Besedeš, T., & Prusa, T. J. (2011). The role of extensive and intensive margins and export growth. *Journal of Development Economics*, *96*(2), 371–379. doi:10.1016/j.jdeveco.2010.08.013

Chow, P. C. (1987). Causality between export growth and industrial development: Empirial evidence from the NICs. *Journal of Development Economics*, *26*(1), 55–63. doi:10.1016/0304-3878(87)90051-4

Competitiveness (In International Trade). (2014). In *OECD Glossary of Statistical Terms*. Retrieved from https://stats.oecd.org/glossary/detail.asp?ID=399

Dekle, R., Jeong, H., & Ryoo, H. (2009). *A Re-Examination of the Exchange Rate Disconnect Puzzle: Evidence from Firm Level Data*. University of Sourthern California mimeo.

Dekle, R., & Ryoo, H. H. (2007). Exchange rate fluctuations, financing constraints, hedging, and exports: Evidence from firm level data. *Journal of International Financial Markets, Institutions and Money*, *17*(5), 437–451. doi:10.1016/j.intfin.2006.04.001

Dethier, J. J., Hirn, M., & Straub, S. (2010). Explaining enterprise performance in developing countries with business climate survey data. *The World Bank Research Observer*, *26*(2), 258–309. doi:10.1093/wbro/lkq007

Dollar, D., Hallward-Driemeier, M., & Mengistae, T. (2006). Investment climate and international integration. *World Development*, *34*(9), 1498–1516. doi:10.1016/j.worlddev.2006.05.001

Dollar, D., & Kraay, A. (2003). Institutions, trade, and growth. *Journal of Monetary Economics*, *50*(1), 133–162. doi:10.1016/S0304-3932(02)00206-4

Dutt, P., & Traca, D. (2010). Corruption and bilateral trade flows: Extortion or evasion? *The Review of Economics and Statistics*, *92*(4), 843–860. doi:10.1162/REST_a_00034

Edwards, S. (1993). Openness, trade liberalization, and growth in developing countries. *Journal of Economic Literature*, *31*(3), 1358–1393.

Eichengreen, B., & Hausmann, R. (2005). *Other People's Money*. University of Chicago Press. doi:10.7208/chicago/9780226194578.001.0001

Evenett, S. J., & Venables, A. (2002). *Export growth by developing economies: Market entry and bilateral trade* (Swiss Institute for International Economics and Applied Economic Research Working Paper). Retrieved from the Swiss Institute for International Economics and Applied Economic Research: https://www.alexandria.unisg.ch/22177/1/setvend.pdf

Forbes, K. J. (2002). *How do large depreciations affect firm performance? (NBER Working Paper 9095)*. Cambridge, MA: National Bureau of Economic Research. Retrieved from the National Bureau of Economic Research. doi:10.3386/w9095

Forlani, E. (2008). *Firms Credit Constraints and Export Propensity*. Mimeo CORE/ Université Catholique de Louvain.

Francois, J., & Manchin, M. (2013). Institutions, infrastructure, and trade. *World Development*, *46*, 165–175. doi:10.1016/j.worlddev.2013.02.009

Giovannetti, G., Marvasi, E., & Sanfilippo, M. (2015). Supply chains and the internationalization of small firms. *Small Business Economics*, *44*(4), 845–865. doi:10.1007/s11187-014-9625-x

Goldberg, P. K., & Knetter, M. M. (1997). Goods Prices and Exchange Rates: What Have We Learned? *Journal of Economic Literature*, *35*(3), 1243–1272.

Gylfason, T. (1999). Exports, inflation and growth. *World Development*, *27*(6), 1031–1057. doi:10.1016/S0305-750X(99)00045-5

Hall, R. E., & Jones, C. I. (1999). Why do some countries produce so much more output per worker than others? *The Quarterly Journal of Economics*, *114*(1), 83–116. doi:10.1162/003355399555954

Hallaert, J. J., Cavazos-Cepeda, R. H., & Kang, G. (2011). *Estimating the constraints to trade of developing countries. (OECD Trade Policy Papers No. 116)*. OECD. doi:10.1787/18166873

Hummels, D., & Klenow, P. J. (2005). The variety and quality of a nation's exports. *The American Economic Review*, *95*(3), 704–723. doi:10.1257/0002828054201396

International Trade Center (ITC). (n.d.). *Trade Performance Index*. Retrieved May 20, 2017, from http://tradecompetitivenessmap.intracen.org/Documents/TradeCompMap-Trade%20Performance%20Index-Technical%20Notes-EN.pdf

Kaufmann, D., Kraay, A., & Mastruzzi, M. (2003). *Governance Matters III: governance indicators for 1996-2002* (World Bank Policy Research Department Working Paper). Retrieved from World Bank website: https://elibrary.worldbank.org/doi/abs/10.1596/1813-9450-3106

Kavoussi, R. M. (1984). Export expansion and economic growth: Further empirical evidence. *Journal of Development Economics*, *14*(1), 241–250. doi:10.1016/0304-3878(84)90052-X

Kowalski, P., Gonzalez, J. L., Ragoussis, A., & Ugarte, C. (2015). *Participation of Developing Countries in Global Value Chains: Implications for Trade and Trade-Related Policies (OECD Trade Policy Papers, No. 179)*. Paris: OECD Publishing. Retrieved from the OECD. doi:10.1787/18166873

Lall, S. (2001). Competitiveness indices and developing countries: An economic evaluation of the global competitiveness report. *World Development*, *29*(9), 1501–1525. doi:10.1016/S0305-750X(01)00051-1

Levchenko, A. A. (2007). Institutional quality and international trade. *The Review of Economic Studies*, *74*(3), 791–819. doi:10.1111/j.1467-937X.2007.00435.x

Limao, N., & Venables, A. J. (2001). Infrastructure, geographical disadvantage, transport costs, and trade. *The World Bank Economic Review*, *15*(3), 451–479. doi:10.1093/wber/15.3.451

Linders, G. J., Slangen, H. L. A., De Groot, H. L., & Beugelsdijk, S. (2005). *Cultural and institutional determinants of bilateral trade flows* (Tinbergen Institute Discussion Paper No. 2005-074/3). Retrieved from the Tinbergen Institute: http://papers.tinbergen.nl/05074.pdf

Manova, K. (2013). Credit constraints, heterogeneous firms, and international trade. *The Review of Economic Studies*, *80*(2), 711–744. doi:10.1093/restud/rds036

Martincus, C. V., & Carballo, J. (2008). Is export promotion effective in developing countries? Firm-level evidence on the intensive and the extensive margins of exports. *Journal of International Economics*, *76*(1), 89–106. doi:10.1016/j.jinteco.2008.05.002

Martincus, C. V., & Carballo, J. (2010). Beyond the average effects: The distributional impacts of export promotion programs in developing countries. *Journal of Development Economics*, *92*(2), 201–214. doi:10.1016/j.jdeveco.2009.02.007

Melitz, M. J. (2003). The impact of trade on intra-industry reallocations and aggregate industry productivity. *Econometrica*, *71*(6), 1695–1725. doi:10.1111/1468-0262.00467

Michaely, M. (1977). Exports and growth: An empirical investigation. *Journal of Development Economics*, *4*(1), 49–53. doi:10.1016/0304-3878(77)90006-2

Minetti, R., & Zhu, S. C. (2011). Credit constraints and firm export: Microeconomic evidence from Italy. *Journal of International Economics*, *83*(2), 109–125. doi:10.1016/j.jinteco.2010.12.004

Moon, H. C. (2000). *From Adam Smith to Michael Porter: Evolution of Competitiveness Theory* (Vol. 2). World Scientific.

Muûls, M. (2008). *Exporters and credit constraints. A firm level approach* (National Bank of Belgium, Working Paper No. 139). Brussels National Bank of Belgium (NBB). Retrieved from the NBB: https://www.nbb.be/doc/ts/publications/wp/wp139en.pdf

Nordås, H. K., & Piermartini, R. (2004). *Infrastructure and trade*. (World Trade Organization Staff Working Paper ERSD-2004-04). Genève: WTO. Retrieved from the WTO: https://www.wto.org/english/res_e/reser_e/ersd200404_e.htm

Porter, M. E. (1999). The Microeconomic Foundations of Economic Development. In *The Global Competitiveness Report*. Geneva, Switzerland: World Economic Forum.

Porter, M. E. (2004). Building the Microeconomic Foundations of Prosperity: Findings from the Business Competitiveness Index. In *The Global Competitiveness Report 2003-2004*. Oxford University Press.

Rodriguez, F., & Rodrik, D. (2000). Trade policy and economic growth: A skeptic's guide to the cross-national evidence. *NBER Macroeconomics Annual*, *15*, 261–325. doi:10.1086/654419

Seker, M. (2011). *Trade policies, investment climate, and exports across countries* (World Bank Policy Research Working Paper No. 5654). Retrieved from World Bank website: https://openknowledge.worldbank.org/bitstream/handle/10986/3415/WPS5654.pdf?sequence=1

Singer, H. W., & Gray, P. (1988). Trade policy and growth of developing countries: Some new data. *World Development*, *16*(3), 395–403. doi:10.1016/0305-750X(88)90006-X

Tyler, W. G. (1981). Growth and export expansion in developing countries: Some empirical evidence. *Journal of Development Economics*, *9*(1), 121–130. doi:10.1016/0304-3878(81)90007-9

Wilson, J. S., Mann, C. L., & Otsuki, T. (2005). Assessing the benefits of trade facilitation: A global perspective. *World Economy*, *28*(6), 841–871. doi:10.1111/j.1467-9701.2005.00709.x

World Bank Group. (2014). *Trade Competitiveness*. World Bank Brief. Retrieved May 20, 2017, from http://www.worldbank.org/en/topic/trade/brief/trade-competitiveness

World Economic Forum. (2014). *The global competitiveness report 2016-2017*. Geneva: World Economic Forum.

Yanikkaya, H. (2003). Trade openness and economic growth: A cross-country empirical investigation. *Journal of Development Economics*, *72*(1), 57–89. doi:10.1016/S0304-3878(03)00068-3

KEY TERMS AND DEFINITIONS

Export Diversification: Expansion of the range of products or markets of a country.

Export-Led Growth Strategy: Economic policy that aims to speed up the industrialization process of a country by exporting goods for which it has a comparative advantage.

Extensive Margin: Entering new export markets or selling new products.

Global Value Chain: Refers to the fragmentation of the production processes in different parts of the world.

Import Substitution Policy: A trade and economic policy that encourages replacing imports with domestic production in order to reduce foreign dependency.

Infant Industry: A newly established industry that is having difficulty in competing with existing competitors abroad.

Intensive Margin: Expansion of the trade of existing products.

Protectionism: The economic policy of restricting trade between countries through different methods including tariffs on imported goods, quotas, and other government regulations.

ENDNOTES

1 Note that when analyzing exchange rate-trade relationship, it is important to distinguish between nominal and real exchange rates. In the developed countries, where inflation rates are low there is little difference between the real and the nominal exchange rates. However, in the context of developing countries, inflation is generally a major problem, therefore real exchange rates have to be taken into consideration. Real exchange rates are calculated as the product of nominal exchange rate (units of foreign currency per domestic currency) and the ratio of domestic price level to foreign price level.

2 Currency mismatch occurs when foreign currency denominated debts are high and the income and assets are mostly denominated in domestic currency.

3 Institutional distance has been calculated based on the 1998 scores on Kaufmann, Kray, and Mastruzzi (2003) six dimensions of governance infrastructure quality.

4 Export diversification has been defined as change in the composition of a country's existing export product mix or export destination (Ali, Alwang, & Siegel, 1991).

Chapter 8
The Status of Foreign Trades Under Globalization in Developing and Developed Countries With Turkey

Nurullah Güleç
Ankara Yıldırım Beyazıt University, Turkey

Cihat Öztürk
Ankara Yıldırım Beyazıt Üniversitesi, Turkey

Deniz Efendioğlu
Marmara University, Turkey

ABSTRACT

In Turkey, the volume of foreign trade, which was very small in the first years of the republic, raised due to the increasing population and the reviving economy. Imports and exports for Turkey, the proportion of equipment, investment goods, and raw materials that would have been used for industrialization has increased. Another type of trade that is desired to be implemented in Turkey in recent years is free trade. The implementations for free trade also bring the question together with themselves. Does globalization always affect developing countries in a positive correlation with their economies? The data taken from KOF Index of Globalization from ETH Zurich are going to be used to see the relationship with the data coming from imports and exports. Then for all developing countries a classification study is done and the relation of developing countries and Turkey is examined. The purpose of the chapter is to examine the number of imports and exports due to globalization indexes to understand the real impact and the direction of globalization from the perspective of Turkey.

DOI: 10.4018/978-1-5225-4032-8.ch008

INTRODUCTION

Fast and stable economic development (growth) and the processes associated with this phenomenon are one of the most prominent topics of discussion in contemporary economics. As developing countries often possess limited foreign exchange reserves, they typically find it difficult to obtain financial resources from international financial markets (Şimşek & Kadılar, 2005).

Emerging economies such as Turkey are also significantly influenced by globalization, a phenomenon characteristic of the 21st century. Globalization has increased the speed of information flow, enabled the dissemination of information to the bottom rungs of society, and enhanced the dynamism of local economies. In general, globalization has increased the number of available jobs and engendered the transformation of local regions into focal points of their respective economies. Local entrepreneurship, mobilization of local resources, knowledge, and skills, and other local potentials enable regions to specialize in specific sectors. Specialization, in turn, is known to make local regions more competent in the world economy, and as a result, local economies can grow and develop at rates higher than the national average.

Global production activity and the global market are based on the various stages of production, which are carried out in different countries to minimize the production costs of raw materials and intermediate goods, labor costs, and external costs. Globalization has also enabled border towns to participate in global production activity, and, as a result, these towns have attracted fixed capital investments and freight manufacturing agreements. Globalization, therefore, has been beneficial to several international companies that outsource their production, and it also enables them to target the whole world as a training field.

In this paper, the authors seek to examine whether the various types of globalization contribute to Turkey's economic growth. To this end, data related to the political, social, and economic globalization of developed and developing economies, including Turkey, shall be examined using regression analysis. Based on the results of this analysis, a classification study shall be undertaken, and the current situation in Turkey shall be examined in the context of this classification of developed countries.

GLOBALIZATION IN TURKEY, DEVELOPING COUNTRIES, AND DEVELOPED COUNTRIES

While globalization is not a new concept, it does possess characteristics that are distinctively contemporary. This concept can be described in different ways. As per one definition, globalization refers to the process by which the world becomes a fully integrated market (Saylan & Kansu, 1997).

Globalization is a concept that involves other issues, such as the development of economic, social, and political relations between countries, recognition of the beliefs and expectations of different societies and cultures, and more frequent international relations. Globalization creates a complex environment and entails conflicts between most field sand disciplines. As a result of globalization, people are more interconnected than ever before (Oman, 1994).

Several political, cultural, technological, and economic factors (McBurnie, 2002) have led to the emergence of globalization. Given the diversity of the factors, it is almost impossible for one to shield himself/herself from the effects of globalization (Karlsen, 2002).

The Effects of Globalization on Turkey's Economy

In spite of the difficulties involved in embracing globalization and policies suited to it, emerging economies need to develop their competitiveness rapidly to comply with the standards of developed countries. In this context, it is important to examine Turkey's economic competency in a globalized world (Yılmaz & Ozdil, 1999).

To examine Turkey's economic policies, it is important to continuously monitor the trajectories of global crises. On the one hand, it is important to ensure that chronic inflation does not become hyperinflation. On the other hand, it is important to highlight the merits of decreasing output when faced with severe contraction. Social and political instability may arise if economic development does not meet societal expectations, or when incomes do not rise in a balanced manner. However, the ineffectiveness of institutionalization makes it easier to address instabilities.

Analyses of Turkey's foreign trade data involving the income structure of its trading partners show that the effects of convergence, brought forth by globalization, are more prominent in Eurasian countries than in the European Union (EU). It is also worth mentioning that Eurasia is primarily constituted by developing economies, whereas the EU represents developed economies. However, in assessing the effects of integrating Turkey's economic growth, it would also be useful to assess its (the integration) functions in terms of technology transfer as well as its advantages in terms of commercial and capital flow. Moreover, it is important to base these assessments on theories of internal growth.

Turkey's innovation performance is directly related to its membership effort with EU. Additionally, when Turkey's integration was compared with the innovation scores using the Global Innovation Index published by INSEAD (Institut Européen D'administratio nDes Affaires), it emerged that the performance of the SEE was less effective compared to Turkey's; the EU's performance, too, was better in this regard. Therefore, Turkey's exports of technologies such as the BSEC, EEC, and D-8 to foreign capital markets are likely to be more than its exports to the EU.

METHODOLOGICAL BACKGROUND OF THE STUDY

Multiple Regression Method

Some applications of regression analysis involve more than one independent variable; and a regression model that contains more than one independent variable is called a multiple regression model (Freund & Simon, 1973).

$$y_i = \beta_0 + \beta_1 x_1 + \beta_2 x_2 + \ldots + e_i, i = 1,\ldots,n \tag{1}$$

For this equation, the expected value of the error term is zero that is $E(e_i) = 0$. The parameter β_0 represents the intercept of the plane. β_1 and β_2 are partial regression coefficients because (i) β_1 measures the expected change in Y per unit change in x_1 when x_2 is held constant, and (ii) β_2 measures the expected change in Y per unit change in x_2 when x_1 is held constant (Montgomery & Rungur, 2010).

Multiple linear regression models are often used as approximating functions. In this equation, the true functional relationship between Y and $x_1, x_2, \ldots, x_k$ is unknown, but beyond certain ranges of the independent variables, the linear regression model becomes an adequate approximation.

Models that are structurally more complex than the above equation may still be analyzed using multiple linear regression techniques (Montgomery & Rungur, 2010). Models involving interaction effects may also be analyzed using multiple linear regression methods.

Least Squares Estimation of the Parameters

The least squares method may be used to estimate the regression coefficients in the multiple regression models. Let us suppose that n>k observations are available, and let x_{ij} denote the i.th observation or level of the variable x_j (Montgomery & Rungur, 2010). The following observation will hold for this scenario.

$$\left(x_{i1}, x_{i2}, \ldots, x_{ik}, y_i\right), i = 1, 2, \ldots, n \ and \ n > k \tag{2}$$

It is customary to present the data for multiple regression models in a table as shown in Table 1.

Each observation $\left(x_{i1}, x_{i2}, \ldots, x_{ik}, y_i\right)$ satisfies the model, or

$$\begin{aligned} y_i &= \beta_0 + \beta_1 x_{i1} + \beta_2 x_{i2} + \ldots + e_i, i = 1, \ldots, n \\ y_i &= \beta_0 + \sum_{i=1}^{n} \beta_j x_{ij} + e_i, i = 1, \ldots, n \end{aligned} \tag{3}$$

The least squares function is

$$L = \sum_{i=1}^{n} e_i^{\ 2} = \sum_{i=1}^{n} \left(y_i - \beta_0 - \sum_{i=1}^{n} \beta_j x_{ij} \right)^2, i = 1, \ldots, n \tag{4}$$

L has to be minimized with respect to $\beta_0, \beta_1, \beta_2, \ldots, \beta_k$. The derivation should be dawn here, and the least squares estimates of $\beta_0, \beta_1, \beta_2, \ldots, \beta_k$ should satisfy

Normal equations in the form p=k+1 are also involved in this analysis, and each of the unknown coefficients is assigned one normal equation. The solution to the normal equations can be found in the least squares estimators of the regression coefficients $\beta_0, \beta_1, \beta_2, \ldots, \beta_k$. The normal equations can be solved using any method appropriate for solving a system of linear equations (Devore, 2015).

Table 1. Data for multiple regression

y	x_1	x_2	$\cdots$	x_k
y_1	x_{11}	x_{12}	$\cdots$	x_{1k}
y_2	x_{21}	x_{22}	$\cdots$	x_{2k}
$\vdots$	$\vdots$	$\vdots$		$\vdots$
y_n	x_{n1}	x_{n2}	$\cdots$	x_{nk}

$$n\hat{\beta}_0 + \hat{\beta}_1 \sum_{i=1}^{n} x_{i1} + \hat{\beta}_2 \sum_{i=1}^{n} x_{i2} + \ldots + \hat{\beta}_k \sum_{i=1}^{n} x_{ik} = \sum_{i=1}^{n} y_i, i = 1, \ldots, n$$

$$\hat{\beta}_0 \sum_{i=1}^{n} x_{i1} + \hat{\beta}_1 \sum_{i=1}^{n} x_{i1}^2 + \hat{\beta}_2 \sum_{i=1}^{n} x_{i1}x_{i2} + \ldots + \hat{\beta}_k \sum_{i=1}^{n} x_{i1}x_{ik} = \sum_{i=1}^{n} x_{i1}y_i, i = 1, \ldots, n$$

$$\vdots$$

$$\hat{\beta}_0 \sum_{i=1}^{n} x_{ik} + \hat{\beta}_1 \sum_{i=1}^{n} x_{ik}x_{i1} + \hat{\beta}_2 \sum_{i=1}^{n} x_{ik}x_{i2} + \ldots + \hat{\beta}_k \sum_{i=1}^{n} x_{ik}^2 = \sum_{i=1}^{n} x_{ik}y_i, i = 1, \ldots, n \tag{5}$$

Matrix Approach to Multiple Linear Regression

In devising multiple regression models, it is convenient to express the mathematical operations using matrix notation. Let us suppose that there are k independent variables and n observations $(x_{i1}, x_{i2}, \ldots, x_{ik}, y_i)$, $i = 1, \ldots, n$; let us then suppose that the following model relates the independents to the response(Montgomery &Rungur, 2010):

$$y_i = \beta_0 + \beta_1 x_{i1} + \beta_2 x_{i2} + \ldots + e_i, i = 1, \ldots, n \tag{6}$$

This model is a system of n equations that can be expressed in matrix notation as

$$\boldsymbol{y} = \boldsymbol{X\beta} + \epsilon \tag{7}$$

where,

$$\boldsymbol{y} = \begin{bmatrix} y_1 \\ y_2 \\ \vdots \\ y_n \end{bmatrix}; \boldsymbol{X} = \begin{bmatrix} x_{11} & x_{12} & x_{13} & \cdots & x_{1k} \\ x_{21} & x_{22} & x_{23} & \cdots & x_{2k} \\ \vdots & \vdots & \vdots & & \vdots \\ x_{n1} & x_{n2} & x_{n3} & \cdots & x_{nk} \end{bmatrix}; \boldsymbol{\beta} = \begin{bmatrix} \beta_1 \\ \beta_2 \\ \vdots \\ \beta_n \end{bmatrix}; \epsilon = \begin{bmatrix} \epsilon_1 \\ \epsilon_2 \\ \vdots \\ \epsilon_n \end{bmatrix} \tag{8}$$

In general, y is an (n x 1) vector of the observations, X is an (n x p) matrix of the levels of the independent variables, β is a (p x 1) vector of the regression coefficients, and ϵ is an (n x 1) vector of random errors (Devore, 2015). The vector of least squares estimators $\hat{\beta}$ should be determined to minimize

$$\sum_{i=1}^{n} \epsilon_i^2 = \epsilon'\epsilon = \left(\boldsymbol{y} - \boldsymbol{X\beta}\right)' \left(\boldsymbol{y} - \boldsymbol{X\beta}\right) \tag{9}$$

The least squares estimator $\hat{\beta}$ is the solution for β in the equation

$$\frac{\partial L}{\partial \boldsymbol{\beta}} = 0 \tag{10}$$

The results will be

$$\boldsymbol{X'y} = \boldsymbol{X'X\hat{\beta}} \tag{11}$$

The least squares normal equations in matrix form are used in this scenario. They are identical to the scalar form of the normal equations given earlier. To solve the normal equations, both sides of the last equations should be multiplied by the inverse of $\boldsymbol{X'X}$. Therefore, the least squares estimate of $\boldsymbol{\beta}$ is

$$\hat{\boldsymbol{\beta}} = \boldsymbol{X'X}^{-1}\boldsymbol{X'y} \tag{12}$$

The result is

$$\begin{pmatrix} n & \sum_{i=1}^{n} x_{i1} & \sum_{i=1}^{n} x_{i2} & \cdots & \sum_{i=1}^{n} x_{ik} \\ \sum_{i=1}^{n} x_{i1} & \sum_{i=1}^{n} x_{i1}^2 & \sum_{i=1}^{n} x_{i1}x_{i2} & \cdots & \sum_{i=1}^{n} x_{i1}x_{ik} \\ \vdots & \vdots & \vdots & & \vdots \\ \sum_{i=1}^{n} x_{ik} & \sum_{i=1}^{n} x_{ik}x_{i1} & \sum_{i=1}^{n} x_{ik}x_{i2} & \cdots & \sum_{i=1}^{n} x_{ik}^2 \end{pmatrix} \begin{bmatrix} \hat{\beta}_0 \\ \hat{\beta}_1 \\ \vdots \\ \hat{\beta}_k \end{bmatrix} = \begin{bmatrix} \sum_{i=1}^{n} y_i \\ \sum_{i=1}^{n} x_{i1}y_i \\ \vdots \\ \sum_{i=1}^{n} x_{ik}y_i \end{bmatrix} \tag{13}$$

The fitted regression model is

$$\hat{y}_i = \hat{\beta}_0 + \sum_{i=1}^{n} \hat{\beta}_j x_{ij} + e_i, i = 1, \ldots, n \tag{14}$$

In matrix notation, the fitted model is

$$\hat{\boldsymbol{y}} = \boldsymbol{X}\hat{\boldsymbol{\beta}} \tag{15}$$

The difference between the observation y_i and the fitted value $\hat{y}_i$ is a residual, say $e_i = y_i - \hat{y}_i$. The (n x 1) vector of residuals is denoted by

$$\boldsymbol{e} = \boldsymbol{y} - \hat{\boldsymbol{y}} \tag{16}$$

As with simple linear regression, it is important to estimate σ^2, the variance of the error term ϵ, in multiple regression models. In simple linear regression, the estimate of σ^2 is obtained by dividing the sum of the squared residuals by n-2. There are two parameters in the simple linear regression model, but for a multiple linear regression with p parameters, the logical estimator for σ^2 (Freund & Simon, 1973), is

$$\hat{\sigma}^2 = \frac{\sum_{i=1}^{n} \epsilon_i^2}{n-p} = \frac{SS_E}{n-p} \tag{17}$$

This is an unbiased estimator of $\hat{\sigma}^2$. As is the case with simple linear regression, the estimate of $\hat{\sigma}^2$ is usually obtained from the analysis of variance for the regression model. The numerator is called the error or residual sum of squares, and the denominator n-p is called the error or residual degrees of freedom (Freund & Simon, 1973).

Hypothesis Tests in Multiple Linear Regression

In multiple linear regression problems, certain tests of hypotheses about the model parameters are useful in measuring model adequacy. In this section, several important hypothesis-testing procedures are described. As is the case with simple linear regression, hypothesis testing requires that the error terms ϵ_i in the regression model are normally and independently distributed with mean zero and variance σ^2 (Montgomery & Rungur, 2010).

Test for Significance of Regression

The test for significance of regression is a test to determine whether a linear relationship exists between the response variable y and a subset of the independent variables $x_1, x_2, \ldots, x_k$. The appropriate hypotheses are

$$H_0 : \beta_1 = \beta_2 = \beta_3 = \ldots = \beta_k = 0$$

$$H_1 : \beta_j \neq 0 \ for \ at \ least \ one \ j$$

Rejection of

$$H_0 : \beta_1 = \beta_2 = \beta_3 = \ldots = \beta_k = 0$$

implies that at least one of the independent variables $x_1, x_2, \ldots, x_k$ contributes significantly to the model. The test for significance of regression is a generalization of the procedure used in the simple linear regression. The total sum of squares SS_T is partitioned into a sum of squares as a result of the regression and error (Montgomery & Rungur, 2010).

$$SS_T = SS_E + SS_R \tag{18}$$

The test statistic for $x_1, x_2, \ldots, x_k$ is

$$F_0 = \frac{\frac{SS_R}{k}}{\frac{SS_E}{n-p}} = \frac{MS_R}{MS_E} \tag{19}$$

R^2 and Adjusted R^2

The coefficient of multiple determinations (R^2) may also be used as a global statistic to assess the fit of the model. Computationally, this is represented as follows.

$$R^2 = \frac{SS_R}{SS_T} = 1 - \frac{SS_E}{SS_T} \tag{20}$$

The R^2 statistic is somewhat problematic as a measure of the quality of the fit for multiple regression models because it always increases when a variable is added to a model. Since R^2 always increases when an independent is added, it can be difficult to judge whether the increase reveals anything useful about the new independent. It is particularly hard to interpret a small increase, such as observed in the pull strength data. Many regression users prefer to use an adjusted R^2 statistic (Montgomery & Rungur, 2010).

$$R^2_{adj} = 1 - \frac{\frac{SS_E}{n-p}}{\frac{SS_T}{n-1}} \tag{21}$$

Given that $SS_E / n - p$ is the error or residual mean square and $SS_T / n - 1$ is a constant, R^2_{adj} will only increase when a variable is added to the model if the new variable reduces the error mean square.

The adjusted R^2 statistic essentially penalizes the analyst for adding terms to the model. It is an easy way to guard against over fitting that is, the inclusion of independents that are not really useful. Consequently, it is very useful in comparing and evaluating competing regression models (Montgomery & Rungur, 2010).

Tests on Individual Regression Coefficients and Subsets of Coefficients

Experts are typically interested in testing hypotheses about the individual regression coefficients. Such tests may be useful in determining the potential value of each independent variable in the regression model. For example, the model might be more effective with the inclusion of additional variables or perhaps with the deletion of one or more independents. Adding a variable to a regression model always causes the sum of squares for regression to increase and the error sum of squares to decrease (this is why R^2 always increases when a variable is added) (Montgomery & Rungur, 2010).

The hypotheses for testing the significance of any individual regression coefficient, say β_j, are

$$H_0 : \beta_j = 0$$

$$H_1 : \beta_j \neq 0$$

If $H_0 : \beta_j = 0$ is not rejected, this indicates that the independent x_j can be deleted from the model. The test statistic for this hypothesis is

$$T_0 = \frac{\hat{\beta}_j}{\sqrt{\hat{\sigma}^2 C_{jj}}} = \frac{\hat{\beta}_j}{se\left(\hat{\beta}_j\right)} \tag{22}$$

In this scenario, C_{jj} is the diagonal element of $(\boldsymbol{X}'\boldsymbol{X})^{-1}$ corresponding to $\hat{\beta}_j$. This is called a partial or marginal test because the regression coefficient $\hat{\beta}_j$ is dependent on all the other independent variables $x_i \left(i \neq j\right)$ in the model.

Moreover, $SS_R(\beta_1 \mid \beta_2)$ is independent of MS_E, and the null hypothesis $\beta_1 = 0$ may be tested by the statistic

$$F_0 = \frac{\dfrac{SS_R(\beta_1 \mid \beta_2)}{r}}{MS_E} \tag{23}$$

If the computed value of the test statistic $f_0 > f_{\alpha,r,n-p}$, H_0 is rejected, and if it is concluded that at least one of the parameters in β_1 is not zero and, then at least one of the variables $x_1, x_2, \ldots, x_k$ in x_1 contributes significantly to the regression model.

The partial F-test is prone to be very useful. It can be used to measure the contribution of each individual independent x_j as if it were the last variable added to the model as a result of computation.

$$SS_R\left(\beta_j \mid \beta_0, \beta_1, \beta_2, \ldots, \beta_{j-1}, \beta_{j+1}, \ldots, \beta_k\right), j = 1, 2, \ldots, k \tag{24}$$

This is the increase in the regression sum of squares due to the addition of x_j to a model that already includes $x_1, x_2, \ldots, x_{j-1}, x_{j+1}, \ldots, x_k$ The partial F-test is a more general procedure in that it can be used to measure the effect of sets of variables.

Confidence Intervals in Multiple Linear Regression

Confidence Intervals on Individual Regression Coefficients

In multiple regression models, it is often useful to construct confidence interval estimates for the regression coefficients $\{\hat{\beta}_j\}$. Developing a procedure to obtain these confidence intervals requires that the errors $\{\epsilon_1\}$ are normally and independently distributed with mean zero and variance σ^2. This is the same assumption required to test a hypothesis. Therefore, the observations $\{Y_i\}$ are normally and independently distributed with mean $\hat{y}_i = \hat{\beta}_0 + \sum_{i=1}^{n} \hat{\beta}_j x_{ij}$ and variance σ^2. Since the least squares estimator $\hat{\beta}$ is a linear combination of the observations, it follows that $\hat{\beta}$ is normally distributed withthe mean vector β and the covariance matrix $\sigma^2(\mathbf{X}'\mathbf{X})^{-1}$ (Montgomery & Rungur, 2010). Each of the statistics is represented as follows.

$$T = \frac{\hat{\beta}_j - \beta_j}{\sqrt{\hat{\sigma}^2 C_{jj}}}, j = 1,2,\ldots,k \tag{25}$$

has a t distribution with n-p degrees of freedom, where C_{jj} is the jj.th element of the $(\boldsymbol{X}'\boldsymbol{X})^{-1}$ matrix, and σ^2 is the estimate of the error variance obtained from equations 12–16. This leads to a 100.(1-α)% confidence interval for the regression coefficient $\beta_j, j = 1,2,\ldots,k$ (Freund & Simon, 1973).

A 100.(1-α)% confidence interval on the regression coefficient $\beta_j, j = 1,2,\ldots,k$ in the multiple linear regression models is given by

$$\hat{\beta}_j - t_{\frac{\alpha}{2},n-p} \sqrt{\hat{\sigma}^2 C_{jj}} \leq \hat{\beta}_j \leq \hat{\beta}_j + t_{\frac{\alpha}{2},n-p} \sqrt{\hat{\sigma}^2 C_{jj}} \tag{26}$$

Confidence Interval on the Mean Response

The confidence interval on the mean response is obtained at a particular point, say, $(x_{01}, x_{02}, \ldots, x_{0k})$. To estimate the mean response at this point, it is necessary to define the vector,

$$\boldsymbol{x}_0 = \begin{bmatrix} 1 \\ x_{01} \\ x_{02} \\ \vdots \\ x_{0k} \end{bmatrix}$$

The mean response $E(Y \mid x_0) = \mu_{(Y|x_0)} = x_0'\beta$ at this point is estimated by

$$\hat{\mu}_{(Y|x_0)} = x_0'\hat{\boldsymbol{\beta}} \tag{27}$$

This estimator is unbiased since

$$E(x_0'\hat{\beta}) = x_0'\beta = E\left(Y \mid x_0\right) = \mu_{(Y|x_0)}$$

and the variance of $\mu_{(Y|x_0)}$ is

$$V\left(\hat{\mu}_{(Y|x_0)}\right) = \sigma^2 x_0'(\boldsymbol{X}'\boldsymbol{X})^{-1} x_0 \tag{28}$$

A 100.(1-α)% confidence interval on $\hat{\mu}_{(Y|x_0)}$ can be constructed from the statistic

$$\frac{\hat{\mu}_{(Y|x_0)} - \mu_{(Y|x_0)}}{\sqrt{\sigma^2 x_0'(\boldsymbol{X}'\boldsymbol{X})^{-1} x_0}} \tag{29}$$

Prediction of New Observations

A 100.(1-α)% confidence interval for future observation is

$$\hat{y}_0 - t_{\frac{\alpha}{2},n-p}\sqrt{\sigma^2 x_0'(\boldsymbol{X}'\boldsymbol{X})^{-1} x_0} \le Y_0 \le \hat{y}_0 + t_{\frac{\alpha}{2},n-p}\sqrt{\sigma^2 x_0'(\boldsymbol{X}'\boldsymbol{X})^{-1} x_0} \tag{30}$$

The confidence interval expresses the error in estimating the mean of a distribution, while the prediction interval expresses the error in predicting a future observation from the distribution at the point x_0. This must include the error in estimating the mean at that point, as well as the inherent variability in the random variable Y at the same value $x = x_0$ (Devore, 2015).

In predicting new observations and in estimating the mean response at a given point $\left(x_{01}, x_{02}, \ldots, x_{0k}\right)$ experts must be careful about extrapolating beyond the region of original observations. It is possible that a model which fits well in the region of the original data will no longer fit well outside that region. In multiple regression, it is often easy to extrapolate inadvertently since the levels of the variables $(x_{i1}, x_{i2}, \ldots, x_{ik})$, $i = 1, 2, \ldots, n$ jointly define the region containing the data (Devore, 2015).

Model Adequacy Checking

Residual Analysis

The residuals from the multiple regression models, defined by $e_t = y_t - \widehat{y_t}$, play an important role in judging the model adequacy, as is the case with simple linear regression. It is also helpful to plot the residuals against variables not present in models that are candidates for inclusion. Patterns in these plots may indicate that the model may be improved by adding the candidate variable (Montgomery & Rungur, 2010).

The standardized residuals are expressed as

$$d_t = \frac{e_t}{\sqrt{MS_E}} = \frac{e_t}{\sqrt{\sigma^2}} \tag{31}$$

Many regression computer programs compute other types of scaled residuals, and studentized residual is one of the most popular scaled residuals.

$$r_t = \frac{e_t}{\sqrt{\sigma^2 \left(1 - h_{ii}\right)}}, i = 1, 2, \ldots, n \tag{32}$$

Since each row of the matrix X corresponds to a vector, say, $x_t' = \left[1, x_{i1}, x_{i2}, \ldots, x_{ik}\right]$, an alternative way to write the diagonal elements of the hat matrix is

$$h_{ii} = x_t'(\boldsymbol{X}'\boldsymbol{X})^{-1} x_t \tag{33}$$

Under the usual assumptions that the model errors are independently distributed with mean zero and variance σ^2, the variance of the i.th residual e_i can be represented in the following manner.

$$V(e_t) = \sigma^2 \left(1 - h_{ii}\right) \tag{34}$$

Furthermore, the h_{ii} elements must fall in the interval $0 < h_{ii} \leq 1$. This implies that the standardized residuals understate the true residual magnitude; thus, the studentized residuals would be a better statistic to examine while evaluating potential outliers.

CLASSIFICATION METHOD

People usually take a step back and try to see the big picture before making important decisions. However, from time to time the big picture can be too complicated. Because a large database can contain a lot of sizes, space, and extremely complex structures, even the best data mining methods may not produce meaningful results. The way to solve very complex problems is to break down the big problem into sub-problems that can be solved more easily. A final solution can be arrived at by combining the solutions for each sub-problem (Koltan & Said, 2011).

Classification is a data mining function that assigns items in a collection to target categories or classes. The goal of classification is to accurately predict the target class for each case in the data (Koltan& Said, 2011). The objective is to determine the value of a qualification using other features. A pattern typically emerges based on the distribution of data sets. The model is used to estimate the future values or the unknown values of the quality; this is typically done after the performance has been determined.

The classification process consists of three steps:

- Creating a model
- Model evaluation
- Using a model

It is assumed that each object belongs to a class specified by the quality of the class tag. The dataset created by the objects, which in turn are used to create the model, is regarded as the learning set. If-Then-Else rules, decision trees, and mathematical formulas can be expressed in different formats. The classification method separates data items into one of the predefined classes and maps the regression data item to a real-valued estimated variable. The evaluation also involves determining the model's performance (correctness) using test set examples. The undetermined class tag is compared with the class tag determined using a known test set instance model (Riedewald, 2015).

As per Tan et al. (2013), the following techniques are used in the classification process.

- Decision Trees
- Statistical Decision Theory

- Nearest Neighbor
- Bayesian Classification
- Artificial Neural Networks
- Support Vector Machines (SVMs)
- Prediction
- Accuracy and Error Measures
- Ensemble Methods

The evaluation of a classification model's performance is based on the correct and incorrect counts of test records predicted by the model. These counts are tabulated using a confusion matrix. Each entry f_{ij} in the table denotes the number of records from class I, which were predicted to belong to class j. Based on the entries in the confusion matrix, the total number of correct predictions made by the model is ($f_{11} + f_{00}$), and the total number of incorrect predictions is ($f_{01} + f_{10}$) (Tan et al., 2013).

Although a confusion matrix provides the information needed to determine the efficacy of a classification model, summarizing this information in a single number would make it more convenient to compare the performance of different models. As per Tan, Steinbach, and Kumar (2013), this can be done using a performance metric such as accuracy, which is defined as follows.

$$Accuracy = \frac{Number\ of\ correct\ predictions}{Total\ number\ of\ predictions} = \frac{\left(f_{11} + f_{00}\right)}{\left(f_{11} + f_{00} + f_{01} + f_{10}\right)} \tag{35}$$

Similarly, the performance of a model can be expressed in terms of its error rates, which is given by the following equation (Tan et al., 2013).

$$Error\ Rate = \frac{Number\ of\ wrong\ predictions}{Total\ number\ of\ predictions} = \frac{\left(f_{01} + f_{10}\right)}{\left(f_{11} + f_{00} + f_{01} + f_{10}\right)} \tag{36}$$

Most classification algorithms seek models that attain the highest accuracy, or equivalently, the lowest error rate when applied to the test set.

Model Overfitting

A good classification model must not fit only the training data but also accurately classify records it has never seen before. In other words, a good model must have low training error as well as low generalization error. This is important because a model that fits the training data too well can have a poorer generalization error than a model with a higher training error. This situation is known as model overfitting (Tan et al., 2013).

Typically, the training and test error rates of the model are large when the size of the tree is very small, a situation known as model underfitting. Underfitting occurs when a model is yet to learn the true structure of the data. As a result, the model performs poorly on both the training and test sets. However, once the tree becomes too large, its test error rate begins to increase even though its training error rate continues to decrease. Model overfitting also refers to this phenomenon (Tan et al., 2013).

Evaluating the Performance of a Classifier

It is often useful to measure the performance of the model on the test set because the measure provides an unbiased estimate of its generalization error. The accuracy or error rate computed from the test set can also be used to compare the relative performance of different classifiers on the same domain. However, to do this, the class labels of the test records must be known. While this process is underway, the following steps should be followed (Tan et al., 2013);

- Holdout Method
- Random Sub-sampling
- Cross-Validation
- Bootstrap

Methods for Comparing Classifiers

It is often useful to compare the performance of different classifiers to identify the classifier that works better on a given data set. However, depending on the size of the data, the observed difference in accuracy between two classifiers may not be statistically significant (Tan et al., 2013).

Estimating a Confidence Interval for Accuracy

To determine the confidence interval, the probability distribution that governs the accuracy measure must be established. For this study, the confidence interval is derived by modeling the classification task as a binomial experiment. Listed below are some of the characteristics of a binomial experiment (Tan et al., 2013).

- The experiment consists of N independent trials, where each trial has two possible outcomes: success or failure.
- The probability of success, p, in each trial is constant.

Based on the normal distribution, the following confidence interval for acc can be derived (Tan et al., 2013).

$$P\left(-Z_{\frac{\alpha}{2}} \leq \frac{acc-p}{\sqrt{p\left(1-p\right)/N}} \leq Z_{1-\frac{\alpha}{2}}\right) = 1-\alpha \quad (37)$$

Comparing the Performance of Two Models

Consider a pair of models, M_1 and M_2, which are evaluated on two independent test sets, D_1 and D_2. Let n_1 denote the number of records in D_1 and n_2 denote the number of records in D_2. In addition, let us suppose that the error rate for M_1 on D_1 is e_1 and $e_2$for the others. The goal is to test whether the observed difference between $e_1$and e_2 is significant (Tan et al., 2013).

If the difference of error rates taken as d

$$\sigma_d^2 \approx \hat{\sigma}_d^2 = \frac{e_1\left(1-e_1\right)}{n_1} + \frac{e_2\left(1-e_2\right)}{n_2} \quad (38)$$

Nearest Neighbor Classifiers

While attempting to classify an email as spam, one possible strategy is to look at existing emails that are similar to the email in question. This process quite amply represents what is called nearest neighbor classifiers (Tan et al., 2013).

Among the various methods of supervised statistical pattern recognition, the Nearest Neighbor rule achieves high performance consistently. This rule does not involve apriori assumptions about the distributions from which the training examples are drawn. It involves a training set of both positive and negative cases. A new sample is classified by calculating the distance to the nearest training case; the sign of that point then determines the classification of the sample (Tan et al., 2013).

The K-nn classifier extends this idea by taking the points nearest to k and attributing the sign of the majority. It is common to select small and odd values of k to break ties (typically 1, 3 or 5). Larger k values help reduce the effects of noisy points within the training data set, and the choice of k is often performed through cross-validation (Tan et al., 2013).

There are many techniques available to improve the performance and speed of the nearest neighbor classification. One approach to this problem is to pre-sort the training sets in some way (such as kd-trees or Voronoi cells). Another solution is to choose a subset of the training data so that classification by the 1-NN rule (using the subset) approximates the Bayes classifier. This can result in significant improvements in speed as k can now be limited to 1 and redundant data points can be removed from the training set. These techniques of data modification can also improve the performance by removing points that cause misclassifications. Several dataset reduction techniques are discussed in the section on target detection (Tan et al., 2013).

Algorithm and Logic

Initially, all training examples are stored in S. Given a new example x to be classified, the training example <x_i, y_i>, whose xi is most similar (or closest) to x, must be located through search. It is also necessary to predict y during this process. To ensure similarity, the distance between the points must be looked at. The most commonly used measure is Euclidean distance.

The Voronoi Diagram

Given a set of points, a Voronoi diagram describes the areas that are nearest to any given point. These areas can be viewed as zones of control. Each example controls its own neighborhood. First, the Voronoi diagram is created. The Decision boundary is formed by retaining only those line segments which separate different classes. The decision boundaries can become more complex as the number of stored training examples increases (Tan et al., 2013).

$$\begin{aligned} D\left(x, x^{i}\right) &= x - x^{i2} \\ &= \left(x - x^{i}\right)^{T}\left(x - x^{i}\right) \\ &= \sum_{j}\left(x_{j} - x_{j}^{i}\right)^{2} \end{aligned} \tag{39}$$

Different k values produce different results. Larger k produces smoother boundaries as the impact of class label noises cancel one another. But when k is too large with oversimplified boundaries, say k=N, the majority class can always be predicted (Tan et al., 2013).

The above discussion focuses on the problems associated with binary classification, in which only two output classes are possible. In the digit recognition example, there are ten output classes, and this changes things slightly. The labeling of training samples and the process of computing the distance are unchanged, but ties can now occur even with odd values of k. If all the neighbors nearest to k are from different classes, then one is no closer to a decision than that which can be arrived at with the single nearest neighbor rule (Tan et al., 2013).

Model Selection

Choosing k for K-nn is just one of the many problems in machine learning in terms of selecting a model. Model selection is about choosing a model: linear regression vs. quadratic regression, or choosing K-nn over LTU. Model selection is widely studied in machine learning, and its practice is of crucial importance (Rojas, 2014).

Complex models are always chosen if training error is used in the selection process. A portion of the labeled data apart can be used as validation data. Different k values are evaluated based on the prediction accuracy of the validation data. Upon the completion of these steps, k is chosen to minimize validation error (Rojas, 2014).

Hashing

Another alternative to a K-nn classifier is to use hash functions to preorder the data points in "buckets" that can be inspected; doing so also reduces the duration of the classification process. Hashing is useful whenever a set of "good" hashing functions can be found and when the dimensionality of the data can be reduced (Rojas, 2014).

If ten-dimensional data points could be mapped straight into n buckets, a significant amount of effort can be saved. However, the hashing method is imprecise. Only probabilistic bounds can be assigned to the result (since the new point in its bucket can be dangerously close to the boundary of the bucket). Nonetheless, the method is prone to be useful in many real-world applications (Rojas, 2014).

BACKGROUND

Past Studies on Regression Analysis on the Topic of Globalization

The commercial impact of globalization is a widely discussed topic. Various methods are used to correlate its effects with globalization. The regression analysis technique is one such method. Regression analysis is used to measure the relationship between two or more variables. If the analysis is performed using a single variable, it is called a univariate regression analysis. If more than one variable is used, it is called a multivariate regression analysis.

Regression analysis is widely used in the analysis of economic and commercial data. For instance, Kose, Prasad, and Terrones (2003) use a data sample consisting of 76 countries 21 developed and 55 developing countries to examine the effects of globalization on business synchronization using regression and correlation analysis.

Aizenman and Jinjarak (2009) examine the relationship between globalization and tax collection. They argue that globalization subjects developing countries to a significant amount of pressure. They used a regression model to probe the links between tax collection and globalization. Vamuakidis (2002) found a positive correlation between economic openness and economic growth in the period between 1920 and 1990.

Trade openness has strong positive effects on growth. Studies also examine the relationship between globalization and trade openness, capital mobility, economic policies, and economic integration (Chang, Lee, & Hsieh, 2014; Aramberri, 2009).

Past Studies on Classification

The aim of classification is to identify and define the class to which unknown samples or observations belong by looking at samples or observations in the training set and the class to which these are classified. Classification is an integral part of machine learning and one of the fundamental techniques involved in supervised learning. Recently, moreover, it has emerged as a popular research topic.

Classification studies are used in many areas, such as image recognition (Glowacz A. & Glowacz Z., 2016), real-time road traffic states measurement (Xu, Wang, Jia, Li, & Zhang, 2016), classification of countries based on economics (de la Paz-Marín, Gutiérrez, & Hervás-Martínez, 2015) or culture (Vanderstraeten & Matthyssens, 2008), and text mining.

The K-nn algorithm, published by Cover T.M. and Hart P.E. in 1967, is an effective lazy algorithm, which is commonly used to solve classification problems (Cover & Hart, 1967). The K-nn is a simple algorithm that takes into account the k-closest sample or observation in the training set to assign each unknown sample or observation to a class. For example, for k=1, the K-nn algorithm considers the nearest point of unknown sample or observation, and this sample or observation is associated with the class of the nearest point in the training set.

Past Studies on Globalization

The concerns embodied in the literature on globalization and regionalization differs vastly from those discussed in the literature on the institutional distinctiveness of national capitalisms. However, a significant number of international and comparative political economists are sensitive to the institutional and cultural variability of contemporary capitalism, and they have identified tendencies of convergence between these two issues often toward an Anglo-US model of deregulated neoliberal capitalism (Hay, 2000).

The literature on globalization has tended to focus on the relations of cultural changes, but it also glosses over the theoretical implications of the relations between knowledge, power, and changing social patterns. Correspondence theories relate changes in world economies to the analysis of the relative autonomy of cultural and social movements engendered by globalization. For instance, Balibar and Walterstein (1991), regard current interests in multiculturalism and ethnicity as the product of changes in notions such as nationalism and capitalism that took place in the late nineteenth century. But when such analyses are used to understand or explain current transformations, there is typically little recognition of the differences in the world capitalist economies between, for example, East Asia, Eastern Europe, Scandinavia, and the United States (Boyer & Drache, 1996).

Nor is there an elaboration of the factors that make the knowledge produced through education and in cultural spheres a constructive element in terms of innovation, health, growth and productivity at a society-wide level (Boyer, 1996, p. 104). Featherstone (1995), for example, asserts that the narratives produced by intellectuals are important elements in defining the boundaries and distinctions of the conditions of globalization, which he calls "post-modernity" (For a counterexample, see Shapiro, 1997).

At first glance, it appears to be the case that globalization has taken form in some parts of the world, while regionalization, a contrast of globalization, is widespread in other parts of the world. In this context, various countries tend to cooperate with each other in different fields, especially in the economic field (Şenyiğit, 2005).

The investigation of empirical evidence carried out in the available literature on this topic reveals a negative relationship between domestic and foreign savings. However, a few studies argue that foreign capital inflow could increase domestic savings (Örnek, 2008).

As economies across the world become more complex, employment in the agriculture and manufacturing sectors is bound to decrease, whereas employment in the service sector is bound to increase (Dogan & Can, 2016).

PROBLEM DESCRIPTION AND METHODOLOGY

The aim of this study is to reveal the effects of social and economic globalization on the foreign trade of developed and developing economies. The second phase of this study involves the classification of countries according to the social and economic effects of globalization on foreign trade. In the first part of this study, the effects of globalization on foreign trade were examined by establishing multiple regression models for developing and developed economies. The classification process was based on the import and export data models. The k-nearest neighborhood algorithm (K-nn algorithm) was used in the classification process, and the extent of globalization and its effects on developing economies were also analyzed. Developing economies were compared with developed economies in this process. The effects of economic and social globalization on foreign trade were examined for each country, and Turkey's position as a developing economy was also examined. Foreign trade information of the various countries was taken from the OECD data. The globalization index was derived from the data published by ETH Zurich KOH.

Economic and social globalization may impact foreign trade data in various ways. Both types of globalization are considered norms, and countries that are more global in these aspects are more prone to experience growth in terms of imports and exports. However, it is also important to observe the current trends in developed economies. Moreover, economic globalization and social globalization influence foreign trade in different ways. For instance, if the social globalization index increases regularly, then imports are expected to increase. Thus, the effects of globalization on imports and exports have been examined from the economic and social perspectives. Additionally, globalization data of countries such as Germany, United Kingdom, United States, Netherlands, and Canada have been used to identify trends in the foreign trade activities of developed countries.

Multiple Regression

It is not possible to describe any dependent variable in the fields of economics and business with a single argument. Economic models are often the result of multiple causes. A large number of variables come together to influence another variable. Multiple linear regression analysis is a method used to (i) explain the cause-effect relationships between two or more independent variables affecting a variable with a linear model and (ii) determine the extent of the effects of independent variables.

The multiple regression models have been established in the first phase of this study. Foreign trade variables are defined as dependent variables, and global variables are defined as independent variables in these models. In the first phase of this study, the aim was to identify the effects of globalization and foreign exchange on foreign trade in advanced and developing countries. In this context, the multiple regression models expressed in Equation1 were used.

In the model expressed in Equation 1, the y_i dependent variable represents the foreign trade (import or export) variable, and β_1 and β_2 independent variables determine the economic and social globalization indexes. The historical range for foreign trade data (import and export) and globalization index data (economic and social) is 1970–2014. Import and export data are taken as a percentage of gross domestic products (% of GDP) and doing so makes it possible to achieve more accurate results. Regression models were established using the IBM SPSS 24 program; the significance and validity test of the model was also calculated using this program. The significance of the coefficients in the model was measured using the t-test. The threshold value for the significance level of the coefficients in the model is determined as 0, 1, and the confidence interval is 90%.

Classification (K-nn Algorithm)

The main purpose of classification is to determine the properties of a new object and to assign the object to a predefined class. There are many different types of classification algorithms: Bayes, decision trees, nearest neighbors, and artificial neural networks, among others. The K-nn algorithm is one of the popular classification algorithms. It classifies a feature that is closest to itself to a selected feature. The value K is expressed, for instance, as 3 or 5. The distances between objects are determined using the following formula:

$$d_{(i,j)} = \sqrt{\sum_{k=1}^{p} \left(x_{ik} - x_{jk}\right)^2} \tag{40}$$

As per this definition, the value of K has to be checked first whenever there is a new object. To avoid equality, K is usually chosen as an odd number. Methods such as Cosinus, Euclidean, or Manhattan distance are used to calculate the distances between new data and older data. In this study, Euclidean distance is used to calculate the distances.

The K-nn classification algorithm is used in the second part of the study. The K-nn algorithm is applied to the coefficients of multiple regression models of developed and developing countries. The globalization variables of the countries are classified according to their influence on foreign trade. The commercial responses of developed countries to globalization are compared with the commercial responses of developing countries. This study operates with the logic that if countries have similar commercial responses to global changes, they should be included in the same class. The K-nn algorithm is run in MATLAB to obtain various k values with multiple regression coefficient data.

COMPUTATIONAL STUDY AND RESULTS

This study is carried out in two phases, and it examines whether there is a meaningful relationship between the globalization indexes of countries and the most basic economic data, such as the import and export data. The regression method is used to examine the relationship between these two factors. In the second phase, countries are classified using coefficients obtained from the regression analysis; separate analyses were conducted for developed and developing countries. The results obtained from the regression analysis are presented in the tables below.

The following table presents the results of regression analysis of the effects of the globalization index on the import-to-GDP ratio for select countries. The political globalization index was excluded from the analysis since it had no effect on the dependent variable, import-to-GDP ratio. Therefore, the analysis was performed using the social and economic globalization index as independent variables. The selected countries are presented in the first column of the table, the R-square values of the regressions in the second column, the regressions constants in the third column, the effect coefficient of the economic globalization index in the fourth column, and the effect coefficient of the social globalization index in the last column. The insignificant coefficients in the 90% confidence interval are indicated in bold.

The results obtained from this analysis indicate that the social globalization index generally has a positive effect on the imports-to-GDP ratio of countries. This means that the index increases imports more than GDP. However, the same cannot be said of the economic globalization index.

It is also possible to determine the efficacy of this index for all developing countries considered in this study, except Israel, whereas the opposite is true of most of the developed countries with a strong industrial infrastructure. In sum, it is feasible to deduce the following: while, compared with GDP, the increase in social globalization increases the imports of all countries; economic globalization reduces the imports of developed countries and increases the imports of developing countries.

In the case of Turkey, too, social and economic globalization increases the imports-to-GDP ratio. For developing countries, economic globalization is less efficacious compared to social globalization. These results indicate that the situation in Turkey should be handled more consciously, especially since Turkey is at the forefront of social media usage.

As Table 2 indicates, the social globalization index has more influence on imports of developed and developing countries than the economic globalization index. The effects of the former are generally positive, although its effects are negative for the Far East economies, which are based on technology exports, such as Korea and Japan. Imports in Japan are negatively affected by economic globalization; on the other hand, in Korea, imports are negatively affected by social globalization. That production in these countries is technology-driven may be the main reason for the negative effects. Moreover, these countries not far and dependent on a supplier to China, which may have created this relationship between globalization and imports.

Table 3 shows the results of regression analyses conducted to determine the effects of the globalization index on the export-to-GDP ratio for select countries. Here too, the political globalization index was not used. This study also examines the effects of economic and social globalization on the export-to-GDP ratio. Columns in the table show selected countries, R-square of regression, regression constant, the coefficient of the effect of economic globalization index, and coefficient of the effect of social globalization index respectively. The coefficients indicated in bold

Table 2. Multiple regression coefficients, constants, and R^2 for import

	Import			
	R-Square	**Constant**	**Coefficient of Economic Globalization Index**	**Coefficient of Social Globalization Index**
Israel	0,333	29,778	**–0,190**	0,740
Korea	0,599	**1,942**	1,865	–1,254
Mexico	0,917	–18,340	0,263	0,712
Turkey	0,931	–3,810	0,266	0,717
South Africa	0,521	–9,968	0,883	**–0,225**
Brazil	0,610	–8,654	**0,271**	0,624
China	0,850	–1,748	0,408	0,529
Chile	0,660	16,161	0,845	**–0,420**
Indonesia	–0,075	23,424	**0,246**	**–0,147**
Canada	0,930	–30,608	1,084	**–0,137**
Germany	0,700	–15,812	**–0,032**	0,863
England	0,300	20,387	**–0,261**	0,766
Japan	0,510	11,081	–0,824	1,210
Netherlands	0,810	14,870	0,200	0,730
USA	0,780	–13,607	0,641	**0,247**

ETH, KOF Index of Globalization 2017.

Table 3. Multiple regression coefficients, constants, and R^2 for export

	Export			
	R-Square	**Constant**	**Coefficient of Economic Globalization Index**	**Coefficient of Social Globalization Index**
Israel	0,273	36,975	**–0,533**	0,937
Korea	0,784	**–11,467**	1,756	–0,969
Mexico	0,894	–19,630	0,749	0,211
Turkey	0,910	–5,369	0,682	0,290
South Africa	0,434	–1,230	0,979	**–0,524**
Brazil	0,770	–28,825	**0,825**	0,111
China	0,870	–6,829	0,493	0,453
Chile	0,720	19,570	1,307	**–0,699**
Indonesia	0,015	26,944	**0,560**	**–0,459**
Canada	0,900	–36,032	1,213	**–0,307**
Germany	0,710	–33,531	**0,170**	0,688
England	0,081	19,691	**0,246**	0,043
Japan	0,460	11,582	–0,728	1,136
Netherlands	0,850	9,164	0,212	0,740
USA	0,580	–4,534	0,625	**0,139**

ETH, KOF Index of Globalization 2017.

are insignificant values in the 90% confidence interval (OECD, Trade in goods and services, 2017).

It can be roughly said that both the social globalization index and the economic globalization index increase the export-to-GDP ratio. When the averages of developed and developing countries are compared, economic globalization has greater effects on the exports of developing countries; the opposite is true of social globalization.

Here, the effects of the social globalization index and economic globalization index on both imports-to-GDP ratio and exports-to-GDP ratio can be evaluated. When the effects on imports-to-GDP ratio and exports-to-GDP ratio of developing countries are evaluated together, economic globalization increases export more than import, whereas social globalization has an adverse effect on imports-to-GDP ratio and exports-to-GDP ratio. It is said that the same situation applies to developing countries.

However, economic globalization has more effects on developing countries than on developed countries. Developed countries, however, are affected by social globalization more than developing countries. As a result, it can be said that social globalization increases the exports-to-GDP ratio more than imports-to-GDP ratio for both developing and developed countries, whereas economic globalization has a more positive effect on exports than on imports.

Economic globalization has limited influence on the exports of developed countries for two reasons. First, the process of economic globalization may have attained a state of saturation in developed economies. Second, exports of developed countries are under the influence of social globalization. For instance, the anti-terrorism policy developed and adopted by some developed countries is a result of social globalization.

As a result, developed countries are required to export goods and services for defense needs. The export and proliferation of computer games and movies are more examples in this context. As a result of social globalization, the trends otherwise particular to developed countries (social life, thought styles, science, culture, etc.) spread to other parts of the world. This affects the exports of developed countries. These examples can be augmented. Developing countries have a weaker impact on exports through social globalization given their limited social impact, inadequate technological infrastructure, and ongoing economic development.

The second phase of this study involves classification using the K-nn algorithm. Up to this point, four different parameters for each country have been obtained: the coefficient of economic globalization on import, the coefficient of social globalization on import, the coefficient of economic globalization on export, and the coefficient of social globalization on export. An attempt is made to classify countries according to their development levels based on the four factors. The attribute table used for this purpose is presented in Table 4.

For the purpose of this study, countries are divided into classes based on their development levels, and developing countries are assigned the code 1, whereas developed countries are assigned 2. It is assumed that the insignificant parameters estimated in the regression analysis are zero (0). As a result, Indonesia is excluded from the analysis as all its parameters turned out to be insignificant.

The data was then normalized to reduce the effect of (i) the range values that change with each parameter and (ii) the extreme values. A K-nn algorithm with different k values is used to compare and classify the countries. The results are detailed below.

Misclassifications are indicated in bold. The best result is obtained at k=1, and the correct classification rate is 71.43%. At k=1, Israel, Canada, England, and Japan are misclassified, whereas the remaining 10 countries are classified correctly.

Another noteworthy point is that, for all k values, Turkey, Korea, Mexico, Brazil, and China are correctly classified, whereas Israel, Canada, and England are misclassified. In this case, the misclassification can be derived from the parameters used. More accurate results can be obtained by focusing on different parameters. A more in-depth analysis of Israel is required given that geographical location and

Table 4. Attributes of each country

	Attributes Table for Classification				
	Attribute 1	**Attribute 2**	**Attribute 3**	**Attribute 4**	**Class**
Israel	**–0,102**	0,590	–0,304	0,825	1
Korea	1,000	–1,000	1,000	–0,853	1
Mexico	0,141	0,568	0,427	0,186	1
Turkey	0,143	0,572	0,388	0,255	1
South Africa	0,473	**–0,179**	0,558	–0,461	1
Brazil	**0,145**	0,498	0,470	**0,098**	1
China	0,219	0,422	0,281	0,399	1
Chile	0,453	**–0,335**	0,744	–0,615	1
Canada	0,581	**–0,109**	0,691	–0,270	2
Germany	**–0,017**	0,688	**0,097**	0,606	2
England	**–0,140**	0,611	**0,140**	**0,038**	2
Japan	–0,442	0,965	–0,415	1,000	2
Netherlands	0,107	0,582	0,121	0,651	2
USA	0,344	**0,197**	0,356	**0,122**	2

Table 5. Classes and accuracy for each k values

	Correct Classes	**Assigned Classes k=1**	**Assigned Classes k=3**	**Assigned Classes k=5**
Israel	1	**2**	**2**	**2**
Korea	1	1	1	1
Mexico	1	1	1	1
Turkey	1	1	1	1
South Africa	1	1	**2**	1
Brazil	1	1	1	1
China	1	1	1	1
Chile	1	1	**2**	1
Canada	2	**1**	**1**	**1**
Germany	2	2	**1**	**1**
England	2	**1**	**1**	**1**
Japan	2	**1**	2	2
Netherlands	2	2	**1**	**1**
USA	2	2	**1**	**1**
	Accuracy	71,43%	42,86%	57,14%

religious and cultural factors are effective for Israel in this classification. However, in general, the classifications are accurate.

In sum, it can be said that globalization index, economic globalization index, and social globalization index have a significant effect on the imports-to-GDP ratio and the exports-to-GDP ratio of both developed and developing countries. The effects moreover are stronger in developing countries.

It is important that developing countries pay attention to the social globalization index given its negative effects on developing economies. Globalization can be an economic power for if it is managed properly.

The Relation of Globalization Over Economic Indicators for Developing Countries and Turkey

First, the effects of globalization will be determined based on the chosen economic indicators. The regression analysis will be conducted at this stage, and the relationship between globalization indices and economic indicators shall be examined. The next step shall be based on the meaningfulness of the outcome. A variance analysis test and significance tests shall be conducted to determine the meaning of the outcome. The significance of the coefficients and the correctness of the general mode suitability of the parameters shall also be tested. The errors shall be determined using the residue analysis, and the analysis of variance shall be based on the results of the former.

The Classification of Countries From Globalization Indexes Over Economic Indicators

In this study, countries shall be classified according to the positive and negative effects of the globalization index on economic indicators. For example, the increase in globalization in Turkey may have a negative impact on Brazil, although it may have a positive impact on the latter's current account deficit. Reasons for the classifications shall also be provided. The reasoning will be based on a set of four indicators. The classification process shall be used to determine the number of groups and the correct classification.

FUTURE RESEARCH DIRECTIONS

This study deals with a lot of factors. Globalization directly impacts the economies of developing and developed countries. More techniques can be employed in studies such as the present one. Particularly, techniques such as decision tree, artificial neural network, statistical decision theory, support vector machines, ensemble method, feature weighting classification, etc. can be used in the classification process. To ensure a mathematical approach, the data clustering technique can be used to determine classified parts. The effects of globalization on developing countries may not be entirely straightforward or visible; hence, the effects of globalization must be investigated from different perspectives.

CONCLUSION

This work examines the relationship between the globalization index and commercial indicators, and the countries were classified based on the relations between these factors. The effects of the globalization index on trade were identified using regression analysis and the classification methods. To measure the relationship between the globalization index and commercial indicators, the effect of globalization on exports-to-GDP ratio and imports-to-GDP ratio were investigated using the regression method. The exports-to-GDP ratio and imports-to-GDP ratio were assigned as dependent variables, and globalization indexes, economic globalization index and social globalization index were assigned as independent variables in the regression model. The importance of the globalization indices for each country has been defined based on the results obtained from this regression analysis. It has been revealed that the effects of globalization indexes are strong on basic economic numbers, the imports-to-GDP ratio, and the exports-to-GDP ratio. Coefficients of the globalization index obtained from regression analysis were used as attributes in the classification method. The countries were classified according to the coefficients of the globalization indexes using the K-nn approach. Three different k values—1,3, and 5—were used in the K-nn classification method, and the countries were assigned to classes according to their development levels. For instance, the impact of the economic globalization index on the exports of developed and developing countries have been compared. The comparative analysis has also been applied to import and export values. It can be said that the effects of social globalization on the import and export items of developed countries are more far-reaching than the effects of economic globalization. For developing countries, economic globalization is more influential in terms of trade. In this context, the results of the classification have proved to be correct for developed and developing countries. Given the occurrence of misclassifications, it is necessary to differentiate the parameters. Future studies can be expanded to include different parameters and methods. In conclusion, this is a comparative study of globalization's impact on the exports and imports of developed and developing economies. It has also been shown that several different types of globalization have an impact on commercial values. The classification based on these effects reveals the commercial responses of developed and developing countries to the various types of globalization.

REFERENCES

Aizenman, J., & Jinjarak, Y. (2009). Globalization and developing countries–a shrinking tax base. *The Journal of Development Studies*, *45*(5), 653–671. doi:10.1080/00220380802582338

Aramberri, J. (2009). The future of tourism and globalization: Some critical remarks. *Futures*, *41*(6), 367–376. doi:10.1016/j.futures.2008.11.015

Balibar, E., & Wallerstein, I. M. (1991). *Race, nation, class: Ambiguous identities*. New York: Verso.

Boyer, R., & Drache, D. (1996). States Against Markets: The Limits of Globalization. New York: Academic Press.

Chang, C. P., Lee, C. C., & Hsieh, M. C. (2015). Does globalization promote real output? Evidence from quantile cointegration regression. *Economic Modelling*, *44*, 25–36. doi:10.1016/j.econmod.2014.09.018

Cover, T., & Hart, P. (1967). Nearest neighbor pattern classification. *IEEE Transactions on Information Theory*, *13*(1), 21–27. doi:10.1109/TIT.1967.1053964

de la Paz-Marín, M., Gutiérrez, P. A., & Hervás-Martínez, C. (2015). Classification of countries' progress toward a knowledge economy based on machine learning classification techniques. *Expert Systems with Applications*, *42*(1), 562–572. doi:10.1016/j.eswa.2014.08.008

Devlet Planlama Teşkilatı. (2000). VII. Beş Yıllık Kalkınma Planı. Küreselleşme Ö.İ.K.Raporu, Ankara.

Devore, J. L. (2015). *Probability and Statistics for Engineering and the Sciences*. Boston: Cengage Learning.

Dogan, B., & Can, M. (2016). The Effects of Economic Structural Transformation on Employment: An Evaluation in the Context of Economic. Handbook of Research on Unemployment and Labor Market Sustainability in the Era of Globalization, 275.

ETH. (2017). *KOF Index of Globalization*. Retrieved from "http://globalization.kof.ethz.ch/query/"

Featherstone, M., Lash, S., & Robertson, R. (1995). *Global modernities* (Vol. 36). Sage.

Freund, J. E., & Simon, G. A. (1973). *Modern elementary statistics* (Vol. 12). Englewood Cliffs, NJ: Prentice-Hall.

Glowacz, A., & Glowacz, Z. (2016). Recognition of images of finger skin with the application of histogram, image filtration, and K-NN classifier. *Biocybernetics and Biomedical Engineering*, *36*(1), 95–101. doi:10.1016/j.bbe.2015.12.005

Gujarati, D. (2008). Temel Ekonometri. Literatür Yayınları.

Hay, C. (2000). Contemporary capitalism, globalization, regionalization and the persistence of national variation. *Review of International Studies*, *26*(4), 509–531. doi:10.1017/S026021050000509X

Kansu, I. (1997). *Emperyalizmin Yeni Masalı: Küreselleşme*. Ankara: İmge Kitabevi.

Karlsen, G. E. (2002). Eğitim Yönetişimi: Küreselleşme ve Demokrasi. Kuram ve Uygulamada Eğitim Bilimleri, 2(1).

Koltan, Ş., & Said, P. (2011). *Kümeleme analizi ve pazarlamada kullanımı*. Retrieved from http://dergipark.ulakbim.gov.tr/ayd/article/view/5000125171/5000115039

Kose, M. A., Prasad, E. S., &Terrones, M. E. (2003). *How does globalization affect the synchronization of business cycles?* Academic Press.

Montgomery, D. C., & Rungur, G. C. (2010). *Applied statistics and probability for engineers*. John Wiley & Sons.

OECD. (2017). *Trade in goods and services*. Retrieved from https://data.oecd.org/trade/trade-in-goods-and-services.htm

Oman, C. (1994). *Globalization and Regionalization*. OECD. Retrieved from http://www.oecd-ilibrary.org/the-policy-challenges-of-globalisation-and-regionalisation_5l9v7frx3m0v.pdf?contentType=%2fns%2fWorkingPaper&itemId=%2fcontent%2fworkingpaper%2f151004514681&mimeType=application%2fpdf&containerItemId=%2fcontent%2fworkingpaperseries%2f20771681&accessItemIds=&option6=imprint&value6=http%3a%2f%2foecd.metastore.ingenta.com%2fcontent%2fimprint%2foecd

Örnek, İ. (2008). Yabancı sermaye akımlarının yurtiçi tasarruf ve ekonomik büyüme üzerine etkisi: Türkiye örneği. *Ankara Üniversitesi SBF Dergisi*, *63*(02), 199–207. doi:10.1501/SBFder_0000002069

Riedewal, M. (2015). *Data Mining Techniques*. Retrieved from http://www.ccs.neu.edu/home /mirek/classes/2012-S-CS6220/Slides/Lecture2-ClassificationPrediction.pdf

Rojas, R. (2013). *Neural networks: A systematic introduction*. Springer Science & Business Media.

Saylan, G. (1997). *Küreselleşmenin Gelişimi*. Ankara: Küreselleşme, İmge Kitabevi.

Şenyiğit, O. (2005). Küreselleşmenin Türkiye'ye etkileri. *Stratejik Araştırmalar Dergisi*, *3*, 35–53.

Shapiro, S. (1997). *Philosophy of mathematics: Structure and ontology*. Oxford University Press on Demand.

Şimşek, M., & Kadilar, C. (2005). Türkiye'nin İhracat Talebi Fonksiyonunun Sınır Testi Yöntemi İle Eşbütünleşme Analizi. *Doğuş Ünv. Dergisi*, *6*(1), 144–152.

Tan, P. N., Steinbach, M., & Kumar, V. (2013). Data mining cluster analysis: basic concepts and algorithms. *Introduction to Data Mining*.

Xu, D. W., Wang, Y. D., Jia, L. M., Li, H. J., & Zhang, G. J. (2016). Real-time road traffic states measurement based on Kernel-KNN matching of regional traffic attractors. *Measurement*, *94*, 862–872. doi:10.1016/j.measurement.2016.08.038

KEY TERMS AND DEFINITIONS

Classification: A data mining function that assigns items in a collection to target categories or classes. The goal of classification is to accurately predict the target class for each case in the data. The objective is to determine the value of a qualification using other features.

Economic Globalization: The abolition of restrictions on international financial markets and the liberalization of international capital movements. Cross-border transactions related to goods and services and international capital movements are steadily increasing as a result of this process. This process also engenders the rapid spread of technology to all parts of the world.

Influential Observation: The influential points are examined to ascertain whether they control the properties of a model. If these influential points are found to be "bad" points or erroneous in any way, they should be eliminated. On the other hand, there may be nothing wrong with these points. However, it is important to determine whether they produce results consistent with the rest of the data.

K-Nearest Neighborhood: According to this classification algorithm, the purpose of feature extraction (feature extraction) is to look at the closeness between the new individual to be categorized to k and the previous individuals.

Least Square Estimation Method: The least squares method (X_i, Y_i) is used to find a function that passes through the points, where i = 0, 1, 2 ... points accumulate. The found function will provide most points but it can calculate the next step where points can be found. In fact, it is an optimization problem.

Multiple Regression Analysis: Many applications of regression analysis involve more than one independent variable. A regression model that contains more than one independent variable is called a multiple regression model.

Political Globalization: This process has effectively challenged the supremacy of the nation-state, which was formerly the main actor at the international level. The nation-state, as a result, has been forced to share its powers with other international and supranational organizations.

Residual Analysis: As is the case with simple linear regression, the residuals from the multiple regression models, defined by $e_t = y_t - \widehat{y_t}$, play an important role in judging the adequacy of a model. It also aids the plotting of the residuals against variables that are not present in the model, but are candidates for inclusion.

Social Globalization: This represents the common understanding among countries about matters that concern humanity, such as democracy, human rights, protection of the environment, drug use and abuse, AIDS, and the fight against terrorism. As a result of social globalization, concepts such as democracy, human rights, market economy, and freedom are now pursued by most countries.

Voronoi Cells: Given a set of points, a Voronoi diagram describes the areas that are nearest to any given point. These areas can be viewed as zones of control. Each example controls its own neighborhood. First, the Voronoi diagram is created. The decision boundary is formed by retaining only those line segments which separate different classes. The higher the number of training examples, the more complex the decision boundaries can become.

Section 3

Financial Analysis in Developing Countries

Chapter 9
Relationship Between Non-Performing Loans, Industry, and Economic Growth of the African Economies and Policy Recommendations for Global Growth

Hasan Dinçer
Istanbul Medipol University, Turkey

Serhat Yuksel
Istanbul Medipol University, Turkey

Zafer Adalı
Artvin Çoruh University, Turkey

ABSTRACT

The main purpose of this chapter is to evaluate the causality relationship between non-performing loans, industry volume, and economic growth and to provide some policy recommendations for global growth. Within this context, annual data of 16 African countries for the periods between 2001 and 2015 was taken into the consideration. Additionally, Dumitrescu Hurlin panel causality test was used to reach the objective. According to the result of this analysis, it was identified that there is a causality relationship between industry volume and economic growth.

DOI: 10.4018/978-1-5225-4032-8.ch009

In addition to this situation, it was also defined that a decrease in economic growth is the main cause of the non-performing loans ratio in African countries. This chapter makes an important contribution to the literature. While considering these results, it can be said that to increase global trade economies of the countries should be improved and banking sectors should work more effectively. As a result, it will be possible to increase the living standards of the people and provide global growth.

INTRODUCTION

Africa is the second biggest continent of the world with respect to population density. There are 54 different countries and more than 1 billion people in this continent which is correspond to 15% of the world population (Toenniessen et. al., 2008). On the other side, Africa combats many different problems at the same time for a long period. Starvation, unfavorable health conditions, migration and civil wars are accepted as the most important problems for Africa (Watts, 1991).

In addition to them, economic problems play a very significant role for this continent. Africa is one of the poorest regions in the world in spite of the fact that it has many natural resources (Kownacki, 2000). According to the World Bank report, most of the people in Africa have less than 2.5 USD incomes per day. This situation underlines the importance of economic problems in this continent. Owing to this condition, it can be said that studies, which focus on economic development in Africa, are essential in order to solve the problems in this continent.

Furthermore, Africa has also significant role in global trade. Especially after the effects of globalization, economic borders among the countries have been disappeared (Yüksel et. al., 2015). This condition gives a chance to all economies to reach new markets in the world. This issue can be accepted as a leading factor to develop global economy. In other words, when the economies of African countries are improved, this will make an important contribution to the global growth. This situation will increase the living standard of the people in the world.

Non-performing loans (NPL) of the banks, industry volume and economic growth are interrelated variables. When non-performing loans ratio of the banks in the country increases, this problem influences industry volume of this country negatively. The main reason behind this situation is that banks will be unwilling to give loans in this aspect (Elegbe, 2013), (Abadi et al., 2014), (Ahmad and Bashir, 2013). Furthermore, when banks reduce the amount of the loans due to the high NPL problem, it will decrease the investment and consumption amount that has a direct effect on economic growth (Balgova et. al., 2016), (Klein, 2013).

Moreover, decrease in industry volume mainly refers that companies have some financial problems. Because of this issue, these countries will face some difficulties in order to pay their loans debt to the banks. This situation will have positive influence on non-performing loans ratio (Karahanoglu and Ercan, 2015), (Ersin and Duran, 2017). Also, these companies will try to decrease their costs to manage this financial problem. Within this context, they mostly prefer to lay off the employees and reduce their investments which lead to decrease in economic growth (Kaldor, 1966), (Drakopoulos and Theodossiou, 1991), (Diaz Bautista, 2003).

Additionally, economic growth has also influences on non-performing loans ratio and industry volume. If there is a decline in economic growth, this situation affects the financial aspects of the people in that country. Due to this issue, both people and countries have some difficulties to pay their debts to the banks that increases non-performing loans ratio (Khemraj and Pasha, 2009), (Louzis et. al., 2012). On the other side, when there is a recession in a country, it will have a negative effect on industry volume in that country (Balgova et. al., 2016).

Although the concepts of economic growth, industry production and nonperforming loans were analyzed in lots of studies separately, there is not a study in the literature which focuses on the relationship between these three different variables together. While considering these aspects, the main purpose of this study is to analyze the causality relationship between non-performing loans ratio, industry volume and economic growth in African countries. In order to reach this objective, annual data for the periods between 2001 and 2015 will be examined by using Dumitrescu Hurlin panel causality test. As a result of this analysis, it will be possible to make some recommendation in order to solve economic problems in Africa. Also, the results will show the ways to increase global growth. Therefore, it can be said that this study will make a significant contribution to the literature by helping to solve important problems.

This paper consists of four different parts. After the introduction, in the second part, similar studies in the literature will be detailed. In this part, the missing area in the literature related to this subject will be underlined. Moreover, in the third part, economic situation in Africa over the years is detailed. In the next part, research and methodology will be explained. Within this context, data and methodology used in the analysis will be detailed. After that, analysis results will be shared. Finally, in the last section, analysis results and the recommendations will be discussed.

BACKGROUND

Economic growth is an important indicator of the economies of the countries. Parallel to this aspect, industry production refers to the development in the industry of these countries. On the other side, nonperforming loans ratio is an important symptom of the financial crisis in banking sector. Economic growth, industry production and

Table 1. Similar studies in the literature

Author	Scope	Method	Result
Kaldor (1966)	UK	Descriptive Statistics	It was concluded that industry volume is the key factor of economic growth.
Drakopoulos and Theodossiou (1991)	Greece	Regression	It was identified that industry volume is the main indicator of economic growth.
Diaz Bautista (2003)	Mexico	Regression	It was determined that increase in industry volume has a positive influence on economic growth.
Fofack (2005)	Sub-Saharan Countries	Pseudo Panel-based Prediction Models	It was analyzed that economic growth is negatively associated with non-performing loans.
Millin and Nichola (2005)	South Africa	Vector Error Correction Model	They reached a conclusion that there is a relationship between industry production and economic growth.
Amediku (2006)	Ghana	VAR	It was determined that adverse output shock causes the NPL ratio to increase.
Arısoy (2008)	Turkey	Vector Error Correction Model	It was identified that there is a relationship between industry development and GDP growth.
Khemraj and Pasha (2009)	Guyana	Regression	It was concluded that GDP growth is adversely associated with non-performing loans.
Espinoza and Prasad (2010)	Gulf Cooperative Council	Regression	They identified that lower economic growth is the main reason of high NPL ratio.
Greenidge and Grosvenor (2010)	Barbados	ARDL	It was defined that GDP growth has an important influence on NPL ratio.
Nkusu (2011)	26 Developed Countries	VAR	It was concluded that a decrease in GDP growth leads to higher NPL ratio.
Terzi and Oltulular (2011)	Turkey	Granger Causality Analysis	It was determined that there is a causality relationship between industry volume and GDP growth.
Adebola et. al. (2011)	Malaysia	Granger Causality Analysis	They reached a conclusion that there is not a significant relationship between industrial production index and NPL ratio.
Louzis et. al. (2012)	Greece	Regression	It was identified that the GDP growth has a powerful impact on NPL ratio.
Saba et. al. (2012)	US	Regression	It was determined that there is a relationship between GDP growth and NPL ratio.
Messai and Jouini (2013)	Italy, Greece and Spain	Regression	It was concluded that higher GDP growth has a decreasing effect on NPL ratio.
Ahmad and Bashir (2013)	Pakistan	Regression	They reached a conclusion that both GDP growth and industry volume in the country lead to decrease NPL ratio.
Elegbe (2013)	Nigeria	Regression	It was defined that there is a negative relationship between industry volume and NPL ratio.
Skarica (2013)	Central and Eastern European Countries	Regression	It was identified that decrease in economic growth is main indicator of high NPL ratio.
Beck et. al. (2013)	75 Different Countries	Regression	It was defined that lower GDP growth is the main determinant of NPL ratio.
Venancio (2013)	17 Developed Countries	Regression	It was concluded that there is a significant relationship between NPL ratio and economic growth.
Vatansever and Hepşen (2013)	Turkey	Engle-Granger Co-integration Analysis	It was determined that industrial production index has negative impact on NPL ratio.
Klein (2013)	Europe	GMM	It was identified that high NPL ratio affects economic growth negatively.
Abadi et al. (2014)	Indonesia	Vector Error Correction Model	They determined that industrial production index influences NPL ratio negatively.
Ghosh (2015)	US	GMM	It was defined that high GDP growth causes NPL ratio to reduce.

continued on following page

Table 1. Continued

Author	Scope	Method	Result
Sheefeni (2015)	Namibia	Granger Causality Analysis	It was determined that there is a causality relationship between economic growth and NPL ratio.
Karahanoglu and Ercan (2015)	Turkey	VAR	It was identified that there is a long run relationship between industrial production index and NPL ratio.
Haniifah (2015)	Uganda	Regression	It was defined that there is a negative relationship between GDP growth and NPL ratio.
Erdogdu (2016)	Turkey	Regression	It was concluded that there is a relationship between NPL ratio and economic growth.
Balgova et. al. (2016)	100 Different Countries	Probit	It was determined that NPL ratio is the most important indicator of economic growth.

nonperforming loans are the subjects that attracted the attention of many different researchers. Because of this situation, there are lots of studies in the literature which focused on these concepts. Some of these studies were detailed on Table 1.

As it can be seen from Table 1, most of the studies focused on the relationship between nonperforming loans and GDP growth. Messai and Jouini (2013) made a study to analyze this relationship in Italy, Greece and Spain. They used regression analysis in order to reach this objective. As a result, it was identified that higher GDP growth has a decreasing effect on NPL ratio. Khemraj and Pasha (2009), Espinoza and Prasad (2010), Louzis et. al. (2012), Saba et. al. (2012), Skarica (2013), Beck et. al. (2013), Venancio (2013), Haniifah (2015) and Erdogdu (2016) also reached the similar conclusion by using the same method.

In addition to those studies, Balgova et. al. (2016) tried to evaluate the determinants of economic growth. Within this context, they analyzed 100 different countries in their study. According to the results of the probit analysis, it was defined that NPL ratio is the most important indicator of economic growth. Also, Klein (2013) and Ghosh (2015) used GMM analysis and emphasized the same conclusion. Furthermore, Amediku (2006) and Nkusu (2011) determined that decrease in GDP growth leads to higher NPL ratio by using GMM approach.

Moreover, it can also be understood that there are also some studies which evaluated the relationship between industry volume and economic growth. Kaldor (1966) concluded that industry volume is the key factor of economic growth in his study. Terzi and Oltulular (2011) also made a study to analyze this relationship in Turkey. As a result of Granger causality analysis, it was identified that there is a causality relationship between industry volume and GDP growth. Additionally, Drakopoulos and Theodossiou (1991) and Diaz Bautista (2003) defined that increase in industry volume has a positive influence on economic growth with the help of regression analysis. Also, Arısoy (2008) and Millin and Nichola (2005) reached the same conclusion with the help of vector error correction method.

Furthermore, some studies in the literature focused on the relationship between industry volume and nonperforming loans. Elegbe (2013) tried to determine this relationship in Nigeria. According to the results of the regression analysis, it was identified that there is a negative relationship between industry volume and NPL ratio. Ahmad and Bashir (2013) emphasized the similar conclusion for Pakistan with the help of similar method. Additionally, Vatansever and Hepşen (2013) and Karahanoglu and Ercan (2015) underlined the same aspect for Turkey. Moreover, Abadi et al. (2014) determined that industrial production index influences NPL ratio negatively. In spite of these studies, Adebola et. al. (2011) analyzed this issue for Malaysia and defined that there is not a significant relationship between industrial production index and NPL ratio.

While considering these studies, it was understood that there are lots of studies in which the relationship between nonperforming loans and economic growth was analyzed. Additionally, it was also seen that the relationship between industry volume and economic growth was also taken into the consideration in many different studies. Similarly, the effect of industry volume on nonperforming loans was also examined. However, it was understood that there is not a study in the literature that considers the causality relationship between these three variables together. In addition to this situation, it was also identified that Africa region was not examined very much in these studies.

MAIN FOCUS OF THE CHAPTER

Socio-Economic Outlook of Africa

Social Conditions of Africa

Regarding the population density, Africa is the second biggest continent in the world. More than 1 billion people live in this continent. This number forms 15% of total population in the world. On the other side, there are 54 different countries in Africa. These countries are listed on Table 2.

On the other side, Table 3 details the information related to the population of African countries in 2015.

Table 3 gives information about the population of African countries in 2015. As seen in this table, Nigeria has the highest population in Africa. In addition to Nigeria, Ethiopia, Egypt and Congo Democratic Republic are the other important countries with respect to the population. On the other hand, Djibouti, Equatorial Guinea, Comoros, Cape Verde, São Tomé & Príncipe and Seychelles are African

Table 2. African countries

Algeria	Angola	Benin	Botswana	Burkina Faso	Burundi	Cabo Verde	Cameroon
Central African Republic	Chad	Comoros	Congo	Cote d'Ivoire	Djibouti	Egypt	Equatorial Guinea
Eritrea	Ethiopia	Gabon	Gambia	Ghana	Guinea	Guinea-Bissau	Kenya
Lesotho	Liberia	Libya	Madagascar	Malawi	Mali	Mauritania	Mauritius
Morocco	Mozambique	Namibia	Niger	Nigeria	Rwanda	Sao Tome and Principe	Senegal
Seychelles	Sierra Leone	Somalia	South Africa	South Sudan	Sudan	Swaziland	Tanzania
Togo	Tunisia	Uganda	Zambia	Zimbabwe			

Table 3. Population of African countries

Country Name	Population (Thousands) in 2015	Country Name	Population (Thousands) in 2015	Country Name	Population (Thousands) in 2015
Nigeria	182,201.96	Burkina Faso	18,105.57	Congo	4,620.33
Ethiopia	99,390.75	Mali	17,599.69	Liberia	4,503.44
Egypt	91,508.08	Malawi	17,215.23	Mauritania	4,067.56
Congo Dem. Rep.	77,266.81	Zambia	16,211.77	Namibia	2,458.83
South Africa	54,490.41	Zimbabwe	15,602.75	Botswana	2,262.49
Tanzania	53,470.42	Senegal	15,129.27	Lesotho	2,135.02
Kenya	46,050.30	Chad	14,037.47	Gambia	1,990.92
Sudan	40,234.88	Guinea	12,608.59	Guinea-Bissau	1,844.33
Algeria	39,666.52	South Sudan	12,339.81	Gabon	1,725.29
Uganda	39,032.38	Rwanda	11,609.67	Swaziland	1,286.97
Morocco	34,377.51	Tunisia	11,253.55	Mauritius	1,273.21
Mozambique	27,977.86	Burundi	11,178.92	Djibouti	887.86
Ghana	27,409.89	Benin	10,879.83	Equatorial Guinea	845.06
Angola	25,021.97	Somalia	10,787.10	Comoros	788.47
Madagascar	24,235.39	Togo	7,304.58	Cape Verde	520.50
Cameroon	23,344.18	Sierra Leone	6,453.18	São Tomé & Príncipe	190.34
Côte d'Ivoire	22,701.56	Libya	6,278.44	Seychelles	96.47
Niger	19,899.12	Eritrea	5,227.79		

Source: African Development Bank.

countries which have low population. Table 4 gives information about the ratio of males to the females of African countries in 2015.

Table 4 shows that in 21 African countries (out of 53), the numbers of males are higher than female people. Within this scope, Equatorial Guinea is the country where the ratio of males to the females is the highest. Nigeria, Côte d'Ivoire and Seychelles are the other significant countries for this situation. Furthermore, Rwanda is also an African country in which the ratio of females to the males is the highest. Mozambique and Namibia are also important African countries where much more males live in comparison with females. Additionally, Table 5 demonstrates the distribution of featured African countries by age.

Table 4. The ratio of males/females African countries in 2015

Country Name	Sex Ratio (Males per 100 Females) in 2015	Country Name	Sex Ratio (Males per 100 Females) in 2015	Country Name	Sex Ratio (Males per 100 Females) in 2015
Equatorial Guinea	105.13	Chad	100.25	Burkina Faso	98.50
Nigeria	103.78	Congo	100.08	Gambia	98.02
Côte d'Ivoire	103.50	Cameroon	100.00	Lesotho	98.01
Seychelles	102.65	Kenya	99.93	Sierra Leone	97.95
Gabon	102.29	Uganda	99.91	Swaziland	97.83
Egypt	102.15	Botswana	99.85	Morocco	97.71
Mali	101.95	Zambia	99.70	Burundi	97.69
Comoros	101.77	Malawi	99.66	Tunisia	97.69
Liberia	101.62	Ethiopia	99.65	Togo	97.66
Niger	101.61	Benin	99.49	Mauritius	97.59
Mauritania	101.29	Congo Dem. Rep.	99.48	Cape Verde	97.40
Algeria	101.26	Madagascar	99.42	Zimbabwe	97.12
Libya	101.12	São Tomé & Príncipe	99.14	South Africa	96.76
Djibouti	100.86	Somalia	99.05	Senegal	96.47
Sudan	100.79	Ghana	98.99	Mozambique	95.49
Guinea	100.57	Tanzania	98.80	Namibia	94.83
Eritrea	100.38	Guinea-Bissau	98.57	Rwanda	91.89
South Sudan	100.30	Angola	98.50		

Source: African Development Bank.

Table 5. Distribution of the population by age in 2015

Country Name	0-14	15-64	65+
Niger	50.47	46.95	2.58
Uganda	48.09	49.42	2.49
Chad	47.72	49.83	2.45
Angola	47.65	50.04	2.31
Mali	47.53	49.95	2.52
Somalia	46.71	50.47	2.82
Gambia	46.18	51.50	2.31
Congo Dem. Rep.	45.99	51.04	2.96
Zambia	45.91	51.18	2.91
Burkina Faso	45.57	52.03	2.39
Gabon	37.13	57.77	5.10
Egypt	33.16	61.62	5.22
Libya	29.83	65.63	4.54
Cape Verde	29.65	65.77	4.58
South Africa	29.24	65.73	5.03
Algeria	28.54	65.52	5.94
Morocco	27.22	66.61	6.17
Seychelles	23.45	69.68	6.88
Tunisia	23.36	69.05	7.59
Mauritius	19.32	71.11	9.56

Source: African Development Bank.

Table 5 shows that 50.47% of the population in Niger is less than 14 years old. This ratio is 48.09% in Uganda, 47.72% in Chad and 57.65% in Angola. This situation identifies that young population is very high in those countries. It can also be understood from Table 5 that the percentage of people who are more than 65 is very low. On the other side, Mauritius is an African country where the percentage of people who are less than 14 years old is 19.32%. However, it can also be understood that 9.56% of people is more than 65 years old. In other words, old population is very high in Mauritius whereas there is very small young population. This situation is also very similar in Tunisia, Seychelles, Morocco and Algeria. As a result, it can be said that countries, which have high young population, are an important opportunity for investment. In other words, they may have a significant contribution to global trade (Fogel, 1994), (Coale and Hoover, 2015), (Bloom et. al., 1998).

Figure 1. Economic growth of Africa
Source: World Bank.

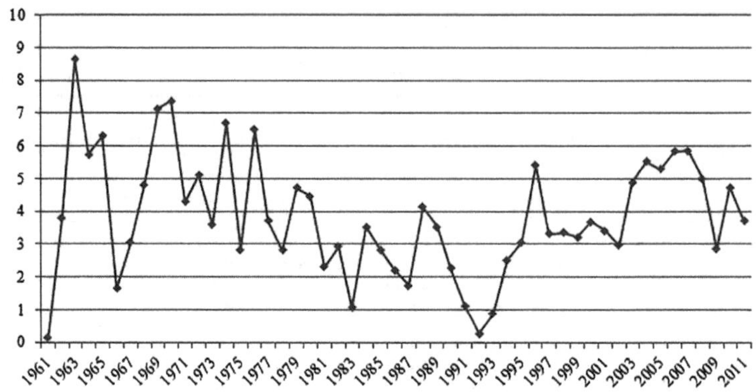

Macroeconomic Conditions of Africa Continent

The importance of Africa with respect to the economic aspect is increasing. Figure 1 gives information about economic growth of Africa over the years.

Figure 1 shows that economic growth is very volatile in Africa. In other words, there are sharp increases and decreases in this ratio over the years. For example, although it was only 0.12% in 1961, it exceeded 8.5% in 1963. However, it decreased dramatically to 1.63% in 1966. Additionally, there was a decreasing trend in economic growth for the periods between 1970 and 1992. In 1970, annual economic growth was 7.37% whereas it declined to 0.26% in 1992. On the other side, it can also be seen that there was a small increasing trend after 1992. From 1997 to 2012, this ratio had values between 3% and 5.89%. In summary, it is understood that economic

Figure 2. Banking sector in Africa (million USD)
Source: World Bank.

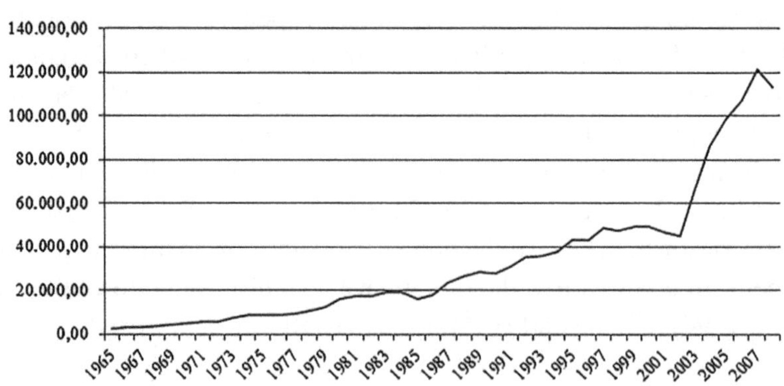

growth in Africa can be changed very fast. Figure 2 shows the amounts of banking sector in Africa.

As it can be seen Figure 2, the importance of banking sector is significantly increasing over the years. In 1965, the amount of banking sector was 2,551 million USD whereas it dramatically increased to 46,769 million USD in 2001. It can also be seen that there was a significant increasing trend after 2001. For example, in 2002 the amount of banking sector was 44,732 million USD, but in went up to 113,554 million USD in 2008. It can be understood that the power of the banks in Africa rises. This situation shows that trade volume in African countries is increasing. Figure 3 gives information about the export volume in Africa over the years.

As it can be seen from Figure 3, there is an important increase in export amount of Africa over the years. In 1962, African countries made 9,245 million USD amount of export. Nonetheless, this amount exceeded to 700 billion USD in 2011. Another important point is that radical increase in the export amount of Africa was mostly stated after 2002. While the export amount was 177 billion USD in 2002, this amount increased to 711 billion USD in 2011. Additionally, it is also understood that there is a decrease in this amount in 2008. The main reason behind this condition is that global mortgage crisis affected the export volume of African countries. These results give information that African countries increased export amount very much especially in the last years. This situation contributes to economic growth of these countries and increase in global trade as well (Kavoussi, 1984), (Yüksel and Zengin, 2016a). Figure 4 shows industry volume in Africa over the years.

As it can be seen from Figure 4, industry volume is significantly increasing in Africa over the years. In 1965, the industry volume in this continent was only 17,763 million USD. However, it is seen that this amount increased to 759 billion USD in 2011. In addition to this aspect, it is also identified that this increase was

Figure 3. Export volume in Africa (million USD)
Source: World Bank.

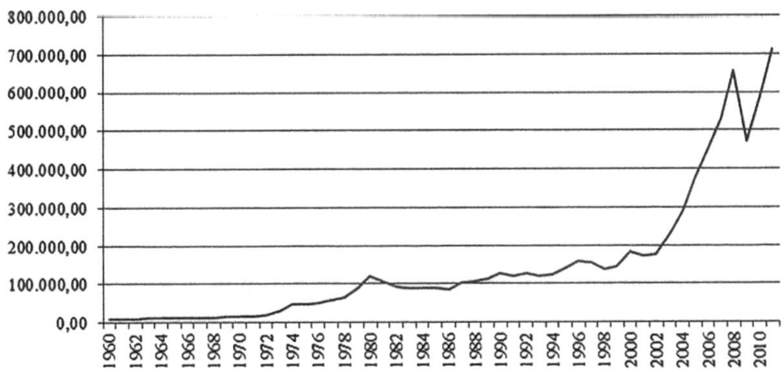

Figure 4. Industry volume in Africa (million USD)
Source: World Bank.

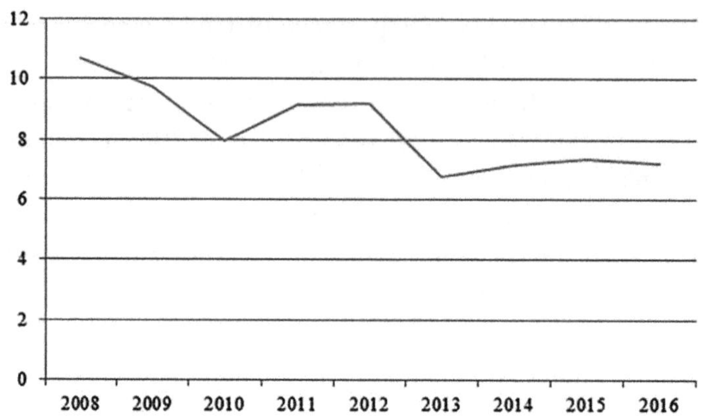

Figure 5. Inflation rates in Africa
Source: African Development Bank.

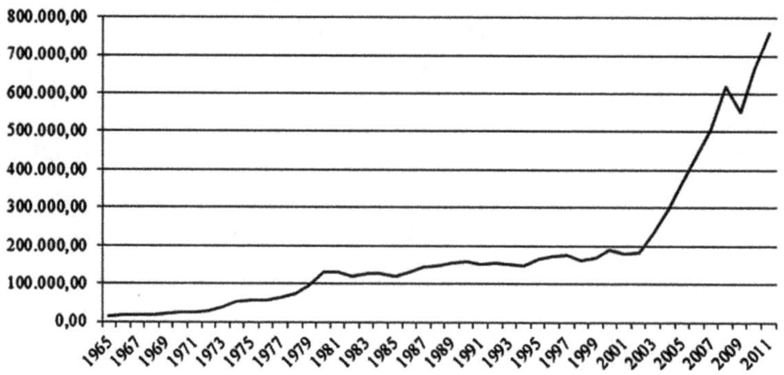

mostly occurred after 2001. While industry volume of Africa was 183 billion USD in 2002, it increased more than 4 times in 2012. It can also be understood that industry volume of Africa was affected negatively form 2008 global mortgage crisis. Figure 5 shows inflation rates of Africa between the years of 2008 and 2016.

As seen in Figure 5, inflation rates have a declining trend in Africa after 2008. For instance, inflation rate was 10.71% in 2008 whereas it decreased to 7.24% in 2016. This decreasing trend in inflation rates shows that economies in African countries started to become more stable. The main reason is that low inflation rates decrease uncertainty in the market. Because of this situation, investors in those countries will be willing to make new investments. This situation will also contribute to trade volume and global growth (Sarel, 1996).

While considering macroeconomic indicators of Africa, it is identified that this continent has a very weak performance in comparison with other continents. It is also understood that the importance of Africa is increasing over the years. In spite of this situation, it can be seen that the economies of African countries had a significant improvement after 2001. This situation makes an important contribution to global growth by increasing the trade volume in the world.

Economic Conditions of Featured African Countries

Table 6 gives information about 15 African countries which have highest GDP amount.

Table 6 shows that Nigeria is the African country which has the highest GDP in 2016. It has 415.080 billion USD amount GDP in this year. On the other hand, Egypt has the second highest GDP with the amount of 346.565 billion USD. In addition to them, South Africa has 280.367 billion USD amount of GDP which is the third highest amount in Africa in 2016. It can also be understood from Table 6 that the rank of Nigeria is 26 in spite of the fact that it has the highest GDP amount in Africa. Moreover, the rank of Egypt is 32 while it has the second highest GDP in Africa. This situation shows that African countries are not successful in the world

Table 6. 15 African countries which have highest GDP (2016)

Country	GDP Amount (Billion USD)	Rank in the World
Nigeria	415.080	26
Egypt	346.565	32
South Africa	280.367	42
Algeria	168.318	54
Morocco	104.908	60
Sudan	94.297	63
Angola	91.939	64
Ethiopia	69.218	69
Kenya	69.170	70
Tanzania	46.695	83
Ghana	42.761	87
Tunisia	42.388	88
Congo	39.820	89
Libya	39.389	91
Côte d'Ivoire	34.649	96

Source: African Development Bank.

with respect to the GDP amount. In other words, Africa has a very weak role in comparison with other countries in the world. Table 7 gives information about the 15 African countries that have highest GDP per capita amount in 2016.

As it can be seen from Table 7, Seychelles is the African country which has the highest GDP per capita amount in 2016 with the amount of 20,804 USD. In addition to Seychelles, Equatorial Guinea is the second best country with the amount of 18,014 USD. Furthermore, Mauritius has 10,699 USD amount of GDP per capita which is the third highest amount. It can be understood from Table 7 that the best countries with respect to GDP per capita are very different than the best countries regarding GDP amount. Table 8 gives information about 10 African countries which have highest inflation rate in 2016.

As it can be understood from Table 8, Sudan is the country which has the highest inflation rate (21.34%) in 2016. On the other side, inflation rate in South Sudan is 14.39% in 2016 which is the second highest rate. In addition to those countries, Eritrea is in the third rank with 12.25% inflation rate. This situation shows that there is high level of uncertainty in these countries. This problem has also negative effect on global trade and global growth. Table 9 gives information about the countries which have the highest real percentage growth of exports.

Table 7. 15 African countries which have highest GDP per capita (2016)

Country	GDP per Capita Amount (USD)
Seychelles	20,804
Equatorial Guinea	18,014
Mauritius	10,699
Gabon	8,296
Libya	6,161
Botswana	5,593
South Africa	4,674
Angola	4,532
Algeria	4,300
Egypt	4,061
Tunisia	3,695
Namibia	3,569
Cape Verde	3,462
Morocco	3,343
Nigeria	2,840

Source: African Development Bank.

Table 8. 10 African countries which have highest inflation rate (2016)

Country	Inflation Rate
Sudan	21.34
South Sudan	14.39
Eritrea	12.25
Malawi	10.08
Zambia	10.75
Egypt	10.05
Ethiopia	9.00
Ghana	8.69
Angola	8.67
Sierra Leone	8.35

Source: African Development Bank.

Table 9. 10 African countries which have the highest export growth (2016)

Country	Real Percentage Export Growth
Niger	16.83
Chad	14.84
Guinea-Bissau	14.51
Namibia	12.59
Liberia	10.27
Seychelles	9.81
Libya	8.63
Senegal	8.44
Democratic Republic of Congo	7.37
Cape Verde	7.18

Source: African Development Bank.

As it can be seen from Table 9, Niger has the highest growth rate (16.83%) of export in 2016. Moreover, Chad has the second highest rate for this aspect. Export amount in this country increased about 14.84% in 2016. In addition to these two countries, Guinea-Bissau and Namibia are other important African countries regarding export growth. Increase in export amount is a very significant factor to contribute global trade. Table 10 shows the ratio of current account balance to GDP amount of African countries in 2016.

Table 10. Current account balance of African in 2016

Country Name	2016	Country Name	2016	Country Name	2016
Botswana	5.61	Tunisia	-5.86	Togo	-11.00
Swaziland	1.64	Burundi	-5.95	Namibia	-11.30
South Sudan	0.90	Senegal	-6.04	Rwanda	-11.87
Morocco	-0.67	Malawi	-6.06	Congo	-12.40
Zambia	-1.09	Kenya	-6.26	Sao Tomé & Príncipe	-13.80
Egypt	-1.12	Sudan	-6.40	Djibouti	-13.96
Madagascar	-1.67	Lesotho	-6.49	Cameroon	-14.58
Equatorial Guinea	-2.33	Comoros	-6.89	Gambia	-14.98
Guinea-Bissau	-2.41	Benin	-7.12	Seychelles	-15.41
Côte d'Ivoire	-3.04	Ghana	-7.66	Algeria	-17.10
Nigeria	-3.16	Tanzania	-8.18	Zimbabwe	-19.78
Mali	-4.07	Sierra Leone	-8.38	Mauritania	-20.26
South Africa	-4.09	Ethiopia	-8.41	Niger	-21.90
Eritrea	-4.10	Chad	-8.60	Guinea	-28.36
Mauritius	-4.71	Uganda	-9.10	Liberia	-31.97
Central Afr. Rep.	-5.08	Gabon	-9.64	Libya	-44.54
Burkina Faso	-5.31	Cape Verde	-9.82	Mozambique	-46.10
Angola	-5.39	Congo Dem. Rep.	-10.85		

Source: African Development Bank.

Table 10 explains current account balance of African countries in 2016. The most important point of this table is that only 3 countries out of 53 have current account surplus. The ratio of current account balance to GDP is 5.61% in Botswana, 1.64% in Swaziland and 0.90% in South Sudan. However, there is current account deficit in other 50 countries. The ratio of current account deficit to GDP amount is less than 5% in 12 different countries.

On the other side, other 37 countries have current account deficit/GDP ratio which is higher than 5%. For example, this ratio is 31.97% in Liberia, 44.54% in Libya and 46.10%. When the ratio of current account deficit to GDP is higher than 5%, it is accepted as a significant indicator of a financial recession in the country (Yüksel and Zengin, 2016b). Because of this situation, these 37 countries are subject to important risks.

In addition to them, Table 11 gives information about trade relationship between Africa and European Union. As it can be seen in this table, there was an increasing trend in the import amount of EU from Africa for the periods between 2006 and

Table 11. Africa and European Union trade relationship

Year	Import of EU From Africa (Million EUR)	Export of EU to Africa (Million EUR)
2006	17,187	15,734
2007	17,210	18,538
2008	22,367	22,436
2009	16,863	19,467
2010	21,759	23,140
2011	34,080	28,891
2012	42,422	28,856
2013	38,257	30,278
2014	37,044	31,133
2015	28,437	29,060
2016	20,412	24,915

Source: European Commission.

2012. Nevertheless, there was a reduce in the amount import form African countries from this year. On the other hand, the export amount of EU to African countries went up until 2014. However, there was a decreasing in this amount in 2015 and 2016.

Issues, Controversies, Problems

Data Set and Variables

In this study, 16 African countries were taken into the consideration because the data for other African countries was not available. In the analysis process, annual data of these 16 African countries for the periods between 2001 and 2015 was used. All data was provided from the website of World Bank. With respect to the "NPL" variable, the ratio of non-performing loans to total loans was considered. Additionally, regarding the variable on "Industry", the ratio of industry volume in GDP amount was used. Moreover, as for the variable of "Economic Growth", annual GDP growth was taken into the consideration. The names of these countries were given on Table 12.

The details of economic growth, industry volume and nonperforming loans data of these countries in 2015 are given on Table 13.

As it can be seen from Table 13, in 2015, Rwanda has the highest GDP growth rate (6.90%) whereas the economy of Sierra Leone is downsizing by 20%. On the

Table 12. 16 African countries analyzed in the study

Egypt	Mauritius	Nigeria	South Africa
Gabon	Morocco	Rwanda	Swaziland
Ghana	Mozambique	Senegal	Tunisia
Kenya	Namibia	Sierra Leone	Uganda

Table 13. The data of economic growth, industry volume and nonperforming loans for selected countries in 2015

Country	NPL (%)	GDP Growth Rate (%)	Industry (%)
Egypt	7.2	4.2	36.3195
Gabon	3.8	3.85668	52.8165
Ghana	14.6736	3.8827	26.3476
Kenya	5.98876	5.6492	19.5245
Mauritius	7.02514	3.50001	22.7061
Morocco	6.53333	4.4	29.1991
Mozambique	4.3	6.26654	20.0823
Namibia	1.55169	5.66377	30.4034
Nigeria	5.32419	2.65269	20.3819
Rwanda	5.83738	6.9042	14.2368
Senegal	21.1733	6.48519	23.5929
Sierra Leone	31.73	-20.301	7.56926
South Africa	3.12083	1.2833	28.7195
Swaziland	7.54107	1.65739	44.2457
Tunisia	16.2	0.8	28.9269
Uganda	5.12696	5.04298	20.4321

other side, industry volume in Gabon is increasing 52% which is the highest ratio among the selected countries. After Gabon, Swaziland is the second country with 44% increase in the industry volume. Furthermore, Sierra Leone has the weakest performance with respect to this concept. In addition to them, Namibia has the lowest nonperforming loans ratio (1.55%) among all selected countries. After Namibia, South Africa is the second successful African country regarding nonperforming loans ratio. On the other hand, Sierra Leone is the worst country for this issue because nonperforming loans ratio of this country is 31.73. It can be understood from Table 12 that Sierra Leone is the worst country for each three variables. However, the best countries are different for each concept.

Dumitrescu Hurlin Panel Causality Tests

Dumitrescu and Hurlin panel causality test is accepted as an advanced form of Granger causality analysis. It tests causality relationship between the variables. The main requisite of this analysis is that the variables, which will be used in the causality analysis, should be stationary. Because of this situation, stationary analysis of the variables should be performed by using panel unit root tests before starting Dumitrescu Hurlin panel causality test. The details of this test were explained below (Dumitrescu and Hurlin, 2012).

$$Y_{i,t} = a_i + \sum_{k=1}^{K} Y_i^k Y_{i,t-k} + \sum_{k=1}^{K} B_i^k X_{i,t-k} + \varepsilon_{i,t} \quad (1)$$

In this equation, K explains optimum lag interval. On the other side, Y and X represents the variables of which causality analysis will be examined. That is to say, the purpose of this analysis is to determine whether X is the cause of Y or not. Because the methodology considered in the analysis is essential (Eti and İnel, 2016), it can be said that Dumitrescu Hurlin panel causality analysis is very helpful in order to achieve the purpose of this study.

Analysis Results

Stationary analysis of the variables is the first step to evaluate the relationship between non-performing loans, industry volume and economic growth. For this purpose, Levin, Lin and Chu (LLC) panel unit root test was used. The results of this test were given on Table 14.

As it can be understood from Table 14, as a result of Levin, Lin and Chu panel unit root test, the probability values of all three variables are less than 0.05. This situation shows that these variables do not have unit root. In other words, they are stationary at their level values. Owing to this situation, these variables were used in the analysis with their original forms. In addition to this condition, to achieve

Table 14. LLC panel unit root test results

Variables	Levin, Lin and Chu Test (p Value)
NPL	0.0000
Industry	0.0002
Economic Growth	0.0000

the objective of the study, Dumitrescu Hurlin panel causality test was taken into the consideration. The results of this test were given on Table 15.

As it can be seen from Table 15, the probability values for the null hypothesis of "Industry volume does not cause economic growth" for 1 lag and 2 lags are less than 0.05. Because of this situation, it was defined that this null hypothesis can be rejected. This result demonstrates that there is a causality relationship between industry volume and economic growth. That is to say, in order for African countries to provide economic growth, increase in industry volume should be provided. It can also be said that when industry is improved in Africa, this will contribute to global trade. Additionally, this situation has a positive influence on global growth.

Another important result of this analysis is that the null hypothesis of "Economic growth does not cause NPL" was rejected since the probability value of this hypothesis is less than 0.05. This result explains that decrease in economic growth is the main cause of the non-performing loans ratio in African countries. This condition shows that when there is a decline in economic growth of these countries, customers started to face some difficulties in order to pay their debts to the banks. Due to this aspect, the non-performing loans ratio increases. Because economic recession has an increasing effect on nonperforming loans, economic growth should be provided to contribute global trade.

In addition to these aspects, the null hypothesis of "Industry volume does not cause NPL" can be rejected as well because the probability values of this hypothesis for 1 lag and 3 lags are less than 0.05. This situation refers that decrease in the industry volume is the key reason of high non-performing loans ratio. This issue explains that when there is decrease in industry volume in African countries, the companies will have lower trade volume and the profitability of them will decline.

Table 15. Dumitrescu Hurlin panel causality test results

Null Hypothesis	Probability Values (lag=1)	Probability Values (lag=2)	Probability Values (lag=3)
"Industry" does not cause *"Economic Growth"*	0.5335	**0.0000**	**0.0003**
"Economic Growth" does not cause *"Industry"*	0.5887	0.4413	0.2233
"NPL" does not cause *"Economic Growth"*	0.8687	0.3226	0.5211
"Economic Growth" does not cause *"NPL"*	**0.0096**	0.8637	0.5078
"NPL" does not cause *"Industry"*	0.6106	0.4218	0.9599
"Industry" does not cause "NPL"	0.0004	0.1482	0.0000

As a result of this aspect, these parties have problems regarding the repayment of the loans taken by the banks. In other words, global trade possibilities should be taken into the consideration to improve the industry. Therefore, it can be possible to minimize the ratio of nonperforming loans.

SOLUTIONS AND RECOMMENDATIONS

In this study, it is concluded that industry growth is the main cause of economic growth which has a decreasing effect on nonperforming loans ratio. As it can be understood these three variables are connected to each other for African countries. Therefore, it is obvious that African countries should focus on improving their industry levels in order to minimize the negative ways of lower economic growth and higher nonperforming loans.

FUTURE RESEARCH DIRECTIONS

In this study, the relationship between nonperforming loans, industry development and economic growth is evaluated for African countries. In addition to this aspect, another study, which makes a comparison developed countries with developing countries with respect to this relationship, will be also very beneficial to the literature.

CONCLUSION

In this paper, it was aimed to identify the causality relationship between non-performing loans, industry volume and economic growth. Within this scope, 16 African countries were analyzed in this study. Because there is not necessary data for other African countries, they had to be eliminated in the analysis. Furthermore, annual data of these 16 African countries for the periods between 2001 and 2015 were taken into the consideration. Additionally, Dumitrescu Hurlin panel causality test was considered in order to reach this objective.

In the analysis process, first of all, unit root test was made to understand whether the variables are stationary or not. Within this context, Levin, Lin and Chu (LLC) panel unit root test was used. As a result of this test, it was defined that probability values of all three variables are less than 0.05. This situation shows that these variables do not have unit roots. In other words, it was seen that they are stationary on their level values. Owing to this situation, it was identified that there are appropriate for Dumitrescu Hurlin panel causality analysis.

According to the results of the panel causality analysis, it was determined that there is a causality relationship between industry volume and economic growth. In other words, it was understood that decrease in the industry volume is the main reason of economic recession. The main reason behind this situation is that when there is a problem in the industry, companies will face financial problems and this issue results in decreasing economic growth. Due to this aspect, it was recommended that African countries should focus on industry development in order to provide economic growth. It can also be understood that when industry is developed in Africa, this will contribute to global trade has an increasing effect on global growth.

In addition to this situation, it was also concluded that decrease in economic growth is the main cause of the non-performing loans ratio in African countries. This condition demonstrates that when economic growth of these countries is declined, customers started to face some financial difficulties in order to pay their debts to the banks. Owing to this situation, the non-performing loans ratio of these banks increases. Therefore, it can be said that when economies of African countries are developed, the problem of high non-performing loans ratios will be minimized. To enhance global growth, banking sector should work effectively. Hence, as it can be understood from the result of the analysis, economies of the countries should be improved to enhance effective banking sector and provide global growth.

Another important result of this study is that decrease in the industry volume is the key reason of high non-performing loans ratio. This issue explains that when industry volume in African countries is decreased, the companies will have lower trade volume. Because of this situation, the profitability of these countries will decline. As a result of this aspect, these parties have problems regarding the repayment of the loans taken by the banks. Thus, it was understood that these countries should also improve their industries to reduce non-performing loans ratio. While considering this result, it can be said that global trade should be developed to have effective banking system and increase life standards of the people. Owing to this situation, it can be possible to reach global growth.

REFERENCES

Abadi, S., Achsan, N. A. I., & Rachmina, D. (2014). The Dynamics of Non-Performing Loan in Indonesian Banking Industry: A Sensitivity Analysis using VECM Approach. *International Journal of Education and Research*, *2*(8).

Adebola, S. S., Sulaiman, W., Yusoff, W., & Dahalan, J. (2011). An ARDL approach to the determinants of nonperforming loans in Islamic banking system in Malaysia. *Kuwait Chapter of Arabian Journal of Business and Management Review*, *1*(2), 20–30.

Ahmad, F., & Bashir, T. (2013). Explanatory Power of Macroeconomic Variables as Determinants of Non-Performing Loans: Evidence form Pakistan. *World Applied Sciences Journal*, *22*(2), 243–255.

Amediku, S. (2006). *Stress tests of the Ghanaian Banking Sector: A VAR Approach.* Working Paper of Bank of Ghana, WP/BOG-2006/02.

Arisoy, I. (2008). *Türkiye'de Sanayi Sektörü-Iktisadi Büyüme Ilişkisinin Kaldor Hipotezi Çerçevesinde Test Edilmesi* (No. 2008/1). Discussion Paper, Turkish Economic Association.

Balgova, M., Nies, M., & Plekhanov, A. (n.d.). *The economic impact of reducing non-performing loans.* EBRD Working Paper No. 193.

Beck, R., Jakubik, P., & Piloiu, A. (2013). *Non-performing loans: What matters in addition to the economic cycle?* Working Paper Series, 1515.

Bloom, D. E., Sachs, J. D., Collier, P., & Udry, C. (1998). Geography, demography, and economic growth in Africa. *Brookings Papers on Economic Activity*, *1998*(2), 207–295. doi:10.2307/2534695 PMID:12295931

Coale, A. J., & Hoover, E. M. (2015). *Population growth and economic development.* Princeton University Press.

Diaz Bautista, A. (2003). México´s Industrial Engine of Growth: Cointegration and Causality. *Revista Momento Economico*, (126).

Drakopoulos, S. A., & Theodossiou, I. (1991). Kaldorian Approach to Greek Economic Growth. *Applied Economics*, *23*(10), 1683–1689. doi:10.1080/00036849100000133

Dumitrescu, E. I., & Hurlin, C. (2012). Testing for Granger non-causality in heterogeneous panels. *Economic Modelling*, *29*(4), 1450–1460. doi:10.1016/j.econmod.2012.02.014

Elegbe, A. (2013). Bank failure and economic development in Nigeria: An empirical approach. *British Journal of Economics. Finance and Management Sciences*, *8*(1), 46–63.

Erdogdu, A. (2016). Assessing the Impact of Non-Performing Loans on Economic Growth in Turkey. *Economic and Social Development: Book of Proceedings*, 309.

Ersin, İ., & Duran, S. (2017). Faizsiz Finans Döngüsünü Oluşturma Açısından Adil Ekonomik Düzen Söyleminin Kredileşme İlkeleri Ve Uygulanabilirliğinin Değerlendirilmesi. *Turkish Studies*, *12*(8), 109–132. doi:10.7827/TurkishStudies.11928

Espinoza, R., & Ananthakri, P. (2010). *Nonperforming Loans in the GCC Banking System and their macroeconomic effects.* IMF Working Paper WP/10/224.

Eti, S., & İnel, M. N. (2016). A Research on Comparison of Regression Models Explaining the Profitability Base on Financial Data. *International Journal of Business and Management*, *4*(10), 470–475.

Fofack, H. (2005). *Nonperforming loans in Sub-Saharan Africa: causal analysis and macroeconomic implications.* World Bank Policy Research Working Paper, 3769.

Fogel, R. W. (1994). *Economic growth, population theory, and physiology: the bearing of long-term processes on the making of economic policy (No. w4638).* National Bureau of Economic Research. doi:10.3386/w4638

Ghosh, A. (2015). Banking-industry specific and regional economic determinants of non-performing loans: Evidence from US states. *Journal of Financial Stability*, *20*, 93–104. doi:10.1016/j.jfs.2015.08.004

Greenidge, K., & Grosvenor, T. (2010). Forecasting non-performing loans in Barbados. *Journal of Business. Finance and Economics in Emerging Economies*, *5*(1), 79–108.

Haniifah, N. (2015). Economic Determinants of Non-performing Loans (NPLs) in Ugandan Commercial Banks. Taylor's. *Business Review (Federal Reserve Bank of Philadelphia)*, *5*(2), 137–153.

Kaldor, N. (1966). *Causes of the Slow Rate of Economic Growth of the United Kingdom: An Inaugural Lecture*. Cambridge University Press.

Karahanoğlu, İ., & Ercan, H. (2015). The Effect of Macroeconomic Variables on Non-Performing Loans in Turkish Banking Sector. *Journal of International Social Research*, *8*(39), 883–892. doi:10.17719/jisr.20153913804

Kavoussi, R. M. (1984). Export expansion and economic growth: Further empirical evidence. *Journal of Development Economics*, *14*(1), 241–250. doi:10.1016/0304-3878(84)90052-X

Klein, N. (2013). *Non-Performing Loans in CESEE: Determinants and Macroeconomic Performance.* IMF Working Paper WP13/72.

Kownacki, P. (2000). Migration phenomena and current social and economic problems of the African countries. *Hemispheres: Studies on Cultures and Societies*, (15), 37-49.

Louzis, D. P., Vouldis, A. T., & Metaxas, V. L. (2012). Macroeconomic and bank-specific determinants of non-performing loans in Greece: A comparative study of mortgage, business and consumer loan portfolios. *Journal of Banking & Finance, 36*(4), 1012–1027. doi:10.1016/j.jbankfin.2011.10.012

Messai, A. S., & Jouini, F. (2013). Micro and macro determinants of non-performing loans. *International Journal of Economics and Financial Issues, 3*(4), 852–860.

Millin, M., & Nichola, T. (2005). Explaining economic growth in South Africa: A Kaldorian approach. *International Journal of Technology Management & Sustainable Development, 4*(1), 47–62. doi:10.1386/ijtm.4.1.47/1

Nkusu, M. (2011). *Nonperforming loans and macrofinancial vulnerabilities in advanced economies*. IMF Working Paper, WP/11/161.

Saba, I., Kouser, R., & Azeem, M. (2012). Determinants of Non Performing Loans: Case of US Banking Sector. *The Romanian Economic Journal, 44*(6), 125–136.

Sarel, M. (1996). Nonlinear effects of inflation on economic growth. *Staff Papers, 43*(1), 199–215. doi:10.2307/3867357

Sheefeni, J. P. S. (2015). The Impact of Macroeconomic Determinants on Non-performing Loans in Namibia. *International Review of Research in Emerging Markets and the Global Economy, 4*, 612–632.

Škarica, B. (2014). Determinants of non-performing loans in Central and Eastern European countries. *Financial Theory and Practice, 38*(1), 37-59.

Terzi, H., & Oltulular, S. (2011). Türkiye'deki Sanayileşme ve Ekonomik Büyüme Arasındaki Nedensel İlişki. *Doğuş Üniversitesi Dergisi, 5*(2), 219–226.

Toenniessen, G., Adesina, A., & DeVries, J. (2008). Building an alliance for a green revolution in Africa. *Annals of the New York Academy of Sciences, 1136*(1), 233–242. doi:10.1196/annals.1425.028 PMID:18579885

Vatansever, M., & Hepsen, A. (2013). Determining impacts on non-performing loan ratio in Turkey. *Journal of Finance and Investment Analysis, 2*(4), 119–129.

Venâncio, S. F. M. (2013). *Does financial development promote economic growth?* (Doctoral dissertation). Instituto Superior de Economia e Gestão.

Watts, M. (1991). Entitlements or empowerment? Famine and starvation in Africa. *Review of African Political Economy, 18*(51), 9–26. doi:10.1080/03056249108703903

Yüksel, S., Dincer, H., & Hacioglu, U. (2015). CAMELS-based Determinants for the Credit Rating of Turkish Deposit Banks. *International Journal of Finance & Banking Studies*, *4*(4), 1–17.

Yüksel, S., & Zengin, S. (2016a). Causality relationship between import, export and growth rate in developing countries. *International Journal of Commerce and Finance*, *2*(1), 147–156.

Yüksel, S., & Zengin, S. (2016b). Leading Indicators of 2008 Global Crisis: An Analysis with Logit and MARS Methods. *Finansal Araştırmalar ve Çalışmalar Dergisi*, *8*(15), 495–518.

KEY TERMS AND DEFINITIONS

Current Account Balance: Gives information about the difference between the incoming and outgoing amounts of foreign exchanges.

Economic Growth: The increase in GDP amount in comparison with the last period.

Export: Selling goods to other countries.

GDP: The first letters of gross domestic product. It gives information about the economic power of the country.

GDP Per Capita: Calculated as the total GDP value divided by the number of people in this country.

Industry Growth: Gives information about the improvement in the industry volume.

Inflation Rate: The increase in the price levels.

Nonperforming Loan: The loan which cannot be paid by the customers within 90 days period after the maturity.

Nonperforming Loans Ratio: Calculated by dividing nonperforming loans to total loans.

Chapter 10
Analyzing the Impact of Oil Price Fluctuations on Vietnam Stock Market

Huynh Viet Khai
Can Tho University, Vietnam

Le Minh Sang
Can Tho University, Vietnam

Phan Thi Anh Nguyet
Can Tho University, Vietnam

ABSTRACT

This chapter covers a study that was conducted to find out the impact of crude oil prices on the Vietnam stock market in the period from March 2006 to June 2015 by using the autoregressive-distributed lag (ARDL) model with dummy variables of the economic crisis. The results revealed that the crude oil prices had positive impacts on VN-Index and HNX-Index in short-run, but negatively in long-run. In addition, the study also found that the economic crisis has affected the relationship between the crude oil prices and the stock market index in the short-run. During the crisis period, the crude oil prices related to the VN-Index and HNX-index more closely than the other stages. However, in the long-run the relationship between oil prices and stock market index was not affected by the economic crisis.

DOI: 10.4018/978-1-5225-4032-8.ch010

INTRODUCTION

Since the existence of oil, one of the most important commodities, is crucial for the world's economy, a change in the price of oil has a significant and large impact on the economy. A high variation of the oil price, in other words the sharp decreases and increases in price, can be seen as high price volatility. This high volatility makes oil one of the major macro-economic factors which create an unstable economic condition for countries around the world (Olivia, 2011). Oil price volatility has an impact on both oil-exporting and oil-importing countries. For oil-importing countries, an increase in the oil prices influences their economy negatively. When the price rises, they will experience harmful impacts such as increase in inflation and economic recession (Ferderer, 1996). On the other hand, the oil-exporting countries are positively correlated to the increase in oil prices. However, a decrease in the oil price exhibits a negative relationship with the economic development and it creates some political and social instability (Yang and Huang, 2002).

Oil price obviously influences the country's economy; the question is how does it effect on stock price on Stock Exchange Market? As stock price on the market is known as the mirror which reflects all changes in the economy, each impact on macro economy somehow influences to stock price on Stock Exchange market. Therefore, whenever fuel price effects on the economy, it makes stock price fluctuate. A large body of academic literature has explained the relationship of oil price and stock price on Stock Exchange Market. Kaul and Seyhun (1990) and Sadorsky (1999) elucidated that the higher oil price volatility tended to cause negative effect on stock market price. Jones and Kaul (1996) indicated that international stock price was not affected by oil shocks. The following study of Huang et al (1996) provided evidences which supported the cause and effect of petroleum price and stock price. Narayan and Narayan (2010) estimated the impact of oil prices on Vietnam's stock prices using daily data for the period 2000–2008 and include the nominal exchange rate as an additional determinant of stock prices. The study found that stock prices, oil prices and nominal exchange rates are cointegrated, and oil prices have a positive and statistically significant impact on stock prices. These diverse impacts and differences can be explained by the differences in importing and exporting petroleum in each country.

Vietnam, an emerging country, is both crude oil exporter and refined- oil importer for domestic use. Vietnam's stock market has grown rapidly in the period of 2000-2008, but has decreased sharply due to economic crisis in the period of 2008-2012. The world's economy is influenced by economic crisis in the period of 2008 and 2012, thus, how this economic crisis affects the relationship of oil prices and Vietnam stock market prices? To answer this question, the study is to examine the relationship between VN-index, HNX-index and world crude oil price from August 2006 to June 2015. The study is to hopefully bring the most accurate overview or whole picture in terms of the correlation of the world oil price and stock market returns on Vietnam stock exchange market in the periods of economic development and recession.

This article is constructed as follows. Section two concentrates on the literature over past works regarding oil price volatility. All the data used are described in section three and methodology in section four. This paper applied the approach of Autoregressive-Distributed Lag (ARDL) to recognize the dynamic relationships between the economic variables. All results and discussion of the analysis are presented and discussed in section five. The final section presents some main conclusions of the study.

BACKGROUND

Literature Review

The relationship between world crude oil price and stock market price becomes research interest of many economists. The relationship between oil-price changes and stock returns still remains a controversial issue. Table 1 summarizes some world and Vietnam's previous studies about the correlation of crude oil price and stock markets.

At first, Hamilton (1983) concluded that oil price shocks are significant causes of economic recession in the US, and then a number of researchers have begun to analyze the importance of oil price fluctuations on economic activity. For instances, the relationship of oil price shocks and stock markets is written by Huang et al (1996), Sadorsky (1999) and Guo and Kliesen (2005) in US, by Papapetrou (2001) in Greece, by Park and Ratti (2008) in US and other 13 European countries.

Table 1. The summary of the studies on the relationship of crude oil prices and stock market prices

Region	Correlation	Related Previous Studies
World	+/-	Jones and Kaul (1996), Sadorsky (1999), Park and Ratti (2008), Killian and Park (2009), Gogineni (2010), Le and Chan (2010), Olivia Prajitno (2011), Mohanty et al (2013), Degiannakis et al (2013).
	Irrelevance	Sawyer and Nandaha (2006), Apergis and Miller (2009).
Vietnam	+	Narayan and Nayaran (2010), Nguyen and Bhatti (2012), Nguyet and Thao (2013).

Nevertheless, these studies are still no consensus. According to the studies of Kaul and Seyhun (1990) and Sadorsky (1999), there is an adverse impact of oil prices on stock market prices. Further, Huang et al. (1996) provided evidence to support a causal impact from oil prices to stock prices. Meanwhile, Narayan and Narayan (2010) reported a positive impact of oil prices on the stock in the long term. So why is there such this difference? This issue can be explained by Gogineni (2007). In his study, oil prices have positive reactions on stock prices if oil shocks reflect all changes in aggregate demand, but on the contrary have a negative impact on the stock price if oil prices reflect the changes in aggregate supply.

Furthermore, stock prices symmetrically react with the fluctuations of oil prices. There are two channels that the changes of oil prices can affect stock market prices and stock market returns (Narayan and Narayan, 2010). First, oil is a crucial input in most firms' production process and leads to changes in costs, affecting earnings and dividends and hence stock prices. Second, oil prices also influence stock market returns through discount rates, which consist of expected inflation rate and real interest rate (Haung et al., 1996). Whenever inflation and interest are influenced by oil prices, in net oil importing countries, hikes in oil price are said to have pressures on exchange rate and inflation. Inflationary pressures caused by increased oil prices may lead central banks to raise interest rates and thus to negatively affect stock prices.

The study by Rafiq et al. (2009) concluded that oil price volatility has influence in the short time horizon and it has a big impact on investment and unemployment rate in Thailand. These results support the theory that oil price volatility has a negative impact on investments, which in turn increases the unemployment rate. Kang et al. (2009) argued that it is very important to forecast the oil price volatility because oil price shocks play an important role in explaining the reason for the recent adverse macroeconomic influence on industrial production, employment, and prices in most countries.

A number of studies on the links between oil prices and stock market are conducted by many researchers. Narayan and Narayan (2010) examined the impact of crude oil prices and foreign exchange rates on the stock market in Vietnam by using daily data of the period from the year 2000 to the year 2008. The results showed that the stock prices, oil prices and nominal exchange rates had a positive relationship; and oil prices had a positive impact on stock prices in the long term. Nevertheless, the studies have not recorded a significant impact of oil prices and Vietnam stock market indices in short term.

Nguyen and Bhatti (2012) studied the relationship between oil price and stock market in China and Vietnam using nonparametric methods of Chi-plot and K-plot, and a parametric approach for copula modeling. The results found out that there was the left tail dependency between international oil prices and Vietnam stock market while Chinese market showed opposite results, proving an existence of relationship between oil prices and stock prices on Vietnam stock market. Nguyen and Thao (2013) tested the correlation of macroeconomic factors and Vietnam stock market. The results showed that there was a linear correlation between monetary supply, inflation, world oil price, industrial output and stock market. However, it remains a reverse relation between interest rate, VND/USD foreign exchange rate and Vietnam stock market.

MAIN FOCUS OF THE CHAPTER

Data Collection

This study uses secondary data, including daily world crude oil prices, VN-index and HNX-index. Data collection and processing methods are shown in Table 2.

After collecting data, the study analyzed the characteristics of the sample, such as mean, maximum, minimum and standard deviation presented in Table 3.

Table 3 shows the characteristics of the data as follows: Firstly, there is sizable difference in value between VN-index and HNX-index. Whereby, the mean of VN-index is 4 times greater than the mean of HNX-index. Moreover, the standard deviation

Table 2. Data description

Variables	Symbol	Data Collection and Processing Methods
World oil price	*POIL*	Monthly average
HNX-index	*HNX*	Monthly average
VN-index	*VNI*	Monthly average
Economic crisis dummy	D_t	D_t=1 in the period of June 2008 to December 2012, D_t =0 in other periods
Interaction variable	D_tLPOIL	The relationship between economic crisis and crude oil prices

Notes: WTI's oil prices were collected on www.intervesting.com. HNX-index and VN-index were collected on www.shbs.com.vn.

Table 3. Descriptive statistics of the sample

Variables	Mean	Maximum	Minimum	Std. Dev.
VNI	543,61	1110,99	261,54	185,17
HNX	135,40	430,72	51,49	84,65
POIL	83,05	133,88	39,09	19,71

Notes: VNI is monthly average value of VN-index. HNX is monthly average value of HNX-index. POIL is mean of world oil prices. All observations are in the period of March 2006 to June 2015.

of VN-index is roughly double in comparison with the HNX-index. It implies that VN-index is more liquid than HNX-index on Vietnam Stock Market. However, the greater standard deviation also indicates that price risks are more likely to be happened on Hochiminh Stock Exchange than on Hanoi Stock Exchange. Secondly, the WTI has greatly fluctuated since 2006. More specifically, during mentioned period, the average value of WTI was 83,05 USD/barrel while the lowest price was 39,09 USD/barrel and standard deviation was 19,71 USD/barrel. The above figures show significant fluctuations of crude oil market over years, especially in economic crisis (2008) and current complex market. In short, the data shows the huge fluctuations of variables during the study's period. All changes on Vietnam Stock Market and world oil market are hardly predictable.

METHODOLOGY

Our study used the popular ARDL method proposed by Pesaran et al. (1999). It has been shown to be a valuable tool for testing for the presence of long-run relationships between economic time-series. The advantage of the ARDL model is its ability to estimate both the long and short-term model parameters. This avoids the problems posed by non-stationary time series. In addition, this approach does not require a prior determination of the order of the cointegration of the variables. Furthermore, the ARDL procedure is robust to small samples, allowing different optimal lags of variables. We conducted our analysis in the sequence shown in Table 4.

In addition, CUSUM and CUSUMSQ graphics were applied to examine the model's stability. The Pesaran et al., (2001) test was applied to test the cointegration among the variables. That procedure first corrects for error, then estimates the model's parameters and uses the F-statistic to test for cointegration.

The study's model is represented by equations (1) and (2) below:

Table 4. The steps of analysis

1. Performed the Augmented Dickey – Fuller test (ADF).
2. Tested the cointegration using the bounds test;
3. Selected an appropriate ARDL Model. The Akaike Information Criteria (AIC) was used in the determination of lag length.
4. Estimated long-term coefficients in the ARDL Model;
5. Estimated short-term coefficients using the Error Correction Models (ECM) developed from the ARDL Model;
6. Tested the stability and errors of the Model, including Autocorrelation and Heteroskedasticity.

ARDL 1:

$$LVNI_t = \alpha_0 + \alpha_1 D_t + \sum_{l=1}^{p_0} \alpha_{2,i} LVNI_{t-i} + \sum_{g=0}^{p_1} \alpha_{3,j} LPOIL_{t-j} + \sum_{h=0}^{p_2} \alpha_{4,k} D_t \cdot LPOIL_{t-k} + \varepsilon_{2t} \tag{1}$$

ARDL 2:

$$LHNX_t = \beta_0 + \beta_1 D_t + \sum_{l=1}^{q_0} \beta_{2,l} LHNX_{t-l} + \sum_{g=0}^{q_1} \beta_{3,g} LPOIL_{t-g} + \sum_{h=0}^{q_2} \beta_{4,h} D_t \cdot LPOIL_{t-h} + \varepsilon_{2t} \tag{2}$$

where *LVNI, LHNX, LPOIL* are respectively *logVNI, logHNX, logPOIL*. D_t is an economic crisis's dummy variable equal to 1 in the period of June 2008 to December 2012 and 0 for the other periods. D_t*.LPOIL* is the interaction variable. p_0, p_1, p_2, q_0, q_1, q_2 represent maximum lag lengths used for *LVNI, LHNX, LPOIL* and $D_t LPOIL$. *i, j, k, l, g, h* are lag lengths of the variables. α_0, β_0 is the model's intercept. α_1, β_1 is the coefficient of D_t. $\alpha_{2,i}$, $\alpha_{3,j}$, $\alpha_{4,k}$, $\beta_{2,l}$, $\beta_{3,g}$, $\beta_{4,h}$ is coefficients of lagged variables. ε_{1t} and ε_{2t} are random error terms.

The bound test was done as follows.

Equation (3) models the cointegration of *logVNI* and *logPOL*.

$$\Delta LVNI_t = \delta_0 + \delta_1 D_t + \sum_{i=1}^{p_0} \delta_{2,i} \Delta LVNI_{t-i} + \sum_{j=0}^{P_1} \delta_{3,j} \Delta LPOIL_{t-j}$$
$$+ \sum_{k=0}^{p_{23}} \delta_{4,k} \Delta D_t \cdot LPOIL_{t-k} + \lambda_0 LVNI_{t-1} + \lambda_1 LPOIL_{t-1} + \lambda_2 D_t LPOIL_{t-1} + \varepsilon_{1t} \tag{3}$$

If $\lambda_0 = \lambda_1 = \lambda_2 = 0$, there is no cointegration.

Equation (4) models the the cointegration of *logHNX* and *logPOIL*.

$$\Delta LHNX_t = \varphi_0 + \varphi_1 D_t + \sum_{l=1}^{q_0} \varphi_{2,l} \Delta LHNX_{t-l} + \sum_{j=0}^{q_1} \varphi_{3,j} \Delta LPOIL_{t-j}$$
$$+ \sum_{k=0}^{q_2} \varphi_{4,k} D_t \cdot LPOIL_{t-k} + \gamma_0 LHNX_{t-1} + \gamma_1 LPOIL_{t-1} + \gamma_2 D_t LPOIL_{t-1} + \varepsilon_{2t} \tag{4}$$

where:

$$\Delta LVNI_t = LVNI_t - LVNI_{t-1};\ \Delta LHNX_t = NX_t - LHNX_{t-1};$$

$$\Delta LPOIL_t = LPOIL_t - LPOIL_{t-1};\ \Delta D_t LPOIL_t = D_t LPOIL_t - D_t LPOIL_{t-1}$$

where: Δ is first-difference operator, $\beta_{0,i}$, $\beta_{1,j}$ are short-term parameters of variables. δ_0, φ_0 are constants. δ_1, δ_2, δ_3, δ_4, φ_1, $\varphi_2\varphi_3$, φ_4 are short-term multipliers. $\lambda_0, \lambda_1, \lambda_2$, $\gamma_0, \gamma_1, \gamma_2$ are long term multipliers of lagged variables in the model.

Equations (3) and (4) were estimated using the OLS method where optimal lag lengths were chosen for each variable. Next, the calculated F-statistics were compared with critical values to determine if there are cointegrating relationships among variables (Persaran, 2001).

According to Persaran (2001), the critical bounds value is calculated based on the number of regressive variables and the model's critical value. There are both upper and lower bounds. The upper critical bounds value assumes that all variables are cointegrated at level 1 or I(1), while all variables' co-integration is at level 0 or I(0) when calculating the lower bound. If the calculated F-statistic exceeds the upper critical bounds value, then H_0 is rejected with the significance at 1%. In this case, there is cointegration among variables. If the F-statistic falls within the bounds, then the test is inconclusive. If the F-statistic falls below the lower bound, then H_0 is accepted. This implies that there is no cointegration. To examine the cointegration of crude oil prices and the HNX-index, a similar test is done with coefficients $\gamma_0, \gamma_1, \gamma_2$ in equation (4).

RESULTS AND DISCUSSION

Stationary or Unit Root Testing

The ADF root unit test, shown in Table 5, indicates that both the VN-index (*LVNI*) and the HNX-index (*LHNX*) are nonstationary in three models. World oil price (*LPOIL*) is stationary in models 2 and 3 the at 1% and 5% significant levels respectively. The difference variables, VN-index (*ΔLVNI*), HNX-index (*ΔLHNX*), and world oil prices (*ΔLPOIL*) are stationary with significance at 1% in the three models.

Table 5. The results of ADF root unit test

Variable	Model 1			Model 2			Model 3		
	Lag Length	t-Value		Lag Length	t-Value		Lag Length	T-Value	
LVNI	1	-0.179		1	-2.458		1	-2.406	
LHNX	1	-1.844		9	-2.606		9	-3.989	
LPOIL	1	-0.230		2	-3.811	***	2	-3.902	**
ΔLVNI	0	-7.164	***	0	-7.128	***	0	-7.093	***
ΔLHNX	0	-7.135	***	0	-7.105	***	0	-7.066	***
ΔLPOIL	0	-6.946	***	0	-6.915	***	0	-6.901	***

Note: ***, **, * denote significance at 1%, 5%, and 10% levels, respectively. All variables (LVNI, LHNX, LPOIL) are natural logs. Δ is first difference of variables. Lag lengths are chosen in line with AIC standards. Model 1 is ADF model with no intercept and trend. Model 2 is ADF model with intercept. Model 3 is ADF model with intercept and trend.

Cointegration Testing

The results of the cointegration test shown in Table 6 present F-values greater than the upper critical bounds at the 5% significance level in both models. Therefore, the null hypothesis (H_0) of no integrating links between variables is rejected in both model 3 and 4. This implies that world oil prices have a long-term relationship with VN-index and HNX-index.

Determination of Lag Lengths

The lag lengths of the variables in models ARDL 1 and ARDL 2 were determined based on the Akaike Information Criterion (AIC). The findings indicate that the models ARDL (12, 4, 3) are most suitable for ARDL 1. The maximum lag lengths

Table 6. The results of Bound test

Model	d.f	F-Value	Critical F-Value					
			10%		5%		1%	
			I(0)	I(1)	I(0)	I(1)	I(0)	I(1)
3	2	8.881***	2.63	3.35	3.1	3.87	4.13	5
4	2	4.632***	2.63	3.35	3.1	3.87	4.13	5

Note: ***, ** and * denote at 1%, 5% and 10% significance levels, respectively. I(1) are upper critical bounds values based on assumption that all variables are cointegration at level 1 or I(1). I(0) are lower critical bounds values based on assumption that all variables are cointegration at level 0 or I(0). Model 3 tests the cointegration between variables in ARDL 1 while Model 4 tests the cointegration between variables in ARDL 2.

for *LVNI, LPOIL,* D_tLPOIL are 12, 4, 3 respectively. Meanwhile, ARDL 2 model has appropriate maximum lag lengths of *LHNX, LPOIL,* D_tLPOIL of 10, 4 and 3, respectively. The results of maximum lag length selection and estimation of models ARDL 1 and 2 are shown in Table 7.

Estimation of Long-Term Coefficients

To estimate long-term coefficients, step 4 (see Table 4) was performed for both ARDL 1 and 2. Table 7 shows the results. The long-term coefficients of LPOIL are less than 0 in both the ARDL models with significance levels at 1% and 5% respectively. This indicates a negative relationship between world oil prices and variables VN-index and HNX-index. This contrasts with former studies that indicated a worldwide long-term positive relationship (Narayan and Nayaran, 2010; Nguyen and Bhatti, 2012). However, our findings agree with most Vietnamese studies. Vietnam imports oil for domestic uses. Thus, an increase in world oil prices results in a rise in Vietnamese domestic oil prices. In long term, when the price of oil increases, production costs increase, and the profits of manufacturing companies decease, negatively affecting the VN-index, and the HNX-index.

The long-term correlation coefficient of economic crisis variable ($D_t = -1.793$) is less than 0 with a significance level of 10% in ARDL 1. However, D_t has no statistical significance in ARDL 2. As a result, the structure of the long-term coefficient in ARDL 1 was different during the economic crisis. Thus, we showed no major impact on the long-term relationship between world crude oil price and the VN-index. During the economic crisis, the VN-index declined more than in the period of no crisis, but there was no change in the HNX-index. The correlation coefficient of the interaction variable (D_tLPOIL) was not significant in either the ARDL 1 or the ARDL 2 models. Therefore, the economic crisis did not affect the long-term relationship between world crude oil prices, the VN-index and the HNX-index.

Estimation of Short-Term Coefficients

To examine the short-term relationship between world oil prices, the VN-index and the HNX-index, we estimated the short-term coefficients in ARDL 1 and ARDL 2. The results are presented in Table 9. The correlation coefficient of the difference variable in the third lag length ($\Delta LPOIL_{t-3}$) is greater than zero with statistical significance at 1% in both models. This implies that the change of world oil prices in the third lag length had a positive relationship with the changes in the VN-index and the HNX-index. In other words, rising world oil prices increased the VN-index and the HNX-index in the following three months. This result is contrary to Narayan and Narayan, (2010), which found no short-term relationship between world oil

Table 7. Results of model selection

ARDL 1: ARDL (12, 4, 3) LVNI Is a Dependent Variable			ARDL 2: ARDL (10, 4, 3) LHNX Is a Dependent Variable		
Variables	**Coefficient**	**t-Value**	**Variables**	**Coefficient**	**t-Value**
$LVNI_{t-1}$	1.077***	10.718	$LHNX_{t-1}$	1,188***	12,173
$LVNI_{t-2}$	-0.231	-1.468	$LHNX_{t-2}$	-0,175	-1,086
$LVNI_{t-3}$	-0.144	-0.931	$LHNX_{t-3}$	-0,261	-1,628
$LVNI_{t-4}$	0.230	1.555	$LHNX_{t-4}$	0,210	1,311
$LVNI_{t-5}$	0.008	0.055	$LHNX_{t-5}$	-0,047	-0,294
$LVNI_{t-6}$	-0.278**	-2.002	$LHNX_{t-6}$	-0,094	-0,609
$LVNI_{t-7}$	0.182	1.383	$LHNX_{t-7}$	0,127	0,837
$LVNI_{t-8}$	-0.046	-0.342	$LHNX_{t-8}$	0,006	0,042
$LVNI_{t-9}$	0.229*	1.704	$LHNX_{t-9}$	0,264*	1,859
$LVNI_{t-10}$	-0.313**	-2.292	$LHNX_{t-10}$	-0,291***	-3,390
$LVNI_{t-11}$	0.233*	1.741	$LPOIL$	0.099	0.835
$LVNI_{t-12}$	-0.166**	-1.998	$LPOIL_{t-1}$	-0.270	-1.552
$LPOIL$	0.072	0.868	$LPOIL_{t-2}$	0.014	0.080
$LPOIL_{t-1}$	-0.243*	-1.957	$LPOIL_{t-3}$	0.363**	2.087
$LPOIL_{t-2}$	0.126	1.024	$LPOIL_{t-4}$	-0.348***	-2.807
$LPOIL_{t-3}$	0.193	1.553	D_tLPOIL	-0.063	-0.905
$LPOIL_{t-4}$	-0.292***	-3.318	D_tLPOIL_{t-1}	0.051***	2.642
D_tLPOIL	0.054	1.089	D_tLPOIL_{t-2}	-0.005	-0.239
D_tLPOIL_{t-1}	0.046***	10.718	D_tLPOIL_{t-3}	-0.026*	-1.720
D_tLPOIL_{t-2}	-0.006	-1.468	D_t	0.166	0.530
D_tLPOIL_{t-3}	-0.020*	-0.931	*Constant*	0.971***	3.216
D_t	-0.392*	1.555			
Constant	2.037***	0.055			
R^2		0.972	R^2		0.982
R^2 adjusted		0.964	R^2 adjusted		0.977
F-value		123.049***	F-value		217.346***

Note: ***.** and * denote significance at 1%. 5% and 10% levels. respectively. Model ARDL 1 invests the link between crude oil prices and VN-index. Model ARDL 2 examines the relationship between crude oil prices and HNX-index. LVNI. LHNX. LPOIL are respectively VN-index. HNX-index and world oil price variables which are taken natural logarithm. D_tLPOIL is an interaction variable.

Table 8. Results of long-term coefficient estimation

ARDL 1 (LVNI Is Dependent Variable)			ARDL 2 (LHNX Is Dependent Variable)		
Variables	Coefficient	t-Value	Variables	Coefficient	t-Value
LPOIL	-0.663***	-3.388	*LPOIL*	-1.951**	-2.316
D_tLPOIL	0.341	1.475	D_tLPOIL	-0.574	-0.593
D_t	-1.793*	-1.744	D_t	2.275	0.532
Constant	9.306***	10.702	*Constant*	13.352**	3.571

Note: ***, **, * denote significance levels of 1%, 5% and 10%. LVNI, LHNX, LPOIL which respectively stand for VN-index, HNX-index and world oil prices are in natural logarithm. D_t is economic crisis dummy variable. D_tLPOIL is interaction variable of economic crisis and world oil prices.

prices and the VN-index. The price of crude oil took about three months to cause an impact on the VN-Index. This is mainly due to the Vietnamese oil price adjustment mechanism, which is less efficient than the world's.

Our results indicate that crude oil prices can be used to assess world economic health in the short-term. Rising oil prices signifies that the world economy is developing well, and will need more oil products for manufacturing. A growing world economy a positively effects the stock market. In contrast, the decline of crude oil prices is usually associated with a decline of the world economy and the stock markets.

The correlation coefficients of the difference of interaction variables at the first and second lag lengths (ΔD_tLPOIL_{t-1}, ΔD_tLPOIL_{t-2}) are significantly greater than zero in both models ARDL 1 and ARDL 2. This indicates that the structure of the short-term relationship between world crude oil prices and VN-Index changed in the examined period. During the crisis period, the change in crude oil prices quickly and positively impacted the VN-Index and and the HNX-Index. It only took a month to realize the impact, and it lasted for two months. In this period, crude oil prices had large variations. This, combined with the herd mentality in the Vietnamese stock market, sped the process.

The correlation coefficient of the crisis dummy variable (ΔD_t) was not statistically significant. Therefore, the change in these indices was the same during the crisis period as it was during the other periods.

Autocorrelation and Heteroskedasticity Tests

The Breusch-Godfrey serial correlation LM test was used to check the presence of Autocorrelations. The Breusch-Pagan-Godfrey method was used to test for heteroskedasticity. The results in Table 10 indicate that the autocorrelation and

Table 9. Results of short-term coefficient estimation

ARDL 1 (ΔLVNI Is Dependent Variable)			ARDL 2 (ΔLHNX Is Dependent Variable)		
Variables	**Coefficient**	**t-Value**	**Variables**	**Coefficient**	**t-Value**
$\Delta LVNI_{t-1}$	0.301***	3.358	$\Delta LHNX_{t-1}$	0.272***	2.896
$\Delta LVNI_{t-2}$	0.053	0.555	$\Delta LHNX_{t-2}$	0.070	0.719
$\Delta LVNI_{t-3}$	-0.074	-0.836	$\Delta LHNX_{t-3}$	-0.167*	-1.738
$\Delta LVNI_{t-4}$	0.150*	1.759	$\Delta LHNX_{t-4}$	0.037	0.395
$\Delta LVNI_{t-5}$	0.151*	1.716	$\Delta LHNX_{t-5}$	-0.015	-0.169
$\Delta LVNI_{t-6}$	-0.124	-1.553	$\Delta LHNX_{t-6}$	-0.111	-1.207
$\Delta LVNI_{t-7}$	0.066	0.829	$\Delta LHNX_{t-7}$	0.031	0.332
$\Delta LVNI_{t-8}$	0.012	0.152	$\Delta LHNX_{t-8}$	0.018	0.215
$\Delta LVNI_{t-9}$	0.242***	3.026	$\Delta LHNX_{t-9}$	0.283***	3.538
$\Delta LVNI_{t-10}$	-0.070	-0.841	$\Delta LPOIL$	0.013	0.086
$\Delta LVNI_{t-11}$	0.157*	1.984	$\Delta LPOIL_{t-1}$	-0.038	-0.349
$\Delta LPOIL$	0.029	0.272	$\Delta LPOIL_{t-2}$	-0.016	-0.142
$\Delta LPOIL_{t-1}$	-0.029	-0.378	$\Delta LPOIL_{t-3}$	0.343***	2.992
$\Delta LPOIL_{t-2}$	0.097	1.241	ΔD_tLPOIL	0.072	0.398
$\Delta LPOIL_{t-3}$	0.286***	3.552	ΔD_tLPOIL_{t-1}	0.029**	2.132
ΔD_tLPOIL	0.124	0.999	ΔD_tLPOIL_{t-2}	0.025*	1.792
ΔD_tLPOIL_{t-1}	0.025***	2.728	ΔD_t	-0.467	-0.553
ΔD_tLPOIL_{t-2}	0.019**	2.072	$ECM2_{t-1}$	-0.070***	-4.333
ΔD_t	-0.720	-1.238			
$ECM1_{t-1}$	-0.210***	-5.997			
$ECM1 = LVNI$ -(-0.6627$LPOIL$ + 0.3414D_t $LPOIL$ -1.793D_t + 9.306)					
ECM2 = LVNI -(-0.574$LPOIL$ -1.951D_tLPOIL + 2.275Dt + 13.352)					

Note: ***, ** and * denote significance levels of 1%, 5% and 10%. LVNI, LHNX, LPOIL, which respectively stand for VN-index, HNX-index and world oil prices are in natural logs. D_t is economic crisis dummy variable. D_tLPOIL is interaction variable of economic crisis and world oil prices. ECM1 and ECM2 are adjusted error variables. Δ is first difference.

heteroskedasticity hypotheses can be rejected at 5% level because all values of F-critical are larger than the F-statistics in both models.

Figures 1 and 2 illustrate the results of CUSUM and CUSUMSQ tests of ARDL 1 and 2. Thus, we conclude, that the models are stable over time, and could be used in analysis and forecasting.

Table 10. Results of autocorrelation and heteroskedasticity tests

Test	ARDL 1			ARDL 2		
	d.f	**F-Critical**	**F-Statistic**	**d.f**	**F-Critical**	**F-Statistic**
Autocorrelation	(1,76)	3.966	0.163	(1,80)	3.960	1.741
Heteroskedasticity	(22,77)	3.426	0.989	(20,81)	1.702	1.248

Figure 1. Results of CUSUM and CUSUMSQ of ARDL 1

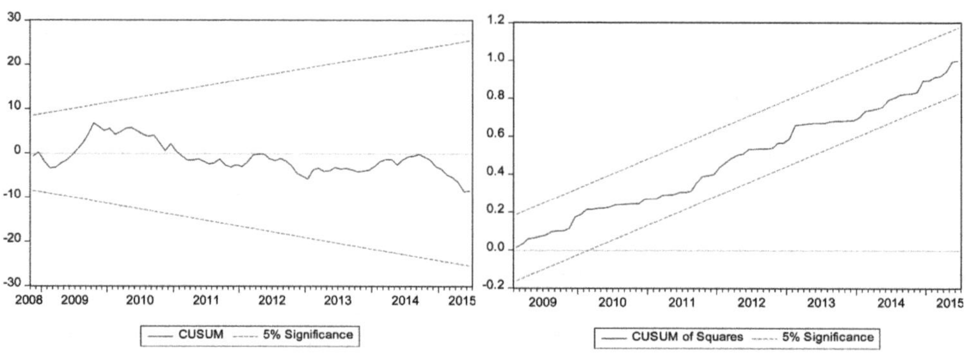

Figure 2. Results of CUSUM and CUSUMSQ of ARDL 2

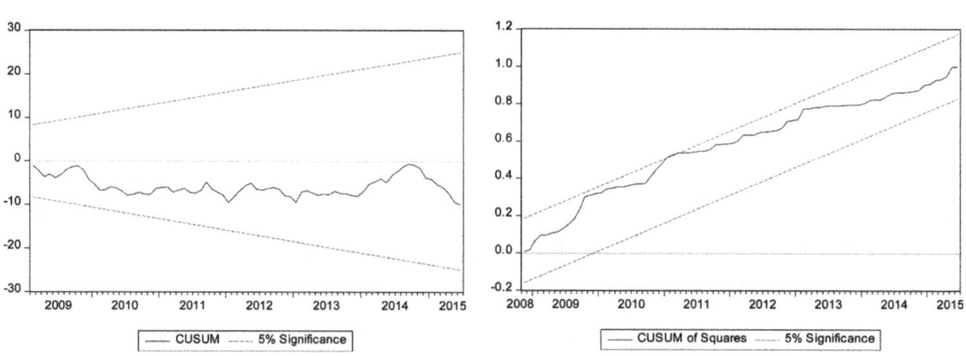

CONCLUSION

Using monthly average data from March 2006 to June 2015, the paper applies Autoregressive-Distributed Lag (ARDL) method (Persaran et al.,1997, 2001), combined with economic crisis dummy variable to empirical examine the relationship between world crude oil prices and Vietnam stock market indices. The results showed that crude oil prices and Vietnam stock market indices had long-term relationship.

The result is similar to the previous studies by Narayan and Narayan (2010), Nguyen and Bhati (2012), Nguyet and Thao (2013). However, when analyzing the long-term and short-term impact, the study results may differ from the results of previous studies. Accordingly, in the short term, crude oil prices and Vietnam stock market indices positively related, whereas previous studies of Narayan and Narayan (2010) did not recognize this relationship in short term. In the long term, the results reported negative relationship between crude oil prices and Vietnam stock market indices, while the findings of Narayan and Narayan (2010) proved they positively correlated. These differences could be explained by the difference in time of the study and the changes in policies on Vietnam oil market and stock market. In addition, this study also showed the differences in the impact of crude oil price between the normal period and economic crisis period. The impact of crude oil prices on the stock market in economic crisis period is faster than in the other periods. Besides, the study also noted the same responses of the HNX-index and VN-index by the impact of crude oil prices in both short term and long term.

ACKNOWLEDGMENT

This chapter is based on an article originally published in Southeast Asia Review of Economics and Business (SAREB) in 2017. This material is reprinted with permission of SAREB.

REFERENCES

Apergis, N., & Miller, S. M. (2009). Do structural oil-market shocks affect stock prices? *Energy Economics*, *31*(4), 569–575. doi:10.1016/j.eneco.2009.03.001

Degiannakis, S., Filis, G., & Kizys, R. (2013). *Oil price shocks and stock market volatility: evidence from European data* (No. 161).

Ferderer, J. P. (1997). Oil price volatility and the macroeconomy. *Journal of Macroeconomics*, *18*(1), 1–26. doi:10.1016/S0164-0704(96)80001-2

Gogineni, S. (2010). Oil and the stock market: An industry level analysis. *Financial Review*, *45*(4), 995–1010. doi:10.1111/j.1540-6288.2010.00282.x

Guo, H., & Kliesen, K. L. (2005). Oil price volatility and US macroeconomic activity. *RE:view*, 87.

Hamilton, J. D. (1983). Oil and the macroeconomy since World War II. *Journal of Political Economy, 91*(2), 228–248. doi:10.1086/261140

Huang, R. D., Masulis, R. W., & Stoll, H. R. (1996). Energy shocks and financial markets. *Journal of Futures Markets, 16*(1), 1–27. doi:10.1002/(SICI)1096-9934(199602)16:1<1::AID-FUT1>3.0.CO;2-Q

Jones, C. M., & Kaul, G. (1996). Oil and the stock markets. *The Journal of Finance, 51*(2), 463–491. doi:10.1111/j.1540-6261.1996.tb02691.x

Kang, S. H., Kang, S. M., & Yoon, S. M. (2009). Forecasting volatility of crude oil markets. *Energy Economics, 31*(1), 119–125. doi:10.1016/j.eneco.2008.09.006

Kaul, G., & Seyhun, H. N. (1990). Relative price variability, real shocks, and the stock market. *The Journal of Finance, 45*(2), 479–496. doi:10.1111/j.1540-6261.1990.tb03699.x

Kilian, L., & Park, C. (2009). The impact of oil price shocks on the US stock market*. *International Economic Review, 50*(4), 1267–1287. doi:10.1111/j.1468-2354.2009.00568.x

Le, T. H., & Chang, Y. (2011). *The impact of oil price fluctuations on stock markets in developed and emerging economies.* Singapore Economic Review Conference 2011.

Mohanty, S. K., Akhigbe, A., Al-Khyal, T. A., & Bugshan, T. (2013). Oil and stock market activity when prices go up and down: The case of the oil and gas industry. *Review of Quantitative Finance and Accounting, 41*(2), 253–272. doi:10.1007/s11156-012-0309-9

Narayan, P. K., & Narayan, S. (2010). Modelling the impact of oil prices on Vietnam's stock prices. *Applied Energy, 87*(1), 356–361. doi:10.1016/j.apenergy.2009.05.037

Nguyen, C. C., & Bhatti, M. I. (2012). Copula model dependency between oil prices and stock markets: Evidence from China and Vietnam. *Journal of International Financial Markets, Institutions and Money, 22*(4), 758–773. doi:10.1016/j.intfin.2012.03.004

Nguyet, P. T. B., & Thao, P. P. (2013). Analyzing the impact of macroeconomic factors on Vietnam stock market. *Journal of Development and Integration, 8*(18), 34–41.

O'Neil, W. J., & Ryan, C. (1988). *How to make money in stocks* (Vol. 10). New York: McGraw-Hill.

Papapetrou, E. (2001). Oil price shocks, stock market, economic activity and employment in Greece. *Energy Economics, 23*(5), 511–532. doi:10.1016/S0140-9883(01)00078-0

Park, J., & Ratti, R. A. (2008). Oil price shocks and stock markets in the US and 13 European countries. *Energy Economics*, *30*(5), 2587–2608. doi:10.1016/j.eneco.2008.04.003

Pesaran, M. H., Shin, Y., & Smith, R. J. (2001). Bounds testing approaches to the analysis of level relationships. *Journal of Applied Econometrics*, *16*(3), 289–326. doi:10.1002/jae.616

Pesaran, M. H., Shin, Y., & Smith, R. P. (1999). Pooled mean group estimation of dynamic heterogeneous panels. *Journal of the American Statistical Association*, *94*(446), 621–634. doi:10.1080/01621459.1999.10474156

Prajitno, O. (2011). *The Effect of the Oil Price Volatility on the US Stock Market* (Thesis). Department of Economics, Erasmus University, Rotterdam, The Netherlands.

Rafiq, S., Salim, R., & Bloch, H. (2009). Impact of crude oil price volatility on economic activities: An empirical investigation in the Thai economy. *Resources Policy*, *34*(3), 121–132. doi:10.1016/j.resourpol.2008.09.001

Sadorsky, P. (1999). Oil price shocks and stock market activity. *Energy Economics*, *21*(5), 449–469. doi:10.1016/S0140-9883(99)00020-1

Sawyer, K. R., & Nandha, M. (2006). *How oil moves stock prices*. Available at SSRN: https://ssrn.com/abstract=910427

Yang, C. W., Hwang, M. J., & Huang, B. N. (2002). An analysis of factors affecting price volatility of the US oil market. *Energy Economics*, *24*(2), 107–119. doi:10.1016/S0140-9883(01)00092-5

Related References

To continue our tradition of advancing academic research, we have compiled a list of recommended IGI Global readings. These references will provide additional information and guidance to further enrich your knowledge and assist you with your own research and future publications.

Adeyemo, O. (2013). The nationwide health information network: A biometric approach to prevent medical identity theft. In *User-driven healthcare: Concepts, methodologies, tools, and applications* (pp. 1636–1649). Hershey, PA: IGI Global. doi:10.4018/978-1-4666-2770-3.ch081

Adler, M., & Henman, P. (2009). Justice beyond the courts: The implications of computerisation for procedural justice in social security. In A. Martínez & P. Abat (Eds.), *E-justice: Using information communication technologies in the court system* (pp. 65–86). Hershey, PA: IGI Global. doi:10.4018/978-1-59904-998-4.ch005

Aflalo, E., & Gabay, E. (2013). An information system for coping with student dropout. In L. Tomei (Ed.), *Learning tools and teaching approaches through ICT advancements* (pp. 176–187). Hershey, PA: IGI Global. doi:10.4018/978-1-4666-2017-9.ch016

Ahmed, M. A., Janssen, M., & van den Hoven, J. (2012). Value sensitive transfer (VST) of systems among countries: Towards a framework. *International Journal of Electronic Government Research*, *8*(1), 26–42. doi:10.4018/jegr.2012010102

Aikins, S. K. (2008). Issues and trends in internet-based citizen participation. In G. Garson & M. Khosrow-Pour (Eds.), *Handbook of research on public information technology* (pp. 31–40). Hershey, PA: IGI Global. doi:10.4018/978-1-59904-857-4.ch004

Aikins, S. K. (2009). A comparative study of municipal adoption of internet-based citizen participation. In C. Reddick (Ed.), *Handbook of research on strategies for local e-government adoption and implementation: Comparative studies* (pp. 206–230). Hershey, PA: IGI Global. doi:10.4018/978-1-60566-282-4.ch011

Aikins, S. K. (2012). Improving e-government project management: Best practices and critical success factors. In *Digital democracy: Concepts, methodologies, tools, and applications* (pp. 1314–1332). Hershey, PA: IGI Global. doi:10.4018/978-1-4666-1740-7.ch065

Akabawi, M. S. (2011). Ghabbour group ERP deployment: Learning from past technology failures. In E. Business Research and Case Center (Ed.), Cases on business and management in the MENA region: New trends and opportunities (pp. 177-203). Hershey, PA: IGI Global. doi:10.4018/978-1-60960-583-4.ch012

Akabawi, M. S. (2013). Ghabbour group ERP deployment: Learning from past technology failures. In *Industrial engineering: Concepts, methodologies, tools, and applications* (pp. 933–958). Hershey, PA: IGI Global. doi:10.4018/978-1-4666-1945-6.ch051

Akbulut, A. Y., & Motwani, J. (2008). Integration and information sharing in e-government. In G. Putnik & M. Cruz-Cunha (Eds.), *Encyclopedia of networked and virtual organizations* (pp. 729–734). Hershey, PA: IGI Global. doi:10.4018/978-1-59904-885-7.ch096

Akers, E. J. (2008). Technology diffusion in public administration. In G. Garson & M. Khosrow-Pour (Eds.), *Handbook of research on public information technology* (pp. 339–348). Hershey, PA: IGI Global. doi:10.4018/978-1-59904-857-4.ch033

Al-Shafi, S. (2008). Free wireless internet park services: An investigation of technology adoption in Qatar from a citizens' perspective. *Journal of Cases on Information Technology*, *10*(3), 21–34. doi:10.4018/jcit.2008070103

Al-Shafi, S., & Weerakkody, V. (2009). Implementing free wi-fi in public parks: An empirical study in Qatar. *International Journal of Electronic Government Research*, *5*(3), 21–35. doi:10.4018/jegr.2009070102

Aladwani, A. M. (2002). Organizational actions, computer attitudes and end-user satisfaction in public organizations: An empirical study. In C. Snodgrass & E. Szewczak (Eds.), *Human factors in information systems* (pp. 153–168). Hershey, PA: IGI Global. doi:10.4018/978-1-931777-10-0.ch012

Aladwani, A. M. (2002). Organizational actions, computer attitudes, and end-user satisfaction in public organizations: An empirical study. *Journal of Organizational and End User Computing*, *14*(1), 42–49. doi:10.4018/joeuc.2002010104

Allen, B., Juillet, L., Paquet, G., & Roy, J. (2005). E-government and private-public partnerships: Relational challenges and strategic directions. In M. Khosrow-Pour (Ed.), *Practicing e-government: A global perspective* (pp. 364–382). Hershey, PA: IGI Global. doi:10.4018/978-1-59140-637-2.ch016

Alshawaf, A., & Knalil, O. E. (2008). IS success factors and IS organizational impact: Does ownership type matter in Kuwait? *International Journal of Enterprise Information Systems*, *4*(2), 13–33. doi:10.4018/jeis.2008040102

Ambali, A. R. (2009). Digital divide and its implication on Malaysian e-government: Policy initiatives. In H. Rahman (Ed.), *Social and political implications of data mining: Knowledge management in e-government* (pp. 267–287). Hershey, PA: IGI Global. doi:10.4018/978-1-60566-230-5.ch016

Amoretti, F. (2007). Digital international governance. In A. Anttiroiko & M. Malkia (Eds.), *Encyclopedia of digital government* (pp. 365–370). Hershey, PA: IGI Global. doi:10.4018/978-1-59140-789-8.ch056

Amoretti, F. (2008). Digital international governance. In A. Anttiroiko (Ed.), *Electronic government: Concepts, methodologies, tools, and applications* (pp. 688–696). Hershey, PA: IGI Global. doi:10.4018/978-1-59904-947-2.ch058

Amoretti, F. (2008). E-government at supranational level in the European Union. In A. Anttiroiko (Ed.), *Electronic government: Concepts, methodologies, tools, and applications* (pp. 1047–1055). Hershey, PA: IGI Global. doi:10.4018/978-1-59904-947-2.ch079

Amoretti, F. (2008). E-government regimes. In A. Anttiroiko (Ed.), *Electronic government: Concepts, methodologies, tools, and applications* (pp. 3846–3856). Hershey, PA: IGI Global. doi:10.4018/978-1-59904-947-2.ch280

Amoretti, F. (2009). Electronic constitution: A Braudelian perspective. In F. Amoretti (Ed.), *Electronic constitution: Social, cultural, and political implications* (pp. 1–19). Hershey, PA: IGI Global. doi:10.4018/978-1-60566-254-1.ch001

Amoretti, F., & Musella, F. (2009). Institutional isomorphism and new technologies. In M. Khosrow-Pour (Ed.), *Encyclopedia of information science and technology* (2nd ed.; pp. 2066–2071). Hershey, PA: IGI Global. doi:10.4018/978-1-60566-026-4.ch325

Andersen, K. V., & Henriksen, H. Z. (2007). E-government research: Capabilities, interaction, orientation, and values. In D. Norris (Ed.), *Current issues and trends in e-government research* (pp. 269–288). Hershey, PA: IGI Global. doi:10.4018/978-1-59904-283-1.ch013

Anderson, K. V., & Henriksen, H. Z. (2005). The first leg of e-government research: Domains and application areas 1998-2003. *International Journal of Electronic Government Research, 1*(4), 26–44. doi:10.4018/jegr.2005100102

Anttiroiko, A. (2009). Democratic e-governance. In M. Khosrow-Pour (Ed.), *Encyclopedia of information science and technology* (2nd ed.; pp. 990–995). Hershey, PA: IGI Global. doi:10.4018/978-1-60566-026-4.ch158

Association, I. R. (2010). *Networking and telecommunications: Concepts, methodologies, tools and applications* (Vols. 1–3). Hershey, PA: IGI Global. doi:10.4018/978-1-60566-986-1

Association, I. R. (2010). *Web-based education: Concepts, methodologies, tools and applications* (Vols. 1–3). Hershey, PA: IGI Global. doi:10.4018/978-1-61520-963-7

Baker, P. M., Bell, A., & Moon, N. W. (2009). Accessibility issues in municipal wireless networks. In C. Reddick (Ed.), *Handbook of research on strategies for local e-government adoption and implementation: Comparative studies* (pp. 569–588). Hershey, PA: IGI Global. doi:10.4018/978-1-60566-282-4.ch030

Becker, S. A., Keimer, R., & Muth, T. (2010). A case on university and community collaboration: The sci-tech entrepreneurial training services (ETS) program. In S. Becker & R. Niebuhr (Eds.), *Cases on technology innovation: Entrepreneurial successes and pitfalls* (pp. 68–90). Hershey, PA: IGI Global. doi:10.4018/978-1-61520-609-4.ch003

Becker, S. A., Keimer, R., & Muth, T. (2012). A case on university and community collaboration: The sci-tech entrepreneurial training services (ETS) program. In Regional development: Concepts, methodologies, tools, and applications (pp. 947-969). Hershey, PA: IGI Global. doi:10.4018/978-1-4666-0882-5.ch507

Bernardi, R. (2012). Information technology and resistance to public sector reforms: A case study in Kenya. In T. Papadopoulos & P. Kanellis (Eds.), *Public sector reform using information technologies: Transforming policy into practice* (pp. 59–78). Hershey, PA: IGI Global. doi:10.4018/978-1-60960-839-2.ch004

Bernardi, R. (2013). Information technology and resistance to public sector reforms: A case study in Kenya. In *User-driven healthcare: Concepts, methodologies, tools, and applications* (pp. 14–33). Hershey, PA: IGI Global. doi:10.4018/978-1-4666-2770-3.ch002

Bolívar, M. P., Pérez, M. D., & Hernández, A. M. (2012). Municipal e-government services in emerging economies: The Latin-American and Caribbean experiences. In Y. Chen & P. Chu (Eds.), *Electronic governance and cross-boundary collaboration: Innovations and advancing tools* (pp. 198–226). Hershey, PA: IGI Global. doi:10.4018/978-1-60960-753-1.ch011

Borycki, E. M., & Kushniruk, A. W. (2010). Use of clinical simulations to evaluate the impact of health information systems and ubiquitous computing devices upon health professional work. In S. Mohammed & J. Fiaidhi (Eds.), *Ubiquitous health and medical informatics: The ubiquity 2.0 trend and beyond* (pp. 552–573). Hershey, PA: IGI Global. doi:10.4018/978-1-61520-777-0.ch026

Borycki, E. M., & Kushniruk, A. W. (2011). Use of clinical simulations to evaluate the impact of health information systems and ubiquitous computing devices upon health professional work. In *Clinical technologies: Concepts, methodologies, tools and applications* (pp. 532–553). Hershey, PA: IGI Global. doi:10.4018/978-1-60960-561-2.ch220

Buchan, J. (2011). Developing a dynamic and responsive online learning environment: A case study of a large Australian university. In B. Czerkawski (Ed.), *Free and open source software for e-learning: Issues, successes and challenges* (pp. 92–109). Hershey, PA: IGI Global. doi:10.4018/978-1-61520-917-0.ch006

Buenger, A. W. (2008). Digital convergence and cybersecurity policy. In G. Garson & M. Khosrow-Pour (Eds.), *Handbook of research on public information technology* (pp. 395–405). Hershey, PA: IGI Global. doi:10.4018/978-1-59904-857-4.ch038

Burn, J. M., & Loch, K. D. (2002). The societal impact of world wide web - Key challenges for the 21st century. In A. Salehnia (Ed.), *Ethical issues of information systems* (pp. 88–106). Hershey, PA: IGI Global. doi:10.4018/978-1-931777-15-5.ch007

Burn, J. M., & Loch, K. D. (2003). The societal impact of the world wide web-Key challenges for the 21st century. In M. Khosrow-Pour (Ed.), *Advanced topics in information resources management* (Vol. 2, pp. 32–51). Hershey, PA: IGI Global. doi:10.4018/978-1-59140-062-2.ch002

Bwalya, K. J., Du Plessis, T., & Rensleigh, C. (2012). The "quicksilver initiatives" as a framework for e-government strategy design in developing economies. In K. Bwalya & S. Zulu (Eds.), *Handbook of research on e-government in emerging economies: Adoption, e-participation, and legal frameworks* (pp. 605–623). Hershey, PA: IGI Global. doi:10.4018/978-1-4666-0324-0.ch031

Cabotaje, C. E., & Alampay, E. A. (2013). Social media and citizen engagement: Two cases from the Philippines. In S. Saeed & C. Reddick (Eds.), *Human-centered system design for electronic governance* (pp. 225–238). Hershey, PA: IGI Global. doi:10.4018/978-1-4666-3640-8.ch013

Camillo, A., Di Pietro, L., Di Virgilio, F., & Franco, M. (2013). Work-groups conflict at PetroTech-Italy, S.R.L.: The influence of culture on conflict dynamics. In B. Christiansen, E. Turkina, & N. Williams (Eds.), *Cultural and technological influences on global business* (pp. 272–289). Hershey, PA: IGI Global. doi:10.4018/978-1-4666-3966-9.ch015

Capra, E., Francalanci, C., & Marinoni, C. (2008). Soft success factors for m-government. In A. Anttiroiko (Ed.), *Electronic government: Concepts, methodologies, tools, and applications* (pp. 1213–1233). Hershey, PA: IGI Global. doi:10.4018/978-1-59904-947-2.ch089

Cartelli, A. (2009). The implementation of practices with ICT as a new teaching-learning paradigm. In A. Cartelli & M. Palma (Eds.), *Encyclopedia of information communication technology* (pp. 413–417). Hershey, PA: IGI Global. doi:10.4018/978-1-59904-845-1.ch055

Charalabidis, Y., Lampathaki, F., & Askounis, D. (2010). Investigating the landscape in national interoperability frameworks. *International Journal of E-Services and Mobile Applications, 2*(4), 28–41. doi:10.4018/jesma.2010100103

Charalabidis, Y., Lampathaki, F., & Askounis, D. (2012). Investigating the landscape in national interoperability frameworks. In A. Scupola (Ed.), *Innovative mobile platform developments for electronic services design and delivery* (pp. 218–231). Hershey, PA: IGI Global. doi:10.4018/978-1-4666-1568-7.ch013

Chen, I. (2005). Distance education associations. In C. Howard, J. Boettcher, L. Justice, K. Schenk, P. Rogers, & G. Berg (Eds.), *Encyclopedia of distance learning* (pp. 599–612). Hershey, PA: IGI Global. doi:10.4018/978-1-59140-555-9.ch087

Chen, I. (2008). Distance education associations. In L. Tomei (Ed.), *Online and distance learning: Concepts, methodologies, tools, and applications* (pp. 562–579). Hershey, PA: IGI Global. doi:10.4018/978-1-59904-935-9.ch048

Chen, Y. (2008). Managing IT outsourcing for digital government. In A. Anttiroiko (Ed.), *Electronic government: Concepts, methodologies, tools, and applications* (pp. 3107–3114). Hershey, PA: IGI Global. doi:10.4018/978-1-59904-947-2.ch229

Chen, Y., & Dimitrova, D. V. (2006). Electronic government and online engagement: Citizen interaction with government via web portals. *International Journal of Electronic Government Research*, *2*(1), 54–76. doi:10.4018/jegr.2006010104

Chen, Y., & Knepper, R. (2005). Digital government development strategies: Lessons for policy makers from a comparative perspective. In W. Huang, K. Siau, & K. Wei (Eds.), *Electronic government strategies and implementation* (pp. 394–420). Hershey, PA: IGI Global. doi:10.4018/978-1-59140-348-7.ch017

Chen, Y., & Knepper, R. (2008). Digital government development strategies: Lessons for policy makers from a comparative perspective. In H. Rahman (Ed.), *Developing successful ICT strategies: Competitive advantages in a global knowledge-driven society* (pp. 334–356). Hershey, PA: IGI Global. doi:10.4018/978-1-59904-654-9.ch017

Cherian, E. J., & Ryan, T. W. (2014). Incongruent needs: Why differences in the iron-triangle of priorities make health information technology adoption and use difficult. In C. El Morr (Ed.), *Research perspectives on the role of informatics in health policy and management* (pp. 209–221). Hershey, PA: IGI Global. doi:10.4018/978-1-4666-4321-5.ch012

Cho, H. J., & Hwang, S. (2010). Government 2.0 in Korea: Focusing on e-participation services. In C. Reddick (Ed.), *Politics, democracy and e-government: Participation and service delivery* (pp. 94–114). Hershey, PA: IGI Global. doi:10.4018/978-1-61520-933-0.ch006

Chorus, C., & Timmermans, H. (2010). Ubiquitous travel environments and travel control strategies: Prospects and challenges. In M. Wachowicz (Ed.), *Movement-aware applications for sustainable mobility: Technologies and approaches* (pp. 30–51). Hershey, PA: IGI Global. doi:10.4018/978-1-61520-769-5.ch003

Chuanshen, R. (2007). E-government construction and China's administrative litigation act. In A. Anttiroiko & M. Malkia (Eds.), *Encyclopedia of digital government* (pp. 507–510). Hershey, PA: IGI Global. doi:10.4018/978-1-59140-789-8.ch077

Ciaghi, A., & Villafiorita, A. (2012). Law modeling and BPR for public administration improvement. In K. Bwalya & S. Zulu (Eds.), *Handbook of research on e-government in emerging economies: Adoption, e-participation, and legal frameworks* (pp. 391–410). Hershey, PA: IGI Global. doi:10.4018/978-1-4666-0324-0.ch019

Ciaramitaro, B. L., & Skrocki, M. (2012). mHealth: Mobile healthcare. In B. Ciaramitaro (Ed.), Mobile technology consumption: Opportunities and challenges (pp. 99-109). Hershey, PA: IGI Global. doi:10.4018/978-1-61350-150-4.ch007

Comite, U. (2012). Innovative processes and managerial effectiveness of e-procurement in healthcare. In A. Manoharan & M. Holzer (Eds.), *Active citizen participation in e-government: A global perspective* (pp. 206–229). Hershey, PA: IGI Global. doi:10.4018/978-1-4666-0116-1.ch011

Cordella, A. (2013). E-government success: How to account for ICT, administrative rationalization, and institutional change. In J. Gil-Garcia (Ed.), *E-government success factors and measures: Theories, concepts, and methodologies* (pp. 40–51). Hershey, PA: IGI Global. doi:10.4018/978-1-4666-4058-0.ch003

Cropf, R. A. (2009). ICT and e-democracy. In M. Khosrow-Pour (Ed.), *Encyclopedia of information science and technology* (2nd ed.; pp. 1789–1793). Hershey, PA: IGI Global. doi:10.4018/978-1-60566-026-4.ch281

Cropf, R. A. (2009). The virtual public sphere. In M. Pagani (Ed.), *Encyclopedia of multimedia technology and networking* (2nd ed.; pp. 1525–1530). Hershey, PA: IGI Global. doi:10.4018/978-1-60566-014-1.ch206

D'Abundo, M. L. (2013). Electronic health record implementation in the United States healthcare industry: Making the process of change manageable. In V. Wang (Ed.), *Handbook of research on technologies for improving the 21st century workforce: Tools for lifelong learning* (pp. 272–286). Hershey, PA: IGI Global. doi:10.4018/978-1-4666-2181-7.ch018

Damurski, L. (2012). E-participation in urban planning: Online tools for citizen engagement in Poland and in Germany. *International Journal of E-Planning Research, 1*(3), 40–67. doi:10.4018/ijepr.2012070103

de Almeida, M. O. (2007). E-government strategy in Brazil: Increasing transparency and efficiency through e-government procurement. In M. Gascó-Hernandez (Ed.), *Latin America online: Cases, successes and pitfalls* (pp. 34–82). Hershey, PA: IGI Global. doi:10.4018/978-1-59140-974-8.ch002

de Juana Espinosa, S. (2008). Empirical study of the municipalitites' motivations for adopting online presence. In A. Anttiroiko (Ed.), *Electronic government: Concepts, methodologies, tools, and applications* (pp. 3593–3608). Hershey, PA: IGI Global. doi:10.4018/978-1-59904-947-2.ch262 de Souza Dias, D. (2002). Motivation for using information technology. In C. Snodgrass & E. Szewczak (Eds.), *Human factors in information systems* (pp. 55–60). Hershey, PA: IGI Global. doi:10.4018/978-1-931777-10-0.ch005

Demediuk, P. (2006). Government procurement ICT's impact on the sustainability of SMEs and regional communities. In S. Marshall, W. Taylor, & X. Yu (Eds.), *Encyclopedia of developing regional communities with information and communication technology* (pp. 321–324). Hershey, PA: IGI Global. doi:10.4018/978-1-59140-575-7.ch056

Devonshire, E., Forsyth, H., Reid, S., & Simpson, J. M. (2013). The challenges and opportunities of online postgraduate coursework programs in a traditional university context. In B. Tynan, J. Willems, & R. James (Eds.), *Outlooks and opportunities in blended and distance learning* (pp. 353–368). Hershey, PA: IGI Global. doi:10.4018/978-1-4666-4205-8.ch026

Di Cerbo, F., Scotto, M., Sillitti, A., Succi, G., & Vernazza, T. (2007). Toward a GNU/Linux distribution for corporate environments. In S. Sowe, I. Stamelos, & I. Samoladas (Eds.), *Emerging free and open source software practices* (pp. 215–236). Hershey, PA: IGI Global. doi:10.4018/978-1-59904-210-7.ch010

Diesner, J., & Carley, K. M. (2005). Revealing social structure from texts: Meta-matrix text analysis as a novel method for network text analysis. In V. Narayanan & D. Armstrong (Eds.), *Causal mapping for research in information technology* (pp. 81–108). Hershey, PA: IGI Global. doi:10.4018/978-1-59140-396-8.ch004

Dologite, D. G., Mockler, R. J., Bai, Q., & Viszhanyo, P. F. (2006). IS change agents in practice in a US-Chinese joint venture. In M. Hunter & F. Tan (Eds.), *Advanced topics in global information management* (Vol. 5, pp. 331–352). Hershey, PA: IGI Global. doi:10.4018/978-1-59140-923-6.ch015

Drnevich, P., Brush, T. H., & Luckock, G. T. (2011). Process and structural implications for IT-enabled outsourcing. *International Journal of Strategic Information Technology and Applications*, *2*(4), 30–43. doi:10.4018/jsita.2011100103

Dwivedi, A. N. (2009). *Handbook of research on information technology management and clinical data administration in healthcare* (Vols. 1–2). Hershey, PA: IGI Global. doi:10.4018/978-1-60566-356-2

Elbeltagi, I., McBride, N., & Hardaker, G. (2006). Evaluating the factors affecting DSS usage by senior managers in local authorities in Egypt. In M. Hunter & F. Tan (Eds.), *Advanced topics in global information management* (Vol. 5, pp. 283–307). Hershey, PA: IGI Global. doi:10.4018/978-1-59140-923-6.ch013

Eom, S., & Fountain, J. E. (2013). Enhancing information services through public-private partnerships: Information technology knowledge transfer underlying structures to develop shared services in the U.S. and Korea. In J. Gil-Garcia (Ed.), *E-government success around the world: Cases, empirical studies, and practical recommendations* (pp. 15–40). Hershey, PA: IGI Global. doi:10.4018/978-1-4666-4173-0.ch002

Esteves, T., Leuenberger, D., & Van Leuven, N. (2012). Reaching citizen 2.0: How government uses social media to send public messages during times of calm and times of crisis. In K. Kloby & M. D'Agostino (Eds.), *Citizen 2.0: Public and governmental interaction through web 2.0 technologies* (pp. 250–268). Hershey, PA: IGI Global. doi:10.4018/978-1-4666-0318-9.ch013

Estevez, E., Fillottrani, P., Janowski, T., & Ojo, A. (2012). Government information sharing: A framework for policy formulation. In Y. Chen & P. Chu (Eds.), *Electronic governance and cross-boundary collaboration: Innovations and advancing tools* (pp. 23–55). Hershey, PA: IGI Global. doi:10.4018/978-1-60960-753-1.ch002

Ezz, I. E. (2008). E-governement emerging trends: Organizational challenges. In A. Anttiroiko (Ed.), *Electronic government: Concepts, methodologies, tools, and applications* (pp. 3721–3737). Hershey, PA: IGI Global. doi:10.4018/978-1-59904-947-2.ch269

Fabri, M. (2009). The Italian style of e-justice in a comparative perspective. In A. Martínez & P. Abat (Eds.), *E-justice: Using information communication technologies in the court system* (pp. 1–19). Hershey, PA: IGI Global. doi:10.4018/978-1-59904-998-4.ch001

Fagbe, T., & Adekola, O. D. (2010). Workplace safety and personnel well-being: The impact of information technology. *International Journal of Green Computing, 1*(1), 28–33. doi:10.4018/jgc.2010010103

Fagbe, T., & Adekola, O. D. (2011). Workplace safety and personnel well-being: The impact of information technology. In *Global business: Concepts, methodologies, tools and applications* (pp. 1438–1444). Hershey, PA: IGI Global. doi:10.4018/978-1-60960-587-2.ch509

Farmer, L. (2008). Affective collaborative instruction with librarians. In S. Kelsey & K. St.Amant (Eds.), *Handbook of research on computer mediated communication* (pp. 15–24). Hershey, PA: IGI Global. doi:10.4018/978-1-59904-863-5.ch002

Favier, L., & Mekhantar, J. (2007). Use of OSS by local e-administration: The French situation. In K. St.Amant & B. Still (Eds.), *Handbook of research on open source software: Technological, economic, and social perspectives* (pp. 428–444). Hershey, PA: IGI Global. doi:10.4018/978-1-59140-999-1.ch033

Fernando, S. (2009). Issues of e-learning in third world countries. In M. Khosrow-Pour (Ed.), *Encyclopedia of information science and technology* (2nd ed.; pp. 2273–2277). Hershey, PA: IGI Global. doi:10.4018/978-1-60566-026-4.ch360

Filho, J. R., & dos Santos, J. R. Jr. (2009). Local e-government in Brazil: Poor interaction and local politics as usual. In C. Reddick (Ed.), *Handbook of research on strategies for local e-government adoption and implementation: Comparative studies* (pp. 863–878). Hershey, PA: IGI Global. doi:10.4018/978-1-60566-282-4.ch045

Fletcher, P. D. (2004). Portals and policy: Implications of electronic access to U.S. federal government information services. In A. Pavlichev & G. Garson (Eds.), *Digital government: Principles and best practices* (pp. 52–62). Hershey, PA: IGI Global. doi:10.4018/978-1-59140-122-3.ch004

Fletcher, P. D. (2008). Portals and policy: Implications of electronic access to U.S. federal government information services. In A. Anttiroiko (Ed.), *Electronic government: Concepts, methodologies, tools, and applications* (pp. 3970–3979). Hershey, PA: IGI Global. doi:10.4018/978-1-59904-947-2.ch289

Forlano, L. (2004). The emergence of digital government: International perspectives. In A. Pavlichev & G. Garson (Eds.), *Digital government: Principles and best practices* (pp. 34–51). Hershey, PA: IGI Global. doi:10.4018/978-1-59140-122-3.ch003

Franzel, J. M., & Coursey, D. H. (2004). Government web portals: Management issues and the approaches of five states. In A. Pavlichev & G. Garson (Eds.), *Digital government: Principles and best practices* (pp. 63–77). Hershey, PA: IGI Global. doi:10.4018/978-1-59140-122-3.ch005

Gaivéo, J. M. (2013). Security of ICTs supporting healthcare activities. In M. Cruz-Cunha, I. Miranda, & P. Gonçalves (Eds.), *Handbook of research on ICTs for human-centered healthcare and social care services* (pp. 208–228). Hershey, PA: IGI Global. doi:10.4018/978-1-4666-3986-7.ch011

Garson, G. D. (1999). *Information technology and computer applications in public administration: Issues and trends*. Hershey, PA: IGI Global. doi:10.4018/978-1-87828-952-0

Garson, G. D. (2003). Toward an information technology research agenda for public administration. In G. Garson (Ed.), *Public information technology: Policy and management issues* (pp. 331–357). Hershey, PA: IGI Global. doi:10.4018/978-1-59140-060-8.ch014

Garson, G. D. (2004). The promise of digital government. In A. Pavlichev & G. Garson (Eds.), *Digital government: Principles and best practices* (pp. 2–15). Hershey, PA: IGI Global. doi:10.4018/978-1-59140-122-3.ch001

Garson, G. D. (2007). An information technology research agenda for public administration. In G. Garson (Ed.), *Modern public information technology systems: Issues and challenges* (pp. 365–392). Hershey, PA: IGI Global. doi:10.4018/978-1-59904-051-6.ch018

Gasco, M. (2007). Civil servants' resistance towards e-government development. In A. Anttiroiko & M. Malkia (Eds.), *Encyclopedia of digital government* (pp. 190–195). Hershey, PA: IGI Global. doi:10.4018/978-1-59140-789-8.ch028

Gasco, M. (2008). Civil servants' resistance towards e-government development. In A. Anttiroiko (Ed.), *Electronic government: Concepts, methodologies, tools, and applications* (pp. 2580–2588). Hershey, PA: IGI Global. doi:10.4018/978-1-59904-947-2.ch190

Ghere, R. K. (2010). Accountability and information technology enactment: Implications for social empowerment. In E. Ferro, Y. Dwivedi, J. Gil-Garcia, & M. Williams (Eds.), *Handbook of research on overcoming digital divides: Constructing an equitable and competitive information society* (pp. 515–532). Hershey, PA: IGI Global. doi:10.4018/978-1-60566-699-0.ch028

Gibson, I. W. (2012). Simulation modeling of healthcare delivery. In A. Kolker & P. Story (Eds.), *Management engineering for effective healthcare delivery: Principles and applications* (pp. 69–89). Hershey, PA: IGI Global. doi:10.4018/978-1-60960-872-9.ch003

Gil-Garcia, J. R. (2007). Exploring e-government benefits and success factors. In A. Anttiroiko & M. Malkia (Eds.), *Encyclopedia of digital government* (pp. 803–811). Hershey, PA: IGI Global. doi:10.4018/978-1-59140-789-8.ch122

Gil-Garcia, J. R., & González Miranda, F. (2010). E-government and opportunities for participation: The case of the Mexican state web portals. In C. Reddick (Ed.), *Politics, democracy and e-government: Participation and service delivery* (pp. 56–74). Hershey, PA: IGI Global. doi:10.4018/978-1-61520-933-0.ch004

Goldfinch, S. (2012). Public trust in government, trust in e-government, and use of e-government. In Z. Yan (Ed.), *Encyclopedia of cyber behavior* (pp. 987–995). Hershey, PA: IGI Global. doi:10.4018/978-1-4666-0315-8.ch081

Goodyear, M. (2012). Organizational change contributions to e-government project transitions. In S. Aikins (Ed.), *Managing e-government projects: Concepts, issues, and best practices* (pp. 1–21). Hershey, PA: IGI Global. doi:10.4018/978-1-4666-0086-7.ch001

Gordon, S., & Mulligan, P. (2003). Strategic models for the delivery of personal financial services: The role of infocracy. In S. Gordon (Ed.), *Computing information technology: The human side* (pp. 220–232). Hershey, PA: IGI Global. doi:10.4018/978-1-93177-752-0.ch014

Gordon, T. F. (2007). Legal knowledge systems. In A. Anttiroiko & M. Malkia (Eds.), *Encyclopedia of digital government* (pp. 1161–1166). Hershey, PA: IGI Global. doi:10.4018/978-1-59140-789-8.ch175

Graham, J. E., & Semich, G. W. (2008). Integrating technology to transform pedagogy: Revisiting the progress of the three phase TUI model for faculty development. In L. Tomei (Ed.), *Adapting information and communication technologies for effective education* (pp. 1–12). Hershey, PA: IGI Global. doi:10.4018/978-1-59904-922-9.ch001

Grandinetti, L., & Pisacane, O. (2012). Web services for healthcare management. In D. Prakash Vidyarthi (Ed.), *Technologies and protocols for the future of internet design: Reinventing the web* (pp. 60–94). Hershey, PA: IGI Global. doi:10.4018/978-1-4666-0203-8.ch004

Groenewegen, P., & Wagenaar, F. P. (2008). VO as an alternative to hierarchy in the Dutch police sector. In G. Putnik & M. Cruz-Cunha (Eds.), *Encyclopedia of networked and virtual organizations* (pp. 1851–1857). Hershey, PA: IGI Global. doi:10.4018/978-1-59904-885-7.ch245

Gronlund, A. (2001). Building an infrastructure to manage electronic services. In S. Dasgupta (Ed.), *Managing internet and intranet technologies in organizations: Challenges and opportunities* (pp. 71–103). Hershey, PA: IGI Global. doi:10.4018/978-1-878289-95-7.ch006

Gronlund, A. (2002). Introduction to electronic government: Design, applications and management. In Å. Grönlund (Ed.), *Electronic government: Design, applications and management* (pp. 1–21). Hershey, PA: IGI Global. doi:10.4018/978-1-930708-19-8.ch001

Gupta, A., Woosley, R., Crk, I., & Sarnikar, S. (2009). An information technology architecture for drug effectiveness reporting and post-marketing surveillance. In J. Tan (Ed.), *Medical informatics: Concepts, methodologies, tools, and applications* (pp. 631–646). Hershey, PA: IGI Global. doi:10.4018/978-1-60566-050-9.ch047

Hallin, A., & Lundevall, K. (2007). mCity: User focused development of mobile services within the city of Stockholm. In I. Kushchu (Ed.), Mobile government: An emerging direction in e-government (pp. 12-29). Hershey, PA: IGI Global. doi:10.4018/978-1-59140-884-0.ch002

Hallin, A., & Lundevall, K. (2009). mCity: User focused development of mobile services within the city of Stockholm. In S. Clarke (Ed.), Evolutionary concepts in end user productivity and performance: Applications for organizational progress (pp. 268-280). Hershey, PA: IGI Global. doi:10.4018/978-1-60566-136-0.ch017

Hallin, A., & Lundevall, K. (2009). mCity: User focused development of mobile services within the city of Stockholm. In D. Taniar (Ed.), Mobile computing: Concepts, methodologies, tools, and applications (pp. 3455-3467). Hershey, PA: IGI Global. doi:10.4018/978-1-60566-054-7.ch253

Hanson, A. (2005). Overcoming barriers in the planning of a virtual library. In M. Khosrow-Pour (Ed.), *Encyclopedia of information science and technology* (pp. 2255–2259). Hershey, PA: IGI Global. doi:10.4018/978-1-59140-553-5.ch397

Haque, A. (2008). Information technology and surveillance: Implications for public administration in a new word order. In T. Loendorf & G. Garson (Eds.), *Patriotic information systems* (pp. 177–185). Hershey, PA: IGI Global. doi:10.4018/978-1-59904-594-8.ch008

Hauck, R. V., Thatcher, S. M., & Weisband, S. P. (2012). Temporal aspects of information technology use: Increasing shift work effectiveness. In J. Wang (Ed.), *Advancing the service sector with evolving technologies: Techniques and principles* (pp. 87–104). Hershey, PA: IGI Global. doi:10.4018/978-1-4666-0044-7.ch006

Hawk, S., & Witt, T. (2006). Telecommunications courses in information systems programs. *International Journal of Information and Communication Technology Education*, *2*(1), 79–92. doi:10.4018/jicte.2006010107

Helms, M. M., Moore, R., & Ahmadi, M. (2009). Information technology (IT) and the healthcare industry: A SWOT analysis. In J. Tan (Ed.), *Medical informatics: Concepts, methodologies, tools, and applications* (pp. 134–152). Hershey, PA: IGI Global. doi:10.4018/978-1-60566-050-9.ch012

Hendrickson, S. M., & Young, M. E. (2014). Electronic records management at a federally funded research and development center. In J. Krueger (Ed.), *Cases on electronic records and resource management implementation in diverse environments* (pp. 334–350). Hershey, PA: IGI Global. doi:10.4018/978-1-4666-4466-3.ch020

Henman, P. (2010). Social policy and information communication technologies. In J. Martin & L. Hawkins (Eds.), *Information communication technologies for human services education and delivery: Concepts and cases* (pp. 215–229). Hershey, PA: IGI Global. doi:10.4018/978-1-60566-735-5.ch014

Hismanoglu, M. (2011). Important issues in online education: E-pedagogy and marketing. In U. Demiray & S. Sever (Eds.), *Marketing online education programs: Frameworks for promotion and communication* (pp. 184–209). Hershey, PA: IGI Global. doi:10.4018/978-1-60960-074-7.ch012

Ho, K. K. (2008). The e-government development, IT strategies, and portals of the Hong Kong SAR government. In A. Anttiroiko (Ed.), *Electronic government: Concepts, methodologies, tools, and applications* (pp. 715–733). Hershey, PA: IGI Global. doi:10.4018/978-1-59904-947-2.ch060

Holden, S. H. (2003). The evolution of information technology management at the federal level: Implications for public administration. In G. Garson (Ed.), *Public information technology: Policy and management issues* (pp. 53–73). Hershey, PA: IGI Global. doi:10.4018/978-1-59140-060-8.ch003

Holden, S. H. (2007). The evolution of federal information technology management literature: Does IT finally matter? In G. Garson (Ed.), *Modern public information technology systems: Issues and challenges* (pp. 17–34). Hershey, PA: IGI Global. doi:10.4018/978-1-59904-051-6.ch002

Holland, J. W. (2009). Automation of American criminal justice. In M. Khosrow-Pour (Ed.), *Encyclopedia of information science and technology* (2nd ed.; pp. 300–302). Hershey, PA: IGI Global. doi:10.4018/978-1-60566-026-4.ch051

Holloway, K. (2013). Fair use, copyright, and academic integrity in an online academic environment. In *Digital rights management: Concepts, methodologies, tools, and applications* (pp. 917–928). Hershey, PA: IGI Global. doi:10.4018/978-1-4666-2136-7.ch044

Horiuchi, C. (2005). E-government databases. In L. Rivero, J. Doorn, & V. Ferraggine (Eds.), *Encyclopedia of database technologies and applications* (pp. 206–210). Hershey, PA: IGI Global. doi:10.4018/978-1-59140-560-3.ch035

Horiuchi, C. (2006). Creating IS quality in government settings. In E. Duggan & J. Reichgelt (Eds.), *Measuring information systems delivery quality* (pp. 311–327). Hershey, PA: IGI Global. doi:10.4018/978-1-59140-857-4.ch014

Hsiao, N., Chu, P., & Lee, C. (2012). Impact of e-governance on businesses: Model development and case study. In *Digital democracy: Concepts, methodologies, tools, and applications* (pp. 1407–1425). Hershey, PA: IGI Global. doi:10.4018/978-1-4666-1740-7.ch070

Huang, T., & Lee, C. (2010). Evaluating the impact of e-government on citizens: Cost-benefit analysis. In C. Reddick (Ed.), *Citizens and e-government: Evaluating policy and management* (pp. 37–52). Hershey, PA: IGI Global. doi:10.4018/978-1-61520-931-6.ch003

Hunter, M. G., Diochon, M., Pugsley, D., & Wright, B. (2002). Unique challenges for small business adoption of information technology: The case of the Nova Scotia ten. In S. Burgess (Ed.), *Managing information technology in small business: Challenges and solutions* (pp. 98–117). Hershey, PA: IGI Global. doi:10.4018/978-1-930708-35-8.ch006

Hurskainen, J. (2003). Integration of business systems and applications in merger and alliance: Case metso automation. In T. Reponen (Ed.), *Information technology enabled global customer service* (pp. 207–225). Hershey, PA: IGI Global. doi:10.4018/978-1-59140-048-6.ch012

Iazzolino, G., & Pietrantonio, R. (2011). The soveria.it project: A best practice of e-government in southern Italy. In D. Piaggesi, K. Sund, & W. Castelnovo (Eds.), *Global strategy and practice of e-governance: Examples from around the world* (pp. 34–56). Hershey, PA: IGI Global. doi:10.4018/978-1-60960-489-9.ch003

Imran, A., & Gregor, S. (2012). A process model for successful e-government adoption in the least developed countries: A case of Bangladesh. In F. Tan (Ed.), *International comparisons of information communication technologies: Advancing applications* (pp. 321–350). Hershey, PA: IGI Global. doi:10.4018/978-1-61350-480-2.ch014

Inoue, Y., & Bell, S. T. (2005). Electronic/digital government innovation, and publishing trends with IT. In M. Khosrow-Pour (Ed.), *Encyclopedia of information science and technology* (pp. 1018–1023). Hershey, PA: IGI Global. doi:10.4018/978-1-59140-553-5.ch180

Islam, M. M., & Ehsan, M. (2013). Understanding e-governance: A theoretical approach. In M. Islam & M. Ehsan (Eds.), *From government to e-governance: Public administration in the digital age* (pp. 38–49). Hershey, PA: IGI Global. doi:10.4018/978-1-4666-1909-8.ch003

Jaeger, B. (2009). E-government and e-democracy in the making. In M. Khosrow-Pour (Ed.), *Encyclopedia of information science and technology* (2nd ed.; pp. 1318–1322). Hershey, PA: IGI Global. doi:10.4018/978-1-60566-026-4.ch208

Jain, R. B. (2007). Revamping the administrative structure and processes in India for online diplomacy. In A. Anttiroiko & M. Malkia (Eds.), *Encyclopedia of digital government* (pp. 1418–1423). Hershey, PA: IGI Global. doi:10.4018/978-1-59140-789-8.ch217

Jain, R. B. (2008). Revamping the administrative structure and processes in India for online diplomacy. In A. Anttiroiko (Ed.), *Electronic government: Concepts, methodologies, tools, and applications* (pp. 3142–3149). Hershey, PA: IGI Global. doi:10.4018/978-1-59904-947-2.ch233

Jauhiainen, J. S., & Inkinen, T. (2009). E-governance and the information society in periphery. In C. Reddick (Ed.), *Handbook of research on strategies for local e-government adoption and implementation: Comparative studies* (pp. 497–514). Hershey, PA: IGI Global. doi:10.4018/978-1-60566-282-4.ch026

Jensen, M. J. (2009). Electronic democracy and citizen influence in government. In C. Reddick (Ed.), *Handbook of research on strategies for local e-government adoption and implementation: Comparative studies* (pp. 288–305). Hershey, PA: IGI Global. doi:10.4018/978-1-60566-282-4.ch015

Jiao, Y., Hurson, A. R., Potok, T. E., & Beckerman, B. G. (2009). Integrating mobile-based systems with healthcare databases. In J. Erickson (Ed.), *Database technologies: Concepts, methodologies, tools, and applications* (pp. 484–504). Hershey, PA: IGI Global. doi:10.4018/978-1-60566-058-5.ch031

Joia, L. A. (2002). A systematic model to integrate information technology into metabusinesses: A case study in the engineering realms. In F. Tan (Ed.), *Advanced topics in global information management* (Vol. 1, pp. 250–267). Hershey, PA: IGI Global. doi:10.4018/978-1-930708-43-3.ch016

Jones, T. H., & Song, I. (2000). Binary equivalents of ternary relationships in entity-relationship modeling: A logical decomposition approach. *Journal of Database Management, 11*(2), 12–19. doi:10.4018/jdm.2000040102

Juana-Espinosa, S. D. (2007). Empirical study of the municipalitites' motivations for adopting online presence. In L. Al-Hakim (Ed.), *Global e-government: Theory, applications and benchmarking* (pp. 261–279). Hershey, PA: IGI Global. doi:10.4018/978-1-59904-027-1.ch015

Jun, K., & Weare, C. (2012). Bridging from e-government practice to e-government research: Past trends and future directions. In K. Bwalya & S. Zulu (Eds.), *Handbook of research on e-government in emerging economies: Adoption, e-participation, and legal frameworks* (pp. 263–289). Hershey, PA: IGI Global. doi:10.4018/978-1-4666-0324-0.ch013

Junqueira, A., Diniz, E. H., & Fernandez, M. (2010). Electronic government implementation projects with multiple agencies: Analysis of the electronic invoice project under PMBOK framework. In J. Cordoba-Pachon & A. Ochoa-Arias (Eds.), *Systems thinking and e-participation: ICT in the governance of society* (pp. 135–153). Hershey, PA: IGI Global. doi:10.4018/978-1-60566-860-4.ch009

Juntunen, A. (2009). Joint service development with the local authorities. In C. Reddick (Ed.), *Handbook of research on strategies for local e-government adoption and implementation: Comparative studies* (pp. 902–920). Hershey, PA: IGI Global. doi:10.4018/978-1-60566-282-4.ch047

Kamel, S. (2001). *Using DSS for crisis management*. Hershey, PA: IGI Global. doi:10.4018/978-1-87828-961-2.ch020

Kamel, S. (2006). DSS for strategic decision making. In M. Khosrow-Pour (Ed.), *Cases on information technology and organizational politics & culture* (pp. 230–246). Hershey, PA: IGI Global. doi:10.4018/978-1-59904-411-8.ch015

Kamel, S. (2009). The software industry in Egypt as a potential contributor to economic growth. In M. Khosrow-Pour (Ed.), *Encyclopedia of information science and technology* (2nd ed.; pp. 3531–3537). Hershey, PA: IGI Global. doi:10.4018/978-1-60566-026-4.ch562

Kamel, S., & Hussein, M. (2008). Xceed: Pioneering the contact center industry in Egypt. *Journal of Cases on Information Technology, 10*(1), 67–91. doi:10.4018/jcit.2008010105

Kamel, S., & Wahba, K. (2003). The use of a hybrid model in web-based education: "The Global campus project. In A. Aggarwal (Ed.), *Web-based education: Learning from experience* (pp. 331–346). Hershey, PA: IGI Global. doi:10.4018/978-1-59140-102-5.ch020

Kardaras, D. K., & Papathanassiou, E. A. (2008). An exploratory study of the e-government services in Greece. In G. Garson & M. Khosrow-Pour (Eds.), *Handbook of research on public information technology* (pp. 162–174). Hershey, PA: IGI Global. doi:10.4018/978-1-59904-857-4.ch016

Kassahun, A. E., Molla, A., & Sarkar, P. (2012). Government process reengineering: What we know and what we need to know. In *Digital democracy: Concepts, methodologies, tools, and applications* (pp. 1730–1752). Hershey, PA: IGI Global. doi:10.4018/978-1-4666-1740-7.ch086

Khan, B. (2005). Technological issues. In B. Khan (Ed.), *Managing e-learning strategies: Design, delivery, implementation and evaluation* (pp. 154–180). Hershey, PA: IGI Global. doi:10.4018/978-1-59140-634-1.ch004

Khasawneh, A., Bsoul, M., Obeidat, I., & Al Azzam, I. (2012). Technology fears: A study of e-commerce loyalty perception by Jordanian customers. In J. Wang (Ed.), *Advancing the service sector with evolving technologies: Techniques and principles* (pp. 158–165). Hershey, PA: IGI Global. doi:10.4018/978-1-4666-0044-7.ch010

Khatibi, V., & Montazer, G. A. (2012). E-research methodology. In A. Juan, T. Daradoumis, M. Roca, S. Grasman, & J. Faulin (Eds.), *Collaborative and distributed e-research: Innovations in technologies, strategies and applications* (pp. 62–81). Hershey, PA: IGI Global. doi:10.4018/978-1-4666-0125-3.ch003

Kidd, T. (2011). The dragon in the school's backyard: A review of literature on the uses of technology in urban schools. In L. Tomei (Ed.), *Online courses and ICT in education: Emerging practices and applications* (pp. 242–257). Hershey, PA: IGI Global. doi:10.4018/978-1-60960-150-8.ch019

Kidd, T. T. (2010). My experience tells the story: Exploring technology adoption from a qualitative perspective - A pilot study. In H. Song & T. Kidd (Eds.), *Handbook of research on human performance and instructional technology* (pp. 247–262). Hershey, PA: IGI Global. doi:10.4018/978-1-60566-782-9.ch015

Kieley, B., Lane, G., Paquet, G., & Roy, J. (2002). e-Government in Canada: Services online or public service renewal? In Å. Grönlund (Ed.), Electronic government: Design, applications and management (pp. 340-355). Hershey, PA: IGI Global. doi:10.4018/978-1-930708-19-8.ch016

Kim, P. (2012). "Stay out of the way! My kid is video blogging through a phone!": A lesson learned from math tutoring social media for children in underserved communities. In *Wireless technologies: Concepts, methodologies, tools and applications* (pp. 1415–1428). Hershey, PA: IGI Global. doi:10.4018/978-1-61350-101-6.ch517

Kirlidog, M. (2010). Financial aspects of national ICT strategies. In S. Kamel (Ed.), *E-strategies for technological diffusion and adoption: National ICT approaches for socioeconomic development* (pp. 277–292). Hershey, PA: IGI Global. doi:10.4018/978-1-60566-388-3.ch016

Kisielnicki, J. (2006). Transfer of information and knowledge in the project management. In E. Coakes & S. Clarke (Eds.), *Encyclopedia of communities of practice in information and knowledge management* (pp. 544–551). Hershey, PA: IGI Global. doi:10.4018/978-1-59140-556-6.ch091

Kittner, M., & Van Slyke, C. (2006). Reorganizing information technology services in an academic environment. In M. Khosrow-Pour (Ed.), *Cases on the human side of information technology* (pp. 49–66). Hershey, PA: IGI Global. doi:10.4018/978-1-59904-405-7.ch004

Knoell, H. D. (2008). Semi virtual workplaces in German financial service enterprises. In P. Zemliansky & K. St.Amant (Eds.), *Handbook of research on virtual workplaces and the new nature of business practices* (pp. 570–581). Hershey, PA: IGI Global. doi:10.4018/978-1-59904-893-2.ch041

Koh, S. L., & Maguire, S. (2009). Competing in the age of information technology in a developing economy: Experiences of an Indian bank. In S. Koh & S. Maguire (Eds.), *Information and communication technologies management in turbulent business environments* (pp. 326–350). Hershey, PA: IGI Global. doi:10.4018/978-1-60566-424-8.ch018

Kollmann, T., & Häsel, M. (2009). Competence of information technology professionals in internet-based ventures. In I. Lee (Ed.), *Electronic business: Concepts, methodologies, tools, and applications* (pp. 1905–1919). Hershey, PA: IGI Global. doi:10.4018/978-1-60566-056-1.ch118

Kollmann, T., & Häsel, M. (2009). Competence of information technology professionals in internet-based ventures. In A. Cater-Steel (Ed.), *Information technology governance and service management: Frameworks and adaptations* (pp. 239–253). Hershey, PA: IGI Global. doi:10.4018/978-1-60566-008-0.ch013

Kollmann, T., & Häsel, M. (2010). Competence of information technology professionals in internet-based ventures. In *Electronic services: Concepts, methodologies, tools and applications* (pp. 1551–1565). Hershey, PA: IGI Global. doi:10.4018/978-1-61520-967-5.ch094

Kraemer, K., & King, J. L. (2006). Information technology and administrative reform: Will e-government be different? *International Journal of Electronic Government Research, 2*(1), 1–20. doi:10.4018/jegr.2006010101

Kraemer, K., & King, J. L. (2008). Information technology and administrative reform: Will e-government be different? In D. Norris (Ed.), *E-government research: Policy and management* (pp. 1–20). Hershey, PA: IGI Global. doi:10.4018/978-1-59904-913-7.ch001

Lampathaki, F., Tsiakaliaris, C., Stasis, A., & Charalabidis, Y. (2011). National interoperability frameworks: The way forward. In Y. Charalabidis (Ed.), *Interoperability in digital public services and administration: Bridging e-government and e-business* (pp. 1–24). Hershey, PA: IGI Global. doi:10.4018/978-1-61520-887-6.ch001

Lan, Z., & Scott, C. R. (1996). The relative importance of computer-mediated information versus conventional non-computer-mediated information in public managerial decision making. *Information Resources Management Journal*, *9*(1), 27–0. doi:10.4018/irmj.1996010103

Law, W. (2004). *Public sector data management in a developing economy*. Hershey, PA: IGI Global. doi:10.4018/978-1-59140-259-6.ch034

Law, W. K. (2005). Information resources development challenges in a cross-cultural environment. In M. Khosrow-Pour (Ed.), *Encyclopedia of information science and technology* (pp. 1476–1481). Hershey, PA: IGI Global. doi:10.4018/978-1-59140-553-5.ch259

Law, W. K. (2009). Cross-cultural challenges for information resources management. In M. Khosrow-Pour (Ed.), *Encyclopedia of information science and technology* (2nd ed.; pp. 840–846). Hershey, PA: IGI Global. doi:10.4018/978-1-60566-026-4.ch136

Law, W. K. (2011). Cross-cultural challenges for information resources management. In *Global business: Concepts, methodologies, tools and applications* (pp. 1924–1932). Hershey, PA: IGI Global. doi:10.4018/978-1-60960-587-2.ch704

Malkia, M., & Savolainen, R. (2004). eTransformation in government, politics and society: Conceptual framework and introduction. In M. Malkia, A. Anttiroiko, & R. Savolainen (Eds.), eTransformation in governance: New directions in government and politics (pp. 1-21). Hershey, PA: IGI Global. doi:10.4018/978-1-59140-130-8.ch001

Mandujano, S. (2011). Network manageability security. In D. Kar & M. Syed (Eds.), *Network security, administration and management: Advancing technology and practice* (pp. 158–181). Hershey, PA: IGI Global. doi:10.4018/978-1-60960-777-7.ch009

Marich, M. J., Schooley, B. L., & Horan, T. A. (2012). A normative enterprise architecture for guiding end-to-end emergency response decision support. In M. Jennex (Ed.), *Managing crises and disasters with emerging technologies: Advancements* (pp. 71–87). Hershey, PA: IGI Global. doi:10.4018/978-1-4666-0167-3.ch006

Markov, R., & Okujava, S. (2008). Costs, benefits, and risks of e-government portals. In G. Putnik & M. Cruz-Cunha (Eds.), *Encyclopedia of networked and virtual organizations* (pp. 354–363). Hershey, PA: IGI Global. doi:10.4018/978-1-59904-885-7.ch047

Martin, N., & Rice, J. (2013). Evaluating and designing electronic government for the future: Observations and insights from Australia. In V. Weerakkody (Ed.), *E-government services design, adoption, and evaluation* (pp. 238–258). Hershey, PA: IGI Global. doi:10.4018/978-1-4666-2458-0.ch014

i. Martinez, A. C. (2008). Accessing administration's information via internet in Spain. In F. Tan (Ed.), *Global information technologies: Concepts, methodologies, tools, and applications* (pp. 2558–2573). Hershey, PA: IGI Global. doi:10.4018/978-1-59904-939-7.ch186

Mbarika, V. W., Meso, P. N., & Musa, P. F. (2006). A disconnect in stakeholders' perceptions from emerging realities of teledensity growth in Africa's least developed countries. In M. Hunter & F. Tan (Eds.), *Advanced topics in global information management* (Vol. 5, pp. 263–282). Hershey, PA: IGI Global. doi:10.4018/978-1-59140-923-6.ch012

Mbarika, V. W., Meso, P. N., & Musa, P. F. (2008). A disconnect in stakeholders' perceptions from emerging realities of teledensity growth in Africa's least developed countries. In F. Tan (Ed.), *Global information technologies: Concepts, methodologies, tools, and applications* (pp. 2948–2962). Hershey, PA: IGI Global. doi:10.4018/978-1-59904-939-7.ch209

Means, T., Olson, E., & Spooner, J. (2013). Discovering ways that don't work on the road to success: Strengths and weaknesses revealed by an active learning studio classroom project. In A. Benson, J. Moore, & S. Williams van Rooij (Eds.), *Cases on educational technology planning, design, and implementation: A project management perspective* (pp. 94–113). Hershey, PA: IGI Global. doi:10.4018/978-1-4666-4237-9.ch006

Melitski, J., Holzer, M., Kim, S., Kim, C., & Rho, S. (2008). Digital government worldwide: An e-government assessment of municipal web sites. In G. Garson & M. Khosrow-Pour (Eds.), *Handbook of research on public information technology* (pp. 790–804). Hershey, PA: IGI Global. doi:10.4018/978-1-59904-857-4.ch069

Memmola, M., Palumbo, G., & Rossini, M. (2009). Web & RFID technology: New frontiers in costing and process management for rehabilitation medicine. In L. Al-Hakim & M. Memmola (Eds.), *Business web strategy: Design, alignment, and application* (pp. 145–169). Hershey, PA: IGI Global. doi:10.4018/978-1-60566-024-0.ch008

Meng, Z., Fahong, Z., & Lei, L. (2008). Information technology and environment. In Y. Kurihara, S. Takaya, H. Harui, & H. Kamae (Eds.), *Information technology and economic development* (pp. 201–212). Hershey, PA: IGI Global. doi:10.4018/978-1-59904-579-5.ch014

Mentzingen de Moraes, A. J., Ferneda, E., Costa, I., & Spinola, M. D. (2011). Practical approach for implementation of governance process in IT: Information technology areas. In N. Shi & G. Silvius (Eds.), *Enterprise IT governance, business value and performance measurement* (pp. 19–40). Hershey, PA: IGI Global. doi:10.4018/978-1-60566-346-3.ch002

Merwin, G. A. Jr, McDonald, J. S., & Odera, L. C. (2008). Economic development: Government's cutting edge in IT. In M. Raisinghani (Ed.), *Handbook of research on global information technology management in the digital economy* (pp. 1–37). Hershey, PA: IGI Global. doi:10.4018/978-1-59904-875-8.ch001

Meso, P., & Duncan, N. (2002). Can national information infrastructures enhance social development in the least developed countries? An empirical investigation. In M. Dadashzadeh (Ed.), *Information technology management in developing countries* (pp. 23–51). Hershey, PA: IGI Global. doi:10.4018/978-1-931777-03-2.ch002

Meso, P. N., & Duncan, N. B. (2002). Can national information infrastructures enhance social development in the least developed countries? In F. Tan (Ed.), *Advanced topics in global information management* (Vol. 1, pp. 207–226). Hershey, PA: IGI Global. doi:10.4018/978-1-930708-43-3.ch014

Middleton, M. (2008). Evaluation of e-government web sites. In G. Garson & M. Khosrow-Pour (Eds.), *Handbook of research on public information technology* (pp. 699–710). Hershey, PA: IGI Global. doi:10.4018/978-1-59904-857-4.ch063

Mingers, J. (2010). Pluralism, realism, and truth: The keys to knowledge in information systems research. In D. Paradice (Ed.), *Emerging systems approaches in information technologies: Concepts, theories, and applications* (pp. 86–98). Hershey, PA: IGI Global. doi:10.4018/978-1-60566-976-2.ch006

Mital, K. M. (2012). ICT, unique identity and inclusive growth: An Indian perspective. In A. Manoharan & M. Holzer (Eds.), *E-governance and civic engagement: Factors and determinants of e-democracy* (pp. 584–612). Hershey, PA: IGI Global. doi:10.4018/978-1-61350-083-5.ch029

Mizell, A. P. (2008). Helping close the digital divide for financially disadvantaged seniors. In F. Tan (Ed.), *Global information technologies: Concepts, methodologies, tools, and applications* (pp. 2396–2402). Hershey, PA: IGI Global. doi:10.4018/978-1-59904-939-7.ch173

Molinari, F., Wills, C., Koumpis, A., & Moumtzi, V. (2011). A citizen-centric platform to support networking in the area of e-democracy. In H. Rahman (Ed.), *Cases on adoption, diffusion and evaluation of global e-governance systems: Impact at the grass roots* (pp. 282–302). Hershey, PA: IGI Global. doi:10.4018/978-1-61692-814-8.ch014

Molinari, F., Wills, C., Koumpis, A., & Moumtzi, V. (2013). A citizen-centric platform to support networking in the area of e-democracy. In H. Rahman (Ed.), *Cases on progressions and challenges in ICT utilization for citizen-centric governance* (pp. 265–297). Hershey, PA: IGI Global. doi:10.4018/978-1-4666-2071-1.ch013

Monteverde, F. (2010). The process of e-government public policy inclusion in the governmental agenda: A framework for assessment and case study. In J. Cordoba-Pachon & A. Ochoa-Arias (Eds.), *Systems thinking and e-participation: ICT in the governance of society* (pp. 233–245). Hershey, PA: IGI Global. doi:10.4018/978-1-60566-860-4.ch015

Moodley, S. (2008). Deconstructing the South African government's ICT for development discourse. In A. Anttiroiko (Ed.), *Electronic government: Concepts, methodologies, tools, and applications* (pp. 622–631). Hershey, PA: IGI Global. doi:10.4018/978-1-59904-947-2.ch053

Moodley, S. (2008). Deconstructing the South African government's ICT for development discourse. In C. Van Slyke (Ed.), *Information communication technologies: Concepts, methodologies, tools, and applications* (pp. 816–825). Hershey, PA: IGI Global. doi:10.4018/978-1-59904-949-6.ch052

Mora, M., Cervantes-Perez, F., Gelman-Muravchik, O., Forgionne, G. A., & Mejia-Olvera, M. (2003). DMSS implementation research: A conceptual analysis of the contributions and limitations of the factor-based and stage-based streams. In G. Forgionne, J. Gupta, & M. Mora (Eds.), *Decision-making support systems: Achievements and challenges for the new decade* (pp. 331–356). Hershey, PA: IGI Global. doi:10.4018/978-1-59140-045-5.ch020

Mörtberg, C., & Elovaara, P. (2010). Attaching people and technology: Between e and government. In S. Booth, S. Goodman, & G. Kirkup (Eds.), *Gender issues in learning and working with information technology: Social constructs and cultural contexts* (pp. 83–98). Hershey, PA: IGI Global. doi:10.4018/978-1-61520-813-5.ch005

Murphy, J., Harper, E., Devine, E. C., Burke, L. J., & Hook, M. L. (2011). Case study: Lessons learned when embedding evidence-based knowledge in a nurse care planning and documentation system. In A. Cashin & R. Cook (Eds.), *Evidence-based practice in nursing informatics: Concepts and applications* (pp. 174–190). Hershey, PA: IGI Global. doi:10.4018/978-1-60960-034-1.ch014

Mutula, S. M. (2013). E-government's role in poverty alleviation: Case study of South Africa. In H. Rahman (Ed.), *Cases on progressions and challenges in ICT utilization for citizen-centric governance* (pp. 44–68). Hershey, PA: IGI Global. doi:10.4018/978-1-4666-2071-1.ch003

Nath, R., & Angeles, R. (2005). Relationships between supply characteristics and buyer-supplier coupling in e-procurement: An empirical analysis. *International Journal of E-Business Research, 1*(2), 40–55. doi:10.4018/jebr.2005040103

Nissen, M. E. (2006). Application cases in government. In M. Nissen (Ed.), *Harnessing knowledge dynamics: Principled organizational knowing & learning* (pp. 152–181). Hershey, PA: IGI Global. doi:10.4018/978-1-59140-773-7.ch008

Norris, D. F. (2003). Leading-edge information technologies and American local governments. In G. Garson (Ed.), *Public information technology: Policy and management issues* (pp. 139–169). Hershey, PA: IGI Global. doi:10.4018/978-1-59140-060-8.ch007

Norris, D. F. (2008). Information technology among U.S. local governments. In G. Garson & M. Khosrow-Pour (Eds.), *Handbook of research on public information technology* (pp. 132–144). Hershey, PA: IGI Global. doi:10.4018/978-1-59904-857-4.ch013

Northrop, A. (1999). The challenge of teaching information technology in public administration graduate programs. In G. Garson (Ed.), *Information technology and computer applications in public administration: Issues and trends* (pp. 1–22). Hershey, PA: IGI Global. doi:10.4018/978-1-87828-952-0.ch001

Northrop, A. (2003). Information technology and public administration: The view from the profession. In G. Garson (Ed.), *Public information technology: Policy and management issues* (pp. 1–19). Hershey, PA: IGI Global. doi:10.4018/978-1-59140-060-8.ch001

Northrop, A. (2007). Lip service? How PA journals and textbooks view information technology. In G. Garson (Ed.), *Modern public information technology systems: Issues and challenges* (pp. 1–16). Hershey, PA: IGI Global. doi:10.4018/978-1-59904-051-6.ch001

Null, E. (2013). Legal and political barriers to municipal networks in the United States. In A. Abdelaal (Ed.), *Social and economic effects of community wireless networks and infrastructures* (pp. 27–56). Hershey, PA: IGI Global. doi:10.4018/978-1-4666-2997-4.ch003

Okunoye, A., Frolick, M., & Crable, E. (2006). ERP implementation in higher education: An account of pre-implementation and implementation phases. *Journal of Cases on Information Technology*, *8*(2), 110–132. doi:10.4018/jcit.2006040106

Olasina, G. (2012). A review of egovernment services in Nigeria. In A. Tella & A. Issa (Eds.), *Library and information science in developing countries: Contemporary issues* (pp. 205–221). Hershey, PA: IGI Global. doi:10.4018/978-1-61350-335-5.ch015

Orgeron, C. P. (2008). A model for reengineering IT job classes in state government. In G. Garson & M. Khosrow-Pour (Eds.), *Handbook of research on public information technology* (pp. 735–746). Hershey, PA: IGI Global. doi:10.4018/978-1-59904-857-4.ch066

Owsinski, J. W., & Pielak, A. M. (2011). Local authority websites in rural areas: Measuring quality and functionality, and assessing the role. In Z. Andreopoulou, B. Manos, N. Polman, & D. Viaggi (Eds.), *Agricultural and environmental informatics, governance and management: Emerging research applications* (pp. 39–60). Hershey, PA: IGI Global. doi:10.4018/978-1-60960-621-3.ch003

Owsiński, J. W., Pielak, A. M., Sęp, K., & Stańczak, J. (2014). Local web-based networks in rural municipalities: Extension, density, and meaning. In Z. Andreopoulou, V. Samathrakis, S. Louca, & M. Vlachopoulou (Eds.), *E-innovation for sustainable development of rural resources during global economic crisis* (pp. 126–151). Hershey, PA: IGI Global. doi:10.4018/978-1-4666-4550-9.ch011

Pagani, M., & Pasinetti, C. (2008). Technical and functional quality in the development of t-government services. In A. Anttiroiko (Ed.), *Electronic government: Concepts, methodologies, tools, and applications* (pp. 2943–2965). Hershey, PA: IGI Global. doi:10.4018/978-1-59904-947-2.ch220

Pani, A. K., & Agrahari, A. (2005). On e-markets in emerging economy: An Indian experience. In M. Khosrow-Pour (Ed.), *Advanced topics in electronic commerce* (Vol. 1, pp. 287–299). Hershey, PA: IGI Global. doi:10.4018/978-1-59140-819-2.ch015

Papadopoulos, T., Angelopoulos, S., & Kitsios, F. (2011). A strategic approach to e-health interoperability using e-government frameworks. In A. Lazakidou, K. Siassiakos, & K. Ioannou (Eds.), *Wireless technologies for ambient assisted living and healthcare: Systems and applications* (pp. 213–229). Hershey, PA: IGI Global. doi:10.4018/978-1-61520-805-0.ch012

Papadopoulos, T., Angelopoulos, S., & Kitsios, F. (2013). A strategic approach to e-health interoperability using e-government frameworks. In *User-driven healthcare: Concepts, methodologies, tools, and applications* (pp. 791–807). Hershey, PA: IGI Global. doi:10.4018/978-1-4666-2770-3.ch039

Papaleo, G., Chiarella, D., Aiello, M., & Caviglione, L. (2012). Analysis, development and deployment of statistical anomaly detection techniques for real e-mail traffic. In T. Chou (Ed.), *Information assurance and security technologies for risk assessment and threat management: Advances* (pp. 47–71). Hershey, PA: IGI Global. doi:10.4018/978-1-61350-507-6.ch003

Papp, R. (2003). Information technology & FDA compliance in the pharmaceutical industry. In M. Khosrow-Pour (Ed.), *Annals of cases on information technology* (Vol. 5, pp. 262–273). Hershey, PA: IGI Global. doi:10.4018/978-1-59140-061-5.ch017

Parsons, T. W. (2007). Developing a knowledge management portal. In A. Tatnall (Ed.), *Encyclopedia of portal technologies and applications* (pp. 223–227). Hershey, PA: IGI Global. doi:10.4018/978-1-59140-989-2.ch039

Passaris, C. E. (2007). Immigration and digital government. In A. Anttiroiko & M. Malkia (Eds.), *Encyclopedia of digital government* (pp. 988–994). Hershey, PA: IGI Global. doi:10.4018/978-1-59140-789-8.ch148

Pavlichev, A. (2004). The e-government challenge for public administration. In A. Pavlichev & G. Garson (Eds.), *Digital government: Principles and best practices* (pp. 276–290). Hershey, PA: IGI Global. doi:10.4018/978-1-59140-122-3.ch018

Penrod, J. I., & Harbor, A. F. (2000). Designing and implementing a learning organization-oriented information technology planning and management process. In L. Petrides (Ed.), *Case studies on information technology in higher education: Implications for policy and practice* (pp. 7–19). Hershey, PA: IGI Global. doi:10.4018/978-1-878289-74-2.ch001

Planas-Silva, M. D., & Joseph, R. C. (2011). Perspectives on the adoption of electronic resources for use in clinical trials. In M. Guah (Ed.), *Healthcare delivery reform and new technologies: Organizational initiatives* (pp. 19–28). Hershey, PA: IGI Global. doi:10.4018/978-1-60960-183-6.ch002

Pomazalová, N., & Rejman, S. (2013). The rationale behind implementation of new electronic tools for electronic public procurement. In N. Pomazalová (Ed.), *Public sector transformation processes and internet public procurement: Decision support systems* (pp. 85–117). Hershey, PA: IGI Global. doi:10.4018/978-1-4666-2665-2.ch006

Postorino, M. N. (2012). City competitiveness and airport: Information science perspective. In M. Bulu (Ed.), *City competitiveness and improving urban subsystems: Technologies and applications* (pp. 61–83). Hershey, PA: IGI Global. doi:10.4018/978-1-61350-174-0.ch004

Poupa, C. (2002). Electronic government in Switzerland: Priorities for 2001-2005 - Electronic voting and federal portal. In Å. Grönlund (Ed.), *Electronic government: Design, applications and management* (pp. 356–369). Hershey, PA: IGI Global. doi:10.4018/978-1-930708-19-8.ch017

Powell, S. R. (2010). Interdisciplinarity in telecommunications and networking. In *Networking and telecommunications: Concepts, methodologies, tools and applications* (pp. 33–40). Hershey, PA: IGI Global. doi:10.4018/978-1-60566-986-1.ch004

Priya, P. S., & Mathiyalagan, N. (2011). A study of the implementation status of two e-governance projects in land revenue administration in India. In M. Shareef, V. Kumar, U. Kumar, & Y. Dwivedi (Eds.), *Stakeholder adoption of e-government services: Driving and resisting factors* (pp. 214–230). Hershey, PA: IGI Global. doi:10.4018/978-1-60960-601-5.ch011

Prysby, C., & Prysby, N. (2000). Electronic mail, employee privacy and the workplace. In L. Janczewski (Ed.), *Internet and intranet security management: Risks and solutions* (pp. 251–270). Hershey, PA: IGI Global. doi:10.4018/978-1-878289-71-1.ch009

Prysby, C. L., & Prysby, N. D. (2003). Electronic mail in the public workplace: Issues of privacy and public disclosure. In G. Garson (Ed.), *Public information technology: Policy and management issues* (pp. 271–298). Hershey, PA: IGI Global. doi:10.4018/978-1-59140-060-8.ch012

Prysby, C. L., & Prysby, N. D. (2007). You have mail, but who is reading it? Issues of e-mail in the public workplace. In G. Garson (Ed.), *Modern public information technology systems: Issues and challenges* (pp. 312–336). Hershey, PA: IGI Global. doi:10.4018/978-1-59904-051-6.ch016

Radl, A., & Chen, Y. (2005). Computer security in electronic government: A state-local education information system. *International Journal of Electronic Government Research, 1*(1), 79–99. doi:10.4018/jegr.2005010105

Rahman, H. (2008). Information dynamics in developing countries. In C. Van Slyke (Ed.), *Information communication technologies: Concepts, methodologies, tools, and applications* (pp. 104–114). Hershey, PA: IGI Global. doi:10.4018/978-1-59904-949-6.ch008

Ramanathan, J. (2009). Adaptive IT architecture as a catalyst for network capability in government. In P. Saha (Ed.), *Advances in government enterprise architecture* (pp. 149–172). Hershey, PA: IGI Global. doi:10.4018/978-1-60566-068-4.ch007

Ramos, I., & Berry, D. M. (2006). Social construction of information technology supporting work. In M. Khosrow-Pour (Ed.), *Cases on information technology: Lessons learned* (Vol. 7, pp. 36–52). Hershey, PA: IGI Global. doi:10.4018/978-1-59140-673-0.ch003

Ray, D., Gulla, U., Gupta, M. P., & Dash, S. S. (2009). Interoperability and constituents of interoperable systems in public sector. In V. Weerakkody, M. Janssen, & Y. Dwivedi (Eds.), *Handbook of research on ICT-enabled transformational government: A global perspective* (pp. 175–195). Hershey, PA: IGI Global. doi:10.4018/978-1-60566-390-6.ch010

Reddick, C. G. (2007). E-government and creating a citizen-centric government: A study of federal government CIOs. In G. Garson (Ed.), *Modern public information technology systems: Issues and challenges* (pp. 143–165). Hershey, PA: IGI Global. doi:10.4018/978-1-59904-051-6.ch008

Reddick, C. G. (2010). Citizen-centric e-government. In C. Reddick (Ed.), *Homeland security preparedness and information systems: Strategies for managing public policy* (pp. 45–75). Hershey, PA: IGI Global. doi:10.4018/978-1-60566-834-5.ch002

Reddick, C. G. (2010). E-government and creating a citizen-centric government: A study of federal government CIOs. In C. Reddick (Ed.), *Homeland security preparedness and information systems: Strategies for managing public policy* (pp. 230–250). Hershey, PA: IGI Global. doi:10.4018/978-1-60566-834-5.ch012

Reddick, C. G. (2010). Perceived effectiveness of e-government and its usage in city governments: Survey evidence from information technology directors. In C. Reddick (Ed.), *Homeland security preparedness and information systems: Strategies for managing public policy* (pp. 213–229). Hershey, PA: IGI Global. doi:10.4018/978-1-60566-834-5.ch011

Reddick, C. G. (2012). Customer relationship management adoption in local governments in the United States. In S. Chhabra & M. Kumar (Eds.), *Strategic enterprise resource planning models for e-government: Applications and methodologies* (pp. 111–124). Hershey, PA: IGI Global. doi:10.4018/978-1-60960-863-7.ch008

Reeder, F. S., & Pandy, S. M. (2008). Identifying effective funding models for e-government. In A. Anttiroiko (Ed.), *Electronic government: Concepts, methodologies, tools, and applications* (pp. 1108–1138). Hershey, PA: IGI Global. doi:10.4018/978-1-59904-947-2.ch083

Riesco, D., Acosta, E., & Montejano, G. (2003). An extension to a UML activity graph from workflow. In L. Favre (Ed.), *UML and the unified process* (pp. 294–314). Hershey, PA: IGI Global. doi:10.4018/978-1-93177-744-5.ch015

Ritzhaupt, A. D., & Gill, T. G. (2008). A hybrid and novel approach to teaching computer programming in MIS curriculum. In S. Negash, M. Whitman, A. Woszczynski, K. Hoganson, & H. Mattord (Eds.), *Handbook of distance learning for real-time and asynchronous information technology education* (pp. 259–281). Hershey, PA: IGI Global. doi:10.4018/978-1-59904-964-9.ch014

Roche, E. M. (1993). International computing and the international regime. *Journal of Global Information Management, 1*(2), 33–44. doi:10.4018/jgim.1993040103

Rocheleau, B. (2007). Politics, accountability, and information management. In G. Garson (Ed.), *Modern public information technology systems: Issues and challenges* (pp. 35–71). Hershey, PA: IGI Global. doi:10.4018/978-1-59904-051-6.ch003

Rodrigues Filho, J. (2010). E-government in Brazil: Reinforcing dominant institutions or reducing citizenship? In C. Reddick (Ed.), *Politics, democracy and e-government: Participation and service delivery* (pp. 347–362). Hershey, PA: IGI Global. doi:10.4018/978-1-61520-933-0.ch021

Rodriguez, S. R., & Thorp, D. A. (2013). eLearning for industry: A case study of the project management process. In A. Benson, J. Moore, & S. Williams van Rooij (Eds.), Cases on educational technology planning, design, and implementation: A project management perspective (pp. 319-342). Hershey, PA: IGI Global. doi:10.4018/978-1-4666-4237-9.ch017

Roman, A. V. (2013). Delineating three dimensions of e-government success: Security, functionality, and transformation. In J. Gil-Garcia (Ed.), *E-government success factors and measures: Theories, concepts, and methodologies* (pp. 171–192). Hershey, PA: IGI Global. doi:10.4018/978-1-4666-4058-0.ch010

Ross, S. C., Tyran, C. K., & Auer, D. J. (2008). Up in smoke: Rebuilding after an IT disaster. In H. Nemati (Ed.), *Information security and ethics: Concepts, methodologies, tools, and applications* (pp. 3659–3675). Hershey, PA: IGI Global. doi:10.4018/978-1-59904-937-3.ch248

Ross, S. C., Tyran, C. K., Auer, D. J., Junell, J. M., & Williams, T. G. (2005). Up in smoke: Rebuilding after an IT disaster. *Journal of Cases on Information Technology*, 7(2), 31–49. doi:10.4018/jcit.2005040103

Roy, J. (2008). Security, sovereignty, and continental interoperability: Canada's elusive balance. In T. Loendorf & G. Garson (Eds.), *Patriotic information systems* (pp. 153–176). Hershey, PA: IGI Global. doi:10.4018/978-1-59904-594-8.ch007

Rubeck, R. F., & Miller, G. A. (2009). vGOV: Remote video access to government services. In A. Scupola (Ed.), Cases on managing e-services (pp. 253-268). Hershey, PA: IGI Global. doi:10.4018/978-1-60566-064-6.ch017

Saekow, A., & Boonmee, C. (2011). The challenges of implementing e-government interoperability in Thailand: Case of official electronic correspondence letters exchange across government departments. In Y. Charalabidis (Ed.), *Interoperability in digital public services and administration: Bridging e-government and e-business* (pp. 40–61). Hershey, PA: IGI Global. doi:10.4018/978-1-61520-887-6.ch003

Saekow, A., & Boonmee, C. (2012). The challenges of implementing e-government interoperability in Thailand: Case of official electronic correspondence letters exchange across government departments. In *Digital democracy: Concepts, methodologies, tools, and applications* (pp. 1883–1905). Hershey, PA: IGI Global. doi:10.4018/978-1-4666-1740-7.ch094

Sagsan, M., & Medeni, T. (2012). Understanding "knowledge management (KM) paradigms" from social media perspective: An empirical study on discussion group for KM at professional networking site. In M. Cruz-Cunha, P. Gonçalves, N. Lopes, E. Miranda, & G. Putnik (Eds.), *Handbook of research on business social networking: Organizational, managerial, and technological dimensions* (pp. 738–755). Hershey, PA: IGI Global. doi:10.4018/978-1-61350-168-9.ch039

Sahi, G., & Madan, S. (2013). Information security threats in ERP enabled e-governance: Challenges and solutions. In *Enterprise resource planning: Concepts, methodologies, tools, and applications* (pp. 825–837). Hershey, PA: IGI Global. doi:10.4018/978-1-4666-4153-2.ch048

Sanford, C., & Bhattacherjee, A. (2008). IT implementation in a developing country municipality: A sociocognitive analysis. *International Journal of Technology and Human Interaction, 4*(3), 68–93. doi:10.4018/jthi.2008070104

Schelin, S. H. (2003). E-government: An overview. In G. Garson (Ed.), *Public information technology: Policy and management issues* (pp. 120–138). Hershey, PA: IGI Global. doi:10.4018/978-1-59140-060-8.ch006

Schelin, S. H. (2004). Training for digital government. In A. Pavlichev & G. Garson (Eds.), *Digital government: Principles and best practices* (pp. 263–275). Hershey, PA: IGI Global. doi:10.4018/978-1-59140-122-3.ch017

Schelin, S. H. (2007). E-government: An overview. In G. Garson (Ed.), *Modern public information technology systems: Issues and challenges* (pp. 110–126). Hershey, PA: IGI Global. doi:10.4018/978-1-59904-051-6.ch006

Schelin, S. H., & Garson, G. (2004). Theoretical justification of critical success factors. In G. Garson & S. Schelin (Eds.), *IT solutions series: Humanizing information technology: Advice from experts* (pp. 4–15). Hershey, PA: IGI Global. doi:10.4018/978-1-59140-245-9.ch002

Scime, A. (2002). Information systems and computer science model curricula: A comparative look. In M. Dadashzadeh, A. Saber, & S. Saber (Eds.), *Information technology education in the new millennium* (pp. 146–158). Hershey, PA: IGI Global. doi:10.4018/978-1-931777-05-6.ch018

Scime, A. (2009). Computing curriculum analysis and development. In M. Khosrow-Pour (Ed.), *Encyclopedia of information science and technology* (2nd ed.; pp. 667–671). Hershey, PA: IGI Global. doi:10.4018/978-1-60566-026-4.ch108

Scime, A., & Wania, C. (2008). Computing curricula: A comparison of models. In C. Van Slyke (Ed.), *Information communication technologies: Concepts, methodologies, tools, and applications* (pp. 1270–1283). Hershey, PA: IGI Global. doi:10.4018/978-1-59904-949-6.ch088

Seidman, S. B. (2009). An international perspective on professional software engineering credentials. In H. Ellis, S. Demurjian, & J. Naveda (Eds.), *Software engineering: Effective teaching and learning approaches and practices* (pp. 351–361). Hershey, PA: IGI Global. doi:10.4018/978-1-60566-102-5.ch018

Seifert, J. W. (2007). E-government act of 2002 in the United States. In A. Anttiroiko & M. Malkia (Eds.), *Encyclopedia of digital government* (pp. 476–481). Hershey, PA: IGI Global. doi:10.4018/978-1-59140-789-8.ch072

Seifert, J. W., & Relyea, H. C. (2008). E-government act of 2002 in the United States. In A. Anttiroiko (Ed.), *Electronic government: Concepts, methodologies, tools, and applications* (pp. 154–161). Hershey, PA: IGI Global. doi:10.4018/978-1-59904-947-2.ch013

Seufert, S. (2002). E-learning business models: Framework and best practice examples. In M. Raisinghani (Ed.), *Cases on worldwide e-commerce: Theory in action* (pp. 70–94). Hershey, PA: IGI Global. doi:10.4018/978-1-930708-27-3.ch004

Shareef, M. A., & Archer, N. (2012). E-government service development. In M. Shareef, N. Archer, & S. Dutta (Eds.), *E-government service maturity and development: Cultural, organizational and technological perspectives* (pp. 1–14). Hershey, PA: IGI Global. doi:10.4018/978-1-60960-848-4.ch001

Shareef, M. A., & Archer, N. (2012). E-government initiatives: Review studies on different countries. In M. Shareef, N. Archer, & S. Dutta (Eds.), *E-government service maturity and development: Cultural, organizational and technological perspectives* (pp. 40–76). Hershey, PA: IGI Global. doi:10.4018/978-1-60960-848-4.ch003

Shareef, M. A., Kumar, U., & Kumar, V. (2011). E-government development: Performance evaluation parameters. In M. Shareef, V. Kumar, U. Kumar, & Y. Dwivedi (Eds.), *Stakeholder adoption of e-government services: Driving and resisting factors* (pp. 197–213). Hershey, PA: IGI Global. doi:10.4018/978-1-60960-601-5.ch010

Shareef, M. A., Kumar, U., Kumar, V., & Niktash, M. (2012). Electronic-government vision: Case studies for objectives, strategies, and initiatives. In M. Shareef, N. Archer, & S. Dutta (Eds.), *E-government service maturity and development: Cultural, organizational and technological perspectives* (pp. 15–39). Hershey, PA: IGI Global. doi:10.4018/978-1-60960-848-4.ch002

Shukla, P., Kumar, A., & Anu Kumar, P. B. (2013). Impact of national culture on business continuity management system implementation. *International Journal of Risk and Contingency Management*, *2*(3), 23–36. doi:10.4018/ijrcm.2013070102

Shulman, S. W. (2007). The federal docket management system and the prospect for digital democracy in U S rulemaking. In G. Garson (Ed.), *Modern public information technology systems: Issues and challenges* (pp. 166–184). Hershey, PA: IGI Global. doi:10.4018/978-1-59904-051-6.ch009

Simonovic, S. (2007). Problems of offline government in e-Serbia. In A. Anttiroiko & M. Malkia (Eds.), *Encyclopedia of digital government* (pp. 1342–1351). Hershey, PA: IGI Global. doi:10.4018/978-1-59140-789-8.ch205

Simonovic, S. (2008). Problems of offline government in e-Serbia. In A. Anttiroiko (Ed.), *Electronic government: Concepts, methodologies, tools, and applications* (pp. 2929–2942). Hershey, PA: IGI Global. doi:10.4018/978-1-59904-947-2.ch219

Singh, A. M. (2005). Information systems and technology in South Africa. In M. Khosrow-Pour (Ed.), *Encyclopedia of information science and technology* (pp. 1497–1502). Hershey, PA: IGI Global. doi:10.4018/978-1-59140-553-5.ch263

Singh, S., & Naidoo, G. (2005). Towards an e-government solution: A South African perspective. In W. Huang, K. Siau, & K. Wei (Eds.), *Electronic government strategies and implementation* (pp. 325–353). Hershey, PA: IGI Global. doi:10.4018/978-1-59140-348-7.ch014

Snoke, R., & Underwood, A. (2002). Generic attributes of IS graduates: An analysis of Australian views. In F. Tan (Ed.), *Advanced topics in global information management* (Vol. 1, pp. 370–384). Hershey, PA: IGI Global. doi:10.4018/978-1-930708-43-3.ch023

Sommer, L. (2006). Revealing unseen organizations in higher education: A study framework and application example. In A. Metcalfe (Ed.), *Knowledge management and higher education: A critical analysis* (pp. 115–146). Hershey, PA: IGI Global. doi:10.4018/978-1-59140-509-2.ch007

Song, H., Kidd, T., & Owens, E. (2011). Examining technological disparities and instructional practices in English language arts classroom: Implications for school leadership and teacher training. In L. Tomei (Ed.), *Online courses and ICT in education: Emerging practices and applications* (pp. 258–274). Hershey, PA: IGI Global. doi:10.4018/978-1-60960-150-8.ch020

Speaker, P. J., & Kleist, V. F. (2003). Using information technology to meet electronic commerce and MIS education demands. In A. Aggarwal (Ed.), *Web-based education: Learning from experience* (pp. 280–291). Hershey, PA: IGI Global. doi:10.4018/978-1-59140-102-5.ch017

Spitler, V. K. (2007). Learning to use IT in the workplace: Mechanisms and masters. In M. Mahmood (Ed.), *Contemporary issues in end user computing* (pp. 292–323). Hershey, PA: IGI Global. doi:10.4018/978-1-59140-926-7.ch013

Stellefson, M. (2011). Considerations for marketing distance education courses in health education: Five important questions to examine before development. In U. Demiray & S. Sever (Eds.), *Marketing online education programs: Frameworks for promotion and communication* (pp. 222–234). Hershey, PA: IGI Global. doi:10.4018/978-1-60960-074-7.ch014

Straub, D. W., & Loch, K. D. (2006). Creating and developing a program of global research. *Journal of Global Information Management, 14*(2), 1–28. doi:10.4018/jgim.2006040101

Straub, D. W., Loch, K. D., & Hill, C. E. (2002). Transfer of information technology to the Arab world: A test of cultural influence modeling. In M. Dadashzadeh (Ed.), *Information technology management in developing countries* (pp. 92–134). Hershey, PA: IGI Global. doi:10.4018/978-1-931777-03-2.ch005

Straub, D. W., Loch, K. D., & Hill, C. E. (2003). Transfer of information technology to the Arab world: A test of cultural influence modeling. In F. Tan (Ed.), *Advanced topics in global information management* (Vol. 2, pp. 141–172). Hershey, PA: IGI Global. doi:10.4018/978-1-59140-064-6.ch009

Suki, N. M., Ramayah, T., Ming, M. K., & Suki, N. M. (2013). Factors enhancing employed job seekers intentions to use social networking sites as a job search tool. In A. Mesquita (Ed.), *User perception and influencing factors of technology in everyday life* (pp. 265–281). Hershey, PA: IGI Global. doi:10.4018/978-1-4666-1954-8.ch018

Suomi, R. (2006). Introducing electronic patient records to hospitals: Innovation adoption paths. In T. Spil & R. Schuring (Eds.), *E-health systems diffusion and use: The innovation, the user and the use IT model* (pp. 128–146). Hershey, PA: IGI Global. doi:10.4018/978-1-59140-423-1.ch008

Swim, J., & Barker, L. (2012). Pathways into a gendered occupation: Brazilian women in IT. *International Journal of Social and Organizational Dynamics in IT*, *2*(4), 34–51. doi:10.4018/ijsodit.2012100103

Tarafdar, M., & Vaidya, S. D. (2006). Adoption and implementation of IT in developing nations: Experiences from two public sector enterprises in India. In M. Khosrow-Pour (Ed.), *Cases on information technology planning, design and implementation* (pp. 208–233). Hershey, PA: IGI Global. doi:10.4018/978-1-59904-408-8.ch013

Tarafdar, M., & Vaidya, S. D. (2008). Adoption and implementation of IT in developing nations: Experiences from two public sector enterprises in India. In G. Garson & M. Khosrow-Pour (Eds.), *Handbook of research on public information technology* (pp. 905–924). Hershey, PA: IGI Global. doi:10.4018/978-1-59904-857-4.ch076

Thesing, Z. (2007). Zarina thesing, pumpkin patch. In M. Hunter (Ed.), *Contemporary chief information officers: Management experiences* (pp. 83–94). Hershey, PA: IGI Global. doi:10.4018/978-1-59904-078-3.ch007

Thomas, J. C. (2004). Public involvement in public administration in the information age: Speculations on the effects of technology. In M. Malkia, A. Anttiroiko, & R. Savolainen (Eds.), *eTransformation in governance: New directions in government and politics* (pp. 67–84). Hershey, PA: IGI Global. doi:10.4018/978-1-59140-130-8.ch004

Treiblmaier, H., & Chong, S. (2013). Trust and perceived risk of personal information as antecedents of online information disclosure: Results from three countries. In F. Tan (Ed.), *Global diffusion and adoption of technologies for knowledge and information sharing* (pp. 341–361). Hershey, PA: IGI Global. doi:10.4018/978-1-4666-2142-8.ch015

van Grembergen, W., & de Haes, S. (2008). IT governance in practice: Six case studies. In W. van Grembergen & S. De Haes (Eds.), *Implementing information technology governance: Models, practices and cases* (pp. 125–237). Hershey, PA: IGI Global. doi:10.4018/978-1-59904-924-3.ch004

van Os, G., Homburg, V., & Bekkers, V. (2013). Contingencies and convergence in European social security: ICT coordination in the back office of the welfare state. In M. Cruz-Cunha, I. Miranda, & P. Gonçalves (Eds.), *Handbook of research on ICTs and management systems for improving efficiency in healthcare and social care* (pp. 268–287). Hershey, PA: IGI Global. doi:10.4018/978-1-4666-3990-4.ch013

Velloso, A. B., Gassenferth, W., & Machado, M. A. (2012). Evaluating IBMEC-RJ's intranet usability using fuzzy logic. In M. Cruz-Cunha, P. Gonçalves, N. Lopes, E. Miranda, & G. Putnik (Eds.), *Handbook of research on business social networking: Organizational, managerial, and technological dimensions* (pp. 185–205). Hershey, PA: IGI Global. doi:10.4018/978-1-61350-168-9.ch010

Villablanca, A. C., Baxi, H., & Anderson, K. (2009). Novel data interface for evaluating cardiovascular outcomes in women. In A. Dwivedi (Ed.), *Handbook of research on information technology management and clinical data administration in healthcare* (pp. 34–53). Hershey, PA: IGI Global. doi:10.4018/978-1-60566-356-2.ch003

Villablanca, A. C., Baxi, H., & Anderson, K. (2011). Novel data interface for evaluating cardiovascular outcomes in women. In *Clinical technologies: Concepts, methodologies, tools and applications* (pp. 2094–2113). Hershey, PA: IGI Global. doi:10.4018/978-1-60960-561-2.ch806

Virkar, S. (2011). Information and communication technologies in administrative reform for development: Exploring the case of property tax systems in Karnataka, India. In J. Steyn, J. Van Belle, & E. Mansilla (Eds.), *ICTs for global development and sustainability: Practice and applications* (pp. 127–149). Hershey, PA: IGI Global. doi:10.4018/978-1-61520-997-2.ch006

Virkar, S. (2013). Designing and implementing e-government projects: Actors, influences, and fields of play. In S. Saeed & C. Reddick (Eds.), *Human-centered system design for electronic governance* (pp. 88–110). Hershey, PA: IGI Global. doi:10.4018/978-1-4666-3640-8.ch007

Wallace, A. (2009). E-justice: An Australian perspective. In A. Martínez & P. Abat (Eds.), *E-justice: Using information communication technologies in the court system* (pp. 204–228). Hershey, PA: IGI Global. doi:10.4018/978-1-59904-998-4.ch014

Wang, G. (2012). E-democratic administration and bureaucratic responsiveness: A primary study of bureaucrats' perceptions of the civil service e-mail box in Taiwan. In K. Kloby & M. D'Agostino (Eds.), *Citizen 2.0: Public and governmental interaction through web 2.0 technologies* (pp. 146–173). Hershey, PA: IGI Global. doi:10.4018/978-1-4666-0318-9.ch009

Wangpipatwong, S., Chutimaskul, W., & Papasratorn, B. (2011). Quality enhancing the continued use of e-government web sites: Evidence from e-citizens of Thailand. In V. Weerakkody (Ed.), *Applied technology integration in governmental organizations: New e-government research* (pp. 20–36). Hershey, PA: IGI Global. doi:10.4018/978-1-60960-162-1.ch002

Wedemeijer, L. (2006). Long-term evolution of a conceptual schema at a life insurance company. In M. Khosrow-Pour (Ed.), *Cases on database technologies and applications* (pp. 202–226). Hershey, PA: IGI Global. doi:10.4018/978-1-59904-399-9.ch012

Whybrow, E. (2008). Digital access, ICT fluency, and the economically disadvantages: Approaches to minimize the digital divide. In F. Tan (Ed.), *Global information technologies: Concepts, methodologies, tools, and applications* (pp. 1409–1422). Hershey, PA: IGI Global. doi:10.4018/978-1-59904-939-7.ch102

Whybrow, E. (2008). Digital access, ICT fluency, and the economically disadvantages: Approaches to minimize the digital divide. In C. Van Slyke (Ed.), *Information communication technologies: Concepts, methodologies, tools, and applications* (pp. 764–777). Hershey, PA: IGI Global. doi:10.4018/978-1-59904-949-6.ch049

Wickramasinghe, N., & Geisler, E. (2010). Key considerations for the adoption and implementation of knowledge management in healthcare operations. In M. Saito, N. Wickramasinghe, M. Fuji, & E. Geisler (Eds.), *Redesigning innovative healthcare operation and the role of knowledge management* (pp. 125–142). Hershey, PA: IGI Global. doi:10.4018/978-1-60566-284-8.ch009

Wickramasinghe, N., & Geisler, E. (2012). Key considerations for the adoption and implementation of knowledge management in healthcare operations. In *Organizational learning and knowledge: Concepts, methodologies, tools and applications* (pp. 1316–1328). Hershey, PA: IGI Global. doi:10.4018/978-1-60960-783-8.ch405

Wickramasinghe, N., & Goldberg, S. (2007). A framework for delivering m-health excellence. In L. Al-Hakim (Ed.), *Web mobile-based applications for healthcare management* (pp. 36–61). Hershey, PA: IGI Global. doi:10.4018/978-1-59140-658-7.ch002

Wickramasinghe, N., & Goldberg, S. (2008). Critical success factors for delivering m-health excellence. In N. Wickramasinghe & E. Geisler (Eds.), *Encyclopedia of healthcare information systems* (pp. 339–351). Hershey, PA: IGI Global. doi:10.4018/978-1-59904-889-5.ch045

Wyld, D. (2009). Radio frequency identification (RFID) technology. In J. Symonds, J. Ayoade, & D. Parry (Eds.), *Auto-identification and ubiquitous computing applications* (pp. 279–293). Hershey, PA: IGI Global. doi:10.4018/978-1-60566-298-5.ch017

Yaghmaei, F. (2010). Understanding computerised information systems usage in community health. In J. Rodrigues (Ed.), *Health information systems: Concepts, methodologies, tools, and applications* (pp. 1388–1399). Hershey, PA: IGI Global. doi:10.4018/978-1-60566-988-5.ch088

Yee, G., El-Khatib, K., Korba, L., Patrick, A. S., Song, R., & Xu, Y. (2005). Privacy and trust in e-government. In W. Huang, K. Siau, & K. Wei (Eds.), *Electronic government strategies and implementation* (pp. 145–190). Hershey, PA: IGI Global. doi:10.4018/978-1-59140-348-7.ch007

Yeh, S., & Chu, P. (2010). Evaluation of e-government services: A citizen-centric approach to citizen e-complaint services. In C. Reddick (Ed.), *Citizens and e-government: Evaluating policy and management* (pp. 400–417). Hershey, PA: IGI Global. doi:10.4018/978-1-61520-931-6.ch022

Young-Jin, S., & Seang-tae, K. (2008). E-government concepts, measures, and best practices. In A. Anttiroiko (Ed.), *Electronic government: Concepts, methodologies, tools, and applications* (pp. 32–57). Hershey, PA: IGI Global. doi:10.4018/978-1-59904-947-2.ch004

Yun, H. J., & Opheim, C. (2012). New technology communication in American state governments: The impact on citizen participation. In K. Bwalya & S. Zulu (Eds.), *Handbook of research on e-government in emerging economies: Adoption, e-participation, and legal frameworks* (pp. 573–590). Hershey, PA: IGI Global. doi:10.4018/978-1-4666-0324-0.ch029

Zhang, N., Guo, X., Chen, G., & Chau, P. Y. (2011). User evaluation of e-government systems: A Chinese cultural perspective. In F. Tan (Ed.), *International enterprises and global information technologies: Advancing management practices* (pp. 63–84). Hershey, PA: IGI Global. doi:10.4018/978-1-60960-605-3.ch004

Zuo, Y., & Hu, W. (2011). Trust-based information risk management in a supply chain network. In J. Wang (Ed.), *Supply chain optimization, management and integration: Emerging applications* (pp. 181–196). Hershey, PA: IGI Global. doi:10.4018/978-1-60960-135-5.ch013

Compilation of References

Abadi, S., Achsan, N. A. I., & Rachmina, D. (2014). The Dynamics of Non-Performing Loan in Indonesian Banking Industry: A Sensitivity Analysis using VECM Approach. *International Journal of Education and Research*, *2*(8).

Acharya, A. (1998). Culture, security, multilateralism: The 'ASEAN way' and regional order. *Contemporary Security Policy*, *19*(1), 55–84. doi:10.1080/13523269808404179

Adebola, S. S., Sulaiman, W., Yusoff, W., & Dahalan, J. (2011). An ARDL approach to the determinants of nonperforming loans in Islamic banking system in Malaysia. *Kuwait Chapter of Arabian Journal of Business and Management Review*, *1*(2), 20–30.

Aggarwal, V. K., & Chow, J. T. (2010). The perils of consensus: How ASEAN's meta-regime undermines economic and environmental cooperation. *Review of International Political Economy*, *17*(2), 262–290. doi:10.1080/09692290903192962

Ahmad, F., & Bashir, T. (2013). Explanatory Power of Macroeconomic Variables as Determinants of Non-Performing Loans: Evidence form Pakistan. *World Applied Sciences Journal*, *22*(2), 243–255.

Ahmed, R., & Islam, T., & Al-Amin. (2013). The effects of market diversification activities on Bangladesh RMG export. *International Journal of Economics and Financial Issues*, *3*(4), 938–948.

Aizenman, J., & Jinjarak, Y. (2009). Globalization and developing countries–a shrinking tax base. *The Journal of Development Studies*, *45*(5), 653–671. doi:10.1080/00220380802582338

Akbas, Y. E., & Sentürk, M. (2013). Dependency of import and export of Turkey: An empirical application for selected countries. *Ege Academic Review*, *13*(2), 195–208.

Alesina, A., Ozler, S., Roubini, N., & Swagel, P. (1996). Political instability and economic growth. *Journal of Economic Growth*, *1*(2), 189–211. doi:10.1007/BF00138862

Ali, R., Alwang, J. R., & Siegel, P. B. (1991). *Is export diversification the best way to achieve export growth and stability? A look at three African countries* (World Bank Working Paper No. 729). Retrieved from World Bank website: http://documents.worldbank.org/curated/en/635281468774612514/pdf/multi0page.pdf

Amediku, S. (2006). *Stress tests of the Ghanaian Banking Sector: A VAR Approach.* Working Paper of Bank of Ghana, WP/BOG-2006/02.

Amurgo-Pacheco, A. (2008). *Patterns of export diversification in developing countries* (World Bank Policy Research Working Paper No. 4473). Retrieved from World Bank website: https://openknowledge.worldbank.org/bitstream/handle/10986/6447/wps4473.pdf?sequence=1

Anderson, J. E., & Marcouiller, D. (2002). Insecurity and the pattern of trade: An empirical investigation. *The Review of Economics and Statistics*, *84*(2), 342–352. doi:10.1162/003465302317411587

Anderson, K., Martin, W. J., & Van der Mensbrugghe, D. (2010). China, the WTO, and the Doha Agenda. *China & World Economy*, 1–18.

Apergis, N., & Miller, S. M. (2009). Do structural oil-market shocks affect stock prices? *Energy Economics*, *31*(4), 569–575. doi:10.1016/j.eneco.2009.03.001

Aramberri, J. (2009). The future of tourism and globalization: Some critical remarks. *Futures*, *41*(6), 367–376. doi:10.1016/j.futures.2008.11.015

Arisoy, I. (2008). *Türkiye'de Sanayi Sektörü-Iktisadi Büyüme Ilişkisinin Kaldor Hipotezi Çerçevesinde Test Edilmesi* (No. 2008/1). Discussion Paper, Turkish Economic Association.

Armenia Trade Statistics. (n.d.). Retrieved February 17, 2017, from http://atlas.media.mit.edu/en/profile/country/arm/

ASEAN Secretariat. (2015). *A Blueprint for Growth. ASEAN Economic Community 2015: Progress and Key Achievements*. Jakarta: ASEAN Secretariat.

ASEAN. (1992). *Singapore Declaration*. Retrieved from http://asean.org/?static_post=singapore-declaration-of-1992-singapore-28-january-1992

ASEAN. (1994). *Joint Press Statement. The Fifth AFTA Council Meeting*. Retrieved from http://asean.org/?static_post=asean-economic-community-asean-free-trade-area-afta-council-press-releases-the-5th-afta-council-ministerial-meeting-1994

Astapenia, R. (2015). *Belarus and Eurasia Economic Union: The view from Minsk*. Retrieved March 28, 2017, from http://www.ecfr.eu/article/commentary_belarus_and_the_eurasian_economic_union_the_view_from_minsk

Aw, B. Y., & Hwang, A. R. M. (1995). Productivity and the export market: A firm-level analysis. *Journal of Development Economics*, *47*(2), 313–332. doi:10.1016/0304-3878(94)00062-H

Bacchetta, M., Jansen, M., Piermartini, R., & Amurgo-Pacheco, A. (2007). *Export diversification as an absorber of external shocks*. Retrieved May 5, 2017, from http://www.etsg.org/ETSG2007/papers/ jansen.pdf

Balassa, B. (1961). *The Theory of Economic Integration. Richard D. Irwin, Inc.*

Balassa, B. (1961). Towards a Theory of Economic Integration. *Kyklos*, *1*(1), 1–5. doi:10.1111/j.1467-6435.1961.tb02365.x

Balassa, B. (1976). Types of economic integration. In *Economic Integration: Worldwide, Regional, Sectoral* (pp. 17–40). Palgrave Macmillan. doi:10.1007/978-1-349-02571-8_2

Balassa, B. (1978). Exports and economic growth: Further evidence. *Journal of Development Economics*, *5*(2), 181–189. doi:10.1016/0304-3878(78)90006-8

Balassa, B. (2011). *The Theory of Economic Integration (Routledge Revivals)*. London: Routledge.

Balchin, L. (2008). Trade-related business climate and manufacturing export performance in Africa: A firm-level analysis. *Journal of Development Perspectives*, *4*(1), 32–66.

Baldwin, J. R., & Yan, B. (2014). *Global value chains and the productivity of Canadian manufacturing firms* (Statistics Canada Economic Research Paper No. 090). Retrieved from Statistics Canada website http://www.statcan.gc.ca/pub/11f0027m/11f0027m2014090-eng.pdf

Baldwin, R. E. (2004). Challenges to Globalization. An Overview. In Challenges to Globalization: Analyzing the Economics (pp. 1-14). University of Chicago Press.

Baldwin, J. R., & Gu, W. (2003). Export-market participation and productivity performance in Canadian manufacturing. *The Canadian Journal of Economics. Revue Canadienne d'Economique*, *36*(3), 634–657. doi:10.1111/1540-5982.t01-2-00006

Baldwin, J. R., & Gu, W. (2004). Trade liberalization: Export-market participation, productivity growth, and innovation. *Oxford Review of Economic Policy*, *20*(3), 372–392. doi:10.1093/oxrep/grh022

Balgova, M., Nies, M., & Plekhanov, A. (n.d.). *The economic impact of reducing non-performing loans*. EBRD Working Paper No. 193.

Balibar, E., & Wallerstein, I. M. (1991). *Race, nation, class: Ambiguous identities*. New York: Verso.

Barieri, izyatia I ogranicheniya EAES. (2016). [Barriers, Exceptions and Limitations of the EEU]. Eurasian Economic Commission. Analitical paper. Retrieved 14 May, 2017, from https://barriers.eaeunion.org/api/info/document/38/file

Beaver, B., Beaver, J., & Wilsey, M. (2017). *The Middle East: United States policy and relations in the latter half of the 20th century*. Retrieved August 6, 2017, from https://web.stanford.edu/class/e297c/war_peace/middleeast/hcentury.html

Beck, R., Jakubik, P., & Piloiu, A. (2013). *Non-performing loans: What matters in addition to the economic cycle?* Working Paper Series, 1515.

Bellone, F., Musso, P., Nesta, L., & Schiavo, S. (2010). Financial constraints and firm export behaviour. *World Economy*, *33*(3), 347–373. doi:10.1111/j.1467-9701.2010.01259.x

Berman, N., & Héricourt, J. (2010). Financial factors and the margins of trade: Evidence from cross-country firm-level data. *Journal of Development Economics*, *93*(2), 206–217. doi:10.1016/j.jdeveco.2009.11.006

Bernard, A. B., & Jensen, J. B. (1999). Exceptional exporter performance: Cause, effect, or both? *Journal of International Economics*, *47*(1), 1–25. doi:10.1016/S0022-1996(98)00027-0

Bernard, A. B., & Jensen, J. B. (2004a). Exporting and Productivity in the USA. *Oxford Review of Economic Policy*, *20*(3), 343–357. doi:10.1093/oxrep/grh020

Bernard, A. B., & Jensen, J. B. (2004b). Why some firms export. *The Review of Economics and Statistics*, *86*(2), 561–569. doi:10.1162/003465304323031111

Bernard, A. B., Jensen, J. B., & Lawrence, R. Z. (1995). Exporters, jobs, and wages in US manufacturing: 1976-1987. *Brookings papers on economic activity. Microeconomics*, *1995*, 67–119.

Bernard, A. B., Jensen, J. B., Redding, S. J., & Schott, P. K. (2007). Firms in international trade. *The Journal of Economic Perspectives*, *21*(3), 105–130. doi:10.1257/jep.21.3.105

Besedeš, T., & Prusa, T. J. (2011). The role of extensive and intensive margins and export growth. *Journal of Development Economics*, *96*(2), 371–379. doi:10.1016/j.jdeveco.2010.08.013

Blockmans, S., Kostanyan, H., & Vorobiov, I. (2012, December). *Towards a Eurasian Economic Union: Integration and cooperation*. CEPS Special Report No. 75.

Bloom, D. E., Sachs, J. D., Collier, P., & Udry, C. (1998). Geography, demography, and economic growth in Africa. *Brookings Papers on Economic Activity*, *1998*(2), 207–295. doi:10.2307/2534695 PMID:12295931

Bondaz, A., Cohen, D., Godement, F., Kratz, A., & Pantucci, R. (2015). *One Belt, One Road: China's Great Leap Outward*. London: European Council on Foreign Relations.

Bowles, P., & MacLean, B. (1996). Understanding Trade Bloc Formation: The Case of the ASEAN Free Trade Area. *Review of International Political Economy*, *3*(2), 319–348. doi:10.1080/09692299608434358

Boyer, R., & Drache, D. (1996). States Against Markets: The Limits of Globalization. New York: Academic Press.

Broz, T., Buturac, G., & Tkalec, M. (2015). To what extent does Croatia really cooperate with SEE countries in he fields of foreign trade, direct investment and tourism? *Ekonomska Istrazivanja*, *28*(1), 879–906. doi:10.1080/1331677X.2015.1092703

Brueckner, M. (2017). *The rise of the middle class and economic growth in ASEAN*. Canberra: Centre for Economic Policy Research, Australian National University. doi:10.1596/1813-9450-8068

Bugajski, J. (2008). *Expanding Eurasia: Russia's European Ambitions*. Washington, DC: CSIS.

Cadot, O., Carrère, C., & Strauss-Kahn, V. (2013). Trade diversification, income, and growth: What do we know? *Journal of Economic Surveys*, *27*(4), 790–812. doi:10.1111/j.1467-6419.2011.00719.x

Cass, D. Z., Williams, B., & Barker, G. R. (2003). *China and the World Trading System: Entering the Millennium*. New York, NY: Cambridge University Press. doi:10.1017/CBO9780511494482

Center for Balkan and Black Sea Studies. (n.d.). *Belarus reportedly mulls leaving the Eurasian Economic Union as relations with Russia worsen*. Retrieved February 3, 2017, from http://bulgariaanalytica.org/cbbss/?p=10497

Cestepe, H., Zildirim, E., & Bahtiyar, B. (2015). The impact of Trade Liberalization on teh Export of MENA Countries to OECD Trade Partners. *Procedia Economics and Finance*, *23*, 1440–1445. doi:10.1016/S2212-5671(15)00427-X

Chamber of Commerce and Industry of Serbia. (2017). *Implementation of CEFTA 2006*. Retrieved May 10, 2017, from http://www.pks.rs/SADRZAJ/Files/CEFTA_ENGLESKI%20DEO.pdf

Chang, C. P., Lee, C. C., & Hsieh, M. C. (2015). Does globalization promote real output? Evidence from quantile cointegration regression. *Economic Modelling*, *44*, 25–36. doi:10.1016/j.econmod.2014.09.018

Characteristics of Kazakh-Russian relations. (n.d.). Embassy of the Republic of Kazakhstan in the Russian Federation. Retrieved 12 April, 2017, from http://www.kazembassy.ru/ru/dvustoronneesotrudnichestvo/harakteristikaotnoshenii

Chauhan, S. (2013). *Vietnam's role in ASEAN*. Retrieved from http://www.eastasiaforum.org/2013/10/23/vietnams-role-in-asean/

Cheng, A., & Lim, H. (n.d.). China and The Eurasian Economic Union: Prospects for The Silk Road Economic Belt. *IPP Review*. Retrieved February 15, 2017, from http://ippreview.com/index.php/Home/Blog/single/id/18.html

Chow, P. C. (1987). Causality between export growth and industrial development: Empirial evidence from the NICs. *Journal of Development Economics*, *26*(1), 55–63. doi:10.1016/0304-3878(87)90051-4

Cinar, S., & Gocer, I. (2014). Towards a new cold war: Global energy policies. Adnan Menderes University. *Journal of Institute of Social Sciences*, *1*(2), 16–29.

Clarete, R., Edmonds, C., & Seddon Wallack, J. (2003). Asian regionalism and its effects on trade in the 1980s and 1990s. *Journal of Asian Economics*, *14*(1), 91–129. doi:10.1016/S1049-0078(02)00242-7

Coale, A. J., & Hoover, E. M. (2015). *Population growth and economic development*. Princeton University Press.

Čokić, M. (2014). *Aktivnosti Bosne i Hercegovine u cilju realizaciji Centralnoevropskog ugovora o slobodnoj trgovini - CEFTA 2006.* Zbornik radova: II Međunarodna konferencija Bosna i Hercegovina i Euroatlantske integracije Trenutni izazovi i perspektive. Retrieved April 29, 2017, from https://ssrc.ibu.edu.ba/assets/ssrc/userfiles/files/ZBORNIK-TOM-II.pdf

Competitiveness (In International Trade). (2014). In *OECD Glossary of Statistical Terms.* Retrieved from https://stats.oecd.org/glossary/detail.asp?ID=399

Cover, T., & Hart, P. (1967). Nearest neighbor pattern classification. *IEEE Transactions on Information Theory, 13*(1), 21–27. doi:10.1109/TIT.1967.1053964

Crisis Group. (2016). *The Eurasian Economic Union: Power, Politics and Trade.* Europe and Central Asia Report N°240. Retrieved January 1, 2017, from https://d2071andvip0wj.cloudfront.net/240-the-eurasian-economic-union-power-politics-and-trade.pdf

Dai, M., Yotov, Y. V., & Zylkin, T. (2014). On the trade-diversion effects of free trade agreements. *Economics Letters, 122*(2), 321–325. doi:10.1016/j.econlet.2013.12.024

de la Paz-Marín, M., Gutiérrez, P. A., & Hervás-Martínez, C. (2015). Classification of countries' progress toward a knowledge economy based on machine learning classification techniques. *Expert Systems with Applications, 42*(1), 562–572. doi:10.1016/j.eswa.2014.08.008

Degiannakis, S., Filis, G., & Kizys, R. (2013). *Oil price shocks and stock market volatility: evidence from European data* (No. 161).

Dekle, R., Jeong, H., & Ryoo, H. (2009). *A Re-Examination of the Exchange Rate Disconnect Puzzle: Evidence from Firm Level Data.* University of Southern California mimeo.

Dekle, R., & Ryoo, H. H. (2007). Exchange rate fluctuations, financing constraints, hedging, and exports: Evidence from firm level data. *Journal of International Financial Markets, Institutions and Money, 17*(5), 437–451. doi:10.1016/j.intfin.2006.04.001

De, P. (2006). *Trade in Northeast Asia: Why Do Trade Costs Matter?* Munich: Leibniz Institute for Economic Research.

Dethier, J. J., Hirn, M., & Straub, S. (2010). Explaining enterprise performance in developing countries with business climate survey data. *The World Bank Research Observer, 26*(2), 258–309. doi:10.1093/wbro/lkq007

Devlet Planlama Teşkilatı. (2000). VII. Beş Yıllık Kalkınma Planı. Küreselleşme Ö.İ.K.Raporu, Ankara.

Devore, J. L. (2015). *Probability and Statistics for Engineering and the Sciences.* Boston: Cengage Learning.

Diaz Bautista, A. (2003). México´s Industrial Engine of Growth: Cointegration and Causality. *Revista Momento Economico*, (126).

Disdier, A. C., Fontagne, L., & Mimouni, M. (2013). *Tariff Liberalization and Trade Integration of Emerging Countries.* CEPII Working paper No. 2013-36. Retrieved May 8, 2017, from http://www.cepii.fr/PDF_PUB/wp/2013/wp2013-36.pdf

Dogan, B., & Can, M. (2016). The Effects of Economic Structural Transformation on Employment: An Evaluation in the Context of Economic. Handbook of Research on Unemployment and Labor Market Sustainability in the Era of Globalization, 275.

Dogovor o Evraziyskom ekonomicheskom soyuze. (2014). [The Treaty on the Eurasian Economic Union]. Signed in Astana on May 29. Retrieved 12 April, 2017, from http://www.eaeunion.org/files/history/2014/2014_2.pdf

Dohmen, H. (1976). China's Foreign Trade Policy. *Inter Economics*, *11*(7), 197–201. doi:10.1007/BF02929005

Dollar, D., Hallward-Driemeier, M., & Mengistae, T. (2006). Investment climate and international integration. *World Development*, *34*(9), 1498–1516. doi:10.1016/j.worlddev.2006.05.001

Dollar, D., & Kraay, A. (2003). Institutions, trade, and growth. *Journal of Monetary Economics*, *50*(1), 133–162. doi:10.1016/S0304-3932(02)00206-4

Drakopoulos, S. A., & Theodossiou, I. (1991). Kaldorian Approach to Greek Economic Growth. *Applied Economics*, *23*(10), 1683–1689. doi:10.1080/00036849100000133

Dreyer, I., & Popescu, N. (2014). *The Eurasian Customs Union: The economics and the politics*. European Union Institute for Security Studies. Retrieved January 15, 2017, from http://www.iss.europa.eu/uploads/media/Brief_11_Eurasian_Union.pdf

Druzhinin, A. (2014). Armenia Joins Eurasian Economic Union. *Sputnik International*. Retrieved January 12, 2017, from https://sputniknews.com/world/20141010193914853-Armenia-Joins-Eurasian-Economic-Union/

Duchatel, M., Godement, F., Liik, K., Shapiro, J., Slavkova, L., Stanzel, A., & Tcherneva, V. (2016). *Eurasian Integration: Caught between Russia and China*. Retrieved April 17, 2017, from http://www.ecfr.eu/article/essay_eurasian

Dumitrescu, E. I., & Hurlin, C. (2012). Testing for Granger non-causality in heterogeneous panels. *Economic Modelling*, *29*(4), 1450–1460. doi:10.1016/j.econmod.2012.02.014

Dunya. (2014). *We bought a $ 1.4 billion toy from China.* Retrieved August 6, 2017, from https://www.dunya.com/ihracat/cin039den-14-milyar-dolarlik-oyuncak-aldik-haberi-234563

Durden, T. (2016). *The oil-gas war over Syria (In 4 Maps).* Retrieved August 6, 2017, from http://www.zerohedge.com/news/2016-10-24/oil-gas-war-over-syria-4-maps

Dutt, P., & Traca, D. (2010). Corruption and bilateral trade flows: Extortion or evasion? *The Review of Economics and Statistics*, *92*(4), 843–860. doi:10.1162/REST_a_00034

EAES I Izrail nachinayut peregovory o sozdanii zony svobodnoy torgovli. (2015, October 16). [The EEU and Israel begin the negotiations on creating a free trade zone]. *Kommersant.ru*. Retrieved from https://www.kommersant.ru/doc/2834675

EAES I Kitay nachinayut peregovory o sozdanii zony svobodnoy torgovli. (2015, May 12). [The EEU and China begin the negotiations on creating a free trade zone]. *GazetaNova.RU*. Retrieved from http://gazetanova.ru/politics/9163-eaes-i-kitay-nachinayut-peregovory-o-sozdanii-zony-svobodnoy-torgovli.html

EAES I Tamojenniy soyuz: komu vigodno? (2016). [The EEU and Customs Union: who benefits?]. Retrieved 21 April, 2017, from http://kazdata.kz/04/2016-03-eaes-ts-kazakhstan-torgovye-otnosheniya.html

EAES ne vedet peregovory s Siriey o sozdanii zony svobodnoy torgovli. (2015, October 12). [The EEU does not negotiate with Syria on the establishment of a free trade zone]. Expert center on WTO issues. Retrieved from http://www.wto.ru/2015/10/12/еаэс-не-ведет-переговоры-с-сирией-о-соз/

Ebrahimzadeh, M.H., Fattahi, A.S. & Nejad, A.B. (2006). Long-term follow-up of Iranian veteran upper extremity amputees from the Iran-Iraq War (1980-1988). *Journal of Trauma-Injury Infection & Critical Care*, *61*(4), 886-888.

EBRD. (2014). *Transition Report 2014 - Innovation in transition.* Retrieved April 29, 2017, from http://www.ebrd.com/news/publications/transition-report/transition-report-2014.html

EBRD. (2015). *Transition Report 2015-16 - Rebalancing finance*. Retrieved April 29, 2017, from http://www.ebrd.com/news/publications/transition-report/ebrd-transition-report-201516.html

Edwards, S. (1993). Openness, trade liberalization, and growth in developing countries. *Journal of Economic Literature*, *31*(3), 1358–1393.

Egger, H., & Kreickemeier, U. (2009). Firm heterogeneity and the labor market effects of trade liberalization. *International Economic Review*, *50*(1), 187–216. doi:10.1111/j.1468-2354.2008.00527.x

Eichengreen, B., & Hausmann, R. (2005). *Other People's Money*. University of Chicago Press. doi:10.7208/chicago/9780226194578.001.0001

Ekspert: zony svobodnoy torgovli mogut obestsenit EAES. (2015, June 2). [An expert: free trade areas can reduce the EEU]. Sovet Federatsii. Retrieved from http://svpressa.ru/economy/news/123895/

Elegbe, A. (2013). Bank failure and economic development in Nigeria: An empirical approach. *British Journal of Economics. Finance and Management Sciences*, *8*(1), 46–63.

Embassy of the People's Republic of China in the United States of America. (2011). *China's Foreign Trade*. Retrieved April 17, 2017, from http://www.china-embassy.org/eng/zt/bps/t943740.htm

Energy Efficiency Association. (2017). *Cost in transportation systems*. Retrieved April 16, 2017, from http://www.enver.org.tr/tr/icerik/ulasim/15

Erdogdu, A. (2016). Assessing the Impact of Non-Performing Loans on Economic Growth in Turkey. *Economic and Social Development: Book of Proceedings*, 309.

Erkan, B. (2014). Product and market diversification in Turkey's foreign trade. *International Journal of Advances in Management and Economics*, *3*(1), 1–15.

Erokhin, V. (2014). Foreign Trade in Russia: Existing Distortions and Potentials of Regional Competitiveness in View of Liberalization. *International Journal of Sustainable Economies Management*, *3*(3), 1–18. doi:10.4018/ijsem.2014070101

Erokhin, V. (2015). Contemporary Reshaping of Eurasian Integration: Russia's Policies and their Implication for the EU and EurAsEC. *Procedia Economics and Finance*, *22*, 402–411. doi:10.1016/S2212-5671(15)00313-5

Erokhin, V. (2016b). Rising Economic Powers among Economies in Transition: Is There Enough Space on the Global Market? In V. Erokhin (Ed.), *Global Perspectives on Trade Integration and Economies in Transition* (pp. 1–25). Hershey, PA: IGI Global. doi:10.4018/978-1-5225-0451-1.ch001

V. Erokhin (Ed.). (2016a). *Global Perspectives on Trade Integration and Economies in Transition*. Hershey, PA: IGI Global. doi:10.4018/978-1-5225-0451-1

Ersin, İ., & Duran, S. (2017). Faizsiz Finans Döngüsünü Oluşturma Açısından Adil Ekonomik Düzen Söyleminin Kredileşme İlkeleri Ve Uygulanabilirliğinin Değerlendirilmesi. *Turkish Studies*, *12*(8), 109–132. doi:10.7827/TurkishStudies.11928

Espinoza, R., & Ananthakri, P. (2010). *Nonperforming Loans in the GCC Banking System and their macroeconomic effects*. IMF Working Paper WP/10/224.

ETH. (2017). *KOF Index of Globalization*. Retrieved from "http://globalization.kof.ethz.ch/query/"

Eti, S., & İnel, M. N. (2016). A Research on Comparison of Regression Models Explaining the Profitability Base on Financial Data. *International Journal of Business and Management*, *4*(10), 470–475.

European Commission. (2012). *10 Benefits of trade for developing countries*. Retrieved May 04, 2017, from http://trade.ec.europa.eu/doclib/docs/2012/january/tradoc_148991.pdf

European Commission. (2016). *Report from the Commission to the Council and the European Parliament on trade and investment barriers and protectionist trends*. Brussels, COM(2016) 406 Final. Retrieved October 11, 2017, from http://trade.ec.europa.eu/doclib/docs/2016/ june/tradoc_154665.pdf

European Union. (2015). *Inside TTIP, The transatlantic trade and investment partnership (TTIP) towards an EU–US trade deal, An overview and chapter-by-chapter guide in plain English*. Retrieved May 03, 2017, from http://trade.ec.europa.eu/doclib/docs/2015/july/tradoc_153635.pdf

Eurostat, International trade in goods in 2014 EU's top trading partners in 2014. (n.d.). Retrieved January 1, 2017, from http://ec.europa.eu/eurostat/documents/2995521/6760204/6-27032015-AP-EN.pdf

Evenett, S. J., & Venables, A. (2002). *Export growth by developing economies: Market entry and bilateral trade* (Swiss Institute for International Economics and Applied Economic Research Working Paper). Retrieved from the Swiss Institute for International Economics and Applied Economic Research: https://www.alexandria.unisg.ch/22177/1/setvend.pdf

Falvey, R., Foster, N., & Greenaway, D. (2012). Trade Liberalization, Econmic Crises, and Growth. *World Development*, *40*(11), 2177–2193. doi:10.1016/j.worlddev.2012.03.020

Fan, H., Li, Y. A., & Yeaple, S. R. (2015). Trade liberalization, quality, and export prices. *The Review of Economics and Statistics*, *97*(5), 1033–1051. doi:10.1162/REST_a_00524

Featherstone, M., Lash, S., & Robertson, R. (1995). *Global modernities* (Vol. 36). Sage.

Fedorenko, V. (2015). *Eurasian Integration: Effects on Central Asia*. Washington, DC: Rethink Institute.

Ferderer, J. P. (1997). Oil price volatility and the macroeconomy. *Journal of Macroeconomics*, *18*(1), 1–26. doi:10.1016/S0164-0704(96)80001-2

Fofack, H. (2005). *Nonperforming loans in Sub-Saharan Africa: causal analysis and macroeconomic implications.* World Bank Policy Research Working Paper, 3769.

Fogel, R. W. (1994). *Economic growth, population theory, and physiology: the bearing of long-term processes on the making of economic policy (No. w4638).* National Bureau of Economic Research. doi:10.3386/w4638

Forbes, K. J. (2002). *How do large depreciations affect firm performance? (NBER Working Paper 9095).* Cambridge, MA: National Bureau of Economic Research. Retrieved from the National Bureau of Economic Research. doi:10.3386/w9095

Forlani, E. (2008). *Firms Credit Constraints and Export Propensity*. Mimeo CORE/Université Catholique de Louvain.

Francisco, C. G. (2013). *What promises does the Eurasian customs union hold for the future? Economic premise. No. 108*. Washington, DC: World Bank.

Francois, J., & Manchin, M. (2013). Institutions, infrastructure, and trade. *World Development*, *46*, 165–175. doi:10.1016/j.worlddev.2013.02.009

Freund, J. E., & Simon, G. A. (1973). *Modern elementary statistics* (Vol. 12). Englewood Cliffs, NJ: Prentice-Hall.

GAIN Report on Eurasian Economic Union One Year On. (n.d.). Retrieved February 20, 2017, from https://gain.fas.usda.gov/Recent%20GAIN%20Publications/Eurasian%20Economic%20Union%20One%20Year%20On_Moscow_Russian%20Federation_3-11-2016.pdf

Gharabegian, A. (2015). The Eurasian Economic Union and Armenia. *The Armenian Weekly*. Retrieved February 10, 2017, from http://armenianweekly.com/2015/10/20/the-eurasian-economic-union-armenia/

Ghosh, A. (2015). Banking-industry specific and regional economic determinants of non-performing loans: Evidence from US states. *Journal of Financial Stability*, *20*, 93–104. doi:10.1016/j.jfs.2015.08.004

Giles, J. A., & Williams, C. L. (2010). Export-led growth: A survey of the empirical literature and some non-causality results. *The Journal of International Trade & Economic Development. An International and Comparative Review*, *9*(3), 261–337.

Giovannetti, G., Marvasi, E., & Sanfilippo, M. (2015). Supply chains and the internationalization of small firms. *Small Business Economics*, *44*(4), 845–865. doi:10.1007/s11187-014-9625-x

Glowacz, A., & Glowacz, Z. (2016). Recognition of images of finger skin with the application of histogram, image filtration, and K-NN classifier. *Biocybernetics and Biomedical Engineering*, *36*(1), 95–101. doi:10.1016/j.bbe.2015.12.005

Gocer, I. (2013). *Productivity and macroeconomic effects of foreign direct investment: The case of Turkey, China and India* (Unpublished PhD dissertation). Adnan Menderes University, Social Sciences Institute, Department of Economics.

Gocer, I., & Cinar, S. (2015). The reasons of Arab Spring, its international dimension and impacts on Turkey's foreign trade and tourism incomes. *The Journal of KAU, IIBF*, *6*(10), 51–68.

Gogineni, S. (2010). Oil and the stock market: An industry level analysis. *Financial Review*, *45*(4), 995–1010. doi:10.1111/j.1540-6288.2010.00282.x

Golam, M. (2013). The concept of 'Eurasia': Kazakhstan's Eurasian policy and its implications. *Journal of Eurasian Studies*, *4*(2), 160–170. doi:10.1016/j.euras.2013.03.006

Goldberg, P. K., & Knetter, M. M. (1997). Goods Prices and Exchange Rates: What Have We Learned? *Journal of Economic Literature*, *35*(3), 1243–1272.

Goldfarb, D. (2006). *Too many eggs in one basket? Evaluating Canada's need to diversify trade*. C.D. Howe Institute, Commentary, No: 236.

Goodman, A. (1996). Vietnam and ASEAN: Who Would Have Thought it Possible? *Asian Survey*, *36*(6), 592–600. doi:10.2307/2645793

Greenidge, K., & Grosvenor, T. (2010). Forecasting non-performing loans in Barbados. *Journal of Business. Finance and Economics in Emerging Economies*, *5*(1), 79–108.

Gujarati, D. (2008). Temel Ekonometri. Literatür Yayınları.

Guo, H., & Kliesen, K. L. (2005). Oil price volatility and US macroeconomic activity. *RE:view*, 87.

Gylfason, T. (1999). Exports, inflation and growth. *World Development*, *27*(6), 1031–1057. doi:10.1016/S0305-750X(99)00045-5

Haberler, G. (1959). The Theory of International Trade. Academic Press.

Hakim, A., & Hamdi, H. (2016). Trade liberalizaction, FDI inflows, environmental quality and ekonomic growth: A comparative analzsis bwteen Tunisaia and Morocco. *Renewable & Sustainable Energy Reviews*, *58*, 1445–1456. doi:10.1016/j.rser.2015.12.280

Hallaert, J. J., Cavazos-Cepeda, R. H., & Kang, G. (2011). *Estimating the constraints to trade of developing countries*. Academic Press.

Hallaert, J. J., Cavazos-Cepeda, R. H., & Kang, G. (2011). *Estimating the constraints to trade of developing countries. (OECD Trade Policy Papers No. 116)*. OECD. doi:10.1787/18166873

Hall, R. E., & Jones, C. I. (1999). Why do some countries produce so much more output per worker than others? *The Quarterly Journal of Economics*, *114*(1), 83–116. doi:10.1162/003355399555954

Hamilton, J. D. (1983). Oil and the macroeconomy since World War II. *Journal of Political Economy*, *91*(2), 228–248. doi:10.1086/261140

Hamrin, C. L., & Zhao, S. (1995). *Decision-making in Deng's China: Perspectives from Insiders*. Armonk, NY: M.E. Sharpe.

Haniifah, N. (2015). Economic Determinants of Non-performing Loans (NPLs) in Ugandan Commercial Banks. Taylor's. *Business Review (Federal Reserve Bank of Philadelphia)*, *5*(2), 137–153.

Harrison, A. (1996). Openness and growth: A time-series, cross-country analysis for developing countries. *Journal of Development Economics*, *48*(2), 419–447. doi:10.1016/0304-3878(95)00042-9

Hay, C. (2000). Contemporary capitalism, globalization, regionalization and the persistence of national variation. *Review of International Studies*, *26*(4), 509–531. doi:10.1017/S026021050000509X

Hillman, A. L. (2015). 12. Rents and international trade policy. *Companion to the Political Economy of Rent Seeking*, 187.

Huang, R. D., Masulis, R. W., & Stoll, H. R. (1996). Energy shocks and financial markets. *Journal of Futures Markets*, *16*(1), 1–27. doi:10.1002/(SICI)1096-9934(199602)16:1<1::AID-FUT1>3.0.CO;2-Q

Hummels, D., & Klenow, P. J. (2005). The variety and quality of a nation's exports. *The American Economic Review*, *95*(3), 704–723. doi:10.1257/0002828054201396

Iglauer, P. (2014). Eastern interest in Eurasian economic deal. *Asia Times*. Retrieved February 11, 2017, from http://www.atimes.com/atimes/Central_Asia/CEN-01-110614.html

IMF. (2017). *World Economic Outlook*. Retrieved May 10, 2017, from http://www.imf.org/en/Data

International Trade Center (ITC). (n.d.). *Trade Performance Index.* Retrieved May 20, 2017, from http://tradecompetitivenessmap.intracen.org/Documents/TradeCompMap-Trade%20Performance%20Index-Technical%20Notes-EN.pdf

Investopedia. (2017). *Financial dictinary.* Retrieved May 5, 2017, from http://www.investopedia.com/terms/e/economic-integration.asp

Islam, R. (2015). *Globalization of production, work and human development: is a race to the bottom inevitable?* UNDP Human Development Report Office, Think Piece.

Jenkins, R. (1996). Trade liberalization and export performance in Bolivia. *Development and Change, 27*(4), 693–716. doi:10.1111/j.1467-7660.1996.tb00608.x

Jones, C. M., & Kaul, G. (1996). Oil and the stock markets. *The Journal of Finance, 51*(2), 463–491. doi:10.1111/j.1540-6261.1996.tb02691.x

Jones, M. (2001). *Conflict and Confrontation in South East Asia, 1961-1965: Britain, the United States, Indonesia and the Creation of Malaysia.* Cambridge, UK: Cambridge University Press. doi:10.1017/CBO9780511497346

Kaboub, F. (2001). The demise and rebirth of laissez-faire capitalism. *Oeconomicus, 4*, 83–86.

Kaczmarski, M. (2015). *China and Russia: Two Approaches to Integration.* Retrieved April 17, 2017, from http://thediplomat.com/2015/03/china-and-russia-two-approaches-to-integration/

Kaldor, N. (1966). *Causes of the Slow Rate of Economic Growth of the United Kingdom: An Inaugural Lecture.* Cambridge University Press.

Kang, S. H., Kang, S. M., & Yoon, S. M. (2009). Forecasting volatility of crude oil markets. *Energy Economics, 31*(1), 119–125. doi:10.1016/j.eneco.2008.09.006

Kansu, I. (1997). *Emperyalizmin Yeni Masalı: Küreselleşme.* Ankara: İmge Kitabevi.

Karahanoğlu, İ., & Ercan, H. (2015). The Effect of Macroeconomic Variables on Non-Performing Loans in Turkish Banking Sector. *Journal of International Social Research, 8*(39), 883–892. doi:10.17719/jisr.20153913804

Karlsen, G. E. (2002). Eğitim Yönetişimi: Küreselleşme ve Demokrasi. Kuram ve Uygulamada Eğitim Bilimleri, 2(1).

Kaufmann, D., Kraay, A., & Mastruzzi, M. (2003). *Governance Matters III: governance indicators for 1996-2002* (World Bank Policy Research Department Working Paper). Retrieved from World Bank website: https://elibrary.worldbank.org/doi/abs/10.1596/1813-9450-3106

Kaul, G., & Seyhun, H. N. (1990). Relative price variability, real shocks, and the stock market. *The Journal of Finance, 45*(2), 479–496. doi:10.1111/j.1540-6261.1990.tb03699.x

Kavoussi, R. M. (1984). Export expansion and economic growth: Further empirical evidence. *Journal of Development Economics, 14*(1), 241–250. doi:10.1016/0304-3878(84)90052-X

Kazakhstan Trade Statistics. (n.d.). Retrieved January 12, 2017, from http://atlas.media.mit.edu/en/profile/country/kaz/

Kazakhstan: Balance of Payments and External Debt for 2015. (n.d.). Retrieved January 1, 2017, from http://bit.ly/29vI5wQ

Khandelwal, P., & Roitman, A. (2013). *The Economics of Political Transitions: Implications for the Arab Spring*. Washington, DC: International Monetary Fund.

Khanna, T., & Palepu, K. G. (2010). *Winning in Emerging Markets: A Road Map for Strategy and Execution*. Boston, MA: Harvard Business Press.

Kilian, L., & Park, C. (2009). The impact of oil price shocks on the US stock market*. *International Economic Review*, *50*(4), 1267–1287. doi:10.1111/j.1468-2354.2009.00568.x

Kindleberger, C. (1974). *Međunarodna ekonomija*. Beograd, Srbija: Vuk Karadžić.

Kit-Katos, K., & Sparrow, R. (2015). Poverty, labour market and trade liberalization in Indonezia. *Journal of Development Economics*, *117*, 94–106. doi:10.1016/j.jdeveco.2015.07.005

Klein, N. (2013). *Non-Performing Loans in CESEE: Determinants and Macroeconomic Performance*. IMF Working Paper WP13/72.

Klimczak, L. (2016). Trade Liberalisation and Export Performance of the Western Balkans 1. *Montenegrin Journal of Economics*, *12*(2), 45–60. doi:10.14254/1800-5845.2016/12-1/3

Kneller, R., Morgan, C. W., & Kanchanahatakij, S. (2008). Trade liberalisation and economic growth. *World Economy*, *31*(6), 701–719. doi:10.1111/j.1467-9701.2008.01101.x

Koen, V. (2017). *Malaysia's economic success story and challenges*. OECD Economics Department Working Papers, 1369. Paris: OECD Publishing.

Koltan, Ş., & Said, P. (2011). *Kümeleme analizi ve pazarlamada kullanımı*. Retrieved from http://dergipark.ulakbim.gov.tr/ayd/article/view/5000125171/5000115039

Korea I. Evraziyskiy ekonomicheskiy soyuz nachali peregovori po soglasheniyu o svobodnoy torgovle. (2017, April 11). [Korea and the Eurasian Economic Union began negotiations on free trade agreement]. Retrieved from http://russian.korea.net/NewsFocus/Business/view?articleId=145305

Korkmaz, P. (2013). *View from London*. Retrieved May 05, 2017, from https://perihankorkmaz.wordpress.com/2013/06/17/ulkelerin-dostlari-ve-cikarlari/

Kose, M. A., Prasad, E. S., &Terrones, M. E. (2003). *How does globalization affect the synchronization of business cycles?* Academic Press.

Kownacki, P. (2000). Migration phenomena and current social and economic problems of the African countries. *Hemispheres: Studies on Cultures and Societies*, (15), 37-49.

Kragulj, D. (2005). *Evropski integracioni i tranzicioni procesi*. Beograd, Srbija: Kragulj.

Kragulj, D. (2016). *Ekonomija – Osnovi mikroekonomske i makroekonomske analize*. Beograd, Srbija: Kragulj.

Krapohl, S. (2016). *Regional Integration in the Global South: External Influence on Economic Cooperation in ASEAN, MERCOSUR and SADC*. Berlin: Springer.

Krugman, P. (1979a). Increasing returns, monopolistic competition and ınternational trade. *Journal of International Economics*, *9*(4), 469–479. doi:10.1016/0022-1996(79)90017-5

Krugman, P. (1979b). A model of balance-of-payment crises. *Journal of Money, Credit and Banking*, *11*(3), 311–325. doi:10.2307/1991793

Krugman, P. (1980). Scale economies, product differentiation, and the pattern of trade. *The American Economic Review*, *70*(5), 950–959.

Krugman, P. (1981). Intra-industry specialization and the gains from trade. *Journal of Political Economy*, *89*(5), 959–973. doi:10.1086/261015

Krugman, P. (1991). Increasing returns and economic geography. *Journal of Political Economy*, *99*(3), 483–499. doi:10.1086/261763

Kuvshinova, O. (2016, December 14). *Snijenie baryerov v torgovle stran EAES mojet uvelichit ih tovarooborot na chetvert* [The reduction of trade barriers in the EEU countries could increase their turnover by a quarter]. Retrieved from https://www.vedomosti.ru/economics/articles/2016/12/14/669499-snizhenie-barerov

Kuzmina, E. M. (2016). Eurasian Economic Union in the New Economy. *Management consulting*, *10*. Retrieved 12 May, 2017, from https://cyberleninka.ru/article/n/evraziyskiy-ekonomicheskiy-soyuz-v-novyh-ekonomicheskih-usloviyah

Kuzmina, E. M. (2017, June 15). *Ekonomicheskoe razvitie stran EAES I perspektivi ekonomicheskoy integrazii do 2025 goda* [Economic development of the EEU countries and prospects of economic integration by 2025]. Working paper. Retrieved from http://russiancouncil.ru/papers/EAEU2025-Policybrief-ru.pdf

Kyrgyzstan Trade Statistics. (n.d.). Retrieved February 17, 2017, from http://atlas.media.mit.edu/en/profile/country/kgz/

Lagutina, M. (2017). Improving relations with Russia and Ukraine. In A. Amighini (Ed.), *China's Belt and Road: a Game Changer?* (pp. 53–75). Milan: ISPI.

Lagutina, M., & Vasilyeva, N. (2016). *The Russian Project of Eurasian Integration. Geopolitical Prospects*. Lexington Books, Rowman and Littlefield.

Lall, S. (2001). Competitiveness indices and developing countries: An economic evaluation of the global competitiveness report. *World Development*, *29*(9), 1501–1525. doi:10.1016/S0305-750X(01)00051-1

Lapenko, M. (2014). Ukrainskiy krizis I ego vliyanie na realizatsiu proekta sozdaniya Evraziyskogo ekonomicheskogo soyuza [Ukrainian crisis and its influence on the development of the Eurasian economic union]. *Connections, 14*(1). Retrieved from http://connections-qj.org/ru/article/ukrainskiy-krizis-i-ego-vliyanie-na-realizaciyu-proekta-sozdaniya-evraziyskogo

Lardy, N. R. (2002). *Integrating China into the World Economy*. Washington, DC: Brookings Institution Press.

Latukhina, K. (2015, August 26). Putin: EAES I Egipet mogut sozdat zonu svobodnoy torgovli [Putin: the EEU and Egypt can create a free trade zone]. *Rossiyskaya gazeta*.

Lawson, C., & Wang, H. (2004). *Economic Transition in Central and Eastern Europe and the Former Soviet Union: Which Policies Worked?* University of Bath.

Le, T. H., & Chang, Y. (2011). *The impact of oil price fluctuations on stock markets in developed and emerging economies*. Singapore Economic Review Conference 2011.

Lee, E. (2005). *Trade liberalization and employment*. UN.

Lemoine, F., & Ünal, D. (2017). China's Foreign Trade: A "New Normal". *China & World Economy, 25*(2), 1–21. doi:10.1111/cwe.12191

Le, T. H., & Tran-Nam, B. (in press). Trade Liberalization, Financial Modernizaation and Economic Development:An Emprical Studz of Selected Asia-Pacific Countries. *Research in Economics*.

Levchenko, A. A. (2007). Institutional quality and international trade. *The Review of Economic Studies, 74*(3), 791–819. doi:10.1111/j.1467-937X.2007.00435.x

Levin Institute. (2017). *Trade and globalization*. Retrieved May 03, 2017, from http://www.globalization101.org/uploads/File/Trade/tradeall.pdf

Liberthal, K. (2004). *Governing China: From Revolution Through Reform*. New York, NY: W. W. Norton.

Limao, N., & Venables, A. J. (2001). Infrastructure, geographical disadvantage, transport costs, and trade. *The World Bank Economic Review, 15*(3), 451–479. doi:10.1093/wber/15.3.451

Linders, G. J., Slangen, H. L. A., De Groot, H. L., & Beugelsdijk, S. (2005). *Cultural and institutional determinants of bilateral trade flows* (Tinbergen Institute Discussion Paper No. 2005-074/3). Retrieved from the Tinbergen Institute: http://papers.tinbergen.nl/05074.pdf

Linn, J. F., & Tiomkin, D. (2006). The New Impetus towards Economic Integration between Europe and Asia. *Asia Europe Journal, 4*(1), 31–41. doi:10.1007/s10308-006-0046-6

Liyanaarachchi, T. S., Naranpanawa, A., & Bandara, J. S. (2016). Impact of trade liberalisation on labour market and poverty in Sri Lanka. An integrated macro-micro modelling approach. *Economic Modelling, 59*, 102–115. doi:10.1016/j.econmod.2016.07.008

Louzis, D. P., Vouldis, A. T., & Metaxas, V. L. (2012). Macroeconomic and bank-specific determinants of non-performing loans in Greece: A comparative study of mortgage, business and consumer loan portfolios. *Journal of Banking & Finance*, *36*(4), 1012–1027. doi:10.1016/j.jbankfin.2011.10.012

Lu, N. (1997). *The Dynamics of Foreign-Policy Decisionmaking in China*. Boulder, CO: Westview Press.

Magee, C. S. (2016). Trade creation, trade diversion, and the general equilibrium effects of regional trade agreements: A study of the European Community–Turkey customs union. *Review of World Economics*, *152*(2), 383–399. doi:10.1007/s10290-015-0239-4

Manni, U. H., Naser, M., & Afzal, M. N. I. (2012). Effect of trade liberalization on economidc growth of developing countries: A case of Bangladesh economy. *Journal of Business. Economics &Finance*, *1*(2), 37–44.

Manova, K. (2013). Credit constraints, heterogeneous firms, and international trade. *The Review of Economic Studies*, *80*(2), 711–744. doi:10.1093/restud/rds036

Manwa, F., & Wijeweera, A. (2016). Trade liberalisation and economic growth link:The case of Southern African Custom Union countries. *Economic Analysis and Policy*, *51*, 13–2. doi:10.1016/j.eap.2016.05.001

Mariani, B. (2013). *China's Role and Interests in Central Asia*. London: Saferworld.

Martincus, C. V., & Carballo, J. (2008). Is export promotion effective in developing countries? Firm-level evidence on the intensive and the extensive margins of exports. *Journal of International Economics*, *76*(1), 89–106. doi:10.1016/j.jinteco.2008.05.002

Martincus, C. V., & Carballo, J. (2010). Beyond the average effects: The distributional impacts of export promotion programs in developing countries. *Journal of Development Economics*, *92*(2), 201–214. doi:10.1016/j.jdeveco.2009.02.007

Matvienko, V. (2015, January 13). *Ryad stran Latinskoy Ameriki proyavlyaut interes k sozdaniyu zony svobodnoy torgovli s EAES* [The number of countries in Latin America show its interest to creating a free trade zone with the EEU]. Sovet Federatsii. Retrieved from http://council.gov.ru/press-center/news/50386/

Melitz, M. J. (2003). The impact of trade on intra-industry reallocations and aggregate industry productivity. *Econometrica*, *71*(6), 1695–1725. doi:10.1111/1468-0262.00467

Messai, A. S., & Jouini, F. (2013). Micro and macro determinants of non-performing loans. *International Journal of Economics and Financial Issues*, *3*(4), 852–860.

Michaely, M. (1977). Exports and growth: An empirical investigation. *Journal of Development Economics*, *4*(1), 49–53. doi:10.1016/0304-3878(77)90006-2

Millin, M., & Nichola, T. (2005). Explaining economic growth in South Africa: A Kaldorian approach. *International Journal of Technology Management & Sustainable Development*, *4*(1), 47–62. doi:10.1386/ijtm.4.1.47/1

Minetti, R., & Zhu, S. C. (2011). Credit constraints and firm export: Microeconomic evidence from Italy. *Journal of International Economics*, *83*(2), 109–125. doi:10.1016/j.jinteco.2010.12.004

Miyamoto, Y. (2014). *Strategic outsourcing and quality choice: Is a vertical integration model sustainable?* Retrieved October 11, 2017, from http://web.iss.u-tokyo.ac.jp/~ matsumur/miyamoto2014.pdf

Mohanty, S. K., Akhigbe, A., Al-Khyal, T. A., & Bugshan, T. (2013). Oil and stock market activity when prices go up and down: The case of the oil and gas industry. *Review of Quantitative Finance and Accounting*, *41*(2), 253–272. doi:10.1007/s11156-012-0309-9

Mongoliya mozhet zakluchit dogovor o zone svobodnoy torgovli s EAES. (2015, May 8). [Mongolia may sign an agreement on free trade zone with the EEU]. BNEWS.KZ. Retrieved from http://bnews.kz/ru/news/post/266141/

Montgomery, D. C., & Rungur, G. C. (2010). *Applied statistics and probability for engineers*. John Wiley & Sons.

Moon, H. C. (2000). *From Adam Smith to Michael Porter: Evolution of Competitiveness Theory* (Vol. 2). World Scientific.

Muûls, M. (2008). *Exporters and credit constraints. A firm level approach* (National Bank of Belgium, Working Paper No. 139). Brussels National Bank of Belgium (NBB). Retrieved from the NBB: https://www.nbb.be/doc/ts/publications/wp/wp139en.pdf

Naranpanawa, A., & Arora, R. (2014). Does trade liberalization promote regional disparities? Evidence from a multiregional CGE model of India. *World Development*, *64*, 339–349. doi:10.1016/j.worlddev.2014.06.001

Narayan, P. K., & Narayan, S. (2010). Modelling the impact of oil prices on Vietnam's stock prices. *Applied Energy*, *87*(1), 356–361. doi:10.1016/j.apenergy.2009.05.037

Nguyen, C. C., & Bhatti, M. I. (2012). Copula model dependency between oil prices and stock markets: Evidence from China and Vietnam. *Journal of International Financial Markets, Institutions and Money*, *22*(4), 758–773. doi:10.1016/j.intfin.2012.03.004

Nguyet, P. T. B., & Thao, P. P. (2013). Analyzing the impact of macroeconomic factors on Vietnam stock market. *Journal of Development and Integration*, *8*(18), 34–41.

Nikolić, G. (2013). Tendency of exports technology structure and exports concentration in the Balkan economies 2000-2012. *Industrija*, *41*(3), 7–24. doi:10.5937/industrija41-4186

Nkusu, M. (2011). *Nonperforming loans and macrofinancial vulnerabilities in advanced economies*. IMF Working Paper, WP/11/161.

Nordås, H. K., & Piermartini, R. (2004). *Infrastructure and trade.* (World Trade Organization Staff Working Paper ERSD-2004-04). Genève: WTO. Retrieved from the WTO: https://www.wto.org/english/res_e/reser_e/ersd200404_e.htm

O Trans-Tikhookeanskom partnerstve. (2015, October 5). [About the Trans-Pacific partnership]. Russian research center of APEC. Retrieved from http://apec-center.ru/о-транстихоокеанском-партнерстве/

O'Neil, W. J., & Ryan, C. (1988). *How to make money in stocks* (Vol. 10). New York: McGraw-Hill.

OECD. (2011). *The Impact of Trade Liberalisation on Jobs and Growth: Technical Note, OECD Trade Policy Papers, No. 107.* Paris: OECD Publishing; doi:10.1787/5kgj4jfj1nq2-

OECD. (2017). *Trade in goods and services.* Retrieved from https://data.oecd.org/trade/trade-in-goods-and-services.htm

Official visit of Vladimir Putin to Kazakhstan. (2015, October 15). Embassy of the Republic of Kazakhstan in the Russian Federation. Retrieved from http://www.kazembassy.ru/ru/mpolitika/7376-2015-10-15-07-19-47

Oman, C. (1994). *Globalization and Regionalization.* OECD. Retrieved from http://www.oecd-ilibrary.org/the-policy-challenges-of-globalisation-and-regionalisation_5l9v7frx3m0v.pdf?contentType=%2fns%2fWorkingPaper&itemId=%2fcontent%2fworkingpaper%2f151004514681&mimeType=application%2fpdf&containerItemId=%2fcontent%2fworkingpaperseries%2f20771681&accessItemIds=&option6=imprint&value6=http%3a%2f%2foecd.metastore.ingenta.com%2fcontent%2fimprint%2foecd

Örnek, İ. (2008). Yabancı sermaye akımlarının yurtiçi tasarruf ve ekonomik büyüme üzerine etkisi: Türkiye örneği. *Ankara Üniversitesi SBF Dergisi, 63*(02), 199–207. doi:10.1501/SBFder_0000002069

Pangestu, M., & Ing, L. Y. (2016). ASEAN: Regional integration and reforms. *Asian Economic Papers, 15*(2), 1–28. doi:10.1162/ASEP_a_00424

Panitchpakdi, S., & Clifford, M. L. (2002). *China and the WTO: Changing China, Changing World Trade.* Singapore: J. Wiley & Sons.

Papapetrou, E. (2001). Oil price shocks, stock market, economic activity and employment in Greece. *Energy Economics, 23*(5), 511–532. doi:10.1016/S0140-9883(01)00078-0

Park, J., & Ratti, R. A. (2008). Oil price shocks and stock markets in the US and 13 European countries. *Energy Economics, 30*(5), 2587–2608. doi:10.1016/j.eneco.2008.04.003

Peng, M. W., Wang, D. Y. L., & Jiang, Y. (2008). An institution-based view of international business strategy: A focus on emerging economies. *Journal of International Business Studies, 39*(5), 920–936. doi:10.1057/palgrave.jibs.8400377

Pesaran, M. H., Shin, Y., & Smith, R. J. (2001). Bounds testing approaches to the analysis of level relationships. *Journal of Applied Econometrics, 16*(3), 289–326. doi:10.1002/jae.616

Pesaran, M. H., Shin, Y., & Smith, R. P. (1999). Pooled mean group estimation of dynamic heterogeneous panels. *Journal of the American Statistical Association*, *94*(446), 621–634. doi:10.1080/01621459.1999.10474156

Petkovic, M., Djedovic-Negre, D., & Lukic, J. (2015). Public-Private Partnerships: Interorganizational Design as Key Success Factor. *Mangement. Journal for Theory and Practice Management*, *77*, 1–11.

Pinder, J. (1968). Positive integration and negative integration: Some problems of economic union in the EEC. *The World Today*, *24*(3), 88–110.

Porter, M. E. (1999). The Microeconomic Foundations of Economic Development. In *The Global Competitiveness Report*. Geneva, Switzerland: World Economic Forum.

Porter, M. E. (2004). Building the Microeconomic Foundations of Prosperity: Findings from the Business Competitiveness Index. In *The Global Competitiveness Report 2003-2004*. Oxford University Press.

Porter, M. E. (1998). *Competitive advantage of nations*. New York: The Free Pres. doi:10.1007/978-1-349-14865-3

Prajitno, O. (2011). *The Effect of the Oil Price Volatility on the US Stock Market* (Thesis). Department of Economics, Erasmus University, Rotterdam, The Netherlands.

Press-konferentsiya po itogam foruma ATES. (2012, September 9). [Press conference on the results of the APEC forum]. President of Russia. Retrieved from http://kremlin.ru/events/president/transcripts/16432

Prezident, T. T. P. RF Sergey Katirin: Kazakhstan – nadejniy partner. (2016, October 14). [President of CCI of Russia Sergei Katyrin: Kazakhstan is a reliable partner]. The Chamber of Commerce and Industry of the Russian Federation. Retrieved from https://tpprf.ru/ru/news/prezident-tpp-rf-sergey-katyrin-kazakhstan-nadezhnyy-partner--i156458/

Pula, G., & Santabarbara, D. (2012). *Is China Climbing Up the Quality Ladder?* Helsinki: Bank of Finland, Institute for Economies in Transition.

Rafiq, S., Salim, R., & Bloch, H. (2009). Impact of crude oil price volatility on economic activities: An empirical investigation in the Thai economy. *Resources Policy*, *34*(3), 121–132. doi:10.1016/j.resourpol.2008.09.001

Raikhan, S. (2013). Eurasian idea of N.A. Nazarbayev as the basis of modern integration. In *Procedia of Social and Behavioral Sciences, 2nd Cyprus International Conference on Educational Research* (*Vol. 89*, pp. 377-386). Academic Press. doi:10.1016/j.sbspro.2013.08.863

Rajsekhar, B., Hulle, F. V., & Jansen, J. C. (1999). Indian wind energy programme: Performance and future directions. *Energy Policy*, *27*(11), 669–678. doi:10.1016/S0301-4215(99)00031-2

Ravenhill, J. (1995). Economic Cooperation in Southeast Asia: Changing Incentives. *Asian Survey*, *35*(9), 850–866. doi:10.2307/2645786

Revenga, A. (1995). *Employment and Wages effect of Trade Liberalization*. Policy Reserach Working Paper 1524. The World Bank. Latin America and the Caribbean.Retrieved May 8, 2017, from https://213.154.74.164/invenio/record/10976/files/wps1524.pdf

Riedewal, M. (2015). *Data Mining Techniques*. Retrieved from http://www.ccs.neu.edu/home / mirek/classes/2012-S-CS6220/Slides/Lecture2-ClassificationPrediction.pdf

Rivera, P. P., & Garashchuk, A. (2016). The Eurasian Economic Union: Prospective regional integration in the post-Soviet space or just geopolitical project? *Eastern Journal of European Studies*, *7*, 91.

Rodriguez, F., & Rodrik, D. (2000). Trade policy and economic growth: A skeptic's guide to the cross-national evidence. *NBER Macroeconomics Annual*, *15*, 261–325. doi:10.1086/654419

Rojas, R. (2013). *Neural networks: A systematic introduction*. Springer Science & Business Media.

Rossiysko-belorusskoe torgovo-ekonomicheskoe sotrudnichestvo. (2015). [Russian-Belorussian trade and economic cooperation]. Retrieved 18 June, 2017, from http://belarus.mid.ru/spravocnye-materialy/-/asset_publisher/9CH6VzS6hIWV/content/rossijsko-belorusskoe-torgovo-ekonomiceskoe-sotrudnicestvo

Rueland, J. (2000). ASEAN and the Asian crisis: Theoretical implications and practical consequences for Southeast Asian regionalism. *The Pacific Review*, *13*(3), 421–451. doi:10.1080/09512740050147942

Russia Trade Statistics. (n.d.). Retrieved February 3, 2017, from http://atlas.media.mit.edu/en/profile/country/rus/

Saavedra-Rivano, N., & Estrada, M. A. R. (2016). An alternative free trade agreement scheme to developing countries: The micro-free trade territory (MFTT). *Quality & Quantity*, *50*(5), 2293–2311. doi:10.1007/s11135-015-0263-4

Saba, I., Kouser, R., & Azeem, M. (2012). Determinants of Non Performing Loans: Case of US Banking Sector. *The Romanian Economic Journal*, *44*(6), 125–136.

Šaban, I. S., & Ušakov, N. A. (1971). *Imperialističeskaja suščnost'zapadnoevropejskoj integracii: meždunarodnopravovye aspekty*. Moskva: Nauka.

Sadorsky, P. (1999). Oil price shocks and stock market activity. *Energy Economics*, *21*(5), 449–469. doi:10.1016/S0140-9883(99)00020-1

Sakaev, V. T. (2016). The political demography of the Eurasian Economic Union. *Journal of Economics and Economic Education Research*, *17*, 169–177.

Sarel, M. (1996). Nonlinear effects of inflation on economic growth. *Staff Papers*, *43*(1), 199–215. doi:10.2307/3867357

Sattar, Z. (2015). *Strategy for export diversification 2015-2020*. Retrieved May 04, 2017, from http://www.plancomm.gov.bd/wp-content/uploads/2015/02/7_Strategy-for-Export-Diversification.pdf

Sawyer, K. R., & Nandha, M. (2006). *How oil moves stock prices*. Available at SSRN: https://ssrn.com/abstract=910427

Saylan, G. (1997). *Küreselleşmenin Gelişimi*. Ankara: Küreselleşme, İmge Kitabevi.

Schott, J. J., & Goodrich, B. (2001). Economic Integration in Northeast Asia. *Proceedings of the KIEP/KEI/CKS Conference on The Challenges of Reconciliation and Reform in Korea*.

Seker, M. (2011). *Trade policies, investment climate, and exports across countries* (World Bank Policy Research Working Paper No. 5654). Retrieved from World Bank website: https://openknowledge.worldbank.org/bitstream/handle/10986/3415/WPS5654.pdf?sequence=1

Şenyiğit, O. (2005). Küreselleşmenin Türkiye'ye etkileri. *Stratejik Araştırmalar Dergisi*, *3*, 35–53.

Shah, A. (2016). Building a Sustainable "Belt and Road." *Horizons, 7*. Retrieved April 17, 2017, from http://www.cirsd.org/en/horizons/horizons-spring-2016--issue-no-7/building-a-sustainable-%E2%80%98belt-and-road-

Shapiro, S. (1997). *Philosophy of mathematics: Structure and ontology*. Oxford University Press on Demand.

Sheefeni, J. P. S. (2015). The Impact of Macroeconomic Determinants on Non-performing Loans in Namibia. *International Review of Research in Emerging Markets and the Global Economy*, *4*, 612–632.

Shein, N. B. (2015). *Nekotorie itogi vzaimnoy torgovli stran-chlenov EAES v 2015 godu* [Some results of mutual trade of member countries of the EEU in 2015]. Retrieved 18 June, 2017, from https://riss.ru/analitycs/34092/

Shpakovsky, A. (2014). *Evraziyskaya integraziya yavlyaetsya dlya Belorusi bezalternativnim vektorom* [Eurasian integration is the only vector for Belarus]. Retrieved 18 June, 2017, from http://www.postkomsg.com/expert_opinion/202548/

Silk Road Trade and Travel Encyclopedia. (n.d.). *Maps*. Retrieved April 18, 2017, from http://www.ipekyollari.com/OBOR/2XinhuaOBOR.jpg

Şimşek, M., & Kadilar, C. (2005). Türkiye'nin İhracat Talebi Fonksiyonunun Sınır Testi Yöntemi İle Eşbütünleşme Analizi. *Doğuş Ünv. Dergisi*, *6*(1), 144–152.

Singer, H. W., & Gray, P. (1988). Trade policy and growth of developing countries: Some new data. *World Development*, *16*(3), 395–403. doi:10.1016/0305-750X(88)90006-X

Škarica, B. (2014). Determinants of non-performing loans in Central and Eastern European countries. *Financial Theory and Practice, 38*(1), 37-59.

Smith, A. (1776). An Inquiry into the Nature and Causes of the Wealth of Nations (5th ed.). London: Methuen & Co., Ltd. doi:10.1093/oseo/instance.00043218

Snorrason, S. (2012). *Asymmetric Economic Integration: Size Characteristics of Economies, Trade Costs and Welfare*. Heidelberg, Germany: Physica. doi:10.1007/978-3-7908-2861-0

Solanko, L. (2016). *Opening up or Closing the Door for Foreign Trade – Russia and China Compared*. Helsinki: Bank of Finland, Institute for Economies in Transition.

Soloaga, I., & Winters, L. A. (2001). Regionalism in the nineties: What effect on trade? *The North American Journal of Economics and Finance*, *12*(1), 1–29. doi:10.1016/S1062-9408(01)00042-0

Sowinski, C., & Parker, L. (2017). WCO Immediate Release Guidelines State of Application in CEFTA. *Global Trade and Customs Journal*, *12*(5), 196–202.

Stančić, D., & Jednak, S. (2003). Privredna transformacija i privatizacija u Poljskoj. *Management*, *29*, 23–28.

State Institute of Statistics Prime Ministry Republic of Turkey. (2003). *Concentration in foreign trade*. Retrieved May 18, 2017 from www.turkstat.gov.tr/IcerikGetir.do%3Fistab_id%3D90

Stuart-Fox, M. (1998). Laos in 1997: Into ASEAN. *Asian Survey*, *38*(1), 75–79. doi:10.2307/2645470

Stubbs, R. (2014). ASEAN's leadership in East Asian region-building: Strength in weakness. *The Pacific Review*, *27*(4), 523–541. doi:10.1080/09512748.2014.924229

Tabuchi, T. (2017). Comparative advantage in the light of the old value theories. In *A new construction of ricardian theory of international values* (pp. 265–280). Springer Singapore. doi:10.1007/978-981-10-0191-8_9

Tan, P. N., Steinbach, M., & Kumar, V. (2013). Data mining cluster analysis: basic concepts and algorithms. *Introduction to Data Mining*.

Tarr, D. G. (2016). The Eurasian Economic Union among Russia, Belarus, Kazakhstan, Armenia and the Kyrgyz Republic: Can it succeed where its predecessor failed? *Eastern European Economics*, *54*(1), 1–22. doi:10.1080/00128775.2015.1105672

Tasch, B. (2014). Russia, Kazakhstan, Belarus sign treaty creating huge economic bloc. *Time Magazine*. Retrieved January 12, 2017, from http://archive.is/4CCJd

Terzi, H., & Oltulular, S. (2011). Türkiye'deki Sanayileşme ve Ekonomik Büyüme Arasındaki Nedensel İlişki. *Doğuş Üniversitesi Dergisi*, *5*(2), 219–226.

Thambipillai, P. (1998). Brunei Darussalam and ASEAN: Regionalism for a small state. *Asian Journal of Political Science*, *6*(1), 80–94. doi:10.1080/02185379808434116

The Central Bank of the Republic of Turkey. (2017). *Electronic data delivery system*. Retrieved May 19 from http://evds.tcmb.gov.tr/index_en.html

The Eurasia Economic Union. (n.d.). Retrieved January 12, 2017, from https://tr.wikipedia.org/wiki/Avrasya_Ekonomik_Birli%C4%9Fi

The Eurasian Economic Commission Statistics. Figures are for Russia, Kazakhstan and Belarus for 2011-2014. (n.d.). Retrieved January 1, 2017, from www.eurasiancommission.org/ru/act/integr_i_makroec/ dep_stat/tradestat/analytics/Pages/default.aspx

The European Free Trade Association. (2016). Retrieved 15 June, 2017, from http://www.efta.int/about-efta/european-free-trade-association

The text of General Agreement on Tariffs and Trade (GATT). (1947, October 30). Retrieved from https://www.wto.org/english/docs_e/legal_e/gatt47_e.pdf

Tinbergen, J. (1959). *On the Theory of Economic Integration*. Amsterdam.

Tkachuk, S. (2016, May 13). *EAES I vse-vse-vse. Vneshniy kontur stanovleniya evraziyskoy integrazii* [The EEU and all. The external contour of the formation of the Eurasian integration]. Retrieved from https://aftershock.news/?q=node/400139

Toenniessen, G., Adesina, A., & DeVries, J. (2008). Building an alliance for a green revolution in Africa. *Annals of the New York Academy of Sciences*, *1136*(1), 233–242. doi:10.1196/annals.1425.028 PMID:18579885

Torgovaya politika EAES. (2016, June 28). [Trade policy of the EEU]. Retrieved from http://eurasiancenter.ru/expert/20160628/1004383194.html

Torgovo-ekonomicheskoe sotrudnichestvo Rossii I Belorussii. (2017, March 30). [Trade and Economic Cooperation of Russia and Belarus]. Retrieved from http://www.tks.ru/news/nearby/2017/03/30/0003

Toševska-Trpčevska, K., & Tevdovski, D. (2016). Trade Facilitation Indicators and Their Potential Impact on Trade between the Countries of South-Eastern Europe. *Scientific Annals of Economics and Business*, *63*(3), 347–362. doi:10.1515/saeb-2016-0127

Trading Economics. (2017). Retrieved May 12, 2017, from http://www.tradingeconomics.com/

Turker, M. (2017). *Economic cooperation organization trade agreement and last development*. Retrieved May 03, 2017 from http://www.mfa.gov.tr/ekonomik-isbirligi-teskilati-ticaret-anlasmasi-_economic-cooperation-organization-trade-agreement-ecota_-ve-son-gelismeler-.tr.mfa

Turkish Statisticial Institute. (2017). *Statistical tables and dynamic interrogation*. Retrieved May 04, 2017, from http://www.tuik.gov.tr/PreTablo.do?alt_id=1046

Turnbull, C., Sun, S., & Anwar, S. (2016). Trade liberalisation, inward FDI and productivity within Australia's manufacturing sector. *Economic Analysis and Policy*, *51*, 12–21.

Tyler, W. G. (1981). Growth and export expansion in developing countries: Some empirical evidence. *Journal of Development Economics*, *9*(1), 121–130. doi:10.1016/0304-3878(81)90007-9

UNCTAD. (2004). *Exports of services and economic growth in developing countries. United Nations Conference on Trade and Development*. Retrieved October 11, 2017, from http://unctad.org/en/docs/ditctncdmisc20036_en.pdf

UNCTAD. (2017a). *United Nations Conference on Trade and Development*. Retrieved May 05, 2017, from http://unctadstat.unctad.org/wds/TableViewer/tableView.aspx?ReportId=97

UNCTAD. (2017b). *United Nations Conference on Trade and Development*. Retrieved May 19, 2017, from http://unctadstat.unctad.org/wds/TableViewer/tableView.aspx

UNCTAD. (2017c). *United Nations Conference on Trade and Development*. Retrieved May 19, 2017, from http://unctadstat.unctad.org/wds/TableViewer/downloadPrompt.aspx

United Nations Conference on Trade and Development. (2017). Statistics Database [Data file]. Retrieved April 17, 2017, from http://unctad.org/en/Pages/Statistics.aspx

United Nations Statistics Division. (2017). *UN Comtrade Database*. Retrieved May 12, 2017, from https://comtrade.un.org/

Vatansever, M., & Hepsen, A. (2013). Determining impacts on non-performing loan ratio in Turkey. *Journal of Finance and Investment Analysis*, *2*(4), 119–129.

Venâncio, S. F. M. (2013). *Does financial development promote economic growth?* (Doctoral dissertation). Instituto Superior de Economia e Gestão.

Videnie i deystvie, napravlennie na prodvizhenie sovmestnogo stroitelstva "Ekonomicheskogo poyasa Shelkovogo puti" i "Morskogo Shelkovogo puti 21 veka". (2015, March 23). [Vision and action aimed at promoting the joint construction of "Economic belt of the Silk road" and "Maritime silk road of the 21st century"]. The official site of the Embassy of the Republic of China in the Russian Federation. Retrieved from http://ru.china-embassy.org/rus/zgxw/t1257296.htm

Vijayasri, G. V. (2013). The importance of international trade in the world. *International Journal of Marketing. Financial Services & Management Research*, *2*(9), 111–119.

Viner, J. (1950). *The Customs Union Issue*. London, UK: Stevens and Son Ltd.

Vinokurov, E. (2014, October 14). *Evropeyskiy I Evraziyskiy soyuzy: povod dlya integratsii* [The European and Eurasian unions: the reason for integration]. TASS Informational agency of Russia. Retrieved from http://tass.ru/opinions/1597482

Vinokurov, E., & Libman, A. (2012). *Eurasia and Eurasian Integration: Beyond the Post-Soviet Borders*. Retrieved April 17, 2017, from http://www.eabr.org/general/upload/CII%20-%20izdania/Yerbook-2012/a_n5_2012_10.pdf

Vinokurov, E. (2014). *Kolichestvenniy analiz ekonomicheskoy integratsii Evropeyskogo soyuza I Evraziyskogo ekonomicheskogo soyuza: metodologicheskie podkhody. Doklad #23* [Quantitative analysis of economic integration of the European Union and the Eurasian Economic Union: methodological approaches. Paper #23]. ZII EABR.

Voprosy I otvety po Soglasheniyu o svobodnoy torgovle mezhdu Evraziyskim ekonomicheskim soyuzom I Sotsialisticheskoy Respublikoy Vietnam. (n.d.). [Questions and answers about the Agreement on the free trade between the Eurasian Economic Union and the Socialist Republic of Vietnam]. Retrieved 14 June, 2017, from http://www.eurasiancommission.org/ru/act/trade/dotp/sogl_torg/Documents/Вопросы%20и%20ответы%20по%20Соглашению%20о%20свободной%20торговле%20между%20странами%20ЕАЭС%20и%20Вьетнамом.pdf

Voskresenskiy, M. (2014, July 17). *Integratsiya, shag vtoroy: zony svobodnoy torgovli v EAES* [Integration, the second step: a free trade zone in EEU]. Evraziyskiy kommunikatsionniy centr. Retrieved from http://eurasiancenter.ru/economyexperts/20140717/1003589939.html

Vozvrashchenie Makkindera – Vengriya prisoedinyaetsya k "Shelkovomu puti." (2015, September 16). [The return of Mackinder – Hungary joins the "Silk road"]. War and Peace. Retrieved from http://www.warandpeace.ru/ru/commentaries/view/105060/

Vzaimnaya torgovlya tovarami. Statistika Evraziyskogo ekonomicheskogo soyuza. (2016). [Mutual trade of goods. Statistics of the Eurasian Economic Union]. Statistical Bulletin. Eurasian Economic Commission. Moscow. Retrieved 18 June, 2017, from http://www.eurasiancommission.org/ru/act/integr_i_makroec/dep_stat/tradestat/publications/Documents/Int_III_2016.pdf

Wacziarg, R., & Welch, K. H. (2008). Trade liberalization and growth: New evidence. *The World Bank Economic Review*, *22*(2), 187–231. doi:10.1093/wber/lhn007

Watts, M. (1991). Entitlements or empowerment? Famine and starvation in Africa. *Review of African Political Economy*, *18*(51), 9–26. doi:10.1080/03056249108703903

Wilson, J. S., Mann, C. L., & Otsuki, T. (2005). Assessing the benefits of trade facilitation: A global perspective. *World Economy*, *28*(6), 841–871. doi:10.1111/j.1467-9701.2005.00709.x

Wong, E., Chi, L. K., Tsui, S., & Tiejun, W. (2017). One Belt, One Road: China's Strategy for a New Global Financial Order. *Monthly Review. An Independent Socialist Magazine*, *68*(8). Retrieved April 17, 2017, from: https://monthlyreview.org/2017/01/01/one-belt-one-road/#en1

World Bank Group. (2014). *Trade Competitiveness*. World Bank Brief. Retrieved May 20, 2017, from http://www.worldbank.org/en/topic/trade/brief/trade-competitiveness

World Bank Group. (2017). *World Bank Open Data*. Retrieved May 12, 2017, from http://data.worldbank.org/

World Bank. (1996). *The political economy of corruption-causes and consequences*. Retrieved October 11, 2017, from http://siteresources.worldbank.org/EXTFINANCIALSECTOR / Resources/282884-1303327122200/074ackerm.pdf

World Bank. (2017). *GDP per capita*. Available from http://data.worldbank.org/data-catalog/world-development-indicators

World Bank. (2017). Retrieved May 05, 2017, from http://data.worldbank.org/indicator/NY.GDP.MKTP.CD?view=chart

World Economic Forum. (2014). *The global competitiveness report 2016-2017*. Geneva: World Economic Forum.

World I. T. S. Russian Federation Exports by Country and Region 2015. (n.d.). Retrieved March 25, 2017, from http://wits.worldbank.org/CountryProfile/en/Country/RUS/Year/LTST/TradeFlow/Export/Partner/all/

Wu, Y. (2006). *Economic Growth, Transition and Globalization in China*. Cheltenham, UK: Edward Elgar Publishing Limited.

Xu, D. W., Wang, Y. D., Jia, L. M., Li, H. J., & Zhang, G. J. (2016). Real-time road traffic states measurement based on Kernel-KNN matching of regional traffic attractors. *Measurement*, *94*, 862–872. doi:10.1016/j.measurement.2016.08.038

Yang, S., & Wang, S. (2014). Development and impacts of the Customs Union of Russia, Belarus and Kazakhstan. *China Institute of International Studies*. Retrieved February 15, 2017, from http://www.ciis.org.cn/english/2014-09/23/content_7254454.htm

Yang, C. W., Hwang, M. J., & Huang, B. N. (2002). An analysis of factors affecting price volatility of the US oil market. *Energy Economics*, *24*(2), 107–119. doi:10.1016/S0140-9883(01)00092-5

Yang, S., & Martinez-Zarzoso, I. (2014). A panel data analysis of trade creation and trade diversion effects: The case of ASEAN–China Free Trade Area. *China Economic Review*, *29*, 138–151. doi:10.1016/j.chieco.2014.04.002

Yanikkaya, H. (2003). Trade openness and economic growth: A cross-country empirical investigation. *Journal of Development Economics*, *72*(1), 57–89. doi:10.1016/S0304-3878(03)00068-3

Yıldız, F. (2007). *Yabancı Uyruklu Gerçek ve Tüzel Kişilere Taşınmaz Mal Satışı. 21. Yüzyıl.* Nisan/Mayıs, 123-136.

Yuan, P.-H. (2017). Trade Strategy Adjustment of China after the Financial Crisis. *Chinese Economy*, *50*(2), 112–118. doi:10.1080/10971475.2016.1227171

Yüksel, S., Dincer, H., & Hacioglu, U. (2015). CAMELS-based Determinants for the Credit Rating of Turkish Deposit Banks. *International Journal of Finance & Banking Studies*, *4*(4), 1–17.

Yüksel, S., & Zengin, S. (2016a). Causality relationship between import, export and growth rate in developing countries. *International Journal of Commerce and Finance*, *2*(1), 147–156.

Yüksel, S., & Zengin, S. (2016b). Leading Indicators of 2008 Global Crisis: An Analysis with Logit and MARS Methods. *Finansal Araştırmalar ve Çalışmalar Dergisi*, *8*(15), 495–518.

Yuzawa, T. (2012). The Fallacy of Socialization? Rethinking the ASEAN Way of Institution-building. In R. Emmers (Ed.), *ASEAN and the Institutionalization of East Asia* (pp. 75–88). London: Routledge.

Zaw, A. (2001). *ASEAN-Burma relations. Challenges to Democratization in Burma - Perspectives on multilateral and bilateral responses*. Washington, DC: National Democratic Institute.

Zbarskaya, I. A., & Gabdrakhimova, R. K. (2016). *Foreign Trade of Countries of The Commonwealth of Independent States 2015*. Moscow, Russia: Interstate Statistical Committee of the CIS.

Zhang, J. (2016). *What's Driving China's One Belt, One Road Initiative?* Retrieved April 17, 2017, from http://www.eastasiaforum.org/2016/09/02/whats-driving-chinas-one-belt-one-road-initiative/

Zhang, T. (2016). *China's Foreign Trade in 2016: Identifying Trends and Opportunities.* Retrieved April 18, 2017, from http://www.china-briefing.com/news/2016/12/22/chinas-foreign-trade-2016-identifying-trends-opportunities.html

Zhong, N. (2015). China vows to enhance trade with Eurasian bloc. *China Daily*. Retrieved February 15, 2017, from http://www.chinadaily.com.cn/world/cn_eu/2015-05/11/content_20676192.htm

Zona svobodnoy torgovli EAES – Indiya – Iran. (2015, October 5). [A free trade zone of the EEU — India — Iran]. NOVORUSMIR.RU. Retrieved from http://novorusmir.ru/archives/4260

About the Contributors

Zafer Adalı is an MA student in Anadolu University in Turkey. He is interested in economics, finance, banking and development. At the same time, he is a research assisstant in the department of Economics in Artvin Çoruh University.

Hasan Dincer is an Associate Professor of finance at Istanbul Medipol University, Faculty of Economics and Administrative Sciences, Istanbul-Turkey. Dr. Dincer has BAs in Financial Markets and Investment Management at Marmara University. He received PhD in Finance and Banking with his thesis entitled "The Effect of Changes on the Competitive Strategies of New Service Development in the Banking Sector". He has work experience in the finance sector as a portfolio specialist and his major academic studies focusing on financial instruments, performance evaluation, and economics.He is the executive editor of the International Journal of Finance and Banking Studies (IJFBS) and the founder member of the Society for the Study of Business and Finance (SSBF).

Deniz Efendioğlu graduated from Industrial Engineering Department of Istanbul University in 2011 with Bachelor Degree and in 2013 with a graduate degree. Along with trying to acquire a place in the academic field, the topics of Operations Research, Decision Making Techniques and Statistical Design in general have been the subjects of his attention. With his double major, Chemical Engineering, he does research in the fields of optimization and regulation of chemical processes. He would like to continue to develop this subject together with the related thesis studies on Renewable Energy Sources. He continues his education in Marmara University in Industrial Engineering Department with Ph.D.

Vasilii Erokhin is an Associate Professor, School of Economics and Management, Harbin Engineering University, China. He holds a Ph.D. degree in Economics and Management (2006) and a Specialist degree in International Economics (2003) from Stavropol State Agrarian University, Russia. Spheres of scientific interests include international trade, globalization, trade integration and liberalization, sustainable development, food security issues with a focus on emerging markets, developing countries, and economies in transition. Vasilii Erokhin is an author of over 150 scientific works in international economics, international trade, sustainable rural development, and regionalization, including 6 books, 10 monographs, over 40 papers in peer-reviewed journals and proceedings (the USA, the Czech Republic, Slovakia, Hungary, Romania, Serbia, Ukraine, Russia). Vasilii Erokhin is an editor of two IGI Global books: Global Perspectives on Trade Integration and Economies in Transition (2016) and Establishing Food Security and Alternatives to International Trade in Emerging Economies (2017). He is also an author of the Series "International Trade from a Russian Perspective" (2014), published online by HSTalks, London. Vasilii Erokhin is a Guest Editor at MDPI Economies, special issue "Macroeconomics and Urban Labour Markets Paradigms"; an Academic Editor at SCIENCEDOMAIN Asian Journal of Economics, Business and Accounting; an Editorial Board Member at SPG Journal of World Economic Research; an Editorial Board Member at IKP Journal of Economics and Trade; a member of the Editorial Review Board at IGI International Journal of Sustainable Economies Management (IJSEM); a member of the Editorial Review Board at IGI International Journal of Social Ecology and Sustainable Development (IJSESD); an Editorial Board Member at SPRINGER Journal of the Knowledge Economy; an Editorial Board Member at SPRINGER Journal of Innovation and Entrepreneurship: A Systems View across Time and Space; an Editorial Board Member at SPRINGER Journal of Technology, Innovation and Education; a member of the International Editorial Review Board at Economics of Agriculture (Ekonomika poljoprivrede); a member of the Editorial Advisory Board at IGI book "Green Economic Structures in Modern Business and Society"; a member of the Editorial Advisory Board at IGI book "Research on Food Science, Production and Engineering in Green Economies"; a member of the Review Board at Applied Research Conference, Koforidua Polytechnic, Ghana. He is a holder of the honorary awards from the Ministry of Agriculture of the Russian Federation (2010), Ministry of Education and Science of the Russian Federation (2012). Vasilii Erokhin is a winner of the 3rd All-Russian competition of business ideas and projects "Creation of Future Russia", project "Efficiency Increasing of the Regional Entrepreneurship in the Conditions of the World Trade Organization Accession" and a scholarship holder of the Vladimir Potanin's Charity Fund among young teachers (2009). Since 2016, Vasilii Erokhin is also a researcher at the Polar Development and Northeast Asian Economic Research Center (PAERC), China and a Specially Invited Expert at the Association of International Economics and Trade of Heilongjiang Province, China.

Nurullah Güleç graduated from Industrial Engineering Department of Istanbul University with first degree in 2012. After two years of experience as ERP consultant in the private sector, he started graduate education in Operations Research at Middle East Technical University in 2014. At the same time, he started second graduate education in Economy at Ankara Yıldırım Beyazıt University, in order to establish the infrastructure for multidisciplinary studies. Gülec have still continued his graduate educations and he is currently as reseach assistant at Industrial Engineering Department of Ankara Yıldırım Beyazıt University, Turkey. His research areas are Operations Research, Data Mining, Machine Learning, Central Banking, Monetary Policies and Production Financing.

Sandra Jednak is an associate professor at the Faculty of Organisational Sciences, University of Belgrade for the undergraduate course Introduction to Economics. She received her bachelor`s, master`s, and doctorate degrees from University of Belgrade. She was visiting lecturer at ISM University of Economics and Management in Lithuania. Her research focus is the economic growth and development of south-eastern European countries. She also does research on knowledge economy, energy economics, international economics and higher education. She has published scientific research papers in international and national journals.

Nazlı Karamollaoğlu is an assistant professor of economics at MEF since March 2014. Previously she has worked at TEB-BNP Paribas İstanbul Office as an economist specializing on GCC countries and Turkey. Karamollaoğlu holds a BA in economics from Boğaziçi University, as well as an MA in international and development economics from Yale University, and a PhD from City University of New York with a concentration in international economics and applied econometrics.

Ina Kayser majored in information systems and international economics. She obtained her PhD from the University of Duisburg-Essen with a thesis on the acceptance of e-government. She worked as a project manager with Germany's largest technical-scientific association and became a professor of economics and information systems in 2016. Her research focuses on interdisciplinary topics in the realm of information systems, politics and economics.

Huynh Viet Khai has received Ph.D. and researched as postdoctoral fellow in Kyushu University, Japan. Now, he is a lecturer at College of Economics, Can Tho University, Vietnam. Dr. Khai has written over twenty scholarly journal articles, two books, and seven book chapters in the areas of agricultural, environmental and resource economics.

Dragana Kragulj is a full professor at the Faculty of Organisational Sciences, University of Belgrade. She is a chair of Department of Economics, Business Planning and International Management. She has been involved in several research projects. In addition to her teaching, she is occupied with research of macroeconomic problems, prices, market, inflation, economic development, investment, international trade, agriculture, energy economics, process of transition, international economic integrations, the European Union. She has published several editions of different textbooks on economics, authored two monographs, and over 100 scientific papers published in reputable national and international journals and conferences.

Maria Lagutina is Associate Professor and Vice-head of World Politics Department at St. Petersburg State University. She holds a Ph.D. in Political Science (2006, St. Petersburg State University, the Russian Federation). Her current research interests are oriented towards Eurasian integration and its regional and global dimensions, including different issues and prospects of the European Union and the Eurasian Economic Union relationships. She is a member of the International Studies Association. Dr. Maria Lagutina is the author of four monographs, one textbook and several chapters in the collective monographs on the world politics issues and Eurasian integration and more than 30 articles in Russian and English. Her latest works were published in the USA: Lagutina M., Vasilyeva N. The Russian Project of Eurasian Integration. Geopolitical Prospects. Lexington Books, Rowman and Littlefield, 2016; Russia and the World: Understanding International Relations. Ed. by N.Tsvetkova. Lexington Books, Rowman and Littlefield, 2017 (2 chapters). In 2016 she was invited as a Visiting Professor at Carleton University (Ottawa, Canada).

Cihat Öztürk is a PHD candidate from the Program in Industrial Engineering at the Marmara University, Turkey. Also, he is research assistant at Engineering and Natural Sciences Faculty, Yıldırım Beyazıt University. His graduated from Industrial Engineering Department at Yildiz Technical University, Istanbul and he has a master degree from Industrial Engineering at Kocaeli University. His research areas are operations Research, optimization, forecasting, metaheuristics, inventory management and statistical analysis.

Miloš Parežanin as is a teaching associate for the scientific area of business economics and macroeconomics at of Organisational Sciences, University of Belgrade since 2011. He graduated from the Faculty of Economics, University of Belgrade in 2009. Currently he is Ph.D. student at same faculty. He received scholarship from: Ministry of Education (academic year 2005/06), city of Belgrade (academic year 2006/07), Foundation „Milivoje Jovanović and Luka Ćelović" (academic year 2007/08) and Fund for Young Talents (academic year 2010/11). He has participated in several national scientific conferences.

Sevgi Sezer has a doctorate in economics. Main research field of author is foreign trade. She has got lots of paper in this area. She has got lots of articles in this area. She likes to work, produce and travel.

Serhat Yüksel is an assistant Professor at Istanbul Medipol University.

Index

F

G

I

K

L

M

N

O

P

R

S

T

V

W

Z

www.ingramcontent.com/pod-product-compliance
Lightning Source LLC
LaVergne TN
LVHW081339300926
849161LV00008B/2026